The

PATRIOT'S

HANDBOOK

THE
PATRIOT'S
HANDBOOK

GEORGE GRANT

Highland Books

Published by Highland Books
229 South Bridge Street
P.O. Box 254
Elkton, Maryland 21922-0254

By license from
Cumberland House Publishing, Inc.
431-433 Harding Industrial Drive
Nashville, Tennessee 37211

Send requests for information to Highland Books at the
above address.

Printed in the United States of America
2 3 4 5 6 7 8—00 99 98 97

To
DAVID DRYE
A Citizen Patriot
and to
HOWARD PHILLIPS
A Statesman Patriot

CONTENTS

PART II: AN EXPERIMENT IN LIBERTY

PART III: MANIFEST DESTINY

PART IV: THE AMERICAN DREAM

ACKNOWLEDGMENTS

"All heaven and earth resound with that subtle and delicately balanced truth that the old paths are the best paths after all."
J. C. Ryle

"Whatever makes a man a good Christian also makes a good citizen," Daniel Webster once asserted. Although the subject of informed public virtue has been much maligned of late, it is no less true today than it was in Webster's day. And thankfully, it is a subject not without its champions. That this book exists at all is substantial evidence of that happy fact.

David Drye first suggested that I make good my long-held hope of revising and publishing a new edition of what was once an American educational tradition: a citizen's handbook of essential historical resources. He encouraged me along the way, supported my efforts, and pushed me forward when other obligations threatened to sidetrack this project. His graciousness and enthusiasm I unhesitatingly count among the greatest gifts in my life.

Likewise, Ron and Julia Pitkin at Cumberland House and Heather Armstrong, Dean Andreola, Phil Hibbard, and Will Wallace at Highland Books prompted me to move apace. Their professionalism, friendship, and constancy have all combined to make this an extraordinarily pleasant publishing experience—a genuine rarity these days.

Robert Fulcher, my colleague at the Franklin Classical School, and his multitalented wife, Kim, helped me immeasurably on this project with their technical expertise. They scanned, translated, and formatted a myriad of scattered scraps, notes, and texts so I could begin to work with them on my computer. Without them, I'm afraid I would have been utterly lost.

Each of these champions of public virtue has taught me what it means to be a good citizen by exemplifying what it means to be a good Christian. Thus I am grateful to them all.

Of course, my family has been my greatest source of inspiration and encouragement. It has been through them that the roots of public virtue have been made known to me—in the guise of private virtue. My wife,

Karen, and my children, Joel, Joanna, and Jesse, are not only my chief joys in life, but they are my first audience and my best critics. All that I am and all that I do, I owe to them.

King's Meadow Farm
Independence Day 1996

INTRODUCTION

*"Politics ought to be the part-time profession of every citizen who would protect
the rights and privileges of free people."*
Dwight D. Eisenhower

G. K. Chesterton once quipped that "America is the only nation in the world that is founded on a creed." Other nations find their identity and cohesion in ethnicity or geography or partisan ideology or cultural tradition. But America was founded on certain ideas—ideas about freedom, about human dignity, and about social responsibility. It was this profound peculiarity that most struck Alexis de Tocqueville during his famous visit to this land at the beginning of the nineteenth century. He called it "American exceptionalism."

· About the same time de Tocqueville penned his sage observations in his classic book *Democracy in America,* educators in the fledgling republic began to realize that if their great experiment in liberty, their extraordinary American exceptionalism, was to be maintained over the course of succeeding generations, then an informed patriotism would have to be instilled in the hearts and minds of the young. Indeed, John Quincy Adams wrote, "Posterity: you will never know how much it has cost my generation to preserve your freedom. I hope you will make good use of it."

Thus, from the middle of the nineteenth century to the middle of the twentieth, rising citizens were presented with small handbooks—brief guides to the essential elements of the American creed. Pastors, statesmen, educators, and parents wanted to somehow pass on to posterity the moral and constitutional tools necessary to make good use of their freedom.

Over the past few years I have tried to collect a representative sample of such handbooks—scouring dusty antiquarian book shops, libraries, and academic collections whenever and wherever I could. Though they varied somewhat over the years in presentation, style, and format, it appears that each was designed to be an introductory and documentary record of the development, confirmation, and establishment of the exceptional American creed. They were offered to the ever-changing citizenry in the hope that the never-changing principles of freedom might be fully comprehended and defended against any and all incursions.

The Patriot's Handbook is an updated version of that vaunted tradition. Containing a concise introduction to the foundational ideas, documents, events, and personalities of American freedom, it is a citizenship primer for a whole new generation of American patriots.

Divided into four chronological sections, the texts, profiles, and samples were selected for their representative overview, not for their comprehensiveness. Part I documents the early settlement of American shores by the colonists and describes the motivations and innovations of their pioneering efforts—efforts that eventually led to the extraordinary freedoms we enjoy today. Part II details the establishment of American independence. Though much of this story has been well documented in our national lore, it is a story worth repeating. Part III surveys the growing pains of America's quick territorial expansion across the continent and its quick economic ascendancy around the world. Here we witness the birth of modernity and the shape of the world we have come to know. Part IV brings the story of American freedom up to date with a documentary snapshot of the modern era—including the titanic struggle to uphold the American creed amid the fierce onslaught of contemporary controversy.

Alexis de Tocqueville has oft been quoted—perhaps apocryphally— saying:

> I sought for the greatness and genius of America in her commodious harbors and her ample rivers, and it was not there; in her fertile fields and boundless prairies, and it was not there; in her rich mines and her vast world commerce, and it was not there. Not until I went to the churches of America and heard her pulpits aflame with righteousness did I understand the secret of her genius and power. America is great because she is good and if America ever ceases to be good, America will cease to be great.

This anthology of historical and citizenship resources is offered in the hope that the ideas that made America both great and good may once again become the common currency of our national life. It is offered in the hope that the secret of our genius and power might be broadcast far and wide— and thus, essentially, cease to be a secret.

PART I
A CITY
ON A HILL

> **A** contempt
> of the monuments
> and the wisdom of
> the past, may be
> justly reckoned one
> of the reigning
> follies of these days,
> to which pride and
> idleness have equally
> contributed.
>
> SAMUEL JOHNSON

APOLOGIA

By Christopher Columbus

In 1492, when he stepped upon the shore of the little Caribbean island of San Salvador, Christopher Columbus ushered in a new age of exploration and settlement the likes of which the world had never seen. He also greatly contributed to the providential perspective of American history—a view that asserts the directing hand of almighty God—through the publication of his Book of Prophesies *some ten years later. This short excerpt gives a glimpse of that perspective and captures the essence of the Admiral of the Ocean Sea's extraordinary worldview.*

At a very early age I went to sea and have continued navigating until today. The art of sailing is favorable for anyone who wants to pursue knowledge of this world's secrets. I have already been at this business for forty years. I have sailed all the waters which up to now, have been navigated. I have had dealings and conversation with learned people—clergymen and laymen, Latins and Greeks, Jews and Moors, and with many others of other sects.

I found our Lord very well disposed toward this, my desire, and he gave me the spirit for it. He prospered me in seamanship and supplied me with the necessary tools of astronomy, as well as geometry and arithmetic and ingenuity of manual skill to draw spherical maps which show cities, rivers and mountains, islands and ports—everything in its proper place.

I have seen and put into study to look into all the Scriptures, cosmography, histories, chronicles, philosophy, and other arts, which our Lord has opened to understanding, so that it became clear to me that it was feasible to navigate from here to the Indies; and He unlocked within me the determination to execute the idea. And I came to the Sovereigns of Castile and Aragon with this ardor. All those who heard about my enterprise rejected it with laughter, scoffing at me. Neither the sciences which I mentioned, nor the authoritative citations from them, were of any avail. In only the sovereigns remained faith and constancy. Who doubts that this illumination was from the Holy Spirit? I attest that He, with marvelous rays of light, consoled me through the holy and sacred Scriptures, a strong and clear testimony, with forty four books of the Old Testament, and four Gospels with twenty three Epistles of those blessed Apostles, encouraging me to proceed, and, continually, without ceasing for a moment, they inflame me with a sense of great urgency.

Our Lord wished to perform the clearest work of providence in this matter—the voyage to the Indies—to console me and others in this matter of the Holy Temple: I have spent seven years in the royal court arguing the case with many persons of such authority and learned in all the arts, and in the end they concluded that all was idle nonsense, and with this they gave up the enterprise; yet the outcome was to be the fulfillment of what our Redeemer Jesus Christ said beforehand through the mouth of the prophets.

And so the prophesy has been made manifest.

AMERICA

By Arthur Cleveland Coxe

From the time of the earliest explorations of the Norse along Ultima Thule and the Spanish in the Caribbean to the settlements of the pioneers in Virginia and Pilgrims in Massachusetts, Americans have always been proud of their courageous heritage and lineage. In this popular nineteenth-century verse, that unique legacy is celebrated.

Oh, who has not heard of the Northmen of yore,
How flew, like the sea-bird, their sails from the shore;
How, westward, they stayed not till, breasting the brine,
They hailed Narragansett, the land of the vine!

Then the war-songs of Rollo, his pennon and glaive,
Were heard as they danced by the moon-lighted wave,
And their golden-haired wives bore them sons of the soil,
While raged with the redskins their feud and turmoil.

And who has not seen, 'mid the summer's gay crowd,
That old pillared tower of their fortalice proud,
How it stands solid proof of the sea chieftains' reign
Ere came with Columbus those galleys of Spain!

Twas a claim for their kindred: an earnest of sway,
By the stout-hearted Cabot made good in its day;
Of the Cross of St. George, on the Chesapeake's tide,
Where lovely Virginia arose like a bride.

Came the Pilgrims with Wintrop; and, saint of the West,
Came Robert of Jamestown, the brave and the blest;
Came Smith, the bold rover, and Rolfe—with his ring,
To wed sweet Matoaka, child of a king.

Undaunted they came, every peril to dare,
Of tribes fiercer far than the wolf in his lair;
Of the wild irksome woods, where in ambush they lay;
Of their terror by night and their arrow by day.

And so where our capes cleave the ice of the poles,
Where groves of the orange scent sea-coast and shoals,
Where the froward Atlantic uplifts its last crest,
Where the sun, when he sets, seeks the East from the West;

The clime that from ocean to ocean expands,
The fields to the snowdrifts that stretch from the sands,
The wilds they have conquered of mountain and plain;
Those Pilgrims have made them fair Freedom's domain.

And the bread of dependence if proudly they spurned,
Twas the soul of their fathers that kindled and burned,
Twas the blood of old Saxon within them that ran;
They held—to be free is the birthright of man.

So oft the old lion, majestic of mane,
sees cubs of his cave breaking loose from his reign;
Unmeet to be his if they braved not his eye,
He gave them the spirit his own to defy.

FLAWLESS HIS HEART

By James Russell Lowell

The great critic and editor James Russell Lowell wrote a number of poems that bear testimony to the tremendous courage and tenacity of America's earliest settlers. This particular verse was a favorite during the halcyon days of optimism at the end of the nineteenth century.

Flawless his Heart and tempered to the core
Who, beckoned by the forward-leaning wave,
First left behind him the firm-footed shore,
And, urged by every nerve of sail and oar,
Steered for the Unknown which gods to mortals gave,
Of thought and action the mysterious door,
Bugbear of fools, a summons to the brave:
Strength found he in the unsympathizing sun,
And strange stars from beneath the horizon won,
and the dumb ocean pitilessly grave:
High-hearted surely he;
But bolder they who first off-cast
Their moorings from the habitable Past
And ventured chartless on the sea
Of storm-engendering Liberty:
For all earth's width of waters is a span,
And their convulsed existence mere repose,
Matched with the unstable heart of man,
Shoreless in wants, mist-girt in all it knows,
Open to every wind of sect or clan,
And sudden-passionate in ebbs and flows.

THE MAYFLOWER COMPACT

Drafted and signed on board the Mayflower as that ship approached Cape Cod on November 11, 1620, the compact is regarded as one of the most important documents in American history. It proves the determination of the small group of English separatist Christians to live under a rule of law based on the consent of the people and to set up their own civil government. The parchment has long since disappeared—the current text was first printed in London in 1622 in a pamphlet generally known as "Mourt's Relation," which contained extracts from the fledgling colony's journals and histories. In an oration delivered at Plymouth in 1802 John Quincy Adams declared that it was "perhaps the only instance, in human history, of that positive, original social compact, which speculative philosophers have imagined as the only legitimate source of government." Thus the Pilgrim Fathers had anticipated the covenantal social contract seventy years before John Locke and 140 years before Jean Jacques Rousseau.

In the name of God Amen. We whose names are underwritten, the loyal subjects of our dread sovereign Lord King James by the grace of God, of Great Britain, France, and Ireland king, defender of the faith, etceteras.

Having undertaken, for the glory of God, and advancements of the Christian faith and honor of our king & country, a voyage to plant the first colony in the Northern parts of Virginia, do by these presents solemnly & mutually in the presence of God, and one of another, covenant & combine our selves together into a civil body politick; for our better ordering, & preservation & furtherance of the ends aforesaid; and by virtue hearof to enact, constitute, and frame such just & equal laws, ordinances, acts, constitutions, and offices, from time to time, as shall be thought most meet and convenient for the general good of the Colony: unto which we promise all due submission and obedience.

In witness whereof we have hereunder subscribed our names at Cape Cod the eleventh of November, in the year the reign of our sovereign Lord King James of England, France, and Ireland the eighteenth and of Scotland the fifty fourth, Anno Dominie, 1620.

John Carver, William Bradford, Edward Winslow, William Brewster, Isaac Allerton, Myles Standish, John Alden, Samuel Fuller, Christopher Martin, William Mullins, William White, Richard Warren, John Howland, Stephen Hopkins, Edward Tilley, John Tilley, Francis Cooke, Thomas Rogers, John Turner, Francis Eaton, James Chilton, John Crakston, John Billington, Moses Fletcher, John Goodman, Degory Priest, Thomas Tinker, John Rigdale, Edward Fuller, Thomas Williams, Gilbert Winslow, Edmund

Margeson, Peter Brown, Richard Britterige, George Soule, Richard Clarke, Richard Gardiner, John Allerton, Thomas English, Edward Doty, Edward Leister.

A MODEL OF CHARITY

By John Winthrop

In the spring of 1630 eleven small cargo vessels set sail across three thousand perilous miles of ocean. On board were some seven hundred men, women, and children who were risking their lives to establish a godly Puritan community on the shores of Massachusetts. John Winthrop, the leader of the group, composed a lay sermon, "A Model of Charity," during the journey, which he probably read to the assembled ship's company. Excerpted here, the sermon expressed his intention to unite his people behind a single purpose—the creation of a due form of government, ecclesiastical as well as civil, so that their community would be a model for the Christian world to emulate. Theirs was to be, he said, a "City upon a Hill."

God Almighty in His most holy and wise providence hath so disposed of the condition of mankind, as in all times some must be rich some poor, some high and eminent in power and dignity; others mean and in subjection.

The reasons hereof: first, to hold conformity with the rest of His works, being delighted to show forth the glory of His wisdom in the variety and difference of the Creatures and the glory of His power, in ordering all these differences for the preservation and good of the whole, and the glory of His greatness that as it is the glory of princes to have many officers, so this great King will have many stewards counting Himself more honored in dispensing His gifts to man by man, than if He did it by His own immediate hand.

Secondly, that He might have the more occasion to manifest the work of His Spirit: first, upon the wicked in moderating and restraining them: so that the rich and mighty should not eat up the poor, nor the poor, and despised rise up against their superiors, and shake off their yoke; secondly, in the regenerate in exercising His graces in them, as in the great ones, their love, mercy, gentleness, temperance, etc., in the poor and inferior sort, their faith, patience, obedience, etc.

Thirdly, that every man might have need of other, and from hence they might be all knit more nearly together in the bond of brotherly affection; from hence it appears plainly that no man is made more honorable than another or more wealthy etc., out of any particular and singular respect to himself but for the glory of his Creator and the common good of the creature, man; Therefore God still reserves the property of these gifts to himself. He calls wealth "His gold and His silver." He claims their service as His due: "Honor the Lord with thy riches." All men being thus, by divine providence, ranked into two sorts, rich and poor; under the first, are comprehended all such as are able to live comfortably by their own means duly improved; and all others are poor according to the former distribution. There are two rules whereby we are to walk one towards another: justice and mercy. These are always distinguished in their act and in their object, yet may they both concur in the same subject in each respect; as sometimes there may be an occasion of showing mercy to a rich man, in some sudden danger of distress, and also doing of mere justice to a poor man in regard of some particular contract. There is likewise a double law by which we are regulated in our conversation one towards another: in both the former respects, the law of nature and the law of grace, or the moral law or the law of the gospel, to omit the rule of justice as not properly belonging to this purpose otherwise than it may fall into consideration in some particular cases; by the first of these laws man as he was enabled so withal is commanded to love his neighbor as himself. Upon this ground stands all the precepts of the moral law, which concerns our dealings with men. To apply this to the works of mercy this law requires two things: first, that every man afford his help to another in every want or distress; secondly, that he perform this out of the same affection, which makes him careful of his own good according to that of our Savior. "Whatsoever ye would that men should do to you." This was practiced by Abraham and Lot in entertaining the Angels and the old man of Gibea.

The law of grace or the gospel hath some difference from the former as in these respects: first, the law of nature was given to man in the estate of innocence; this of the gospel in the estate of regeneracy; secondly, the former propounds one man to another, as the same flesh and image of God, this as a brother in Christ also, and in the communion of the same Spirit and so teacheth us to put a difference between Christians and others. "Do good to all especially to the household of faith." Upon this ground the Israelites were to put a difference between the brethren of such as were stranger though not of the Canaanites. Thirdly, the law of nature could give no rules for dealing with enemies for all to be considered as friends in the estate of innocence, but the gospel commands love to an enemy. "If thine enemy hunger feed him; love your enemies, do good to them that hate you."

This law of the gospel propounds likewise a difference of seasons and occasions: there is a time when a Christian must sell all and give to the poor as they did in the Apostles times. There is a time also when a Christian—though they give not all yet—must give beyond their ability, as they of Macedonia. Likewise, a community of perils calls for extraordinary liberality and so doth the community in some special service for the church. Lastly, when there is no other means whereby our Christian brother may be relieved in this distress, we must help him beyond our ability, rather than tempt God, in putting him upon help by miraculous or extraordinary means.

This duty of mercy is exercised in the kinds: giving, lending, and forgiving.

What rule shall a man observe in giving in respect of the measure? If the time and occasion be ordinary he is to give out of his abundance—let him lay aside as God hath blessed him. If the time and occasion be extraordinary he must be ruled by them; taking this withal, that then a man cannot likely do too much especially, if he may leave himself and his family under probable means of comfortable subsistence.

Some though, may object, "A man must lay up for posterity, the fathers lay up for posterity and children and he is worse than an Infidel that provideth not for his own." But it is plain, first that the command is being spoken by way of comparison. It must be meant of the ordinary and usual course of fathers and cannot extend to times and occasions extraordinary. In addition, the Apostle speaks against such as walked inordinately, and it is without question, that he is worse than an infidel who through his own sloth and voluptuousness shall neglect to provide for his family.

Another may object: "The wise man's eyes are in his head and foreseeth the plague, therefore we must forecast and lay up against evil times when he or his may stand in need of all he can gather." Yet, this very argument Solomon useth to persuade to liberality: "Cast thy bread upon the waters, for thou knowest not what evil may come upon the land." Make you friends of the riches of iniquity; you will ask how this shall be; very well for first, "He that gives to the poor lends to the Lord," and He will repay him even in this life an hundred fold to him or his. The righteous is ever merciful and lendeth and his seed enjoyeth the blessing; and besides we know what advantage it will be to us in the day of account when many such witnesses shall stand forth for us to witness the improvement of our talent. And I would know of those who plead so much for laying up for time to come, whether they hold that to be. "Lay not up for yourselves Treasures upon Earth." If they acknowledge it what extent will they allow it; if only to those primitive times let them consider the reason whereupon our Savior grounds it: the first is that they are subject to the moth, the rust, the thief; secondly, they will steal away the hearse, where the treasure is there will the heart be also. The reasons are of like force at all times therefore the exhortation must be general and perpetual which applies always in respect of the love and affection to riches and in regard of the things themselves when any special service for the church or particular distress of our brother do call for the use of them; otherwise it is not only lawful but necessary to lay up as Joseph did to have ready upon such occasions, as the Lord—whose stewards we are of them—shall call for them from us: Christ gives us an instance of the first, when He sent His disciples for the ass, and bids them answer the owner thus, "The Lord hath need of him"; so when the Tabernacle was to be built He sends to his people to call for their silver and gold, and yields them no other reason but that it was for His work. When Elisha comes to the widow of Sareptah and finds her preparing to make ready her pittance for herself and family, he bids her first provide for him. He challengeth first God's purse, which she must give before she can serve her own family. All these teach us that the Lord looks that when He is pleased to call for His right in any thing we have, our own interest we have must stand aside, till His turn be served, for the other we need look no further than: "He who hath this worlds goodies and seeth his brother to need, and shuts up his compassion from him, how dwelleth the love of God in him," which comes punctually to this conclusion; "If thy brother be in want and thou canst help him, thou needst not make doubt, what thou shouldst do; if thou lovest God, thou must help him."

What rule must we observe in lending? Thou must observe whether thy brother hath present or probable, or possible means of repaying thee. If there be none of these, thou must give him according to his necessity, rather than lend him as he requires: if he hath present means of repaying thee, thou art to look at him, not as an act of mercy, but by way of commerce; wherein thou art to walk by the rule of justice, but, if his means of repaying thee be only probable or possible then is he an object of thy mercy thou must lend him, though there be danger of loosing it: "If any of thy brethren be poor, thou shalt lend him sufficient" that men might not shift off this duty by the apparent hazard, he tells them that though the Year of Jubilee were at hand—when he must remit it, if he were not able to repay it before—yet he must lend him and that cheerfully; it may not grieve thee to give him and because some might object, "Why so I should soon impoverish my self and my family," he adds with all thy work for our Savior? From him that would borrow of thee turn not away.

What rule must we observe in forgiving? Whether thou didst lend by way of commerce or in mercy, if he have nothing to pay thou must forgive him—except in cause where thou hast a surety or a lawful pledge. Every seventh year the creditor was to quit that which he lent to his brother if he were poor as appears: save when there shall be no poor with thee. In all these and like cases Christ was a general rule. "Whatsoever ye would that men should do to you do ye the same to them also."

What rule must we observe and walk by in cause of Community of peril? The same as before, but with more enlargement towards others and less respect towards our selves, and our own right hence it was that in the primitive church, "They sold all, had all things in common, neither did any man say that that which he possessed was his own." Likewise, in their return out of the captivity, because the work was great for the restoring of the church and the danger of enemies was common to all, Nehemiah exhorts the Jews to liberality and readiness in remitting their debts to their brethren, and disposeth liberally of his own to such as wanted and stands not upon his own due, which he might have demanded of them. Thus did some of our forefathers in times of persecution in England, and so did many of the faithful in other churches whereof we keep an honorable remembrance of them, and it is to be observed that both in Scriptures and latter stories of the churches that such as have been most bountiful. To the poor saints especially in these extraordinary times and occasions God hath left them highly commended to posterity, and Zacheus, Cornelius, Dorcas, Bishop Hooper, the Cuttler of Brussells and divers others. Observe again that the Scripture gives no caution to restrain any from being over liberal this way; but all men to the liberal and cheerful practice hereof by the sweetest promises as to instance one for many. "Is not this the fast that I have chosen to loose the bonds of wickedness, to take off the heavy burdens to let the oppressed go free and to break every yoke, to deal thy bread to the hungry and to bring the poor that wander into thy house, when thou seest the naked to cover them? Then shall thy light break forth as the morning, and thy health shall grow speedily, thy righteousness shall go before thee, and the glory of the Lord shall embrace thee, then thou shalt call and the Lord shall answer thee. If thou pour out thy soul to the hungry, then shall thy light spring out in darkness, and the Lord shall guide thee continually, and satisfy thy soul in draught, and make fat thy bones; thou shalt be like a watered garden, and they shall be of thee that shall build the old west places." On the contrary most heavy curses are laid upon such as are straightened towards the Lord and his people: "Curse ye Meroshe because they came not to help the Lord." He who shutteth his ears from hearing the cry of the poor, he shall cry and shall not be heard: "Go ye cursed into everlasting fire. I was hungry and ye fed me not. He that soweth sparingly shall reap sparingly."

The end is to improve our lives to do more service to the Lord the comfort and increase of the body of Christ whereof we are members that our selves and posterity may be the better preserved from the common corruptions of this evil world to serve the Lord and work out our salvation under the power and purity of His holy ordinances.

Now the only way to accomplish this end and to provide for our posterity is to follow the counsel of Micah, "to do justly, to love mercy, and to walk humbly with our God." For this end we must be knit together in this work as one man, we must entertain each other in brotherly affection, we must be willing to abridge our selves of our superfluities, for the supply of others necessities, we must uphold a familiar commerce together in all meekness, gentleness, patience and liberality, we must delight in each another, make others conditions our own, rejoice together, mourn together, labor, and suffer together, always having before our eyes our commission and community in the work, our community as members of the same body. So shall we keep the unity of the Spirit in the bond of peace. The Lord will be our God and delight to dwell among us, as His own people and will command a blessing upon us in all our ways, so that we shall see much more of his wisdom power goodness and truth than formerly we have been acquainted with. We shall find that the God of Israel is among us—when ten of us shall be able to resist a thousand of our enemies, when he shall make us a praise and glory, that men shall say of succeeding plantations: The Lord make it like that of New England. For we must consider that we shall be as a "City upon a Hill." The eyes of all people are upon us; so that if we shall deal falsely with our God in this work, we have undertaken and so cause Him to withdraw His present help from us, we shall be made a story and a by-word through the world; we shall open the mouths of enemies to speak evil of the ways of God and all professors for God's sake; we shall shame the faces of many of God's worthy servants, and cause their prayers to be turned into curses upon us till we be consumed out of the good land whither we are going.

"Beloved there is now set before us life, and good, death and evil in that we are commanded this day to love the Lord our God, and to love one another to walk in His ways and to keep His commandments and His ordinance, and His laws, and the articles of our covenant with Him that we may live and be multiplied, and that the Lord our God may bless us in the land whither we go to possess it. But if our hearts shall turn away so that we will not obey, but shall be seduced and worship other gods, our pleasures, and profits, and serve them; it is propounded unto us this day, we shall surely perish out of the good land whither we pass over this vast sea to possess it."

Therefore let us choose life that we, and our seed may live; by obeying His voice, and cleaving to Him, for He is our life, and our prosperity.

THE FIRST PROCLAMATION

By Margaret Preston

The Mayflower was not the first ship of colonists to arrive in the New World. It was not even the first in the English domains. Yet it retains a place of first importance in the lore and legend of this land. In this romantic verse we catch a glimpse of the faith, resolve, and bold sense of providence that the passengers of that little ship brought with them from across the Atlantic—and that they endowed upon all those who would follow.

"Ho, Rose! " quoth the stout Miles Standish,
    As he stood on the Mayflower's deck,
And gazed on the sandy coast-line
    That loomed as a misty speck.

"On the edge of the distant offing;
    See! yonder we have in view
Bartholomew Gosnold's 'headlands.'
    'Twas in sixteen hundred and two

"That the Concord of Dartmouth anchored
    Just there where the beach is broad,
And the merry old captain named it
    (Half swamped by the fish)—Cape Cod.

"And so as his mighty 'headlands'
    are scarcely a league away,
What say you to landing, sweetheart,
    And having a washing-day?"

"Dear heart"—and the sweet Rose Standish
    Looked up with a tear in her eye;
She was back in the flag-stoned kitchen
    Where she watched, in the days gone by:

Her mother among her maidens
    (She should watch them no more, alas!),
And saw as they stretched the linen
    To bleach on the Suffolk grass.

In a moment her brow was cloudless,
  As she leaned on the vessel's rail,
And thought of the sea-stained garments,
  Of coif and farthingale;

And the doublets of fine Welsh flannel,
  The tuckers and homespun gowns,
And the piles of the hose knitted
  From the wool of the Devon downs.

So the matrons aboard the Mayflower
  Made ready with eager hand
To drop from the deck their baskets
  As soon as the prow touched land.

And there did the Pilgrim Mothers,
  "On a Monday," the record says,
Ordain for their new-found England
  The first of her washing-days.

And there did the Pilgrim Fathers,
  With matchlock and axe well slung,
Keep guard o'er the smoking kettles
  That propt on the crotches hung.

For the trail of the startle savage
  Was over the marshy grass,
And the glint of his eyes kept peering
  Through cedar and sassafras.

And the children were mad with pleasure
  As they gathered the twigs in sheaves,
And piled on the fire the fagots,
  And heaped up the autumn leaves.

"Do the thing that is next," saith the proverb,
  And a nobler shall yet succeed:
'Tis the motive exalts the action;
  'Tis the doing, and not the deed;

For the earliest act of the heroes
Whose fame has a world-wide sway
Was—to fashion a crane for a kettle,
  And order a washing-day!

THANKSGIVING IN BOSTON

By Hezekiah Butterworth

Early on the settlers expressed their thanksgiving for the evidence of God's good providence in their lives. Despite all the hardships they faced, they recognized the peculiar opportunity they had been afforded. Thus they outwardly affirmed their fealty to God and His ways. In this verse a renowned historical poet captures that predisposition toward gratitude in early Boston.

"Praise ye the Lord!" The Psalm today
    Still rises on our ears,
Borne from the hills of Boston Bay
    Through five times fifty years,
When Wintrop's fleet from Yarmouth crept
    Out to the open main,
And through the widening waters swept,
    In April sun and rain.
"Pray to the Lord with fervent lips,"
    The leader shouted, "pray";
And prayer arose from all the ships
    As faded Yarmouth Bay.
They passed the Scilly Isles that day,
    And May-days came, and June,
And trice upon the ocean lay
    The full orb of the moon.
And as that day, on Yarmouth Bay,
    Ere England sunk from view,
While yet the rippling Solent lay
    In April skies of blue.
"Pray to the Lord with fervent lips,"
    Each morn was shouted, "pray";
And prayer arose from all the ships,
    As first in Yarmouth Bay;
Blew warm the breeze o'er Western seas,
    Through Maytime morns, and June,
Till hailed these souls the Isles of Shoals,
    Low 'neath the summer moon;

And as Cape Ann arose to view,
    And Norman's Woe they passed,
The wood-doves came the white mists through,
    And circled round each mast.
"Pray to the Lord with fervent lips,"
    Then called the leader, "pray";
And prayer arose from all the ships,
    As first in Yarmouth Bay.

Above the sea the hill-tops fair;
    God's towers—began to rise,
And odors rare breathe through the air,
    Like balms of Paradise.
Through burning skies the ospreys flew,
    And near the pine-cooled shores
Danced airy boat and thin canoe,
    To flash of sunlit oars.

"Pray to the Lord with fervent lips,"
    The leader shouted, "pray!"
Then prayer arose, and all the ships
    Sailed in Boston Bay.

The white wings folded, anchors down,
    The sea-worn fleet in line,
Fair rose the hills where Boston town
    Should rise from clouds of pine:
Fair was the harbor, summit-walled,
    And placid lay the sea.
"Praise ye the Lord," the leader called;
    "Praise ye the Lord," spake he.

"Give thanks to God with fervent lips,
    Give thanks to God today,"
The anthem rose from all the ships,
    Safe moored in Boston Bay.

ESSAYS TO DO GOOD

By Cotton Mather

One of the most brilliant and prolific of the early colonists, Cotton Mather was the scion of a prominent family of academics and clerics. His more than three hundred published works, spanning an astonishing array of subjects and disciplines, helped to establish the substantive cultural tenor of the Massachusetts colony. Perhaps his most famous book, Essays to Do Good, *excerpted here, reiterated Governor Winthrop's call for America to be a beacon light of charity and grace to the world.*

S uch glorious things are spoken in the oracles of our good God, concerning them who devise good, that a book of good devices, may very reasonably demand attention and acceptance from them that have any impressions of the most reasonable religion upon them. I am devising such a book; but at the same time offering a sorrowful demonstration, that if men would set themselves to devise good, a world of good might be done, more than there is in this present evil world.

It is very sure the world has need enough. There needs abundance to be done, that the great God and His Christ may be more known and served in the world; and that the errors which are impediments to the acknowledgment wherewith men ought to glorify their Creator and Redeemer may be rectified. There needs abundance to be done, that the evil manners of the world, by which men are drowned in perdition, may be reformed; and mankind rescued from the epidemical corruption and slavery which has overwhelmed it. There needs abundance to be done, that the miseries of the world may have remedies and abatements provided for them; and that miserable people may be relieved and comforted.

The world has according to the computation of some, above seven hundred millions of people now living in it. What an ample field among all these, to do good upon! In a word, the kingdom of God in the world, calls for innumerable services from us. To do such things is to do good. Those men devise good, who shape any devices to do things of such a tendency, whether the things be of a spiritual importance, or of a temporal.

You see, the general matter, appearing as yet, but as a chaos, which is to be wrought upon. Oh! that the good Spirit of God may now fall upon us, and carry on the glorious work which lies before us.

SIR HUMPHREY GILBERT

By Henry Wadsworth Longfellow

The grave dangers of those first few adventures in colonization and settlement were highlighted in the songs, legends, and folklore of the American experience. This verse from one of the nation's greatest poets captures the sense of this peril—and the tragedy that often accompanied it.

S outhward with fleet of ice
    Sailed the corsair, Death;
Wild and fast blew the blast,
    And the East Wind was his breath.

His lordly ships of ice
    Glisten in the sun;
On each side, like pinions wide,
    Flashing crystal streamlets run.

His sails of white sea-mist
    Dripped with silver rain;
But where he passed there were cast
    Leaden shadows o'er the main.

Eastward from Campobello
    Sir Humphrey Gilbert sailed;
Three days or more seaward he bore,
    Then, alas! the land wind failed.

Alas! the land wind failed,
    And ice-cold grew the night;
And nevermore, on sea or shore,
    Should Sir Humphrey see the light.

He sat upon the deck,
    The Book was in his hand;
"Do not fear! Heaven is as near,"
    He said, "by water as by land!"

In the first watch of the night,
    Without a signal's sound,
Out of the sea, mysteriously,
    The fleet of Death rose all around.

The moon and the evening star
    Were hanging in the shrouds;
Every mast, as it passed,
    Seemed to rake the passing clouds.

They grappled with their prize,
    At midnight black and cold!
As of a rock was the shock;
    Heavily the ground swell rolled.

Southward through day and dark,
    They drift in close embrace,
With mist and rain, o'er the open main;
    Yet there seems no change of place.

Southward, forever southward,
    They drift through dark and day;
And like a dream, in the Gulf Stream
    Sinking, vanish all away.

POCAHONTAS

By William Makepeace Thackeray

The story of the Indian princess Pocahontas is among the greatest romances of the American frontier. In this retelling of the story a famed English author highlights the valor demonstrated by all the inhabitants of the rugged land—both the native and the newly arrived.

W earied arm and broken sword
    Wage in vain the desperate fight;
Round him press a countless horde,
    He is but a single knight.

Hark! A cry of triumph shrill
  Through the wilderness resounds,
As, with twenty bleeding wounds,
  Sinks the warrior, fighting still.

Now they heap the funeral pyre,
  And the torch of death they light;
Ah! Tis hard to die by fire!
  Who will shield the captive knight?
Round the stake with fiendish cry
  Wheel and dance the savage crowd,
  Cold the victim's mien and proud,
  And his breast is bared to die.

Who will shield the fearless heart?
  Who avert the murderous blade?
From the throng with sudden start
  See, there springs an Indian maid.
Quick she stands before the knight:
  "Loose the chain, unbind the ring!
  I am daughter of the King,
  And claim the Indian right!"

Dauntlessly aside she flings
  Lifted axe and thirsty knife,
Fondly to his heart she clings,
  And her bosom guards his life!
In the woods of Powhatan,
  Still tis told by Indian fires
  How a daughter of their sires
  Saved a captive Englishman.

FIVE KERNELS OF CORN

By Hezekiah Butterworth

*The first few winters in the New World were treacherous for the new colonists.
The settlers of the Plymouth colony died in droves from both sickness and
starvation. In this verse the necessity of rationing the meager food resources is
set alongside the abundant moral reserves of the people. Long a part of New*

England holiday tradition—before the turkey is carved each member of the family is served a mere five kernels of corn, after which this inspiring poem is recited— the remembrance of Plymouth has become a symbol of the incredible blessing of this land.

T was the year of the famine in Plymouth of old,
    The ice and the snow from the thatched roofs had rolled;
Through the warm purple skies steered the geese o'er the seas,
    And the woodpeckers tapped in the clocks of the trees;
And the boughs on the slopes to the south winds lay bare,
    And dreaming of summer, the buds swelled in the air.
The pale Pilgrims welcomed each reddening morn;
    There were left but for rations Five Kernels of Corn.
    Five Kernels of Corn!
    Five Kernels of Corn!
But to Bradford a feast were Five Kernels of Corn!

"Five Kernels of Corn! Five Kernels of Corn!
    Ye people, be glad for Five Kernels of Corn!"
So Bradford cried out on bleak Burial Hill,
    And the thin women stood in their doors, white and still.
"Lo, the harbor of Plymouth rolls bright in the Spring,
    The maples grow red, and the wood robins sing,
The west wind is blowing, and fading the snow
    And the pleasant pines sing, and arbutuses blow.
    Five Kernels of Corn!
    Five Kernels of Corn!
To each one be given Five Kernels of Corn!"

O Bradford of Austerfield haste on thy way.
    The west winds are blowing o'er Provincetown Bay,
The white avens bloom, but the pine domes are chill,
    And new graves have furrowed Precisioners' Hill!
"Give thanks, all ye people, the warm skies have come,
    The hilltops are sunny, and green grows the holm,
And the trumpets of winds, and the white March is gone,
    And ye still have left you Five Kernels of Corn.
    Five Kernels of Corn!
    Five Kernels of Corn!
Ye have for Thanksgiving Five Kernels of Corn!

"The raven's gift eat and be humble and pray,
    A new light is breaking, and Truth leads your way;
One taper a thousand shall kindle: rejoice
    That to you has been given the wilderness voice!"
O Bradford of Austerfield, daring the wave,
    And safe though the sounding blasts leading the brave,
Of deeds such as thine was the free nation born,
    And the festal world sings the "Five Kernels of Corn."
    Five Kernels of Corn!
    Five Kernels of Corn!
The nation gives thanks for Five Kernels of Corn!
To the Thanksgiving Feast bring Five Kernels of Corn!

THE COURTSHIP OF MILES STANDISH

By Henry Wadsworth Longfellow

One of the most beautiful of Longfellow's many historical epics, this poem describes not only the romance of two young Puritans in the New World, but also the way of life and state of mind the colonists possessed. It is one of the best and most delightful snapshots of those early heroic days.

I: MILES STANDISH

In the Old Colony days, in Plymouth the land of the Pilgrims,
To and fro in a room of his simple and primitive dwelling,
Clad in doublet and hose, and boots of Cordovan leather,
Strode, with a martial air, Miles Standish the Puritan Captain.
Buried in thought he seemed, with his hands behind him, and pausing,
Ever and anon to behold his glittering weapons of warfare,
Hanging in shining array along the walls of the chamber,
Cutlass and corselet of steel, and his trusty sword of Damascus,
Curved at the point and inscribed with its mystical Arabic sentence,
While underneath, in a corner, were fowling-piece, musket, and matchlock.
Short of stature he was, but strongly built and athletic,
Broad in the shoulders, deep-chested, with muscles and sinews of iron,
Brown as a nut was his face, but his russet beard was already
Flaked with patches of snow, as hedges sometimes in November.

Near him was seated John Alden, his friend and household companion,
Writing with diligent speed at a table of pine by the window;
Fair-haired, azure-eyed, with delicate Saxon complexion,
Having the dew of his youth, and the beauty thereof, as the captives,
Whom Saint Gregory saw, and exclaimed, "Not Angles, but Angels."
Youngest of all was he of the men who came in the Mayflower.

Suddenly breaking the silence, the diligent scribe interrupting,
Spake, in the pride of his heart, Miles Standish the Captain of Plymouth.
"Look at these arms," he said, "the warlike weapons that hang here
Burnished and bright and clean, as if for parade or inspection!
This is the sword of Damascus I fought with in Flanders; this breastplate,
Well I remember the day! once saved my life in a skirmish;
Here in front you can see the very dint of the bullet
Fired point-blank at my heart by a Spanish arcabucero.
Had it not been of sheer steel, the forgotten bones of Miles Standish
Would at this moment be mould, in their grave in the Flemish morasses."
Thereupon answered John Alden, but looked not up from his writing:
"Truly the breath of the Lord hath slackened the speed of the bullet
He in his mercy preserved you, to be our shield and our weapon!"
Still the Captain continued, unheeding the words of the stripling:
"See, how bright they are burnished, as if in an arsenal hanging;
That is because I have done it myself, and not left it to others.
Serve yourself, would you be well served, is an excellent adage;
So I take care of my arms, as you of your pens and your inkhorn.
Then, too, there are my soldiers, my great, invincible army,
Twelve men, all equipped, having each his rest and his matchlock
Eighteen shillings a month, together with diet and pillage,
And, like Cæsar, I know the name of each of my soldiers!"
This he said with a smile, that danced in his eyes, as the sunbeams
Dance on the waves of the sea, and vanish again in a moment.
Alden laughed as he wrote, and still the Captain continued:
"Look! you can see from this window my brazen howitzer planted
High on the roof of the church, a preacher who speaks to the purpose,
Steady, straightforward, and strong, with irresistible logic,
Orthodox, flashing conviction right into the hearts of the heathen.
Now we are ready, I think, for any assault of the Indians
Let them come, if they like, and the sooner they try it the better,
Let them come, if they like, be it sagamore, sachem, or pow-wow,
Aspinet, Samoset, Corbitant, Squanto, or Tokamahamon!"

Long at the window he stood, and wistfully gazed on the landscape,
Washed with a cold gray mist, the vapory breath of the east-wind,
Forest and meadow and hill, and the steel-blue rim of the ocean,
Lying silent and sad, in the afternoon shadows and sunshine.
Over his countenance flitted a shadow like those on the landscape,
Gloom intermingled with light; and his voice was subdued with emotion,
Tenderness, pity, regret, as after a pause he proceeded:
"Yonder there, on the hill by the sea, lies buried Rose Standish;
Beautiful rose of love, that bloomed for me by the wayside!
She was the first to die of all who came in the Mayflower!
Green above her is growing the field of wheat we have sown there,
Better to hide from the Indian scouts the graves of our people,
Lest they should count them and see how many already have perished!"
Sadly his face he averted, and strode up and down, and was thoughtful.

Fixed to the opposite wall was a shelf of books, and among them
Prominent three, distinguished alike for bulk and for binding
Bariffe's Artillery Guide, and the Commentaries of Cæsar
Out of the Latin translated by Arthur Goldinge of London
And, as if guarded by these, between them was standing the Bible.
Musing a moment before them, Miles Standish paused, as if doubtful
Which of the three he should choose for his consolation and comfort,
Whether the wars of the Hebrews, the famous campaigns of the Romans,
Or the Artillery practice, designed for belligerent Christians.
Finally down from its shelf he dragged the ponderous Roman,
Seated himself at the window, and opened the book, and in silence
Turned o'er the well-worn leaves, where thumb-marks thick on the margin,
Like the trample of feet, proclaimed the battle was hottest.
Nothing was heard in the room but the hurrying pen of the stripling,
Busily writing epistles important, to go by the Mayflower,
Ready to sail on the morrow, or next day at latest, God willing!
Homeward bound with the tidings of all that terrible winter,
Letters written by Alden, and full of the name of Priscilla!
Full of the name and the fame of the Puritan maiden Priscilla!

II: Love and Friendship

Nothing was heard in the room but the hurrying pen of the stripling,
Or an occasional sigh from the laboring heart of the Captain
Reading the marvellous words and achievements of Julius Cæsar.
After a while he exclaimed, as he smote with his hand, palm downwards,

Heavily on the page: "A wonderful man was this Cæsar!
You are a writer, and I am a fighter, but here is a fellow
Who could both write and fight, and in both was equally skilful!"
Straightway answered and spake John Alden, the comely, the youthful:
"Yes, he was equally skilled, as you say, with his pen and his weapons.
Somewhere have I read, but where I forget, he could dictate
Seven letters at once, at the same time writing his memoirs."
"Truly," continued the Captain, not heeding or hearing the other,
"Truly a wonderful man was Caius Julius Cæsar!
Better be first, he said, in a little Iberian village,
Than be second in Rome, and I think he was right when he said it.
Twice was he married before he was twenty, and many times after;
Battles five hundred he fought, and a thousand cities he conquered;
He, too, fought in Flanders, as he himself has recorded
Finally he was stabbed by his friend, the orator Brutus!
Now, do you know what he did on a certain occasion in Flanders,
When the rear-guard of his army retreated, the front giving way too
And the immortal Twelfth Legion was crowded so closely together
There was no room for their swords? Why, he seized a shield from a soldier
Put himself straight at the head of his troops, and commanded the captains,
Calling on each by his name, to order forward the ensigns;
Then to widen the ranks, and give more room for their weapons;
So he won the day, the battle of something-or-other.
That's what I always say; if you wish a thing to be well done,
You must do it yourself, you must not leave it to others!"

All was silent again; the Captain continued his reading.
Nothing was heard in the room but the hurrying pen of the stripling
Writing epistles important to go next day by the Mayflower,
Filled with the name and the fame of the Puritan maiden Priscilla
Every sentence began or closed with the name of Priscilla,
Till the treacherous pen, to which he confided the secret,
Strove to betray it by singing and shouting the name of Priscilla!
Finally closing his book, with a bang of the ponderous cover,
Sudden and loud as the sound of a soldier grounding his musket,
Thus to the young man spake Miles Standish the Captain of Plymouth:
"When you have finished your work, I have something important to tell you.
Be not however in haste; I can wait; I shall not be impatient!"
Straightway Alden replied, as he folded the last of his letters,
Pushing his papers aside, and giving respectful attention:
"Speak; for whenever you speak, I am always ready to listen,
Always ready to hear whatever pertains to Miles Standish."

Thereupon answered the Captain, embarrassed, and culling his phrases:
"Tis not good for a man to be alone, say the Scriptures.
This I have said before, and again and again I repeat it;
Every hour in the day, I think it, and feel it, and say it.
Since Rose Standish died, my life has been weary and dreary;
Sick at heart have I been, beyond the healing of friendship;
Oft in my lonely hours have I thought of the maiden Priscilla.
She is alone in the world; her father and mother and brother
Died in the winter together; I saw her going and coming,
Now to the grave of the dead, and now to the bed of the dying,
Patient, courageous, and strong, and said to myself, that if ever
There were angels on earth, as there are angels in heaven,
Two have I seen and known; and the angel whose name is Priscilla
Holds in my desolate life the place which the other abandoned.
Long have I cherished the thought, but never have dared to reveal it
Being a coward in this though valiant enough for the most part.
Go to the damsel Priscilla, the loveliest maiden of Plymouth,
Say that a blunt old Captain, a man not of words but of actions,
Offers his hand and his heart, the hand and heart of a soldier.
Not in these words, you know, but this in short is my meaning;
I am a maker of war, and not a maker of phrases.
You, who are bred as a scholar, can say it in elegant language,
Such as you read in your books of the pleadings and wooings of lovers,
Such as you think best adapted to win the heart of a maiden."

When he had spoken, John Alden, the fair-haired, taciturn stripling,
All aghast at his words, surprised, embarrassed, bewildered,
Trying to mask his dismay by treating the subject with lightness,
Trying to smile, and yet feeling his heart stand still in his bosom,
Just as a timepiece stops in a house that is stricken by lightning,
Thus made answer and spake, or rather stammered than answered:
"Such a message as that, I am sure I should mangle and mar it;
If you would have it well done, I am only repeating your maxim,
You must do it yourself, you must not leave it to others!"
But with the air of a man whom nothing can turn from his purpose,
Gravely shaking his head, made answer the Captain of Plymouth:
"Truly the maxim is good, and I do not mean to gainsay it;
But we must use it discreetly, and not waste powder for nothing.
Now, as I said before, I was never a maker of phrases.
I can march up to a fortress and summon the place to surrender,
But march up to a woman with such a proposal, I dare not.
I'm not afraid of bullets, nor shot from the mouth of a cannon,

But of a thundering 'No!' point-blank from the mouth of woman,
That I confess I'm afraid of, nor am I ashamed to confess it!
So you must grant my request, for you are an elegant scholar,
Having the graces of speech, and skill in the turning of phrases."
Taking the hand of his friend, who still was reluctant and doubtful,
Holding it long in his own, and pressing it kindly, he added:
"Though I have spoken thus lightly, yet deep is the feeling that prompts me;
Surely you cannot refuse what I ask in the name of our friendship!"
Then made answer John Alden: "The name of friendship is sacred;
What you demand in that name, I have not the power to deny you!"
So the strong will prevailed, subduing and moulding the gentler,
Friendship prevailed over love, and Alden went on his errand.

III: THE LOVER'S ERRAND

So the strong will prevailed, and Alden went on his errand,
Out of the street of the village, and into the paths of the forest,
Into the tranquil woods, where bluebirds and robins were building
Towns in the populous trees, with hanging gardens of verdure,
Peaceful, aerial cities of joy and affection and freedom.
All around him was calm, but within him commotion and conflict,
Love contending with friendship, and self with each generous impulse.
To and fro in his breast his thoughts were heaving and dashing,
As in a foundering ship, with every roll of the vessel,
Washes the bitter sea, the merciless surge of the ocean!
"Must I relinquish it all," he cried with a wild lamentation,
"Must I relinquish it all, the joy, the hope, the illusion?
Was it for this I have loved, and waited, and worshiped in silence?
Was it for this I have followed the flying feet and the shadow
Over the wintry sea, to the desolate shores of New England?
Truly the heart is deceitful, and out of its depths of corruption
Rise, like an exhalation, the misty phantoms of passion;
Angels of light they seem, but are only delusions of Satan.
All is clear to me now; I feel it, I see it distinctly!
This is the hand of the Lord; it is laid upon me in anger,
For I have followed too much the heart's desires and devices,
Worshiping Astaroth blindly, and impious idols of Baal.
This is the cross I must bear; the sin and the swift retribution."
So through the Plymouth woods John Alden went on his errand;
Crossing the brook at the ford, where it brawled over pebble and shallow,

Gathering still, as he went, the May-flowers blooming around him,
Fragrant, filling the air with a strange and wonderful sweetness,
Children lost in the woods, and covered with leaves in their slumber.
"Puritan flowers," he said, "and the type of Puritan maidens,
Modest and simple and sweet, the very type of Priscilla!
So I will take them to her; to Priscilla the Mayflower of Plymouth
Modest and simple and sweet, as a parting gift will I take them
Breathing their silent farewells, as they fade and wither and perish
Soon to be thrown away as is the heart of the giver."

So through the Plymouth woods John Alden went on his errand;
Came to an open space, and saw the disk of the ocean,
Sailless, sombre and cold with the comfortless breath of the east-wind;
Saw the new-built house, and people at work in a meadow;
Heard, as he drew near the door, the musical voice of Priscilla
Singing the hundredth Psalm, the grand old Puritan anthem,
Music that Luther sang to the sacred words of the Psalmist,
Full of the breath of the Lord, consoling and comforting many.
Then, as he opened the door, he beheld the form of the maiden
Seated beside her wheel, and the carded wool like a snow-drift
Piled at her knee, her white hands feeding the ravenous spindle,
While with her foot on the treadle she guided the wheel in its motion.
Open wide on her lap lay the well-worn psalm-book of Ainsworth,
Printed in Amsterdam, the words and the music together,
Rough-hewn, angular notes, like stones in the wall of a churchyard,
Darkened and overhung by the running vine of the verses.
Such was the book from whose pages she sang the old Puritan anthem
She, the Puritan girl, in the solitude of the forest,
Making the humble house and the modest apparel of homespun
Beautiful with her beauty, and rich with the wealth of her being!
Over him rushed, like a wind that is keen and cold and relentless,
Thoughts of what might have been, and the weight and woe of his errand;
All the dreams that had faded, and all the hopes that had vanished,
All his life henceforth a dreary and tenantless mansion,
Haunted by vain regrets, and pallid, sorrowful faces.
Still he said to himself, and almost fiercely he said it,
"Let not him that putteth his hand to the plough look backwards;
Though the ploughshare cut through the flowers of life to its fountains
Though it pass o'er the graves of the dead and the hearths of the living,
It is the will of the Lord; and his mercy endureth forever!"

So he entered the house: and the hum of the wheel and the singing
Suddenly ceased, for Priscilla, aroused by his step on the threshold,
Rose as he entered; and gave him her hand, in signal of welcome,
Saying, "I knew it was you, when I heard your step in the passage;
For I was thinking of you, as I sat there singing and spinning."
Awkward and dumb with delight, that a thought of him had been mingled
Thus in the sacred psalm, that came from the heart of the maiden,
Silent before her he stood, and gave her the flowers for an answer,
Finding no words for his thought. He remembered that day in the winter
After the first great snow, when he broke a path from the village,
Reeling and plunging along through the drifts that encumbered the doorway,
Stamping the snow from his feet as he entered the house, and Priscilla
Laughed at his snowy locks, and gave him a seat by the fireside,
Grateful and pleased to know he had thought of her in the snowstorm.
Had he but spoken then! perhaps not in vain had he spoken
Now it was all too late; the golden moment had vanished!
So he stood there abashed, and gave her the flowers for an answer.

Then they sat down and talked of the birds and the beautiful Spring-time,
Talked of their friends at home, and the Mayflower that sailed on the
     morrow.
"I have been thinking all day," said gently the Puritan maiden
"Dreaming all night, and thinking all day, of the hedge-rows of England,
They are in blossom now, and the country is all like a garden:
Thinking of lanes and fields, and the song of the lark and the linnet,
Seeing the village street, and familiar faces of neighbors
Going about as of old, and stopping to gossip together,
And, at the end of the street, the village church, with the ivy
Climbing the old gray tower, and the quiet graves in the church-yard.
Kind are the people I live with, and dear to me my religion;
Still my heart is so sad, that I wish myself back in Old England.
You will say it is wrong, but I cannot help it: I almost
Wish myself back in Old England, I feel so lonely and wretched."
Thereupon answered the youth: "Indeed I do not condemn you;
Stouter hearts than a woman's have quailed in this terrible winter.
Yours is tender and trusting, and needs a stronger to lean on;
So I have come to you now, with an offer and proffer of marriage
Made by a good man and true, Miles Standish the Captain of Plymouth!"

Thus he delivered his message, the dexterous writer of letters,
Did not embellish the theme, nor array it in beautiful phrases,
But came straight to the point, and blurted it out like a school-boy;

Even the Captain himself could hardly have said it more bluntly.
Mute with amazement and sorrow, Priscilla the Puritan maiden
Looked into Alden's face, her eyes dilated with wonder,
Feeling his words like a blow, that stunned her and rendered her
    speechless;
Till at length she exclaimed, interrupting the ominous silence:
"If the great Captain of Plymouth is so very eager to wed me,
Why does he not come himself, and take the trouble to woo me?
If I am not worth the wooing, I surely am not worth the winning!"
Then John Alden began explaining and smoothing the matter,
Making it worse as he went, by saying the Captain was busy,
Had no time for such things—such things! the words grating harshly
Fell on the ear of Priscilla; and swift as a flash she made answer:
"Has he no time for such things, as you call it, before he is married,
Would he be likely to find it, or make it, after the wedding?
That is the way with you men; you don't understand us, you cannot.
When you have made up your minds, after thinking of this one and that one,
Choosing, selecting, rejecting, comparing one with another,
Then you make known your desire, with abrupt and sudden avowal,
And are offended and hurt, and indignant perhaps, that a woman
Does not respond at once to a love that she never suspected,
Does not attain at a bound the height to which you have been climbing.
This is not right nor just: for surely a woman's affection
Is not a thing to be asked for, and had for only the asking.
When one is truly in love, one not only says it, but shows it.
Had he but waited awhile, had he only showed that he loved me,
Even this Captain of yours—who knows?—at last might have won me,
Old and rough as he is; but now it never can happen."

Still John Alden went on, unheeding the words of Priscilla,
Urging the suit of his friend, explaining, persuading, expanding;
Spoke of his courage and skill, and of all his battles in Flanders,
How with the people of God he had chosen to suffer affliction;
How, in return for his zeal, they had made him Captain of Plymouth;
He was a gentleman born, could trace his pedigree plainly
Back to Hugh Standish of Duxbury Hall, in Lancashire, England,
Who was the son of Ralph, and the grandson of Thurston de Standish;
Heir unto vast estates, of which he was basely defrauded,
Still bore the family arms, and had for his crest a cock argent,
Combed and wattled gules, and all the rest of the blazon.
He was a man of honor, of noble and generous nature;
Though he was rough, he was kindly; she knew how during the winter

He had attended the sick, with a hand as gentle as woman's;
Somewhat hasty and hot, he could not deny it, and headstrong,
Stern as a soldier might be, but hearty, and placable always,
Not to be laughed at and scorned, because he was little of stature;
For he was great of heart, magnanimous, courtly, courageous;
Any woman in Plymouth, nay, any woman in England,
Might be happy and proud to be called the wife of Miles Standish!

But as he warmed and glowed, in his simple and eloquent language,
Quite forgetful of self, and full of the praise of his rival,
Archly the maiden smiled, and, with eyes overrunning with laughter
Said, in a tremulous voice, "Why don't you speak for yourself, John?"

IV: JOHN ALDEN

Into the open air John Alden, perplexed and bewildered,
Rushed like a man insane, and wandered alone by the sea-side;
Paced up and down the sands, and bared his head to the east-wind,
Cooling his heated brow, and the fire and fever within him.
Slowly as out of the heavens, with apocalyptical splendors,
Sank the City of God, in the vision of John the Apostle,
So, with its cloudy walls of chrysolite, jasper, and sapphire,
Sank the broad red sun, and over its turrets uplifted
Glimmered the golden reed of the angel who measured the city.
"Welcome, O wind of the East!" he exclaimed in his wild exultation,
"Welcome, O wind of the East, from the caves of the misty Atlantic!
Blowing o'er fields of dulse, and measureless meadows of sea-grass,
Blowing o'er rocky wastes, and the grottoes and gardens of ocean!
Lay thy cold, moist hand on my burning forehead, and wrap me
Close in thy garments of mist, to allay the fever within me!"

Like an awakened conscience, the sea was moaning and tossing,
Beating remorseful and loud the mutable sands of the sea-shore.
Fierce in his soul was the struggle and tumult of passions contending
Love triumphant and crowned, and friendship wounded and bleeding,
Passionate cries of desire, and importunate pleadings of duty!
"Is it my fault," he said, "that the maiden has chosen between us?
Is it my fault that he failed,—my fault that I am the victor?"
Then within him there thundered a voice, like the voice of the Prophet:
"It hath displeased the Lord!"—and he thought of David's transgression,

Bathsheba's beautiful face, and his friend in the front of the battle!
Shame and confusion of guilt, and abasement and self-condemnation,
Overwhelmed him at once; and he cried in the deepest contrition:
"It hath displeased the Lord! It is the temptation of Satan!"

Then, uplifting his head, he looked at the sea, and beheld there
Dimly the shadowy form of the Mayflower riding at anchor,
Rocked on the rising tide, and ready to sail on the morrow;
Heard the voices of men through the mist, the rattle of cordage
Thrown on the deck, the shouts of the mate, and the sailors' "Ay, ay, Sir!"
Clear and distinct, but not loud, in the dripping air of the twilight.
Still for a moment he stood, and listened, and stared at the vessel,
Then went hurriedly on, as one who, seeing a phantom
Stops, then quickens his pace, and follows the beckoning shadow.
"Yes, it is plain to me now," he murmured; "the hand of the Lord is
Leading me out of the land of darkness, the bondage of error,
Through the sea, that shall lift the walls of its waters around me
Hiding me, cutting me off, from the cruel thoughts that pursue me.
Back will I go o'er the ocean, this dreary land will abandon
Her whom I may not love, and him whom my heart has offended.
Better to be in my grave in the green old churchyard in England,
Close by my mother's side, and among the dust of my kindred;
Better be dead and forgotten, than living in shame and dishonor;
Sacred and safe and unseen, in the dark of the narrow chamber
With me my secret shall lie, like a buried jewel that glimmers
Bright on the hand that is dust, in the chambers of silence and darkness,
Yes, as the marriage ring of the great espousal hereafter!"

Thus as he spake, he turned, in the strength of his strong resolution
Leaving behind him the shore, and hurried along in the twilight,
Through the congenial gloom of the forest silent and sombre,
Till he beheld the lights in the seven houses of Plymouth,
Shining like seven stars in the dusk and mist of the evening.
Soon he entered his door, and found the redoubtable Captain
Sitting alone, and absorbed in the martial pages of Cæsar,
Fighting some great campaign in Hainault or Brabant or Flanders.
"Long have you been on your errand," he said with a cheery demeanor,
Even as one who is waiting an answer, and fears not the issue.
"Not far off is the house, although the woods are between us;
But you have lingered so long, that while you were going and coming
I have fought ten battles and sacked and demolished a city.
Come, sit down, and in order relate to me all that has happened."

Then John Alden spake, and related the wondrous adventure,
From beginning to end, minutely, just as it happened;
How he had seen Priscilla, and how he had sped in his courtship,
Only smoothing a little, and softening down her refusal.
But when he came at length to the words Priscilla had spoken,
Words so tender and cruel: "Why don't you speak for yourself, John?"
Up leaped the Captain of Plymouth, and stamped on the floor, till his armor
Clanged on the wall, where it hung, with a sound of sinister omen.
All his pent-up wrath burst forth in a sudden explosion,
E'en as a hand-grenade, that scatters destruction around it.
Wildly he shouted, and loud: "John Alden! you have betrayed me!
Me, Miles Standish, your friend! have supplanted, defrauded, betrayed me!
One of my ancestors ran his sword through the heart of Wat Tyler;
Who shall prevent me from running my own through the heart of a traitor?
Yours is the greater treason, for yours is a treason to friendship!
You, who lived under my roof, whom I cherished and loved as a brother
You, who have fed at my board, and drunk at my cup, to whose keeping
I have entrusted my honor, my thoughts the most sacred and secret,—
You too, Brutus! ah woe to the name of friendship hereafter!
Brutus was Cæsar's friend, and you were mine, but henceforward
Let there be nothing between us save war, and implacable hatred!"

So spake the Captain of Plymouth, and strode about in the chamber,
Chafing and choking with rage; like cords were the veins on his temples.
But in the midst of his anger a man appeared at the doorway,
Bringing in uttermost haste a message of urgent importance,
Rumors of danger and war and hostile incursions of Indians!
Straightway the Captain paused, and, without further question or parley,
Took from the nail on the wall his sword with its scabbard of iron,
Buckled the belt round his waist, and, frowning fiercely, departed.
Alden was left alone. He heard the clank of the scabbard
Growing fainter and fainter, and dying away in the distance.
Then he arose from his seat, and looked forth into the darkness,
Felt the cool air blow on his cheek, that was hot with the insult,
Lifted his eyes to the heavens, and, folding his hands as in childhood,
Prayed in the silence of night to the Father who seeth in secret.

Meanwhile the choleric Captain strode wrathful away to the council,
Found it already assembled, impatiently waiting his coming;
Men in the middle of life, austere and grave in deportment,
Only one of them old, the hill that was nearest to heaven,
Covered with snow, but erect, the excellent Elder of Plymouth.

God had sifted three kingdoms to find the wheat for this planting,
Then had sifted the wheat, as the living seed of a nation;
So say the chronicles old, and such is the faith of the people!
Near them was standing an Indian, in attitude stern and defiant,
Naked down to the waist, and grim and ferocious in aspect
While on the table before them was lying unopened a Bible,
Ponderous, bound in leather, brass-studded, printed in Holland,
And beside it outstretched the skin of a rattlesnake glittered,
Filled, like a quiver, with arrows; a signal and challenge of warfare,
Brought by the Indian, and speaking with arrowy tongues of defiance.
This Miles Standish beheld, as he entered, and heard them debating
What were an answer befitting the hostile message and menace,
Talking of this and of that, contriving, suggesting, objecting;
One voice only for peace, and that the voice of the Elder,
Judging it wise and well that some at least were converted,
Rather than any were slain, for this was but Christian behavior!
Then out spake Miles Standish, the stalwart Captain of Plymouth,
Muttering deep in his throat, for his voice was husky with anger,
"What! do you mean to make war with milk and the water of roses?
Is it to shoot red squirrels you have your howitzer planted
There on the roof of the church, or is it to shoot red devils?
Truly the only tongue that is understood by a savage
Must be the tongue of fire that speaks from the mouth of the cannon!"
Thereupon answered and said the excellent Elder of Plymouth,
Somewhat amazed and alarmed at this irreverent language;
"Not so thought St. Paul, nor yet the other Apostles;
Not from the cannon's mouth were the tongues of fire they spake with!"
But unheeded fell this mild rebuke on the Captain,
Who had advanced to the table, and thus continued discoursing:
"Leave this matter to me, for to me by right it pertaineth.
War is a terrible trade; but in the cause that is righteous,
Sweet is the smell of powder; and thus I answer the challenge!"
Then from the rattlesnake's skin, with a sudden, contemptuous gesture
Jerking the Indian arrows, he filled it with powder and bullets
Full to the very jaws, and handed it back to the savage,
Saying, in thundering tones: "Here, take it! this is your answer!"
Silently out of the room then glided the glistening savage,
Bearing the serpent's skin, and seeming himself like a serpent,
Winding his sinuous way in the dark to the depths of the forest.

V: THE SAILING OF THE MAYFLOWER

Just in the gray of the dawn, as the mists uprose from the meadows,
There was a stir and a sound in the slumbering village of Plymouth;
Clanging and clicking of arms, and the order imperative, "Forward!"
Given in tone suppressed, a tramp of feet, and then silence.
Figures ten, in the mist, marched slowly out of the village.
Standish the stalwart it was, with eight of his valorous army,
Led by their Indian guide, by Hobomok, friend of the white men,
Northward marching to quell the sudden revolt of the savage.
Giants they seemed in the mist, or the mighty men of King David;
Giants in heart they were, who believed in God and the Bible,—
Ay, who believed in the smiting of Midianites and Philistines.
Over them gleamed far off the crimson banners of morning;
Under them loud on the sands, the serried billows, advancing,
Fired along the line, and in regular order retreated.

Many a mile had they marched, when at length the village of Plymouth
Woke from its sleep, and arose, intent on its manifold labors.
Sweet was the air and soft; and slowly the smoke from the chimneys
Rose over roofs of thatch, and pointed steadily eastward;
Men came forth from the doors, and paused and talked of the weather
Said that the wind had changed, and was blowing fair for the Mayflower;
Talked of their Captain's departure, and all the dangers that menaced,
He being gone, the town, and what should be done in his absence.
Merrily sang the birds, and the tender voices of women
Consecrated with hymns the common cares of the household.
Out of the sea rose the sun, and the billows rejoiced at his coming;
Beautiful were his feet on the purple tops of the mountains;
Beautiful on the sails of the Mayflower riding at anchor,
Battered and blackened and worn by all the storms of the winter.
Loosely against her masts was hanging and flapping her canvas,
Rent by so many gales, and patched by the hands of the sailors.
Suddenly from her side, as the sun rose over the ocean
Darted a puff of smoke, and floated seaward, anon rang
Loud over field and forest the cannon's roar, and the echoes
Heard and repeated the sound, the signal-gun of departure!
Ah! but with louder echoes replied the hearts of the people!
Meekly, in voices subdued, the chapter was read from the Bible
Meekly the prayer was begun, but ended in fervent entreaty!
Then from their houses in haste came forth the Pilgrims of Plymouth,
Men and women and children, all hurrying down to the sea-shore

Eager, with tearful eyes, to say farewell to the Mayflower
Homeward bound o'er the sea, and leaving them here in the desert.

Foremost among them was Alden. All night he had lain without slumber,
Turning and tossing about in the heat and unrest of his fever.
He had beheld Miles Standish, who came back late from the council
Stalking into the room, and heard him mutter and murmur;
Sometimes it seemed a prayer, and sometimes it sounded like swearing.
Once he had come to the bed, and stood there a moment in silence;
Then he had turned away, and said: "I will not awake him
Let him sleep on, it is best; for what is the use of more talking!"
Then he extinguished the light, and threw himself down on his pallet,
Dressed as he was, and ready to start at the break of the morning,
Covered himself with the cloak he had worn in his campaigns in
    Flanders,—
Slept as a soldier sleeps in his bivouac, ready for action.
But with the dawn he arose; in the twilight Alden beheld him
Put on his corselet of steel, and all the rest of his armor,
Buckle about his waist his trusty blade of Damascus
Take from the corner his musket, and so stride out of the chamber,
Often the heart of the youth had burned and yearned to embrace him,
Often his lips had essayed to speak, imploring for pardon,
All the old friendship came back, with its tender and grateful emotions;
But his pride overmastered the nobler nature within him,
Pride, and the sense of his wrong, and the burning fire of the insult.
So he beheld his friend departing in anger, but spake not,
Saw him go forth to danger, perhaps to death, and he spake not!
Then he arose from his bed, and heard what the people were saying,
Joined in the talk at the door, with Stephen and Richard and Gilbert,
Joined in the morning prayer, and in the reading of Scripture,
And, with the others, in haste went hurrying down to the seashore
Down to the Plymouth Rock, that had been to their feet as a doorstep
Into a world unknown,—the corner-stone of a nation!

There with his boat was the Master, already a little impatient
Lest he should lose the tide, or the wind might shift to the eastward,
Square-built, hearty, and strong, with an odor of ocean about him,
Speaking with this one and that, and cramming letters and parcels
Into his pockets capacious, and messages mingled together
Into his narrow brain, till at last he was wholly bewildered.
Nearer the boat stood Alden, with one foot placed on the gunwale,
One still firm on the rock, and talking at times with the sailors,

Seated erect on the thwarts, all ready and eager for starting.
He too was eager to go, and thus put an end to his anguish,
Thinking to fly from despair, that swifter than keel is or canvas,
Thinking to drown in the sea the ghost that would rise and pursue him.
But as he gazed on the crowd, he beheld the form of Priscilla
Standing dejected among them, unconscious of all that was passing.
Fixed were her eyes upon his, as if she divined his intention,
Fixed with a look so sad, so reproachful, imploring, and patient,
That with a sudden revulsion his heart recoiled from its purpose,
As from the verge of a crag, where one step more is destruction.
Strange is the heart of man, with its quick, mysterious instincts!
Strange is the life of man, and fatal or fated are moments,
Whereupon turn, as on hinges, the gates of the wall adamantine!
"Here I remain!" he exclaimed, as he looked at the heavens above him,
Thanking the Lord whose breath had scattered the mist and the madness,
Wherein, blind and lost, to death he was staggering headlong.
"Yonder snow-white cloud, that floats in the ether above me,
Seems like a hand that is pointing and beckoning over the ocean.
There is another hand, that is not so spectral and ghost-like,
Holding me, drawing me back, and clasping mine for protection.
Float, O hand of cloud, and vanish away in the ether!
Roll thyself up like a fist, to threaten and daunt me; I heed not
Either your warning or menace, or any omen of evil!
There is no land so sacred, no air so pure and so wholesome
As is the air she breathes, and the soil that is pressed by her footsteps.
Here for her sake will I stay, and like an invisible presence
Hover around her forever, protecting, supporting her weakness;
Yes! as my foot was the first that stepped on this rock at the landing,
So, with the blessing of God, shall it be the last at the leaving!"

Meanwhile the Master alert, but with dignified air and important,
Scanning with watchful eye the tide and the wind and the weather,
Walked about on the sands, and the people crowded around him
Saying a few last words, and enforcing his careful remembrance.
Then, taking each by the hand, as if he were grasping a tiller,
Into the boat he sprang, and in haste shoved off to his vessel,
Glad in his heart to get rid of all this worry and flurry,
Glad to be gone from a land of sand and sickness and sorrow,
Short allowance of victual, and plenty of nothing but Gospel!
Lost in the sound of the oars was the last farewell of the Pilgrims.
O strong hearts and true! not one went back in the Mayflower!
No, not one looked back, who had set his hand to this ploughing!

Soon were heard on board the shouts and songs of the sailors
Heaving the windlass round, and hoisting the ponderous anchor.
Then the yards were braced, and all sails set to the west-wind,
Blowing steady and strong; and the Mayflower sailed from the harbor,
Rounded the point of the Gurnet, and leaving far to the southward
Island and cape of sand, and the Field of the First Encounter,
Took the wind on her quarter, and stood for the open Atlantic,
Borne on the send of the sea, and the swelling hearts of the Pilgrims.

Long in silence they watched the receding sail of the vessel,
Much endeared to them all, as something living and human;
Then, as if filled with the spirit, and wrapt in a vision prophetic,
Baring his hoary head, the excellent Elder of Plymouth
Said, "Let us pray!" and they prayed, and thanked the Lord and took
      courage.
Mournfully sobbed the waves at the base of the rock, and above them
Bowed and whispered the wheat on the hill of death, and their kindred
Seemed to awake in their graves, and to join in the prayer that they uttered.
Sun-illumined and white, on the eastern verge of the ocean
Gleamed the departing sail, like a marble slab in a graveyard;
Buried beneath it lay forever all hope of escaping.
Lo! as they turned to depart, they saw the form of an Indian,
Watching them from the hill; but while they spake with each other,
Pointing with outstretched hands, and saying, "Look!" he had vanished.
So they returned to their homes; but Alden lingered a little,
Musing alone on the shore, and watching the wash of the billows
Round the base of the rock, and the sparkle and flash of the sunshine,
Like the spirit of God, moving visibly over the waters.

VI: PRISCILLA

Thus for a while he stood, and mused by the shore of the ocean,
Thinking of many things, and most of all of Priscilla;
And as if thought had the power to draw to itself, like the loadstone,
Whatsoever it touches, by subtile laws of its nature,
Lo! as he turned to depart, Priscilla was standing beside him.

"Are you so much offended, you will not speak to me?" said she.
"Am I so much to blame, that yesterday, when you were pleading
Warmly the cause of another, my heart, impulsive and wayward,
Pleaded your own, and spake out, forgetful perhaps of decorum?

Certainly you can forgive me for speaking so frankly, for saying
What I ought not to have said, yet now I can never unsay it;
For there are moments in life, when the heart is so full of emotion
That if by chance it be shaken, or into its depths like a pebble
Drops some careless word, it overflows, and its secret,
Spilt on the ground like water, can never be gathered together.
Yesterday I was shocked, when I heard you speak of Miles Standish,
Praising his virtues, transforming his very defects into virtues,
Praising his courage and strength, and even his fighting in Flanders,
As if by fighting alone you could win the heart of a woman,
Quite overlooking yourself and the rest, in exalting your hero.
Therefore I spake as I did, by an irresistible impulse.
You will forgive me, I hope, for the sake of the friendship between us
Which is too true and too sacred to be so easily broken!"
Thereupon answered John Alden, the scholar, the friend of Miles Standish:
"I was not angry with you, with myself alone I was angry,
Seeing how badly I managed the matter I had in my keeping."
"No!" interrupted the maiden, with answer prompt and decisive
"No; you were angry with me, for speaking so frankly and freely.
It was wrong, I acknowledge; for it is the fate of a woman
Long to be patient and silent, to wait like a ghost that is speechless,
Till some questioning voice dissolves the spell of its silence.
Hence is the inner life of so many suffering women
Sunless and silent and deep, like subterranean rivers
Running through caverns of darkness, unheard, unseen, and unfruitful,
Chafing their channels of stone, with endless and profitless murmurs.
Thereupon answered John Alden, the young man, the lover of women:
"Heaven forbid it, Priscilla; and truly they seem to me always
More like the beautiful rivers that watered the garden of Eden,
More like the river Euphrates, through deserts of Havilah flowing,
Filling the land with delight, and memories sweet of the garden!"
"Ah, by these words, I can see," again interrupted the maiden,
"How very little you prize me, or care for what I am saying.
When from the depths of my heart, in pain and with secret misgiving,
Frankly I speak to you, asking for sympathy only and kindness,
Straightway you take up my words, that are plain and direct and in earnest,
Turn them away from their meaning, and answer with flattering phrases.
This is not right, is not just, is not true to the best that is in you;
For I know and esteem you, and feel that your nature is noble,
Lifting mine up to a higher, a more ethereal level.
Therefore I value your friendship, and feel it perhaps the more keenly
If you say aught that implies I am only as one among many,

If you make use of those common and complimentary phrases
Most men think so fine, in dealing and speaking with women,
But which women reject as insipid, if not as insulting."

Mute and amazed was Alden; and listened and looked at Priscilla,
Thinking he never had seen her more fair, more divine in her beauty.
He who but yesterday pleaded so glibly the cause of another,
Stood there embarrassed and silent, and seeking in vain for an answer.
So the maiden went on, and little divined or imagined
What was at work in his heart, that made him so awkward and speechless.
"Let us, then, be what we are, and speak what we think, and in all things
Keep ourselves loyal to truth, and the sacred professions of friendship,
It is no secret I tell you, nor am I ashamed to declare it:
I have liked to be with you, to see you, to speak with you always.
So I was hurt at your words, and a little affronted to hear you
Urge me to marry your friend, though he were the Captain Miles Standish.
For I must tell you the truth: much more to me is your friendship
Than all the love he could give, were he twice the hero you think him."
Then she extended her hand, and Alden, who eagerly grasped it,
Felt all the wounds in his heart, that were aching and bleeding so sorely,
Healed by the touch of that hand, and he said, with a voice full of feeling:
"Yes, we must ever be friends; and of all who offer you friendship
Let me be ever the first, the truest, the nearest and dearest!"

Casting a farewell look at the glimmering sail of the Mayflower,
Distant, but still in sight, and sinking below the horizon,
Homeward together they walked, with a strange, indefinite feeling,
That all the rest had departed and left them alone in the desert.
But, as they went through the fields in the blessing and smile of the
    sunshine,
Lighter grew their hearts, and Priscilla said very archly:
"Now that our terrible Captain has gone in pursuit of the Indians,
Where he is happier far than he would be commanding a household,
You may speak boldly, and tell me of all that happened between you
When you returned last night, and said how ungrateful you found me."
Thereupon answered John Alden, and told her the whole of the story,
Told her his own despair, and the direful wrath of Miles Standish.
Whereat the maiden smiled, and said between laughing and earnest,
"He is a little chimney, and heated hot in a moment!"
But as he gently rebuked her, and told her how he had suffered,
How he had even determined to sail that day in the Mayflower,
And had remained for her sake, on hearing the dangers that threatened,

All her manner was changed, and she said with a faltering accent,
"Truly I thank you for this: how good you have been to me always!"

Thus, as a pilgrim devout, who toward Jerusalem journeys,
Taking three steps in advance, and one reluctantly backward,
Urged by importunate zeal, and withheld by pangs of contrition;
Slowly but steadily onward, receding yet ever advancing,
Journeyed this Puritan youth to the Holy Land of his longings,
Urged by the fervor of love, and withheld by remorseful misgivings.

VII: THE MARCH OF MILES STANDISH

Meanwhile the stalwart Miles Standish was marching steadily northward,
Winding through forest and swamp, and along the trend of the seashore,
All day long, with hardly a halt, the fire of his anger
Burning and crackling within, and the sulphurous odor of powder
Seeming more sweet to his nostrils than all the scents of the forest.
Silent and moody he went, and much he revolved his discomfort;
He who was used to success, and to easy victories always,
Thus to be flouted, rejected, and laughed to scorn by a maiden,
Thus to be mocked and betrayed by the friend whom most he had trusted!
Ah! 't was too much to be borne, and he fretted and chafed in his armor!

"I alone am to blame," he muttered, "for mine was the folly.
What has a rough old soldier, grown grim and gray in the harness,
Used to the camp and its ways, to do with the wooing of maidens?
'T was but a dream, let it pass, let it vanish like so many others!
What I thought was a flower, is only a weed, and is worthless;
Out of my heart will I pluck it, and throw it away, and henceforward
Be but a fighter of battles, a lover and wooer of dangers!"
Thus he revolved in his mind his sorry defeat and discomfort,
While he was marching by day or lying at night in the forest,
Looking up at the trees, and the constellations beyond them.

After a three days' march he came to an Indian encampment
Pitched on the edge of a meadow, between the sea and the forest;
Women at work by the tents, and warriors, horrid with war-paint,
Seated about a fire, and smoking and talking together;
Who, when they saw from afar the sudden approach of the white men,
Saw the flash of the sun on breastplate and sabre and musket,

Straightway leaped to their feet, and two, from among them advancing,
Came to parley with Standish, and offer him furs as a present;
Friendship was in their looks, but in their hearts there was hatred.
Braves of the tribe were these, and brothers, gigantic in stature,
Huge as Goliath of Gath, or the terrible Og, king of Bashan;
One was Pecksuot named, and the other was called Wattawamat.
Round their necks were suspended their knives in scabbards of wampum,
Two-edged, trenchant knives, with points as sharp as a needle.
Other arms had they none, for they were cunning and crafty.
"Welcome, English!" they said, these words they had learned from the
     traders
Touching at times on the coast, to barter and chaffer for peltries.
Then in their native tongue they began to parley with Standish,
Through his guide and interpreter, Hobomok, friend of the white man
Begging for blankets and knives, but mostly for muskets and powder
Kept by the white man, they said, concealed, with the plague, in his cellars,
Ready to be let loose, and destroy his brother the red man!
But when Standish refused, and said he would give them the Bible
Suddenly changing their tone, they began to boast and to bluster.
Then Wattawamat advanced with a stride in front of the other,
And, with a lofty demeanor, thus vauntingly spake to the Captain:
"Now Wattawamat can see, by the fiery eyes of the Captain,
Angry is he in his heart; but the heart of the brave Wattawamat
Is not afraid at the sight. He was not born of a woman,
But on a mountain at night, from an oak-tree riven by lightning
Forth he sprang at a bound, with all his weapons about him,
Shouting, 'Who is there here to fight with the brave Wattawamat?'"
Then he unsheathed his knife, and, whetting the blade on his left hand,
Held it aloft and displayed a woman's face on the handle;
Saying, with bitter expression and look of sinister meaning:
"I have another at home, with the face of a man on the handle;
By and by they shall marry; and there will be plenty of children!"

Then stood Pecksuot forth, self-vaunting, insulting Miles Standish:
While with his fingers he patted the knife that hung at his bosom,
Drawing it half from its sheath, and plunging it back, as he muttered,
"By and by it shall see; it shall eat; ah, ha! but shall speak not!
This is the mighty Captain the white men have sent to destroy us!
He is a little man; let him go and work with the women!"

Meanwhile Standish had noted the faces and figures of Indians
Peeping and creeping about from bush to tree in the forest,

Feigning to look for game, with arrows set on their bow-strings,
Drawing about him still closer and closer the net of their ambush.
But undaunted he stood, and dissembled and treated them smoothly;
So the old chronicles say, that were writ in the days of the fathers.
But when he heard their defiance, the boast, the taunt, and the insult,
All the hot blood of his race, of Sir Hugh and of Thurston de Standish,
Boiled and beat in his heart, and swelled in the veins of his temples.
Headlong he leaped on the boaster, and, snatching his knife from its
    scabbard,
Plunged it into his heart, and, reeling backward, the savage
Fell with his face to the sky, and a fiendlike fierceness upon it.
Straight there arose from the forest the awful sound of the war-whoop.
And, like a flurry of snow on the whistling wind of December,
Swift and sudden and keen came a flight of feathery arrows.
Then came a cloud of smoke, and out of the cloud came the lightning,
Out of the lightning thunder, and death unseen ran before it.
Frightened the savages fled for shelter in swamp and in thicket,
Hotly pursued and beset; but their sachem, the brave Wattawamat,
Fled not, he was dead. Unswerving and swift had a bullet
Passed through his brain, and he fell with both hands clutching the
    greensward,
Seeming in death to hold back from his foe the land of his fathers.

There on the flowers of the meadow the warriors lay, and above them,
Silent, with folded arms, stood Hobomok, friend of the white man.
Smiling at length he exclaimed to the stalwart Captain of Plymouth:
"Pecksuot bragged very loud, of his courage, his strength, and his stature,
Mocked the great Captain, and called him a little man; but I see now
Big enough have you been to lay him speechless before you!"

Thus the first battle was fought and won by the stalwart Miles Standish.
When the tidings thereof were brought to the village of Plymouth,
And as a trophy of war the head of the brave Wattawamat
Scowled from the roof of the fort, which at once was a church and a
    fortress,
All who beheld it rejoiced, and praised the Lord, and took courage.
Only Priscilla averted her face from this spectre of terror,
Thanking God in her heart that she had not married Miles Standish;
Shrinking, fearing almost, lest, coming home from his battles,
He should lay claim to her hand, as the prize and reward of his valor.

VIII: THE SPINNING-WHEEL

Month after month passed away, and in Autumn the ships of the merchants
Came with kindred and friends, with cattle and corn for the Pilgrims.
All in the village was peace; the men were intent on their labors,
Busy with hewing and building, with garden-plot and with mere-stead,
Busy with breaking the glebe, and mowing the grass in the meadows,
Searching the sea for its fish, and hunting the deer in the forest.
All in the village was peace; but at times the rumor of warfare
Filled the air with alarm, and the apprehension of danger.
Bravely the stalwart Standish was scouring the land with his forces,
Waxing valiant in fight and defeating the alien armies,
Till his name had become a sound of fear to the nations.
Anger was still in his heart, but at times the remorse and contrition
Which in all noble natures succeed the passionate outbreak,
Came like a rising tide, that encounters the rush of a river,
Staying its current awhile, but making it bitter and brackish.
Meanwhile Alden at home had built him a new habitation,
Solid, substantial, of timber rough-hewn from the firs of the forest.
Wooden-barred was the door, and the roof was covered with rushes;
Latticed the windows were, and the window-panes were of paper,
Oiled to admit the light, while wind and rain were excluded.
There too he dug a well, and around it planted an orchard:
Still may be seen to this day some trace of the well and the orchard.
Close to the house was the stall, where, safe and secure from annoyance,
Raghorn, the snow-white bull, that had fallen to Alden's allotment
In the division of cattle, might ruminate in the night-time
Over the pastures he cropped, made fragrant by sweet pennyroyal.

Oft when his labor was finished, with eager feet would the dreamer
Follow the pathway that ran through the woods to the house of Priscilla,
Led by illusions romantic and subtile deceptions of fancy,
Pleasure disguised as duty, and love in the semblance of friendship.
Ever of her he thought, when he fashioned the walls of his dwelling;
Ever of her he thought, when he delved in the soil of his garden;
Ever of her he thought, when he read in his Bible on Sunday
Praise of the virtuous woman, as she is described in the Proverbs,
How the heart of her husband doth safely trust in her always,
How all the days of her life she will do him good, and not evil,
How she seeketh the wool and the flax and worketh with gladness,
How she layeth her hand to the spindle and holdeth the distaff,

How she is not afraid of the snow for herself or her household,
Knowing her household are clothed with the scarlet cloth of her weaving!

So as she sat at her wheel one afternoon in the Autumn,
Alden, who opposite sat, and was watching her dexterous fingers,
As if the thread she was spinning were that of his life and his fortune,
After a pause in their talk, thus spake to the sound of the spindle.
"Truly, Priscilla,' he said, "when I see you spinning and spinning,
Never idle a moment, but thrifty and thoughtful of others,
Suddenly you are transformed, are visibly changed in a moment;
You are no longer Priscilla, but Bertha the Beautiful Spinner."
Here the light foot on the treadle grew swifter and swifter; the spindle
Uttered an angry snarl, and the thread snapped short in her fingers;
While the impetuous speaker, not heeding the mischief, continued:
"You are the beautiful Bertha, the spinner, the queen of Helvetia;
She whose story I read at a stall in the streets of Southampton,
Who, as she rode on her palfrey, o'er valley and meadow and mountain
Ever was spinning her thread from a distaff fixed to her saddle.
She was so thrifty and good, that her name passed into a proverb.
So shall it be with your own, when the spinning-wheel shall no longer
Hum in the house of the farmer, and fill its chambers with music.
Then shall the mothers, reproving, relate how it was in their childhood,
Praising the good old times, and the days of Priscilla the spinner!"
Straight uprose from her wheel the beautiful Puritan maiden
Pleased with the praise of her thrift from him whose praise was the
          sweetest,
Drew from the reel on the table a snowy skein of her spinning,
Thus making answer, meanwhile, to the flattering phrases of Alden:
"Come, you must not be idle; if I am a pattern for housewives
Show yourself equally worthy of being the model of husbands.
Hold this skein on your hands, while I wind it, ready for knitting;
Then who knows but hereafter, when fashions have changed and the
          manners,
Fathers may talk to their sons of the good old times of John Alden!"
Thus, with a jest and a laugh, the skein on his hands she adjusted
He sitting awkwardly there, with his arms extended before him,
She standing graceful, erect, and winding the thread from his fingers,
Sometimes chiding a little his clumsy manner of holding,
Sometimes touching his hands, as she disentangled expertly
Twist or knot in the yarn, unawares—for how could she help it?
Sending electrical thrills through every nerve in his body.

Lo! in the midst of this scene, a breathless messenger entered,
Bringing in hurry and heat the terrible news from the village.
Yes; Miles Standish was dead!—an Indian had brought them the tidings,
Slain by a poisoned arrow, shot down in the front of the battle,
Into an ambush beguiled, cut off with the whole of his forces;
All the town would be burned, and all the people be murdered!
Such were the tidings of evil that burst on the hearts of the hearers.
Silent and statue-like stood Priscilla, her face looking backward
Still at the face of the speaker, her arms uplifted in horror;
But John Alden, upstarting, as if the barb of the arrow
Piercing the heart of his friend had struck his own, and had sundered
Once and forever the bonds that held him bound as a captive,
Wild with excess of sensation, the awful delight of his freedom,
Mingled with pain and regret, unconscious of what he was doing,
Clasped, almost with a groan, the motionless form of Priscilla
Pressing her close to his heart, as forever his own, and exclaiming:
"Those whom the Lord hath united, let no man put them asunder!"

Even as rivulets twain, from distant and separate sources,
Seeing each other afar, as they leap from the rocks, and pursuing
Each one its devious path, but drawing nearer and nearer,
Rush together at last, at their trysting-place in the forest;
So these lives that had run thus far in separate channels,
Coming in sight of each other, then swerving and flowing asunder,
Parted by barriers strong, but drawing nearer and nearer,
Rushed together at last, and one was lost in the other.

IX: The Wedding-Day

Forth from the curtain of clouds, from the tent of purple and scarlet
Issued the sun, the great High-Priest, in his garments resplendent,
Holiness unto the Lord, in letters of light, on his forehead,
Round the hem of his robe the golden bells and pomegranates.
Blessing the world he came, and the bars of vapor beneath him
Gleamed like a grate of brass, and the sea at his feet was a laver!
This was the wedding morn of Priscilla the Puritan maiden.
Friends were assembled together; the Elder and Magistrate also
Graced the scene with their presence, and stood like the Law and the
    Gospel,
One with the sanction of earth and one with the blessing of heaven.
Simple and brief was the wedding, as that of Ruth and of Boaz.

Softly the youth and the maiden repeated the words of betrothal
Taking each other for husband and wife in the Magistrate's presence,
After the Puritan way, and the laudable custom of Holland.
Fervently then, and devoutly, the excellent Elder of Plymouth
Prayed for the hearth and the home, that were founded that day in
    affection,
Speaking of life and of death, and imploring Divine benedictions.

Lo! when the service was ended, a form appeared on the threshold,
Clad in armor of steel, a sombre and sorrowful figure!
Why does the bridegroom start and stare at the strange apparition?
Why does the bride turn pale, and hide her face on his shoulder?
Is it a phantom of air, a bodiless, spectral illusion?
Is it a ghost from the grave, that has come to forbid the betrothal?
Long had it stood there unseen, a guest uninvited, unwelcomed;
Over its clouded eyes there had passed at times an expression
Softening the gloom and revealing the warm heart hidden beneath them,
As when across the sky the driving rack of the rain-cloud
Grows for a moment thin, and betrays the sun by its brightness.
Once it had lifted its hand, and moved its lips, but was silent,
As if an iron will had mastered the fleeting intention.
But when were ended the troth and the prayer and the last benediction,
Into the room it strode, and the people beheld with amazement
Bodily there in his armor Miles Standish, the Captain of Plymouth
Grasping the bridegroom's hand, he said with emotion, "Forgive me!
I have been angry and hurt,—too long have I cherished the feeling;
I have been cruel and hard, but now, thank God! it is ended.
Mine is the same hot blood that leaped in the veins of Hugh Standish,
Sensitive, swift to resent, but as swift in atoning for error.
Never so much as now was Miles Standish the friend of John Alden."
Thereupon answered the bridegroom: "Let all be forgotten between us,
All save the dear old friendship, and that shall grow older and dearer!"
Then the Captain advanced, and, bowing, saluted Priscilla,
Gravely, and after the manner of old-fashioned gentry in England,
Something of camp and of court, of town and of country, commingled,
Wishing her joy of her wedding, and loudly lauding her husband.
Then he said with a smile: "I should have remembered the adage,
If you would be well served, you must serve yourself; and moreover,
No man can gather cherries in Kent at the season of Christmas!"

Great was the people's amazement, and greater yet their rejoicing,
Thus to behold once more the sunburnt face of their Captain,

Whom they had mourned as dead; and they gathered and crowded about
    him,
Eager to see him and hear him, forgetful of bride and of bridegroom,
Questioning, answering, laughing, and each interrupting the other,
Till the good Captain declared, being quite overpowered and bewildered,
He had rather by far break into an Indian encampment
Than come again to a wedding to which he had not been invited!

Meanwhile the bridegroom went forth and stood with the bride at the
    doorway,
Breathing the perfumed air of that warm and beautiful morning.
Touched with autumnal tints, but lonely and sad in the sunshine,
Lay extended before them the land of toil and privation;
There were the graves of the dead, and the barren waste of the seashore.
There the familiar fields, the groves of pine, and the meadows;
But to their eyes transfigured, it seemed as the Garden of Eden,
Filled with the presence of God, whose voice was the sound of the ocean.

Soon was their vision disturbed by the noise and stir of departure,
Friends coming forth from the house, and impatient of longer delaying,
Each with his plan for the day, and the work that was left uncompleted.
Then from a stall near at hand, amid exclamations of wonder,
Alden the thoughtful, the careful, so happy, so proud of Priscilla,
Brought out his snow-white bull, obeying the hand of its master,
Led by a cord that was tied to an iron ring in its nostrils,
Covered with crimson cloth, and a cushion placed for a saddle.
She should not walk, he said, through the dust and heat of the noonday;
Nay, she should ride like a queen, not plod along like a peasant.
Somewhat alarmed at first, but reassured by the others,
Placing her hand on the cushion, her foot in the hand of her husband,
Gayly, with joyous laugh, Priscilla mounted her palfrey.
"Nothing is wanting now," he said with a smile, "but the distaff;
Then you would be in truth my queen, my beautiful Bertha!"

Onward the bridal procession now moved to their new habitation,
Happy husband and wife, and friends conversing together.
Pleasantly murmured the brook, as they crossed the ford in the forest,
Pleased with the image that passed, like a dream of love, through its
    bosom,
Tremulous, floating in air, o'er the depths of the azure abysses.
Down through the golden leaves the sun was pouring his splendors,
Gleaming on purple grapes, that, from branches above them suspended

Mingled their odorous breath with the balm of the pine and the fir-tree,
Wild and sweet as the clusters that grew in the valley of Eshcol.
Like a picture it seemed of the primitive, pastoral ages,
Fresh with the youth of the world, and recalling Rebecca and Isaac,
Old and yet ever new, and simple and beautiful always,
Love immortal and young in the endless succession of lovers.
So through the Plymouth woods passed onward the bridal procession.

NED BRADDOCK

By John Williamson Palmer

By the end of the colonial era the little settlements had grown into considerable political, economic, and military forces. When the grave conflict between France and England spread to the Americas, what we call the French and Indian War began. One of the most heroic and romantic English leaders in that struggle— who also happened to be young George Washington's commanding officer—is celebrated in this verse. The remarkable growth and maturity of the colonies is also highlighted here.

S aid the sword to the axe,
    "Twixt the whacks and the hacks,
Who's your bold Berserker, cleaving of tracks?
Hewing a highway through greenwood and glen,
Foot-free for cattle and heart-free for men?"
    "Braddock of Fontenoy, stubborn and grim,
Carving a cross on the wilderness rim;
In his own doom building large for the Lord
Steeple and State!" said the axe to the sword.

Said the blade to the axe,
    "And shall none say him nay?
Never a broadsword to bar him the way?
Never a bush where a Huron may hide,
Or the shot of Shawnee spit red on his side?"
    Down the long trail from the Fort to the ford,
Naked and streaked, plunge a moccasined horde:
Huron and Wyandot, hot for the bout;
Shawnee and Ottawa, barring him out!

Red'ning the ridge,
    Twixt a gorge and a gorge
Bold to the sky, loom the ranks of Saint George;
Braddock of Fontenoy, belted and horsed,
For a foe to be struck and a pass to be forced
    Twixt the pit and the crest, twixt the rocks and the grass,
Where the bush hides the foe, and the foe holds the pass,
Beaujeu and Pontiac, striving amain;
Huron and Wyandot, jeering the slain!

Beaujeu, bon camarade!
    Beaujeu the Gay!
Beaujeu and Death cast their blades in the fray.
Never a rifle that spared when they spoke,
Never a scalp-knife that balked in its stroke.
    Till the red hillocks marked
Where their sabers had glanced.
But Braddock raged fierce in that storm by the ford,
And railed at his "curs" with the flat of his sword!

Said the sword to the axe,
    "Where's your Berserker now?
Lo! His bones mark a path for a countryman's cow.
And Beaujeu the Gay? Give him place, right or wrong,
In your tale of a camp, or your stave of a song."
    "But Braddock of Fontenoy, stubborn and grim,
Who but he carved a cross on the wilderness rim?
In his own doom building large for the Lord,
Steeple and State!" said the axe to the sword.

PART II
AN EXPERIMENT IN LIBERTY

The Constitution is not an instrument for government to restrain the people, it is an instrument for the people to restrain the government—lest it come to dominate our lives and interests.

PATRICK HENRY

THE METHOD OF GRACE

By George Whitefield

The transformation of American life from the colonial era to the national era did not so much hinge upon the prosecution of the Revolutionary War as it did the presupposition of a unique worldview. That worldview was inculcated in the colonies largely by the widespread Great Awakening—a dramatic revival of interest in, concern for, and practice of spiritual things. Sparked largely by the preaching of George Whitefield, an English evangelist, it was the single most significant cultural event leading up to the drive for independence. In this prototypical sermon, preached innumerable times throughout the colonies during the three decades of the revival, the peculiar Reformation vision of providence and grace is clearly propounded.

"They have healed also the hurt of the daughter of my people slightly, saying, 'Peace, peace,' when there is no peace" (Jeremiah 5:14). As God can send a nation or people no greater blessing than to give them faithful, sincere, and upright ministers, so the greatest curse that God can possibly send upon a people in this world, is to give them over to blind, unregenerate, carnal, lukewarm, and unskillful guides. And yet, in all ages, we find that there have been many wolves in sheep's clothing, many that daubed with untempered mortar, that prophesied smoother things than God did allow. As it was formerly, so it is now; there are many that corrupt the Word of God and deal deceitfully with it. It was so in a special manner in the prophet Jeremiah's time; and he, faithful to his Lord, faithful to that God who employed him, did not fail from time to time to open his mouth against them, and to bear a noble testimony to the honor of that God in whose name he from time to time spake. If you will read His prophecy, you will find that none spake more against such ministers than Jeremiah, and here especially in the chapter out of which the text is taken, he speaks very severely against them—he charges them with several crimes; particularly, he charges them with covetousness: "For," says he in the thirteenth verse, "from the least of them even to the greatest of them, every one is given to covetousness; and from the prophet even unto the priest, every one dealeth falsely." And then, in the words of the text, in a more special manner, he exemplifies how they had dealt falsely, how they had behaved treacherously to poor souls: says he, "They have healed also the hurt of the daughter of my people slightly, saying, Peace, peace, when there is no peace." The prophet, in the name of God, had been denouncing war against the people, he had been telling them that their house should be left desolate, and that the Lord would certainly visit the land with war. "Therefore," says he, in the eleventh verse, "I am full of the fury of the Lord; I am weary with holding in; I will pour it out upon the children abroad, and upon the assembly of young men together; for even the husband with the wife shall be taken, the aged with him that is full of days. And their houses shall be turned unto others, with their fields and wives together; for I will stretch out my hand upon the inhabitants of the land, saith the Lord." The prophet gives a thundering message, that they might be terrified and have some convictions and inclinations to repent; but it seems that the false prophets, the false priests, went about stifling people's convictions, and when they were hurt or a little terrified, they were for daubing over the wound, telling them that Jeremiah was but an enthusiastic preacher, that there could be no such thing as war among them, and saying to people, Peace, peace, be still, when the prophet told them there was no peace. The words, then, refer primarily unto outward things, but I verily believe have also a further reference to the soul, and are to be referred to those false teachers, who, when people were under conviction of sin, when people were beginning to look towards heaven, were for stifling their convictions and telling them they were good enough before. And, indeed, people generally love to have it so; our hearts are exceedingly deceitful, and desperately wicked; none but the eternal God knows how treacherous they are. How many of us cry, peace, peace, to our souls, when there is no peace! How many are there who are now settled upon their lees, that now think they are Christians, that now flatter themselves that they have an interest in Jesus Christ; whereas if we come to examine their experiences, we shall find that their peace is but a peace of the devil's making—it is not a peace of God's giving—it is not a peace that passeth human understanding. It is matter, therefore, of great importance, my dear hearers, to know whether we may speak peace to our hearts. We are all desirous of peace; peace is an unspeakable blessing; how can we live without peace? And, therefore, people from time to time must be taught how far they must go, and what must be wrought in them, before they can speak peace to their hearts. This is what I design at present, that I may deliver my soul, that I may be free from the blood of all those to whom I preach—that I may not fail to declare the whole counsel of God. I shall, from the words of the text, endeavor to show you what you must undergo, and what must be wrought in you before you can speak peace to your hearts.

But before I come directly to this, give me leave to premise a caution or two. And the first is, that I take it for granted you believe religion to be an inward thing; you believe it to be a work in the heart, a work wrought in the soul by the power of the Spirit of God. If you do not believe this, you do not believe your Bibles. If you do not believe this, though you have got your Bibles in your hand, you hate the Lord Jesus Christ in your heart; for religion is everywhere represented in Scripture as the work of God in the heart. "The kingdom of God is within us," says our Lord; and, "He is not a Christian who is one outwardly; but he is a Christian who is one inwardly." If any of you place religion in outward things, I shall not perhaps please you this morning; you will understand me no more when I speak of the work of God upon a poor sinner's heart, than if I were talking in an unknown tongue. I would further premise a caution, that I would by no means confine God to one way of acting. I would by no means say, that all persons, before they come to have a settled peace in their hearts, are obliged to undergo the same degrees of conviction. No; God has various ways of bringing his children home; his sacred Spirit bloweth when, and where, and how it listeth. But, however, I will venture to affirm this, that before ever you can speak peace to your heart, whether by shorter or longer continuance of your convictions, whether in a more pungent or in a more gentle way, you must undergo what I shall hereafter lay down in the following discourse.

First, then, before you can speak peace to your hearts, you must be made to see, made to feel, made to weep over, made to bewail, your actual transgressions against the law of God. According to the covenant of works, "The soul that sinneth, it shall die; cursed is that man, be he what he may, be he who he may, that continueth not in all things that are written in the book of the law to do them." We are not only to do some things, but we are to do all things, and we are to continue so to do; so that the least deviation from the moral law, according to the covenant of works, whether in thought, word, or deed, deserves eternal death at the hand of God. And if one evil thought, if one evil word, if one evil action, deserves eternal damnation, how many hells, my friends, do every one of us deserve, whose whole lives have been one continued rebellion against God! Before ever, therefore, you can speak peace to your hearts, you must be brought to see, brought to believe, what a dreadful thing it is to depart from the living God. And now, my dear friends, examine your hearts, for I hope you came hither with a design to have your souls made better. Give me leave to ask you, in the presence of God, whether you know the time, and if you do not know exactly the time, do you know there was a time, when God wrote bitter things against you, when the arrows of the Almighty were within you? Was ever the remembrance of your sins grievous to you? Was the burden of your sins intolerable to your thoughts? Did you ever see that God's wrath might justly fall upon you, on account of your actual transgressions against God? Were you ever in all your life sorry for your sins? Could you ever say, My sins are gone over my head as a burden too heavy for me to bear? Did you ever experience any such thing as this? Did ever any such thing as this pass between God and your soul? If not, for Jesus Christ's sake, do not call yourselves Christians; you may speak peace to your hearts, but there is no peace. May the Lord awaken you, may the Lord convert you, may the Lord give you peace, if it be his will, before you go home!

But further: you may be convinced of your actual sins, so as to be made to tremble, and yet you may be strangers to Jesus Christ, you may have no true work of grace upon your hearts. Before ever, therefore, you can speak peace to your hearts, conviction must go deeper; you must not only be convinced of your actual transgressions against the law of God, but likewise of the foundation of all your transgressions. And what is that? I mean original sin, that original corruption each of us brings into the world with us, which renders us liable to God's wrath and damnation. There are many poor souls that think themselves fine reasoners, yet they pretend to say there is no such thing as original sin; they will charge God with injustice in imputing Adam's sin to us; although we have got the mark of the beast and of the devil upon us, yet they tell us we are not born in sin. Let them look abroad into the world and see the disorders in it, and think, if they can, if this is the paradise in which God did put man. No! everything in the world is out of order. I have often thought, when I was abroad, that if there were no other argument to prove original sin, the rising of wolves and tigers against man, nay, the barking of a dog against us, is a proof of original sin. Tigers and lions durst not rise against us, if it were not for Adam's first sin; for when the creatures rise up against us, it is as much as to say, You have sinned against God, and we take up our Master's quarrel. If we look inwardly, we shall see enough of lusts, and man's temper contrary to the temper of God. There is pride, malice, and revenge, in all our hearts; and this temper cannot come from God; it comes from our first parent, Adam, who, after he fell from God, fell out of God into the devil. However, therefore, some people may deny this, yet when conviction comes, all carnal reasonings are battered down immediately and the poor soul begins to feel and see the fountain from which all the polluted streams do flow. When the sinner is first awakened, he begins to wonder—How came I to be so wicked? The Spirit of God then strikes in, and shows that he has no good thing in him by nature; then he sees that he is altogether gone out of the way, that he is altogether become abominable, and the poor creature is made to lie down at the foot of the throne of God, and to acknowledge that God would be just to damn him, just to cut him off, though he never had committed one actual sin in his life. Did you ever feel and experience this, any of you—to justify God in your damnation—to own that you are by nature children of wrath, and that God may justly cut you off, though you never actually had offended him in all your life? If you were ever truly convicted, if your hearts were ever truly cut, if self were truly taken out of you, you would be made to see and feel this. And if you have never felt the weight of original sin, do not call yourselves Christians. I an verily persuaded original sin is the greatest burden of a true convert; this ever grieves the regenerate soul, the sanctified soul. The indwelling of sin in the heart is the burden of a converted person; it is the burden of a true Christian. He continually cries out, "O! who will deliver me from this body of death," this indwelling corruption in my heart? This is that which disturbs a poor soul most. And, therefore, if you never felt this inward corruption, if you never saw that God might justly curse you for it, indeed, my dear friends, you may speak peace to your hearts, but I fear, nay, I know, there is no true peace.

Further: before you can speak peace to your hearts, you must not only be troubled for the sins of your life, the sin of your nature, but likewise for the sins of your best duties and performances. When a poor soul is somewhat awakened by the terrors of the Lord, then the poor creature, being born under the covenant of works, flies directly to a covenant of works again. And as Adam and Eve hid themselves among the trees of the garden, and sewed fig leaves together to cover their nakedness, so the poor sinner, when awakened, flies to his duties and to his performances, to hide himself from God, and goes to patch up a righteousness of his own. Says he, I will be mighty good now—I will reform—I will do all I can; and Jesus Christ will have mercy on me. But before you can speak peace to your heart, you must be brought to see that God may damn you for the best prayer you ever put up; you must be brought to see that all your duties— all your righteousness—as the prophet elegantly expresses it—put them all together, are so far from recommending you to God, are so far from being any motive and inducement to God to have mercy on your poor soul, that he will see them to be filthy rags, a menstruous cloth—that God hates them, and cannot away with them, if you bring them to him in order to recommend you to his favor. My dear friends, what is there in our performances to recommend us unto God? Our persons are in an unjustified state by nature, we deserve to be damned ten thousand times over; and what must our performances be? We can do no good thing by nature: "They that are in the flesh cannot please God." You may do things materially good, but you cannot do a thing formally and rightly good; because nature cannot act above itself. It is impossible that a man who is unconverted can act for the glory of God; he cannot do anything in faith, and "whatsoever is not of faith is sin." After we are renewed, yet we are renewed but in part, indwelling sin continues in us, there is a mixture of corruption in every one of our duties; so that after we are converted, were Jesus Christ only to accept us according to our works, our works would damn us, for we cannot put up a prayer but it is far from that perfection which the moral law requireth. I do not know what you may think, but I can say that I cannot pray but I sin—I cannot preach to you or any others but I sin—I can do nothing without sin; and, as one expresseth it, my repentance wants to be repented of, and my tears to be washed in the precious blood of my dear Redeemer. Our best duties are as so many splendid sins. Before you can speak peace to your heart, you must not only be sick of your original and actual sin, but you must be made sick of your righteousness, of all your duties and performances. There must be a deep conviction before you can be brought out of your self-righteousness; it is the last idol taken out of our heart. The pride of our heart will not let us submit to the righteousness of Jesus Christ. But if you never felt that you had no righteousness of your own, if you never felt the deficiency of your own righteousness, you cannot come to Jesus Christ. There are a great many now who may say, Well, we believe all this; but there is a great difference betwixt talking and feeling. Did you ever feel the want of a dear Redeemer? Did you ever feel the want of Jesus Christ, upon the account of the deficiency of your own righteousness? And can you now say from your heart, Lord, thou mayst justly damn me for the best duties that ever I did perform? If you are not thus brought out of self, you may speak peace to yourselves, but yet there is no peace.

But then, before you can speak peace to your souls, there is one particular sin you must be greatly troubled for, and yet I fear there are few of you think what it is; it is the reigning, the damning sin of the Christian world, and yet the Christian world seldom or never think of it. And pray what is that? It is what most of you think you are not guilty of—and that is, the sin of unbelief. Before you can speak peace to your heart, you must be troubled for the unbelief of your heart. But, can it be supposed that any of you are unbelievers here in this church-yard, that are born in Scotland, in a reformed country, that go to church every Sabbath? Can any of you that receive the sacrament once a year—O that it were administered oftener! Can it be supposed that you who had tokens for the sacrament, that you who keep up family prayer, that any of you do not believe in the Lord Jesus Christ? I appeal to your own hearts, if you would not think me uncharitable, if I doubted whether any of you believed in Christ; and yet, I fear upon examination, we should find that most of you have not so much faith in the Lord Jesus Christ as the devil himself. I am persuaded the devil believes more of the Bible than most of us do. He believes the divinity of Jesus Christ; that is more than many who call themselves Christians do; nay, he believes and trembles, and that is more than thousands amongst us do. My friends, we mistake a historical faith for a true faith, wrought in the heart by the Spirit of God. You fancy you believe, because you believe there is such a book as we call the Bible—because you go to church; all this you may do, and have no true faith in Christ. Merely to believe there was such a person as Christ, merely to believe there is a book called the Bible, will do you no good, more than to believe there was such a man as Caesar or Alexander the Great. The Bible is a sacred depository. What thanks have we to give to God for these lively oracles! But yet we may have these, and not believe in the Lord Jesus Christ. My dear friends, there must be a principle wrought in the heart by the Spirit of the living God. Did I ask you how long it is since you believed in Jesus Christ, I suppose most of you would tell me, you believed in Jesus Christ as long as ever you remember—you never did misbelieve. Then, you could not give me a better proof that you never yet believed in Jesus Christ, unless you were sanctified early, as from the womb; for, they that otherwise believe in Christ know there was a time when they did not believe in Jesus Christ. You say you love God with all your heart, soul, and strength. If I were to ask you how long it is since you loved God, you would say, As long as you can remember; you never hated God, you know no time when there was enmity in your heart against God. Then, unless you were sanctified very early, you never loved God in your life. My dear friends, I am more particular in this, because it is a most deceitful delusion, whereby so many people are carried away, that they believe already. Therefore, it is remarked of Mr. Marshall, giving account of His experiences, that he had been working for life, and he had ranged all his sins under the ten commandments, and then coming to a minister, asked him the reason why he could not get peace. The minister looked to His catalogue, Away, says he, I do not find one word of the sin of unbelief in all your catalogue. It is the peculiar work of the Spirit of God to convince us of our unbelief—that we have got no faith. Says Jesus Christ, "I will send the Comforter; and when he is come, he will reprove the world" of the sin of unbelief; "of sin," says Christ, "because they believe not on me." Now, my dear friends, did God ever show you that you had no faith? Were you ever made to bewail a hard heart of unbelief? Was it ever the language of your heart, Lord, give me faith; Lord, enable me to lay hold on thee; Lord, enable me to call thee my Lord and my God? Did Jesus Christ ever convince you in this manner? Did he ever convince you of your inability to close with Christ, and make you to cry out to God to give you faith? If not, do not speak peace to your heart. May the Lord awaken you, and give you true, solid peace before you go hence and be no more!

Once more then: before you can speak peace to your heart, you must not only be convinced of your actual and original sin, the sins of your own righteousness, the sin of unbelief, but you must be enabled to lay hold upon the perfect righteousness, the all-sufficient righteousness, of the Lord Jesus Christ; you must lay hold by faith on the righteousness of Jesus Christ, and then you shall have peace. "Come," says Jesus, "unto me, all ye that are weary and heavy laden, and I will give you rest." This speaks encouragement to all that are weary and heavy laden; but the promise of rest is made to them only upon their coming and believing, and taking him to be their God and their all. Before we can ever have peace with God, we must be justified by faith through our Lord Jesus Christ, we must be enabled to apply Christ to our hearts, we must have Christ brought home to our souls, so as His righteousness may be made our righteousness, so as his merits may be imputed to our souls. My dear friends, were you ever married to Jesus Christ? Did Jesus Christ ever give himself to you? Did you ever close with Christ by a lively faith, so as to feel Christ in your hearts, so as to hear him speaking peace to your souls? Did peace ever flow in upon your hearts like a river? Did you ever feel that peace that Christ spoke to his disciples? I pray God he may come and speak peace to you. These things you must experience. I am now talking of the invisible realities of another world, of inward religion, of the work of God upon a poor sinner's heart. I am now talking of a matter of great importance, my dear hearers; you are all concerned in it, your souls are concerned in it, your eternal salvation is concerned in it. You may be all at peace, but perhaps the devil has lulled you asleep into a carnal lethargy and security, and will endeavor to keep you there, till he get you to hell, and there you will be awakened; but it will be dreadful to be awakened and find yourselves so fearfully mistaken, when the great gulf is fixed, when you will be calling to all eternity for a drop of water to cool your tongue, and shall not obtain it.

Give me leave, then, to address myself to several sorts of persons; and O may God, of his infinite mercy, bless the application! There are some of you perhaps can say, Through grace we can go along with you. Blessed be God, we have been convinced of our actual sins, we have been convinced of original sin, we have been convinced of self-righteousness, we have felt the bitterness of unbelief, and through grace we have closed with Jesus Christ; we can speak peace to our hearts, because God hath spoken peace to us. Can you say so? Then I will salute you, as the angels did the women the first day of the week, All hail! fear not ye, my dear brethren, you are happy souls; you may be down and be at peace indeed, for God hath given you peace; you may be content under all the dispensations of providence, for nothing can happen to you now, but what shall be the effect of God's love to your soul; you need not fear what fightings may be without, seeing there is peace within. Have you closed with Christ? Is God your friend? Is Christ your friend? Then, look up with comfort; all is yours, and you are Christ's, and Christ is God's. Everything shall work together for your good; the very hairs of your head are numbered; he that toucheth you, toucheth the apple of God's eye. But then, my dear friends, beware of resting on your first conversion. You that are young believers in Christ, you should be looking out for fresh discoveries of the Lord Jesus Christ every moment; you must not build upon your past experiences, you must not build upon a work within volt, but always come out of yourselves to the righteousness of Jesus Christ without you; you must be always coming as poor sinners to draw water out of the wells of salvation; you must be forgetting the things that are behind, and be continually pressing forward to the things that are before. My dear friends, you must keep up a tender, close walk with the Lord Jesus Christ. There are many of us who lose our peace by our untender walk; something or other gets in betwixt Christ and us, and we fall into darkness; something or other steals our hearts from God, and this grieves the Holy Ghost, and the Holy Ghost leaves us to ourselves. Let me, therefore, exhort you that have got peace with God, to take care that you do not lose this peace. It is true, if you are once in Christ, you cannot finally fall from God: "There is no condemnation to them that are in Christ Jesus;" but if you cannot fall finally, you may fall foully, and may go with broken bones all your days. Take care of backslidings; for Jesus Christ's sake, do not grieve the Holy Ghost—you may never recover your comfort while you live. O take care of going a gadding and wandering from God, after you have closed with Jesus Christ. My dear friends, I have paid dear for backsliding. Our hearts are so cursedly wicked, that if you take not care, if you do not keep up a constant watch, your wicked hearts will deceive you, and draw you aside. It will be sad to be under the scourge of a correcting Father; witness the visitations of Job, David, and other saints in Scripture. Let me, therefore, exhort you that have got peace to keep a close walk with Christ. I am grieved with the loose walk of those that are Christians, that have had discoveries of Jesus Christ; there is so little difference betwixt them and other people, that I scarce know which is the true Christian. Christians are afraid to speak for God—they run down with the stream; if they come into worldly company, they will talk of the world as if they were in their element; this you would not do when you had the first discoveries of Christ's love; you could talk then of Christ's love for ever, when the candle of the Lord shined upon your soul. That time has been when you had something to say for your dear Lord; but now you can go into company and hear others speaking about the world bold enough, and you are afraid of being laughed at if you speak for Jesus Christ. A great many people have grown conformists now in the worst sense of the word; they will cry out against the ceremonies of the church, as they may justly do; but then you are mighty fond of ceremonies in your behavior; you will conform to the world, which is a great deal worse. Many will stay till the devil bring up new fashions. Take care, then, not to be conformed to the world. What have Christians to do with the world? Christians should be singularly good, bold for their Lord, that all who are with you may take notice that you have been with Jesus. I would exhort you to come to a settlement in Jesus Christ, so as to have a continual abiding of God in your heart. We go a-building on our faith of adherence, and lose our comfort; but we should be growing up to a faith of assurance, to know that we are God's, and so walk in the comfort of the Holy Ghost and be edified. Jesus Christ is now much wounded in the house of his friends. Excuse me in being particular; for, my friends, it grieves me more that Jesus Christ should be wounded by His friends than by his enemies. We cannot expect anything else from Deists; but for such as have felt his power, to fall away, for them not to walk agreeably to the vocation wherewith they are called—by these means we bring our Lord's religion into contempt, to be a byword among the heathen. For Christ's sake, if you know Christ keep close by him; if God have spoken peace, O keep that peace by looking up to Jesus Christ every moment. Such as have got peace with God, if you are under trials, fear not, all things shall work for your good; if you are under temptations, fear not, if he has spoken peace to your hearts, all these things shall be for your good.

But what shall I say to you that have got no peace with God? and these are, perhaps, the most of this congregation: it makes me weep to think of it. Most of you, if you examine your hearts, must confess that God never yet spoke peace to you; you are children of the devil, if Christ is not in you, if God has not spoken peace to your heart. Poor soul! what a cursed condition are you in. I would not be in your case for ten thousand, thousand worlds. Why? You are just hanging over hell. What peace can you have when God is your enemy, when the wrath of God is abiding upon your poor soul? Awake, then, you that are sleeping in a false peace; awake, ye carnal professors, ye hypocrites that go to church, receive the sacrament, read your Bibles, and never felt the power of God upon your hearts; you that are formal professors, you that are baptized heathens awake, awake, and do not rest on a false bottom. Blame me not for addressing myself to you; indeed, it is out of love to your souls. I see you are lingering in your Sodom, and wanting to stay there; but I come to you as the angel did to Lot, to take you by the hand. Come away, my dear brethren—fly, fly, fly for your lives to Jesus Christ, fly to a bleeding God, fly to a throne of grace; and beg of God to break your hearts, beg of God to convince you of your actual sins, beg of God to convince you of your original sin, beg of God to convince you of your self-righteousness—beg of God to give you faith, and to enable you to close with Jesus Christ. O you that are secure, I must be a son of thunder to you, and O that God may awaken you, though it be with thunder; it is out of love, indeed, that I speak to you. I know by sad experience what it is to be lulled asleep with a false peace; long was I lulled asleep, long did

I think myself a Christian, when I knew nothing of the Lord Jesus Christ. I went perhaps farther than many of you do; I used to fast twice a week, I used to pray sometimes nine times a-day, I used to receive the sacrament constantly every Lord's-day; and yet I knew nothing of Jesus Christ in my heart, I knew not that I must be a new creature—I knew nothing of inward religion in my soul. And perhaps, many of you may be deceived as I, poor creature, was; and, therefore, it is out of love to you indeed, that I speak to you. O if you do not take care, a form of religion will destroy your soul; you will rest in it, and will not come to Jesus Christ at all; whereas, these things are only the means, and not the end of religion; Christ is the end of the law for righteousness to all that believe. O, then, awake, you that are settled on your lees; awake you Church professors; awake you that have got a name to live, that are rich and think you want nothing, not considering that you are poor, and blind, and naked; I counsel you to come and buy of Jesus Christ gold, white raiment, and eye-salve. But I hope there are some that are a little wounded; I hope God does not intend to let me preach in vain; I hope God will reach some of your precious souls, and awaken some of you out of your carnal security; I hope there are some who are willing to come to Christ, and beginning to think that they have been building upon a false foundation. Perhaps the devil may strike in, and bid you despair of mercy; but fear not, what I have been speaking to you is only out of love to you—is only to awaken you, and let you see your danger. If any of you are willing to be reconciled to God, God the Father, Son, and Holy Ghost, is willing to be reconciled to you. O then, though you have no peace as yet, come away to Jesus Christ; he is our peace, he is our peace-maker—he has made peace betwixt God and offending man. Would you have peace with God? Away, then, to God through Jesus Christ, who has purchased peace; the Lord Jesus has shed his heart's blood for this. He died for this; he rose again for this; he ascended into the highest heaven, and is now interceding at the right hand of God. Perhaps you think there will be no peace for you. Why so? Because you are sinners? because you have crucified Christ—you have put him to open shame—you have trampled under foot the blood of the Son of God? What of all this? Yet there is peace for you. Pray, what did Jesus Christ say to His disciples, when he came to them the first day of the week? The first word he said was, "Peace be unto you;" he showed them his hands and His side, and said, "Peace be unto you." It is as much as if he had said, Fear not, my disciples; see my hands and my feet how they have been pierced for your sake; therefore, fear not. How did Christ speak to His disciples? "Go tell my brethren, and tell broken-hearted Peter in particular, that Christ is risen, that he is ascended unto His Father and your Father, to His God and your God." And after Christ rose from the dead, he came preaching peace, with

an olive branch of peace, like Noah's dove: "My peace I leave with you."
Who were they? They were enemies of Christ as well as we, they were
deniers of Christ once as well as we. Perhaps some of you have
backslidden and lost your peace, and you think you deserve no peace; and
no more you do. But, then, God will heal your backslidings, he will love
you freely. As for you that are wounded, if you are made willing to come
to Christ, come away. Perhaps some of you want to dress yourselves in
your duties, that are but rotten rags. No, you had better come naked as you
are, for you must throw aside your rags, and come in your blood. Some of
you may say, We would come, but we have got a hard heart. But you will
never get it made soft till we come to Christ; he will take away the heart of
stone, and give you an heart of flesh; he will speak peace to your souls;
though ye have betrayed him, yet he will be your peace. Shall I prevail
upon any of you this morning to come to Jesus Christ? There is a great
multitude of souls here; how shortly must you all die, and go to judgment!
Even before night, or tomorrow's night, some of you may be laid out for
this kirk-yard. And how will you do if you be not at peace with God—if
the Lord Jesus Christ has not spoken peace to your heart? If God speak not
peace to you here, you will be damned for ever. I must not flatter you, my
dear friends; I will deal sincerely with your souls. Some of you may think
I carry things too far. But, indeed, when you come to judgment, you will
find what I say is true, either to your eternal damnation or comfort. May
God influence your hearts to come to him! I am not willing to go away
without persuading you. I cannot be persuaded but God may make use of
me as a mean of persuading some of you to come to the Lord Jesus Christ.
O did you but feel the peace which they have that love the Lord Jesus
Christ! "Great peace have they," says the psalmist, "that love thy law;
nothing shall offend them." But there is no peace to the wicked. I know
what it is to live a life of sin; I was obliged to sin in order to stifle
conviction. And I am sure this is the way many of you take; if you get into
company, you drive off conviction. But you had better go to the bottom at
once; it must be done; your wound must be searched, or you must be
damned. If it were a matter of indifference, I would not speak one word
about it. But you will be damned without Christ. He is the way, he is the
truth, and the life. I cannot think you should go to hell without Christ. How
can you dwell with everlasting burnings? How can you abide the thought
of living with the devil for ever? Is it not better to have some soul-trouble
here, than to be sent to hell by Jesus Christ hereafter? What is hell, but to
be absent from Christ? If there were no other hell, that would be hell
enough. It will be hell to be tormented with the devil for ever. Get
acquaintance with God, then, and be at peace. I beseech you, as a poor
worthless ambassador of Jesus Christ, that you would be reconciled to

God. My business this morning, the first day of the week, is to tell you that Christ is willing to be reconciled to you. Will any of you be reconciled to Jesus Christ? Then, he will forgive you all your sins, he will blot out all your transgressions. But if you will go on and rebel against Christ, and stab him daily—if you will go on and abuse Jesus Christ, the wrath of God you must expect will fall upon you. God will not be mocked; that which a man soweth, that shall he also reap. And if you will not be at peace with God, God will not be at peace with you. Who can stand before God when he is angry? It is a dreadful thing to fall into the hands of an angry God. When the people came to apprehend Christ, they fell to the ground when Jesus said, "I am he." And if they could not bear the sight of Christ when clothed with the rags of mortality, how will they bear the sight of him when he is on His Father's throne? Methinks I see the poor wretches dragged out of their graves by the devil; methinks I see them trembling, crying out to the hills and rocks to cover them. But the devil will say, Come, I will take you away; and then they shall stand trembling before the judgment-seat of Christ. They shall appear before him to see him once, and hear him pronounce that irrevocable sentence, "Depart from me, ye cursed." Methinks I hear the poor creatures saying, Lord, if we must be damned, let some angel pronounce the sentence. No, the God of love, Jesus Christ, will pronounce it. Will ye not believe this? Do not think I am talking at random, but agreeably to the Scriptures of truth. If you do not, then show yourselves men, and this morning go away with full resolution, in the strength of God, to cleave to Christ. And may you have no rest in your souls till you rest in Jesus Christ! I could still go on, for it is sweet to talk of Christ. Do you not long for the time when you shall have new bodies—when they shall be immortal, and made like Christ's glorious body? and then they will talk of Jesus Christ for evermore. But it is time, perhaps, for you to go and prepare for your respective worship, and I would not hinder any of you. My design is, to bring poor sinners to Jesus Christ. O that God may bring some of you to himself! May the Lord Jesus now dismiss you with his blessing, and may the dear Redeemer convince you that are unawakened, and turn the wicked from the evil of their way! And may the love of God, that passeth all understanding, fill your hearts. Grant this, O Father, for Christ's sake; to whom, with thee and the blessed Spirit, be all honor and glory, now and for evermore. Amen.

AWAKEN

By Lawrence Tribble

The Great Awakening touched every section of the colonial domains of England in the New World—from northernmost New England to southernmost Georgia. And its impact was enormous. Interestingly, this cultural and spiritual phenomenon was entirely driven by grassroots evangelism and community cooperation, as this famous verse illustrates.

One man awake,
Awakens another.
The second awakens
His next-door brother.
The three awake can rouse a town
By turning
The whole place
Upside down.

The many awake
Can make such a fuss
It finally awakens
The rest of us.
One man up,
With dawn in his eyes,
Surely then
Multiplies.

A BALLAD OF THE BOSTON TEA PARTY

By Oliver Wendell Holmes

On December 16, 1773, colonial leaders grown weary with England's increasingly intrusive government carried out a remarkable protest in Boston Harbor. Disguised as Indians, they boarded a British ship and threw its cargo of imported tea overboard. This action, more than almost any other, demonstrated the resolve of the colonists to maintain the standard of liberty—guaranteed by English common law—in their American homeland. Here this well-known tale is set to popular verse by one of the masters of the nineteenth-century American literary scene.

No! never such a draught was poured
    Since Hebe served with nectar
The bright Olympians and their Lord,
    Her over-kind protector,
Since Father Noah squeezed the grape
    And took to such behaving
As would have shamed our grand-sire ape
    Before the days of shaving,
No! ne'er was mingled such a draught
    In palace, hall, or arbor,
As freemen brewed and tyrants quaffed
    That night in Boston Harbor!
It kept King George so long awake
    His brain at last got addled,
It made the nerves of Britain shake,
    With seven score millions saddled;
Before that bitter cup was drained,
    Amid the roar of cannon,
The Western war-cloud's crimson stained
    The Thames, the Clyde, the Shannon;
Full many a six-foot grenadier
    The flattened grass had measured,
And, many a mother many a year
    Her tearful memories treasured;
Fast spread the tempest's darkening pall,
    The mighty realms were troubled,

The storm broke loose, but first of all
    The Boston teapot bubbled!

An evening party—only that,
    No formal invitation,
No gold-laced coat, no stiff cravat,
    No feast in contemplation,
No silk-robed dames, no fiddling band,
    No flowers, no songs, no dancing,
A tribe of red men, axe in hand,
    Behold the guests advancing!
How fast the stragglers join the throng,
    From stall and workshop gathered!
The lively barber skips along
    And leaves a chin half-lathered;
The smith has flung his hammer down,
    The horseshoe still is glowing;
The truant tapster at the Crown
    Has left a beer-cask flowing;
The cooper's boys have dropped the adze,
    And trot behind their master;
Up run the tarry shipyard lads,
    The crowd is hurrying faster,
Out from the millpond's purlieus gush
    The streams of white-faced millers,
And down their slippery alleys rush
    The lusty young Fort-Hillers;
The ropewalk lends its 'prentice crew,
    The Tories seize the omen:
"Ay, boys, you'll soon have work to do
    For England's rebel foemen,
'King Hancock,' Adams, and their gang,
That fire the mob with treason,
When these we shoot and those we hang
    The town will come to reason."
    On—on to where the ten-ships ride!
And now their ranks are forming,
    A rush, and up the Dartmouth's side
    The Mohawk band is swarming!
See the fierce natives! What a glimpse
    Of paint and fur and feather,

As all at once the full-grown imps
    Light on the deck together!
A scarf the pigtail's secret keeps,
    A blanket hides the breeches,
And out the cursed cargo leaps,
    And overhead it pitches!

O woman, at the evening board
    So gracious, sweet, and purring,
So happy while the tea is poured,
    So blest while spoons are stirring,
What martyr can compare with thee,
    The mother, wife, or daughter,
That night, instead of best Bohea,
    Condemned to milk and water!

Ah, little dreams the quiet dame
    Who plies with rock and spindle
The patient flax, how great a flame
    Yon little spark shall kindle!
The lurid morning shall reveal
    A fire no king can smother
Where British flint and Boston steel
    Have clashed against each other!
Old charters shrivel in its track,
    His Worship's bench has crumbled,
It climbs and clasps the Union Jack,
    Its blazoned pomp is humbled,
The flags go down on land and sea
    Like corn before the reapers;
So burned the fire that brewed the tea
    That Boston served her keepers!

The waves that wrought a century's wreck
    Have rolled o'er Whig and Tory;
The Mohawks on the Dartmouth's deck
    Still live in song and story;
The waters in the rebel bay
    Have kept the tea-leaf savor;
Our old North-Enders in their spray
    Still taste a Hyson flavor;

And Freedom's teacup still o'erflows
    With ever fresh libations,
To cheat of slumber all her foes
    And cheer the wakening nations!

THE DIVINE SOURCE OF LIBERTY

By Samuel Adams

Samuel Adams was one of the firebrands of the Revolution. The founder of the Committees of Correspondence and the Sons of Liberty, he challenged the authority of the English to violate the common law tradition in the colonies and eventually led the armed resistance to the king's tyranny following the Boston Massacre. In this widely circulated verse, he detailed the standards for the American demand for freedom.

All temporal power is of God,
And the magistratal, His institution, laud,
To but advance creaturely happiness aubaud:

    Let us then affirm the Source of Liberty.

Ever agreeable to the nature and will,
Of the Supreme and Guardian of all yet still
Employed for our rights and freedom's thrill:

    Thus proves the only Source of Liberty.

Though our civil joy is surely expressed
Through hearth, and home, and church manifest,
Yet this too shall be a nation's true test:

    To acknowledge the divine Source of Liberty.

LIBERTY OR DEATH

By Patrick Henry

This famous speech by the first governor of the state of Virginia, a member of the First Continental Congress, was delivered at Richmond's historic St. John's Church in the year before the signing of the Declaration of Independence. It was a fiery call to arms against British oppression and cry for a "well-regulated militia" for the colony of Virginia. It caused an immediate and rousing reaction and subsequently became one of the great clarion cries for freedom that circulated throughout the colonies. The convention subsequently passed his resolution.

Mr. President: No man thinks more highly than I do of the patriotism, as well as abilities, of the very worthy gentlemen who have just addressed the House. But different men often see the same subjects in different lights; and, therefore, I hope that it will not be thought disrespectful to those gentlemen, if, entertaining as I do, opinions of a character very opposite to theirs, I shall speak forth my sentiments freely and without reserve. This is no time for ceremony. The question before the House is one of awful moment to this country. For my own part I consider it as nothing less than a question of freedom or slavery, and in proportion to the magnitude of the subject ought to be the freedom of the debate. It is only in this way that we can hope to arrive at truth and fulfill the great responsibility which we hold to God and our country. Should I keep back my opinions at such a time, through fear of giving offense, I should consider myself as guilty of treason toward my country and of an act of disloyalty toward the majesty of heaven, which I revere above all earthly kings.

Mr. President, it is natural to man to indulge in the illusions of hope. We are apt to shut our eyes against a painful truth and listen to the song of that siren, till she transforms us into beasts. Is this the part of wise men, engaged in a great and arduous struggle for liberty? Are we disposed to be of the number of those who, having eyes, see not, and having ears, hear not, the things which so nearly concern their temporal salvation? For my part, whatever anguish of spirit it may cost, I am willing to know the whole truth, to know the worst and to provide for it.

I have but one lamp by which my feet are guided, and that is the lamp of experience. I know of no way of judging of the future but by the past. And judging by the past, I wish to know what there has been in the conduct of the British ministry for the last ten years to justify those hopes with which gentlemen have been pleased to solace themselves and the House? Is it that insidious smile with which our petition has been lately received? Trust it not, sir; it will prove a snare to your feet. Suffer not yourselves to be betrayed with a kiss. Ask yourselves how this gracious reception of our petition comports with these warlike preparations which cover our waters and darken our land. Are fleets and armies necessary to a work of love and reconciliation? Have we shown ourselves so unwilling to be reconciled that force must be called in to win back our love?

Let us not deceive ourselves, sir. These are the implements of war and subjugation, the last arguments to which kings resort. I ask gentlemen, sir, what means this martial array, if its purpose be not to force us to submission? Can gentlemen assign any other possible motives for it? Has Great Britain any enemy, in this quarter of the world, to call for all this accumulation of navies and armies? No, sir, she has none. They are meant for us; they can be meant for no other. They are sent over to bind and rivet upon us those chains which the British ministry have been so long forging. And what have we to oppose to them? Shall we try argument? Sir, we have been trying that for the last ten years. Have we anything new to offer on the subject? Nothing. We have held the subject up in every light of which it is capable, but it has been all in vain. Shall we resort to entreaty and humble supplication? What terms shall we find which have not been already exhausted? Let us not, I beseech you, sir, deceive ourselves longer. Sir, we have done everything that could be done to avert the storm which is now coming on. We have petitioned; we have remonstrated; we have supplicated; we have prostrated ourselves before the tyrannical hands of the ministry and parliament. Our petitions have been slighted; our remonstrances have produced additional violence and insult; our supplications have been disregarded; and we have been spurned, with contempt, from the foot of the throne.

In vain, after these things, may we indulge the fond hope of peace and reconciliation. There is no longer any room for hope. If we wish to be free—if we mean to preserve inviolate those inestimable privileges for which we have been so long contending—if we mean not basely to abandon the noble struggle in which we have been so long engaged, and which we have pledged ourselves never to abandon until the glorious object of our contest shall be obtained, we must fight! I repeat it, sir, we must fight! An appeal to arms and to the God of Hosts is all that is left us!

They tell us, sir, that we are weak, unable to cope with so formidable an adversary. But when shall we be stronger? Will it be the next week, or the next year? Will it be when we are totally disarmed, and when a British guard shall be stationed in every house? Shall we gather strength by irresolution and inaction? Shall we acquire the means of effectual resistance by lying supinely on our backs and hugging the delusive phantom of hope, until our enemies shall have bound us hand and foot? Sir, we are not weak, if we make a proper use of the means which the God of nature hath placed in our power. Three millions of people, armed in the holy cause of liberty, and in such a country as that which we possess, are invincible by any force which our enemy can send against us. Besides, sir, we shall not fight our battles alone. There is a just God who presides over the destinies of nations, and who will raise friends to fight our battles for us. The battle, sir, is not to the strong alone; it is to the vigilant, the active, the brave. Besides, sir, we have no election. If we were base enough to desire it, it is now too late to retire from the contest. There is no retreat but in submission and slavery! Our chains are forged! Their clanking may be heard on the plains of Boston! The war is inevitable—and let it come! I repeat it, sir, let it come!

It is in vain, sir, to extenuate the matter. Gentlemen may cry, peace, peace!—but there is no peace. The war is actually begun! The next gale that sweeps from the north will bring to our ears the clash of resounding arms! Our brethren are already in the field! Why stand we here idle? What is it that gentlemen wish? What would they have? Is life so dear, or peace so sweet, as to be purchased at the price of chains and slavery? Forbid it, Almighty God! I know not what course others may take, but as for me: Give me liberty, or give me death!

PAUL REVERE'S RIDE

By Henry Wadsworth Longfellow

This tale, one of the most legendary in all the Founding Era, was set to verse by one of America's foremost poets. It immediately became a popular anthem celebrating both the great valor of the revolutionaries and the great virtue of the revolutionary cause.

Listen, my children, and you shall hear
Of the midnight ride of Paul Revere
On the eighteenth of April, in Seventy-five;
Hardly a man is now alive
Who remembers that famous day and year.

He said to his friend, "If the British march
By land or sea from the town to-night,
Hang a lantern aloft in the belfry arch
Of the North Church tower as a signal light,
One, if by land, and two, if by sea;
And I on the opposite shore will be,
Ready to ride and spread the alarm
Through every Middlesex village and farm,
For the country folk to be up and to arm."

Then he said, "Good night!" and with muffled oar
Silently rowed to the Charlestown shore,
Just as the moon rose over the bay,
Where swinging wide at her moorings lay
The Somerset, British man-of-war;
A phantom ship, with each mast and spar
Across the moon like a prison bar
And a huge black hulk, that was magnified
By its own reflection in the tide.

Meanwhile, his friend, through alley and street,
Wanders and watches with eager ears,
Till in the silence around him he hears
The muster of men at the barrack door,
The sound of arms, and the tramp of feet,
And the measured tread of the grenadiers,
Marching down to their boats on the shore.

Then he climbed the tower of the Old North Church,
By the wooden stairs, with stealthy tread,
To the belfry-chamber overhead,
And startled the pigeons from their perch
On the sombre rafters, that round him made
Masses and moving shapes of shade,
By the trembling ladder, steep and tall,
To the highest window in the wall,
Where he paused to listen and look down
A moment on the roofs of the town,
And the moonlight flowing over all.

Beneath, in the churchyard, lay the dead,
In their night-encampment on the hill,

Wrapped in silence so deep and still
That he could hear, like a sentinel's tread,
The watchful night-wind, as it went
Creeping along from tent to tent,
And seeming to whisper, "All is well!"
A moment only he feels the spell
Of the place and the hour, and the secret dread
Of the lonely belfry and the dead;
For suddenly all his thoughts are bent
On a shadowy something far away,
Where the river widens to meet the bay,
A line of black that bends and floats
On the rising tide, like a bridge of boats.

Meanwhile, impatient to mount and ride,
Booted and spurred, with a heavy stride
On the opposite shore walked Paul Revere.
Now he patted his horse's side,
Now gazed at the landscape far and near,
Then, impetuous, stamped the earth,
And turned and tightened his saddle-girth;
But mostly he watched with eager search
The belfry-tower of the Old North Church,
As it rose above the graves on the hill,
Lonely and spectral and sombre and still.
And lo! as he looks, on the belfry's height
A glimmer, and then a gleam of light!
He springs to the saddle, the bridle he turns,
But lingers and gazes, till full on his sight
A second lamp in the belfry burns!

A hurry of hoofs in a village street,
A shape in the moonlight, a bulk in the dark,
And beneath, from the pebbles, in passing, a spark
Struck out by a steed flying fearless and fleet:
That was all! And yet, through the gloom and the light,
The fate of a nation was riding that night,
And the spark struck out by that steed, in his flight,
Kindled the land into flame with its heat.

He has left the village and mounted the steep,
And beneath him, tranquil and broad and deep,

Is the Mystic, meeting the ocean tides;
And under the alders that skirt its edge,
Now soft on the sand, now loud on the ledge,
Is heard the tramp of his steed as he rides.

It was twelve by the village clock,
When he crossed the bridge into Medford town.
He heard the crowing of the cock,
And the barking of the farmer's dog,
And felt the damp of the river fog,
That rises after the sun goes down.

It was one by the village clock,
When he galloped into Lexington.
He saw the gilded weathercock
Swim in the moonlight as he passed,
And the meeting-house windows, blank and bare,
Gaze at him with a spectral glare,
As if they already stood aghast
At the bloody work they would look upon.

It was two by the village clock,
When he came to the bridge in Concord town.
He heard the bleating of the flock,
And the twitter of birds among the trees,
And felt the breath of the morning breeze
Blowing over the meadows brown.
And one was safe and asleep in his bed
Who at the bridge would be first to fall,
Who that day would be lying dead,
Pierced by a British musket-ball.

You know the rest. In the books you have read,
How the British Regulars fired and fled,
How the farmers gave them ball for ball,
From behind each fence and farm-yard wall,
Chasing the red-coats down the lane,
Then crossing the fields to emerge again
Under the trees at the turn of the road,
And only pausing to fire and load.

So through the night rode Paul Revere;

And so through the night went his cry of alarm
To every Middlesex village and farm,—
A cry of defiance and not of fear,
A voice in the darkness, a knock at the door,
And a word that shall echo forevermore!
For, borne on the night-wind of the Past,
Through all our history, to the last,
In the hour of darkness and peril and need,
The people will waken and listen to hear
The hurrying hoof-beats of that steed,
And the midnight message of Paul Revere.

THE DOMINION OF PROVIDENCE OVER THE PASSIONS OF MEN

By John Witherspoon

Born in Scotland, educated at Edinburgh, and a leader among the Presbyterian Jacobites during the great Rising of 1745, John Witherspoon came to America in 1768 to become president of Princeton College. He has been called the most influential professor in American history, not only because of his powerful writing and speaking style, but because of the vast number of leaders he trained and sent forth. Nine of the fifty-five participants in the Federal Convention in 1787 were his students—including James Madison. Moreover, his pupils included a president and a vice president, twenty-one senators, twenty-nine representatives, fifty-six state legislators, and thirty-three judges, three of whom were appointed to the Supreme Court. This sermon caused a great stir when first preached in Princeton and published in Philadelphia in 1776, about a month before he was elected to the Continental Congress.

"Surely the wrath of man shall praise thee; the remainder of wrath shalt thou restrain" (Psalm 76:10). There is not a greater evidence either of the reality or the power of religion, than a firm belief of God's universal presence, and a constant attention to the influence and operation of his providence. It is by this means that the Christian may be said, in the emphatical scripture language, "to walk with God, and to endure as seeing him who is invisible."

The doctrine of divine providence is very full and complete in the sacred oracles. It extends not only to things which we may think of great moment, and therefore worthy of notice, but to things the most indifferent and inconsiderable; "Are not two sparrows sold for a farthing," says our Lord, "and one of them falleth not to the ground without your heavenly Father"; nay, "the very hairs of your head are all numbered." It extends not only to things beneficial and salutary, or to the direction and assistance of those who are the servants of the living God; but to things seemingly most hurtful and destructive, and to persons the most refractory and disobedient. He overrules all his creatures, and all their actions. Thus we are told, that "fire, hail, snow, vapor, and stormy wind, fulfill his word," in the course of nature; and even so the most impetuous and disorderly passions of men, that are under no restraint from themselves, are yet perfectly subject to the dominion of Jehovah. They carry his commission, they obey his orders, they are limited and restrained by his authority, and they conspire with every thing else in promoting his glory. There is the greater need to take notice of this, that men are not generally sufficiently aware of the distinction between the law of God and his purpose; they are apt to suppose, that as the temper of the sinner is contrary to the one, so the outrages of the sinner are able to defeat the other; than which nothing can be more false. The truth is plainly asserted, and nobly expressed by the psalmist in the text, "Surely the wrath of man shall praise thee; the remainder of wrath shalt thou restrain."

This psalm was evidently composed as a song of praise for some signal victory obtained, which was at the same time a remarkable deliverance from threatening danger. The author was one or other of the later prophets, and the occasion probably the unsuccessful assault of Jerusalem, by the army of Sennacherib king of Assyria, in the days of Hezekiah. Great was the insolence and boasting of his generals and servants against the city of the living God, as may be seen in the thirty-sixth chapter of Isaiah. Yet it pleased God to destroy their enemies, and, by his own immediate interposition, to grant them deliverance. Therefore the Psalmist says in the fifth and sixth verses of this psalm, "The stout-hearted are spoiled, they have slept their sleep. None of the men of might have found their hands. At thy rebuke, O God of Jacob! both the chariot and the horse are cast into a deep sleep." After a few more remarks to the same purpose, he draws the inference, or makes the reflection in the text, "Surely the wrath of man shall praise thee; the remainder of wrath shalt thou restrain": which may be paraphrased thus, The fury and injustice of oppressors shall bring in a tribute of praise to thee; the influence of thy righteous providence shall be clearly discerned; the countenance and support thou wilt give to thine own people shall be gloriously illustrated; thou shalt set the bounds which the boldest cannot pass.

I am sensible, my brethren, that the time and occasion of this psalm, may seem to be in one respect ill suited to the interesting circumstances of this country at present. It was composed after the victory was obtained; whereas we are now but putting on the harness and entering upon an important contest, the length of which it is impossible to foresee, and the issue of which it will perhaps be thought presumption to foretell. But as the truth, with respect to God's moral government, is the same and unchangeable; as the issue, in the case of Sennacherib's invasion, did but lead the prophet to acknowledge it; our duty and interest conspire in calling upon us to improve it. And I have chosen to insist upon it on this day of solemn humiliation, as it will probably help us to a clear and explicit view of what should be the chief subject of our prayers and endeavors, as well as the great object of our hope and trust, in our present situation.

The truth, then, asserted in this text, which I propose to illustrate and improve, is, That all the disorderly passions of men, whether exposing the innocent to private injury, or whether they are the arrows of divine judgment in public calamity, shall, in the end, be to the praise of God: Or, to apply it more particularly to the present state of the American colonies, and the plague of war, The ambition of mistaken princes, the cunning and cruelty of oppressive and corrupt ministers, and even the inhumanity of brutal soldiers, however dreadful, shall finally promote the glory of God, and in the mean time, while the storm continues, his mercy and kindness shall appear in prescribing bounds to their rage and fury.

In discoursing on this subject, it is my intention, through the assistance of divine grace:

First, to point out to you in some particulars, how the wrath of man praises God;

Second, to apply these principles to our present situation, by inferences of truth for your instruction and comfort, and by suitable exhortations to duty in the important crisis.

In the first place, I am to point out to you in some particulars, how the wrath of man praises God. I say in some instances, because it is far from being in my power, either to mention or explain the whole. There is an unsearchable depth in the divine counsels, which it is impossible for us to penetrate. It is the duty of every good man to place the most unlimited confidence in divine wisdom, and to believe that those measures of providence that are most unintelligible to him, are yet planned with the same skill, and directed to the same great purposes as others, the reason and tendency of which he can explain in the clearest manner. But where revelation and experience enables us to discover the wisdom, equity, or mercy of divine providence, nothing can be more delightful or profitable to a serious mind, and therefore I beg your attention to the following remarks.

In the first place, the wrath of man praises God, as it is an example and illustration of divine truth, and clearly points out the corruption of our nature, which is the foundation stone of the doctrine of redemption. Nothing can be more absolutely necessary to true religion, than a clear and full conviction of the sinfulness of our nature and state. Without this there can be neither repentance in the sinner, nor humility in the believer. Without this all that is said in scripture of the wisdom and mercy of God in providing a Savior, is without force and without meaning. Justly does our Savior say, "The whole have no need of a physician, but those that are sick. I came not to call the righteous, but sinners to repentance." Those who are not sensible that they are sinners, will treat every exhortation to repentance, and every offer of mercy, with disdain or defiance.

But where can we have a more affecting view of the corruption of our nature, than in the wrath of man, when exerting itself in oppression, cruelty and blood? It must be owned, indeed, that this truth is abundantly manifest in times of the greatest tranquillity. Others may, if they please, treat the corruption of our nature as a chimera: for my part, I see it every where, and I feel it every day. All the disorders in human society, and the greatest part even of the unhappiness we are exposed to, arises from the envy, malice, covetousness, and other lusts of man. If we and all about us were just what we ought to be in all respects, we should not need to go any further for heaven, for it would be upon earth. But war and violence present a spectacle still more awful. How affecting is it to think, that the lust of domination should be so violent and universal? That men should so rarely be satisfied with their own possessions and acquisitions, or even with the benefit that would arise from mutual service, but should look upon the happiness and tranquillity of others, as an obstruction to their own? That, as if the great law of nature, were not enough, "Dust thou art, and to dust thou shalt return," they should be so furiously set for the destruction of each other? It is shocking to think, since the first murder of Abel by his brother Cain, what havoc has been made of man by man in every age. What is it that fills the pages of history, but the wars and contentions of princes and empires? What vast numbers has lawless ambition brought into the field, and delivered as a prey to the destructive sword?

If we dwell a little upon the circumstances, they become deeply affecting. The mother bears a child with pain, rears him by the laborious attendance of many years; yet in the prime of life, in the vigor of health, and bloom of beauty, in a moment he is cut down by the dreadful instruments of death. "Every battle of the warrior is with confused noise, and garments rolled in blood"; but the horror of the scene is not confined to the field of slaughter. Few go there unrelated, or fall unlamented; in every hostile encounter, what must be impression upon the relations of the deceased? The bodies of the dead can only be seen, or the cries of the dying heard for a single day, but many days shall not put an end to the mourning of a parent for a beloved son, the joy and support of his age, or of the widow and helpless offspring, for a father taken away in the fullness of health and vigor.

But if this may be justly said of all wars between man and man, what shall we be able to say that is suitable to the abhorred scene of civil war between citizen and citizen? How deeply affecting is it, that those who are the same in complexion, the same in blood, in language, and in religion, should, notwithstanding, butcher one another with unrelenting rage, and glory in the deed? That men should lay waste the fields of their fellow subjects, with whose provision they themselves had been often fed, and consume with devouring fire those houses in which they had often found a hospitable shelter.

These things are apt to overcome a weak mind with fear, or overwhelm it with sorrow, and in the greatest number are apt to excite the highest indignation, and kindle up a spirit of revenge. If this last has no other tendency than to direct and invigorate the measures of self-defense, I do not take upon me to blame it, on the contrary, I call it necessary and laudable.

But what I mean at this time to prove by the preceding reflections, and wish to impress on your minds, is the depravity of our nature. James 4:1. "From whence come wars and fighting among you? come they not hence even from your lusts that war in your members?" Men of lax and corrupt principles, take great delight in speaking to the praise of human nature, and extolling its dignity, without distinguishing what it was, at its first creation, from what it is in its present fallen state. These fine speculations are very grateful to a worldly mind. They are also much more pernicious to incautious and unthinking youth, than even the temptations to a dissolute and sensual life, against which they are fortified by the dictates of natural conscience, and a sense of public shame. But I appeal from these visionary reasonings to the history of all ages, and the inflexible testimony of daily experience. These will tell us what men have been in their practice, and from thence you may judge what they are by nature, while unrenewed. If I am not mistaken, a cool and candid attention, either to the past history, or present state of the world, but above all, to the ravages of lawless power, ought to humble us in the dust. It should at once lead us to acknowledge the just view given us in scripture of our lost state; to desire the happy influence of renewing grace each for ourselves; and to long for the dominion of righteousness and peace, when "men shall beat their swords into plow-shares, and their spears into pruning hooks; when nation shall not lift up sword against nation, neither shall they learn war any more."

I cannot help embracing this opportunity of making a remark or two upon a virulent reflection thrown out against this doctrine, in a well known pamphlet, Common Sense. The author of that work expresses himself thus: "If the first king of any country was by election, that likewise establishes a precedent for the next; for to say, that the right of all future generations is taken away, by the act of the first electors, in their choice not only of a king, but of a family of kings forever, hath no parallel in or out of scripture, but the doctrine of original sin, which supposes the free will of all men lost in Adam, and from such comparison, and it will admit of no other, hereditary succession can derive no glory. For as in Adam all sinned, and as in the first electors all men obeyed: as in the one all mankind were subjected to Satan, and in the other to sovereignty; as our innocence was lost in the first, and our authority in the last; and as both disable us from re-assuming some former state and privilege, it unanswerably follows that original sin and hereditary succession are parallels. Dishonorable rank! Inglorious connection! Yet the most subtle sophist cannot produce a juster simile." Without the shadow of reasoning, he is pleased to represent the doctrine of original sin as an object of contempt or abhorrence. I beg leave to demur a little to the candor, the prudence, and the justice of this proceeding.

Was it modest or candid for a person without name or character, to talk in this supercilious manner of a doctrine that has been espoused and defended by many of the greatest and best men that the world ever saw, and makes an essential part of the established creeds and confessions of all the Protestant churches without exception? I thought the grand modern plea had been freedom of sentiment, and charitable thoughts of one another. Are so many of us, then, beyond the reach of this gentleman's charity? I do assure him that such presumption and self-confidence are no recommendation to me, either of his character or sentiments.

Was it prudent, when he was pleading a public cause, to speak in such opprobrious terms of a doctrine, which he knew, or ought to have known, was believed and professed by, I suppose, a great majority of very different denominations? Is this gentleman ignorant of human nature, as well as an enemy to the Christian faith? Are men so little tenacious of their religious sentiments, whether true or false? The prophet thought otherwise, who said, Hath a nation changed their gods which yet are no gods? Was it the way to obtain the favor of the public, to despise what they hold sacred? Or shall we suppose this author so astonishingly ignorant, as to think that all men now, whose favor is worth asking, have given up the doctrine of the New Testament? If he does, he is greatly mistaken.

In fine, I ask, where was the justice of this proceeding? Is there so little to be said for the doctrine of original sin, that it is not to be refuted, but despised? Is the state of the world such, as to render this doctrine not only false, but incredible? Has the fruit been of such a quality as to exclude all doubts of the goodness of the tree? On the Contrary, I cannot help being of opinion, that such has been the visible state of the World in every age, as cannot be accounted for on any other principles than what we learn from the word of God, that the imagination of the heart of man is only evil from his youth, and that continually.

The wrath of man praiseth God, as it is the instrument in his hand for bringing sinners to repentance, and for the correction and improvement of his own children. Whatever be the nature of the affliction with which he visits either persons, families, or nations; whatever be the disposition or intention of those whose malice he employs as a scourge; the design on his part is, to rebuke men for iniquity, to bring them to repentance, and to promote their holiness and peace. The salutary nature and sanctifying influence of affliction in general is often taken notice of in scripture, both as making a part of the purpose of God, and the experience of his saints.

"Now, no affliction for the present seemeth to be joyous, but grievous: Nevertheless, afterwards it yieldeth the peaceable fruit of righteousness unto them which are exercised thereby." But what we are particularly led to observe by the subject of this discourse is, that the wrath of man, or the violence of the oppressor that praiseth God in this respect, it has a peculiar tendency to alarm the secure conscience, to convince and humble the obstinate sinner. This is plain from the nature of the thing, and from the testimony of experience. Public calamities, particularly the destroying sword, are so awful that it cannot but have a powerful influence in leading men to consider the presence and the power of God. It threatens them not only in themselves, but touches them in all that is dear to them, whether relations or possessions. The prophet Isaiah says, "Yea, in the way of thy judgments, O Lord, have we waited for thee—for when thy judgments are in the earth, the inhabitants of the world will learn righteousness." He considers it as the most powerful means of alarming the secure and subduing the obstinate. "Lord when thy hand is lifted up, they will not see, but they shall see and be ashamed, for their envy at the people, yea the fire of thine enemies shall devour them." It is also sometimes represented as a symptom of a hopeless and irrecoverable state, when public judgments have no effect. Thus says the prophet Jeremiah, "O Lord, are not thine eyes upon the truth? thou hast stricken them, but they have not grieved; thou hast consumed them, but they have refused to receive correction: they have made their faces harder than a rock, they have refused to return." We can easily see in the history of the children of Israel, how severe strokes brought them to submission and penitence. "When he slew them, then they sought him, and they returned and inquired early after God, and they remembered that God was their rock, and the high God their redeemer."

Both nations in general, and private persons, are apt to grow remiss and lax in a time of prosperity and seeming security; but when their earthly comforts are endangered or withdrawn, it lays them under a kind of necessity to seek for something better in their place. Men must have comfort from one quarter or another. When earthly things are in a pleasing and promising condition, too many are apt to find their rest, and be satisfied with them as their only portion. But when the vanity and passing nature of all created comfort is discovered, they are compelled to look for something more durable as well as valuable. What therefore, can be more to the praise of God, than that when a whole people have forgotten their resting place, when they have abused their privileges, and despised their mercies, they should by distress and suffering be made to hearken to the rod, and return to their duty?

There is an inexpressible depth and variety in the judgments of God, as in all his other works; but we may lay down this as a certain principle, that if there were no sin, there could be no suffering. Therefore they are certainly for the correction of sin, or for the trial, illustration, and perfecting of the grace and virtue of his own people. We are not to suppose, that those who suffer most, or who suffer soonest, are therefore more criminal than others. Our Savior himself thought it necessary to give a caution against this rash conclusion, as we are informed by the evangelist Luke. "There were present at that season some that told him of the Galileans, whose blood Pilate had mingled with their sacrifices. And Jesus answering said unto them, Suppose ye that these Galileans were sinners above all the Galileans, because they suffered such things? I tell you nay, but except ye repent, ye shall all likewise perish." I suppose we may say with sufficient warrant, that it often happens, that those for whom God hath designs of the greatest mercy, are first brought to the trial, that they may enjoy in due time the salutary effect of the unpalatable medicine.

I must also take leave to observe, and I hope no pious humble sufferer will be unwilling to make the application, that there is often a discernible mixture of sovereignty and righteousness in providential dispensations. It is the prerogative of God to do what he will with his own, but he often displays his justice itself, by throwing into the furnace those, who though they may not be visibly worse than others, may yet have more to answer for, as having been favored with more distinguished privileges, both civil and sacred. It is impossible for us to make a just and full comparison of the character either of persons or nations, and it would be extremely foolish for any to attempt it, either for increasing their own security, or impeaching the justice of the Supreme Ruler. Let us therefore neither forget the truth, nor go beyond it. "His mercy fills the earth." He is also "known by the judgment which he executeth." The wrath of man in its most tempestuous rage, fulfills his will, and finally promotes the good of his chosen.

The wrath of man praiseth God, as he sets bounds to it, or restrains it by his providence, and sometimes makes it evidently a means of promoting and illustrating his glory.

There is no part of divine providence in which a greater beauty and majesty appears, than when the Almighty Ruler turns the counsels of wicked men into confusion, and makes them militate against themselves. If the psalmist may be thought to have had a view in this text to the truths illustrated in the two former observations, there is no doubt at all that he had a particular view to this, as he says in the latter part of the verse, "the remainder of wrath shalt thou restrain." The scripture abounds with instances, in which the designs of oppressors were either wholly disappointed, or in execution fell far short of the malice of their intention, and in some they turned out to the honor and happiness of the persons or the people, whom they were intended to destroy. We have an instance of the first of these in the history to which my text relates. We have also an instance in Esther, in which the most mischievous designs of Haman, the son of Hammedatha the Agagite against Mordecai the Jew, and the nation from which he sprung, turned out at last to his own destruction, the honor of Mordecai, and the salvation and peace of his people.

From the New Testament I will make choice of that memorable event on which the salvation of believers in every age rests as its foundation, the death and sufferings of the Son of God. This the great adversary and all his agents and instruments prosecuted with unrelenting rage. When they had blackened him with slander, when they scourged him with shame, when they had condemned him in judgment, and nailed him to the cross, how could they help esteeming their victory complete? But oh the unsearchable wisdom of God! they were but perfecting the great design laid for the salvation of sinners. Our blessed Redeemer by his death finished his work, overcame principalities and powers, and made a shew of them openly, triumphing over them in his cross. With how much justice do the apostles and their company offer this doxology to God, "They lifted up their voice with one accord, and said, Lord thou art God which hast made heaven and earth, and the sea, and all that in them is; Who by the mouth of thy servant David hast said, Why did the Heathen rage, and the people imagine vain things? The kings of the earth stood up, and the rulers were gathered together against the Lord, and against his Christ. For of a truth, against thy holy child Jesus, whom thou hast anointed, both Herod and Pontius Pilate, with the Gentiles, and the people of Israel were gathered together, for to do whatsoever thy hand and thy counsel determined before to be done."

In all after ages, in conformity to this, the deepest laid contrivances of the prince of darkness, have turned out to the confusion of their author; and

I know not, but considering his malice and pride, this perpetual disappointment, and the superiority of divine wisdom, may be one great source of his suffering and torment. The cross hath still been the banner of truth, under which it hath been carried through the world. Persecution has been but as the furnace to the gold, to purge it of its dross, to manifest its purity, and increase its luster. It was taken notice of very early, that the blood of the martyrs was the seed of Christianity; the more abundantly it was shed, the more plentifully did the harvest grow.

So certain has this appeared, that the most violent infidels, both of early and later ages, have endeavored to account for it, and have observed that there is a spirit of obstinacy in man which inclines him to resist violence, and that severity doth but increase opposition, be the cause what it will. They suppose that persecution is equally proper to propagate truth and error. This though in part true, will by no means generally hold. Such an apprehension, however, gave occasion to a glorious triumph of divine providence of an opposite kind, which I must shortly relate to you. One of the Roman emperors, Julian, surnamed the apostate, perceiving how impossible it was to suppress the gospel by violence, endeavored to extinguish it by neglect and scorn. He left the Christians unmolested for sometime, but gave all manner of encouragement to those of opposite principles, and particularly to the Jews, out of hatred to the Christians; and that he might bring public disgrace upon the Galileans, as he affected to stile them, he encouraged the Jews to rebuild the temple of Jerusalem, and visibly refute the prophecy of Christ, that it should lie under perpetual desolation. But this profane attempt was so signally frustrated, that it served, as much as any one circumstance, to spread the glory of our Redeemer, and establish the faith of his saints. It is affirmed by some ancient authors, particularly by Ammianus Marcellinus, a heathen historian, that fire came out of the earth and consumed the workmen when laying the foundation. But in whatever way it was prevented, it is beyond all controversy, from the concurring testimony of heathens and Christians, that little or no progress was ever made in it, and that in a short time, it was entirely defeated.

It is proper here to observe, that at the time of the reformation, when religion began to revive, nothing contributed more to facilitate its reception and increase its progress than the violence of its persecutors. Their cruelty and the patience of the sufferers, naturally disposed men to examine and weigh the cause to which they adhered with so much constancy and resolution. At the same time also, when they were persecuted in one city, they fled to another, and carried the discoveries of popish fraud to every part of the world. It was by some of those who were persecuted in Germany, that the light of the reformation was brought so early into Britain.

The power of divine providence appears with the most distinguished luster, when small and inconsiderable circumstances, and sometimes, the weather and seasons, have defeated the most formidable armaments, and frustrated the best concerted expeditions. Near two hundred years ago, the monarchy of Spain was in the height of its power and glory, and determined to crush the interest of the reformation. They sent out a powerful armament against Britain, giving it ostentatiously, and in my opinion profanely, the name of the Invincible Armada. But it pleased God so entirely to discomfit it by tempests, that a small part of it returned home, though no British force had been opposed to it at all.

We have a remarkable instance of the influence of small circumstances in providence in the English history. The two most remarkable persons in the civil wars had earnestly desired to withdraw themselves from the contentions of the times, Mr. Hampden and Oliver Cromwell. They had actually taken their passage in a ship for New England, when by an arbitrary order of council they were compelled to remain at home. The consequence of this was, that one of them was the soul of the republican opposition to monarchical usurpation during the civil wars, and the other in the course of that contest, was the great instrument in bringing the tyrant to the block.

The only other historical remark I am to make, is, that the violent persecution which many eminent Christians met with in England from their brethren, who called themselves Protestants, drove them in great numbers to a distant part of the world, where the light of the gospel and true religion were unknown. Some of the American settlements, particularly those in New England, were chiefly made by them; and as they carried the knowledge of Christ to the dark places of the earth, so they continue themselves in as great a degree of purity, of faith, and strictness of practice, or rather a greater, than is to be found in any Protestant church now in the world. Does not the wrath of man in this instance praise God? Was not the accuser of the brethren, who stirs up their enemies, thus taken in his own craftiness, and his kingdom shaken by the very means which he employed to establish it.

Proceed now to the second general head, which was to apply the principles illustrated above to our present situation, by inferences of truth for your instruction and comfort, and by suitable exhortations to duty in this important crisis.

In the first place, I would take the opportunity on this occasion, and from this subject, to press every hearer to a sincere concern for his own soul's salvation. There are times when the mind may be expected to be more awake to divine truth, and the conscience more open to the arrows of conviction, than at others. A season of public judgment is of this kind, as appears from what has been already said. That curiosity and attention at least are raised in some degree, is plain from the unusual throng of this assembly. Can you have a clearer view of the sinfulness of your nature, than when the rod of the oppressor is lifted up, and when you see men putting on the habit of the warrior, and collecting on every hand the weapons of hostility and instruments of death? I do not blame your ardor in preparing for the resolute defense of your temporal rights. But consider I beseech you, the truly infinite importance of the salvation of your souls. Is it of much moment whether you and your children shall be rich or poor, at liberty or in bonds? Is it of much moment whether this beautiful country shall increase in fruitfulness from year to year, being cultivated by active industry, and possessed by independent freemen, or the scanty produce of the neglected fields shall be eaten up by hungry publicans, while the timid owner trembles at the tax gatherers approach? And is it of less moment my brethren, whether you shall be the heirs of glory or the heirs of hell? Is your state on earth for a few fleeting years of so much moment? And is it of less moment, what shall be your state through endless ages? Have you assembled together willingly to hear what shall be said on public affairs, and to join in imploring the blessing of God on the counsels and arms of the united colonies, and can you be unconcerned, what shall become of you for ever, when all the monuments of human greatness shall be laid in ashes, for "the earth itself and all the works that are therein shall be burnt up."

Wherefore my beloved hearers, as the ministry of reconciliation is committed to me, I beseech you in the most earnest manner, to attend to "the things that belong to your peace, before they are hid from your eyes." How soon and in what manner a seal shall be set upon the character and state of every person here present, it is impossible to know; for he who only can know does not think proper to reveal it. But you may rest assured that there is no time more suitable, and there is none so safe, as that which is present, since it is wholly uncertain whether any other shall be yours. Those who shall first fall in battle, have not many more warnings to receive. There are some few daring and hardened sinners who despise eternity itself, and set their Maker at defiance, but the far greater number by staving off their convictions to a more convenient season, have been taken unprepared, and thus eternally lost. I would therefore earnestly press the apostles exhortation. "We then, as workers together with him, beseech you also, that ye receive not the grace of God in vain: For he saith, I have heard thee in a time accepted, and in the day of salvation have I succored thee: Behold, now is the accepted time; behold, now is the day of salvation."

Suffer me to beseech you, or rather to give you warning, not to rest satisfied with a form of godliness, denying the power thereof. There can be no true religion, till there be a discovery of your lost state by nature and practice, and an unfeigned acceptance of Christ Jesus, as he is offered in the gospel. Unhappy they who either despise his mercy, or are ashamed of his cross! Believe it, "there is no salvation in any other. There is no other name under heaven given amongst men by which we must be saved." Unless you are united to him by a lively faith, not the resentment of a haughty monarch, but the sword of divine justice hangs over you, and the fullness of divine vengeance shall speedily overtake you. I do not speak this only to the heaven, daring profligate, or groveling sensualist, but to every insensible secure sinner; to all those, however decent and orderly in their civil deportment, who live to themselves and have their part and portion in this life; in fine to all who are yet in a state of nature, for "except a man be born again, he cannot see the kingdom of God." The fear of man may make you hide your profanity: prudence and experience may make you abhor intemperance and riot; as you advance in life, one vice may supplant another and hold its place; but nothing less than the sovereign grace of God can produce a saving change of heart and temper, or fit you for his immediate presence.

From what has been said upon this subject, you may see what ground there is to give praise to God for his favors already bestowed on us, respecting the public cause. It would be a criminal inattention not to observe the singular interposition of Providence hitherto, in behalf of the American colonies. It is however impossible for me, in a single discourse, as well as improper at this time, to go through every step of our past transactions. I must therefore content myself with a few remarks. How many discoveries have been made of the designs of enemies in Britain and among ourselves, in a manner as unexpected to us as to them, and in such season as to prevent their effect? What surprising success has attended our encounters in almost every instance? Has not the boasted discipline of regular and veteran soldiers been turned into confusion and dismay, before the new and maiden courage of freemen, in defense of their property and right? In what great mercy has blood been spared on the side of this injured country? Some important victories in the south have been gained with so little loss, that enemies will probably think it has been dissembled; as many, even of ourselves thought, till time rendered it undeniable. But these were comparatively of small moment. The signal advantage we have gained by the evacuation of Boston, and the shameful flight of the army and navy of Britain, was brought about without the loss of a man. To all this we may add, that the counsels of our enemies have been visibly confounded, so that I believe that I may say with truth, that there is hardly any step which they have taken, but it has operated strongly against themselves, and been more in our favor, than if they had followed a contrary course.

While we give praise to God the supreme disposer of all events, for his interposition in our behalf, let us guard against the dangerous error of trusting in, or boasting of an arm of flesh. I could earnestly wish, that while our arms are crowned with success, we might content ourselves with a modest ascription of it to the power of the Highest. It has given me great uneasiness to read some ostentatious, vaunting expressions in our newspapers, though happily I think, much restrained of late. Let us not return to them again. If I am not mistaken, not only the holy scriptures in general, and the truths of the glorious gospel in particular, but the whole course of Providence, seem intended to abase the pride of man, and lay the vainglorious in the dust. How many instances does history furnish us with, of those who after exulting over, and despising their enemies, were signally and shamefully defeated. The truth is, I believe, the remark may be applied universally, and we may say, that through the whole frame of nature, and the whole system of human life, that which promises most, performs the least. The flowers of finest color seldom have the sweetest fragrance. The trees of quickest growth or fairest form, are seldom of the greatest value or duration. Deep waters move with least noise. Men who think most are seldom talkative. And I think it holds as much in war as in any thing, that every boaster is a coward.

Pardon me, my brethren, for insisting so much upon this, which may seem but an immaterial circumstance. It is in my opinion of very great moment. I look upon ostentation and confidence to be a sort of outrage upon Providence, and when it becomes general, and infuses itself into the spirit of a people, it is a forerunner of destruction. How does Goliath the champion, armed in a most formidable manner, express his disdain of David the stripling with his sling and his stone? "And when the Philistine looked about and saw David, he disdained him: for he was but a youth, and ruddy, and of a fair countenance. And the Philistine said unto David, Am I a dog, that thou comest to me with staves? And the Philistine cursed David by his gods, and the Philistine said to David, come to me, and I will give thy flesh unto the fowls of the air, and to the beasts of the field." But how just and modest the reply? "Then said David to the Philistine, thou comest to me with a sword and with a spear, and with a shield, but I come unto thee in the name of the Lord of hosts, the God of the armies of Israel, whom thou hast defied." I was well pleased with a remark of this kind thirty years ago in a pamphlet, in which it was observed, that there was a great deal of profane ostentation in the names given to ships of war, as the Victory, the Valiant, the Thunderer, the Dreadnought, the Terrible, the Firebrand, the Furnace, the Lightning, the Infernal, and many more of the same kind. This the author considered as a symptom of the national character and manners very unfavorable, and not likely to obtain the blessing of the God of heaven.

From what has been said you may learn what encouragement you have to put your trust in God, and hope for his assistance in the present important conflict. He is the Lord of hosts, great in might, and strong in battle. Whoever hath his countenance and approbation, shall have the best at last. I do not mean to speak prophetically, but agreeably to the analogy of faith, and the principles of God's moral government. Some have observed that true religion, and in her train, dominion, riches, literature, and arts, have taken their course in a slow and gradual manner, from east to west, since the earth was settled after the flood, and from thence forebode the future glory of America. I leave this as a matter rather of conjecture than certainty, but observe, that if your cause is just, if your principles are pure, and if your conduct is prudent, you need not fear the multitude of opposing hosts.

If your cause is just—you may look with confidence to the Lord and entreat him to plead it as his own. You are all my witnesses, that this is the first time of my introducing any political subject into the pulpit. At this season however, it is not only lawful but necessary, and I willingly embrace the opportunity of declaring my opinion without any hesitation, that the cause in which America is now in arms, is the cause of justice, of liberty, and of human nature. So far as we have hitherto proceeded, I am satisfied that the confederacy of the colonies, has not been the effect of pride, resentment, or sedition, but of a deep and general conviction, that our civil and religious liberties, and consequently in a great measure the temporal and eternal happiness of us and our posterity, depended on the issue. The knowledge of God and his truths have from the beginning of the world been chiefly, if not entirely, confined to those parts of the earth, where some degree of liberty and political justice were to be seen, and great were the difficulties with which they had to struggle from the imperfection of human society, and the unjust decisions of usurped authority. There is not a single instance in history in which civil liberty was lost, and religious liberty preserved entire. If therefore we yield up our temporal property, we at the same time deliver the conscience into bondage.

You shall not, my brethren, hear from me in the pulpit, what you have never heard from me in conversation, I mean railing at the king personally, or even his ministers and the parliament, and people of Britain, as so many barbarous savages. Many of their actions have probably been worse than their intentions. That they should desire unlimited dominion, if they can obtain or preserve it, is neither new nor wonderful. I do not refuse submission to their unjust claims, because they are corrupt or profligate, although probably many of them are so, but because they are men, and therefore liable to all the selfish bias inseparable from human nature. I call this claim unjust, of making laws to bind us in all cases whatsoever, because they are separated from us, independent of us, and have an interest in opposing us. Would any man who could prevent it, give up his estate, person, and family, to the disposal of his neighbor, although he had liberty to choose the wisest and the best master? Surely not. This is the true and proper hinge of the controversy between Great Britain and America. It is however to be added, that such is their distance from us, that a wise and prudent administration of our affairs is as impossible as the claim of authority is unjust. Such is and must be their ignorance of the state of things here, so much time must elapse before an error can be seen and remedied, and so much injustice and partiality must be expected from the arts and misrepresentation of interested persons, that for these colonies to depend wholly upon the legislature of Great Britain, would be, like many other oppressive connections, injury to the master, and ruin to the slave.

The management of the war itself on their part, would furnish new proof of this, if any were needful. Is it not manifest with what absurdity and impropriety they have conducted their own designs? We had nothing so much to fear as dissension, and they have by wanton and unnecessary cruelty forced us into union. At the same time to let us see what we have to expect, and what would be the fatal consequence of unlimited submission, they have uniformly called those acts lenity, which filled this whole continent with resentment and horror. The ineffable disdain expressed by our fellow subject, in saying, "That he would not harken to America, till she was at his feet," has armed more men, and inspired more deadly rage, than could have been done by laying waste a whole province with fire and sword. Again we wanted not numbers, but time, and they sent over handful after handful till we were ready to oppose a multitude greater than they have to send. In fine, if there was one place stronger than the rest, and more able and willing to resist, there they made the attack, and left the others till they were duly informed, completely incensed, and fully furnished with every instrument of war.

I mention these things, my brethren, not only as grounds of confidence in God, who can easily overthrow the wisdom of the wise, but as decisive proofs of the impossibility of these great and growing states, being safe and happy when every part of their internal polity is dependent on Great Britain. If, on account of their distance, and ignorance of our situation, they could not conduct their own quarrel with propriety for one year, how can they give direction and vigor to every department of our civil constitutions from age to age? There are fixed bounds to every human thing. When the branches of a tree grow very large and weighty, they fall off from the trunk.

The sharpest sword will not pierce when it cannot reach. And there is a certain distance from the seat of government, where an attempt to rule will either produce tyranny and helpless subjection, or provoke resistance and effect a separation.

I have said, if your principles are pure—the meaning of this is, if your present opposition to the claims of the British ministry does not arise from a seditious and turbulent spirit, or a wanton contempt of legal authority; from a blind and factious attachment to particular persons or parties; or from a selfish rapacious disposition, and a desire to turn public confusion to private profit but from a concern for the interest of your country, and the safety of yourselves and your posterity. On this subject I cannot help observing, that though it would be a miracle if there were not many selfish persons among us, and discoveries now and then made of mean and interested transactions, yet they have been comparatively inconsiderable both in number and effect. In general, there has been so great a degree of public spirit, that we have much more reason to be thankful for its vigor and prevalence, than to wonder at the few appearances of dishonesty or disaffection. It would be very uncandid to ascribe the universal ardor that has prevailed among all ranks of men, and the spirited exertions in the most distant colonies, to any thing else than public spirit. Nor was there ever perhaps in history so general a commotion from which religious differences have been so entirely excluded. Nothing of this kind has as yet been heard, except of late in the absurd, but malicious and detestable attempts of our few remaining enemies to introduce them. At the same time I must also, for the honor of this country observe, that though government in the ancient forms has been so long unhinged, and in some colonies not sufficient care taken to substitute another in its place; yet has there been, by common consent, a much greater degree of order and public peace, than men of reflection and experience foretold or expected. From all these circumstances I conclude favorably of the principles of the friends of liberty, and do earnestly exhort you to adopt and act upon those which have been described, and resist the influence of every other.

Once more, if to the justice of your cause, and the purity of your principles, you add prudence in your conduct, there will be the greatest reason to hope, by the blessing of God, for prosperity and success. By prudence in conducting this important struggle, I have chiefly in view union, firmness, and patience. Every body must perceive the absolute necessity of union. It is indeed in every body's mouth, and therefore instead of attempting to convince you of its importance, I will only caution you against the usual causes of division. If persons of every rank, instead of implicitly complying with the orders of those whom they themselves have chosen to direct, will needs judge every measure over again, when it comes to be put in execution; if different classes of men intermix their little private views, or clashing interest with public affairs, and marshal into parties, the merchant against the landholder, and the landholder against the merchant; if local provincial pride and jealousy arise, and you allow yourselves to speak with contempt of the courage, character, manners, or even language of particular places, you are doing a greater injury to the common cause, than you are aware of. If such practices are admitted among us, I shall look upon it as one of the most dangerous symptoms, and if they become general, a presage of approaching ruin.

By firmness and patience, I mean a resolute adherence to your duty, and laying your account with many difficulties, as well as occasional disappointments. In a former part of this discourse, I have cautioned you against ostentation and vain glory. Be pleased farther to observe that extremes often beget one another, the same persons who exult extravagantly on success, are generally most liable to despondent timidity on every little inconsiderable defeat. Men of this character are the bane and corruption of every society or party to which they belong, but they are especially the ruin of an army, if suffered to continue in it. Remember the vicissitude of human things, and the usual course of Providence. How often has a just cause been reduced to the lowest ebb, and yet when firmly adhered to, has become finally triumphant. I speak this now while the affairs of the colonies are in so prosperous a state, lest this propriety itself should render you less able to bear unexpected misfortunes—the sum of the whole is, that the blessing of God is only to be looked for by those who are not wanting in the discharge of their own duty. I would neither have you to trust in an arm of flesh, nor sit with folded hands and expect that miracles should be wrought in your defense—this is a sin which is in scripture styled tempting God. In opposition to it, I would exhort you as Joab did the host of Israel, who, though he does not appear to have had a spotless character throughout, certainly in this instance spoke like a prudent general and a pious man. "Be of good courage, and let us behave ourselves valiantly for our people and for the cities of our God, and let the Lord do that which is good in his sight."

I shall now conclude this discourse by some exhortations to duty, founded upon the truths which have been illustrated above, and suited to the interesting state of this country at the present time.

Suffer me to recommend to you an attention to the public interest of religion, or in other words, zeal for the glory of God and the good of others. I have already endeavored to exhort sinners to repentance; what I have here in view is to point out to you the concern which every good man ought to take in the national character and manners, and the means which he ought to use for promoting public virtue, and bearing down impiety and vice.

This is a matter of the utmost moment, and which ought to be well understood, both in its nature and principles. Nothing is more certain than that a general profligacy and corruption of manners make a people ripe for destruction. A good form of government may hold the rotten materials together for some time, but beyond a certain pitch, even the best constitution will be ineffectual, and slavery must ensue. On the other hand, when the manners of a nation are pure, when true religion and internal principles maintain their vigor, the attempts of the most powerful enemies to oppress them are commonly baffled and disappointed. This will be found equally certain, whether we consider the great principles of God's moral government, or the operation and influence of natural causes.

What follows from this? That he is the best friend to American liberty, who is most sincere and active in promoting true and undefiled religion, and who sets himself with the greatest firmness to bear down profanity and immorality of every kind. Whoever is an avowed enemy to God, I scruple not to call him an enemy to his country. Do not suppose, my brethren, that I mean to recommend a furious and angry zeal for the circumstantials of religion, or the contentions of one sect with another about their peculiar distinctions. I do not wish you to oppose any body's religion, but every body's wickedness. Perhaps there are few surer marks of the reality of religion, than when a man feels himself more joined in spirit to a true holy person of a different denomination, than to an irregular liver of his own. It is therefore your duty in this important and critical season to exert yourselves, every one in his proper sphere, to stem the tide of prevailing vice, to promote the knowledge of God, the reverence of his name and worship, and obedience to his laws.

Perhaps you will ask, what it is that you are called to do for this purpose farther than your own personal duty? I answer this itself when taken in its proper extent is not a little. The nature and obligation of visible religion is, I am afraid, little understood and less attended to.

Many from a real or pretended fear of the imputation of hypocrisy, banish from their conversation and carriage every appearance of respect and submission to the living God. What a weakness and meanness of spirit does it discover, for a man to be ashamed in the presence of his fellow sinners, to profess that reverence to almighty God which he inwardly feels: The truth is, he makes himself truly liable to the accusation which he means to avoid. It is as genuine and perhaps a more culpable hypocrisy to appear to have less religion than you really have, than to appear to have more. This false shame is a more extensive evil than is commonly apprehended. We contribute constantly, though insensibly, to form each others character and manners; and therefore, the usefulness of a strictly holy and conscientious deportment is not confined to the possessor, but spreads its happy influence to all that are within its reach. I need scarcely add, that in proportion as men are distinguished by understanding, literature, age, rank, office, wealth, or any other circumstance, their example will be useful on the one hand, or pernicious on the other.

But I cannot content myself with barely recommending a silent example. There is a dignity in virtue which is entitled to authority, and ought to claim it. In many cases it is the duty of a good man, by open reproof and opposition, to wage war with profaneness. There is a scripture precept delivered in very singular terms, to which I beg your attention; "Thou shalt not hate thy brother in thy heart, but shalt in any wise rebuke him, and not suffer sin upon him." How prone are many to represent reproof as flowing from ill nature and surliness of temper? The spirit of God, on the contrary, considers it as the effect of inward hatred, or want of genuine love, to forbear reproof, when it is necessary or may be useful. I am sensible there may in some cases be a restraint from prudence, agreeably to that caution of our Savior, "Cast not your pearls before swine, lest they trample them under their feet, and turn again and rent you." Of this every man must judge as well as he can for himself; but certainly, either by open reproof, or expressive silence, or speedy departure from such society, we ought to guard against being partakers of other men's sins.

To this let me add, that if all men are bound in some degree, certain classes of men are under peculiar obligations, to the discharge of this duty. Magistrates, ministers, parents, heads of families, and those whom age has rendered venerable, are called to use their authority and influence for the glory of God and the good of others. Bad men themselves discover an inward conviction of this, for they are often liberal in their reproaches of persons of grave characters or religious profession, if they bear with patience the profanity of others. Instead of enlarging on the duty of men in authority in general, I must particularly recommend this matter to those who have the command of soldiers enlisted for the defense of their country. The cause is sacred, and the champions for it ought to be holy. Nothing is more grieving to the heart of a good man, than to hear from those who are going to the field, the horrid sound of cursing and blasphemy; it cools the ardor of his prayers, as well as abates his confidence and hope in God. Many more circumstances affect me in such a case, than I can enlarge upon, or indeed easily enumerate at present; the glory of God, the interest of the deluded sinner, going like a devoted victim, and imprecating vengeance on his own head, as well as the cause itself committed to his care. We have sometimes taken the liberty to forebode the downfall of the British empire, from the corruption and degeneracy of the people. Unhappily the British soldiers have been distinguished among all the nations in Europe, for the most shocking profanity. Shall we then pretend to emulate them in this internal distinction, or rob them of the horrid privilege? God forbid. Let the officers of the army in every degree remember, that as military subjection, while it lasts, is the most complete of any, it is in their power greatly to restrain, if not wholly to banish, this flagrant enormity.

I exhort all who are not called to go into the field, to apply themselves with the utmost diligence to works of industry. It is in your power by this means not only to supply the necessities, but to add to the strength of your country. Habits of industry prevailing in a society, not only increase its wealth, as their immediate effect, but they prevent the introduction of many vices, and are intimately connected with sobriety and good morals. Idleness is the mother or nurse of almost every vice; and want, which is its inseparable companion, urges men on to the most abandoned and destructive courses. Industry, therefore is a moral duty of the greatest moment, absolutely necessary to national prosperity, and the sure way of obtaining the blessing of God. I would also observe, that in this, as in every other part of God's government, obedience to his will is as much a natural means, as a meritorious cause, of the advantage we wish to reap from it. Industry brings up a firm and hardy race. He who is inured to the labor of the field, is prepared for the fatigues of a campaign. The active farmer who rises with the dawn and follows his team or plow, must in the end be an overmatch for those effeminate and delicate soldiers, who are nursed in the lap of self-indulgence, and whose greatest exertion is in the important preparation for, and tedious attendance on, a masquerade, or midnight ball.

In the last place, suffer me to recommend to you frugality in your families, and every other article of expense. This the state of things among us renders absolutely necessary, and it stands in the most immediate connection both with virtuous industry, and active public spirit. Temperance in meals, moderation and decency in dress, furniture and equipage, have, I think, generally been characteristics of a distinguished patriot. And when the same spirit pervades a people in general, they are fit for every duty, and able to encounter the most formidable enemy. The general subject of the preceding discourse has been the wrath of man praising God. If the unjust oppression of your enemies, which withholds from you many of the usual articles of luxury and magnificence, shall contribute to make you clothe yourselves and your children with the works of your own hands, and cover your tables with the salutary productions of your own soil, it will be a new illustration of the same truth, and a real happiness to yourselves and your country.

I could wish to have every good thing done from the purest principles and the noblest views. Consider, therefore, that the Christian character, particularly the self-denial of the gospel, should extend to your whole deportment. In the early times of Christianity, when adult converts were admitted to baptism, they were asked among other questions, Do you renounce the world, its shews, its pomp, and its vanities? I do. The form of this is still preserved in the administration of baptism, where we renounce the devil, the world, and the flesh. This certainly implies not only abstaining from acts of gross intemperance and excess, but a humility of carriage, a restraint and moderation in all your desires. The same thing, as it is suitable to your Christian profession, is also necessary to make you truly independent in yourselves, and to feed the source of liberality and charity to others, or to the public. The riotous and wasteful liver, whose craving appetites make him constantly needy, is and must be subject to many masters, according to the saying of Solomon, "The borrower is servant to the lender." But the frugal and moderate person, who guides his affairs with discretion, is able to assist in public counsels by a free and unbiased judgment, to supply the wants of his poor brethren, and sometimes, by his estate and substance to give important aid to a sinking country.

Upon the whole, I beseech you to make a wise improvement of the present threatening aspect of public affairs, and to remember that your duty to God, to your country, to your families, and to yourselves, is the same. True religion is nothing else but an inward temper and outward conduct suited to your state and circumstances in providence at any time. And as peace with God and conformity to him, adds to the sweetness of created comforts while we possess them, so in times of difficulty and trial, it is in the man of piety and inward principle, that we may expect to find the uncorrupted patriot, the useful citizen, and the invincible soldier. God grant that in America true religion and civil liberty may be inseparable, and that the unjust attempts to destroy the one, may in the issue tend to the support and establishment of both.

LIBERTY TREE

By Thomas Paine

One of the most popular booklets to circulate throughout America during the Revolutionary War was written by this English radical who later played a significant part in the French Revolution. His non-Christian libertarian ideals were particularly influential with men such as Thomas Jefferson and John Adams. This verse extols the Enlightenment principle of natural liberty.

In a chariot of light from the regions of day,
The goddess of Liberty came;
Ten thousand celestials directed the way
and hither conducted the dame.
A fair budding branch from the gardens above,
where millions with millions agree,
she brought in her hand as a pledge of her love,
And the plant she named Liberty Tree.

The celestial exotic struck deep in the ground,
Like a native it flourished and bore;
The fame of its fruit drew the nations around,
To seek out this peaceable shore.
Unmindful of names or distinction they came,
For freemen like brothers agree;
With one spirit endures, they one friendship pursued,
And their temple was Liberty Tree.

Beneath this fair tree, like the patriarchs of old
Their bread in contentment they ate,
Unvexed with the troubles of silver and gold,
The cares of the grand and the great,
With timber and tar they Old England supplied,
And supported her power on the sea;
Her battles they fought, without getting a goat,
For the honor of Liberty Tree.

But hear, O ye swains, 'tis a tale most profane,
How all the tyrannical powers,
Kings, Commons, and Lords, are uniting again
To cut down this guardian of ours;
From the east to the west blow the trumpet to arms
Through the land let the sound of it flee,
Let the far and the near, all unite with a cheer,
In defense of our Liberty Tree.

THE DECLARATION OF INDEPENDENCE

On June 9, 1776, the Continental Congress accepted a resolution of Virginia delegate Richard Henry Lee, appointing a committee to draft a declaration of secession from the dominions of the English king and parliament. On June 29 the committee—composed of Thomas Jefferson, John Adams, Benjamin Franklin, Roger Sherman, and Robert Livingston—presented their draft for debate and a vote. On July 4 an amended version of that draft was accepted. The war that had been raging for more than a year had finally driven the reluctant revolutionaries to sever all ties with their motherland.

When in the course of human events, it becomes necessary for one people to dissolve the political bands which have connected them with another, and to assume among the powers of the earth the separate and equal station to which the laws of nature and of nature's God entitle them, a decent respect to the opinions of mankind requires that they should declare the causes which impel them to the separation.

We hold these truths to be self-evident: that all men are created equal, that they are endowed by their Creator with certain unalienable rights, that among these are life, liberty, and the pursuit of happiness. That to secure these rights, governments are instituted among men, deriving their just powers from the consent of the governed; that whenever any form of government becomes destructive of these ends, it is the right of the people to alter or to abolish it, and to institute new government, laying its foundation on such principles and organizing its powers in such form, as to them shall seem most likely to effect their safety and happiness.

Prudence, indeed, will dictate that governments long established should not be changed for light and transient causes; and accordingly all experience hath shown, that mankind are more disposed to suffer, while evils are sufferable, than to right themselves by abolishing the forms to which they are accustomed. But when a long train of abuses and usurpations, pursuing invariably the same object, evinces a design to reduce them under absolute despotism, it is their right, it is their duty, to throw off such government, and to provide new guards for their future security. Such has been the patient sufferance of these colonies; and such is now the necessity which constrains them to alter their former systems of government.

The history of the present king of Great Britain is a history of repeated injuries and usurpations, all having in direct object the establishment of an absolute tyranny over these states. To prove this, let facts be submitted to a candid world.

He has refused his assent to laws, the most wholesome and necessary for the public good.

He has forbidden his governors to pass laws of immediate and pressing importance, unless suspended in their operation till his assent should be obtained; and when so suspended, he has utterly neglected to attend to them.

He has refused to pass other laws for the accommodation of large districts of people, unless those people would relinquish the right of representation in the legislature, a right inestimable to them and formidable to tyrants only.

He has called together legislative bodies at places unusual, uncomfortable, and distant from the depository of their public records, for the sole purpose of fatiguing them into compliance with his measures.

He has dissolved representative houses repeatedly for opposing with manly firmness his invasions on the rights of the people.

He has refused for a long time, after such dissolutions, to cause others to be elected; whereby the legislative powers, incapable of annihilation, have returned to the people at large for their exercise; the state remaining in the meantime exposed to all the dangers of invasion from without, and convulsions within.

He has endeavored to prevent the population of these states; for that purpose obstructing the laws for naturalization of foreigners; refusing to pass others to encourage their migration hither, and raising the conditions of new appropriations of lands.

He has obstructed the administration of justice, by refusing his assent to laws for establishing judiciary powers.

He has made judges dependent on his will alone, for the tenure of their offices, and the amount and payment of their salaries.

He has erected a multitude of new offices, and sent hither swarms of officers to harass our people and eat out their substance.

He has kept among us, in times of peace, standing armies without the consent of our legislature.

He has affected to render the military independent of and superior to the civil power.

He has combined with others to subject us to a jurisdiction foreign to our constitution, and unacknowledged by our laws; giving his assent to their acts of pretended legislation:

For quartering large bodies of armed troops among us;

For protecting them, by a mock trial, from punishment for any murders which they should commit on the inhabitants of these states;

For cutting off our trade with all parts of the world;

For imposing taxes on us without our consent;

For depriving us, in many cases, of the benefits of trial by jury;

For transporting us beyond seas to be tried for pretended offenses;

For abolishing the free system of English laws in a neighboring province, establishing therein an arbitrary government, and enlarging its boundaries so as to render it at once an example and fit instrument for introducing the same absolute rule into these colonies;

For taking away our charters, abolishing our most valuable laws, and altering fundamentally the forms of our governments;

For suspending our own legislatures, and declaring themselves invested with power to legislate for us in all cases whatsoever.

He has abdicated government here by declaring us out of his protection and waging war against us.

He has plundered our seas, ravaged our coasts, burnt our towns, and destroyed the lives of our people.

He is at this time transporting large armies of foreign mercenaries to complete the works of death, desolation, and tyranny, already begun with circumstances of cruelty and perfidy scarcely paralleled in the most barbarous ages, and totally unworthy of the head of a civilized nation.

He has constrained our fellow citizens taken captive on the high seas to bear arms against their country, to become the executioners of their friends and brethren, or to fall themselves by their hands.

He has excited domestic insurrections amongst us, and has endeavored to bring on the inhabitants of our frontiers, the merciless Indian savages, whose known rule of warfare is an undistinguished destruction of all ages, sexes, and conditions.

In every stage of these oppressions we have petitioned for redress in the most humble terms; our repeated petitions have been answered only by repeated injury. A prince, whose character is thus marked by every act which may define a tyrant, is unfit to be the ruler of a free people.

Nor have we been wanting in attention to our British brethren. We have warned them from time to time of attempts by their legislature to extend an unwarrantable jurisdiction over us. We have reminded them of the circumstances of our emigration and settlement here. We have appealed to their native justice and magnanimity, and we have conjured them by the ties of our common kindred to disavow these usurpations, which would inevitably interrupt our connections and correspondence. They too have been deaf to the voice of justice and of consanguinity. We must, therefore, acquiesce in the necessity which denounces our separation, and hold them, as we hold the rest of mankind, enemies in war, in peace, friends.

We, therefore, the representatives of the United States of America, in general congress assembled, appealing to the Supreme Judge of the world for the rectitude of our intentions, do, in the name and by authority of the good people of these colonies, solemnly publish and declare, that these united colonies are, and of right ought to be, free and independent states; that they are absolved from all allegiance to the British crown, and that all political connection between them and the state of Great Britain is, and ought to be, totally dissolved; and that as free and independent states they have full power to levy war, conclude peace, contract alliances, establish commerce, and to do all other acts and things which independent states may of right do. And for the support of this declaration, with a firm reliance on the protection of Divine Providence, we mutually pledge to each other our lives, our fortunes, and our sacred honor.

ON THE RIGHT TO REBEL

By Samuel West

One of New England's most revered and highly influential clergymen, Samuel West was repeatedly sought out for advice on political matters. This sermon was preached before the Council and House of Representatives in 1776 and later reprinted widely throughout the colonies. Not surprisingly, it quickly became one of the most significant justifications for the struggle for independence.

"Put them in mind to be subject to principalities and powers, to obey magistrates, to be ready to every good work" (Titus 3:1). The great Creator, having designed the human race for society, has made us dependent on one another for happiness. He has so constituted us that it becomes both our duty and interest to seek the public good; and that we may be the more firmly engaged to promote each other's welfare, the Deity has endowed us with tender and social affections, with generous and benevolent principles: hence the pain that we feel in seeing an object of distress; hence the satisfaction that arises in relieving the afflictions, and the superior pleasure which we experience in communicating happiness to the miserable. The Deity has also invested us with moral powers and faculties, by which we are enabled to discern the difference between right and wrong, truth and falsehood, good and evil: hence the approbation of mind that arises upon doing a good action, and the remorse of conscience which we experience when we counteract the moral sense and do that which is evil. This proves that, in what is commonly called a state of nature, we are the subjects of the divine law and government; that the Deity is our supreme magistrate, who has written his law in our hearts, and will reward or punish us according as we obey or disobey his commands. Had the human race uniformly persevered in a state of moral rectitude, there would have been little or no need of any other law besides that which is written in the heart—for every one in such a state would be a law unto himself. There could be no occasion for enacting or enforcing of penal laws; for such are "not made for the righteous man, but for the lawless and disobedient, for the ungodly, and for sinners, for the unholy and profane, for murderers of fathers and murderers of mothers, for manslayers, for whoremongers, for them that defile themselves with mankind, for men-stealers, for liars, for perjured persons, and if there be any other thing that is contrary to" moral rectitude and the happiness of mankind. The necessity of forming ourselves into politic bodies, and granting to our rulers a power to enact laws for the public safety, and to enforce them by proper penalties, arises from our being in a fallen and degenerate state. The slightest view of the present state and condition of the human race is abundantly sufficient to convince any person of common sense and common honesty that civil government is absolutely necessary for the peace and safety of mankind; and, consequently, that all good magistrates, while they faithfully discharge the trust reposed in them, ought to be religiously and conscientiously obeyed. An enemy to good government is an enemy not only to his country, but to all mankind; for he plainly shows himself to be divested of those tender and social sentiments which are characteristic of a human temper, even of that generous and benevolent disposition which is the peculiar glory of a rational creature. An enemy to good government has degraded himself below the rank and dignity of a man, and deserves to be classed with the lower creation. Hence we find that wise and good men, of all nations and religions, have ever inculcated subjection to good government, and have borne their testimony against the licentious disturbers of the public peace.

Nor has Christianity been deficient in this capital point. We find our blessed Savior directing the Jews to render to Caesar the things that were Caesar's; and the apostles and first preachers of the gospel not only exhibited a good example of subjection to the magistrate, in all things that were just and lawful, but they have also, in several places in the New Testament, strongly enjoined upon Christians the duty of submission to that government under which Providence had placed them. Hence we find that those who despise government, and are not afraid to speak evil of dignities, are, by the apostles Peter and Jude, classed among those presumptuous, self-willed sinners that are reserved to the judgment of the great day. And the apostle Paul judged submission to civil government to be a matter of such great importance, that he thought it worth his while to charge Titus to put his hearers in mind to be submissive to principalities and powers, to obey magistrates, to be ready to every good work; as much as to say, none can be ready to every good work, or be properly disposed to perform those actions that tend to promote the public good, who do not obey magistrates, and who do not become good subjects of civil government. If, then, obedience to the civil magistrates is so essential to the character of a Christian, that without it he cannot be disposed to perform those good works that are necessary for the welfare of mankind, if the despisers of governments are those presumptuous, self-willed sinners who are reserved to the judgment of the great day, it is certainly a matter of the utmost importance to us all to be thoroughly acquainted with the nature and extent of our duty, that we may yield the obedience required; for it is impossible that we should properly discharge a duty when we are strangers to the nature and extent of it.

In order, therefore, that we may form a right judgment of the duty enjoined in our text, I shall consider the nature and design of civil government, and shall show that the same principles which oblige us to submit to government do equally oblige us to resist tyranny; or that tyranny and magistracy are so opposed to each other that where the one begins the other ends. I shall then apply the present discourse to the grand controversy that at this day subsists between Great Britain and the American colonies.

That we may understand the nature and design of civil government, and discover the foundation of the magistrate's authority to command, and the duty of subjects to obey, it is necessary to derive civil government from its original, in order to which we must consider what "state all men are naturally in, and that is (as Mr. Locke observes) a state of perfect freedom to order all their actions, and dispose of their possessions and persons as they think fit, within the bounds of the law of nature, without asking leave or depending upon the will of any man." It is a state wherein all are equal, no one having a right to control another, or oppose him in what he does, unless it be in his own defense, or in the defense of those that, being injured, stand in need of his assistance.

Had men persevered in a state of moral rectitude, every one would have been disposed to follow the law of nature, and pursue the general good. In such a state, the wisest and most experienced would undoubtedly be chosen to guide and direct those of less wisdom and experience than themselves, there being nothing else that could afford the least show or appearance of any one's having the superiority or precedency over another; for the dictates of conscience and the precepts of natural law being uniformly and regularly obeyed, men would only need to be informed what things were most fit and prudent to be done in those cases where their inexperience or want of acquaintance left their minds in doubt what was the wisest and most regular method for them to pursue. In such cases it would be necessary for them to advise with those who were wiser and more experienced than themselves. But these advisers could claim no authority to compel or to use any forcible measures to oblige any one to comply with their direction or advice. There could be no occasion for the exertion of such a power; for every man, being under the government of right reason, would immediately feel himself constrained to comply with everything that appeared reasonable or fit to be done, or that would any way tend to promote the general good. This would have been the happy state of mankind had they closely adhered to the law of nature, and persevered in their primitive state.

Thus we see that a state of nature, though it be a state of perfect freedom, yet is very far from a state of licentiousness. The law of nature gives men no right to do anything that is immoral, or contrary to the will of God, and injurious to their fellow-creatures; for a state of nature is properly a state of law and government, even a government founded upon the unchangeable nature of the Deity, and a law resulting from the eternal fitness of things. Sooner shall heaven and earth pass away, and the whole frame of nature be dissolved, than any part even the smallest iota, of this law shall ever be abrogated; it is unchangeable as the Deity himself, being a transcript of his moral perfections. A revelation, pretending to be from God, that contradicts any part of natural law, ought immediately to be rejected as an imposture; for the Deity cannot make a law contrary to the law of nature without acting contrary to himself, a thing in the strictest sense impossible, for that which implies contradiction is not an object of the divine power. Had this subject been properly attended to and understood, the world had remained free from a multitude of absurd and pernicious principles, which have been industriously propagated by artful and designing men, both in politics and divinity. The doctrine of nonresistance and unlimited passive obedience to the worst of tyrants could never have found credit among mankind had the voice of reason been hearkened to for a guide, because such a doctrine would immediately have been discerned to be contrary to natural law.

In a state of nature we have a right to make the persons that have injured us repair the damages that they have done us; and it is just in us to inflict such punishment upon them as is necessary to restrain them from doing the like for the future, the whole end and design of punishing being either to reclaim the individual punished, or to deter others from being guilty of similar crimes. Whenever punishment exceeds these bounds it becomes cruelty and revenge, and directly contrary to the law of nature. Our wants and necessities being such as to render it impossible in most cases to enjoy life in any tolerable degree without entering into society, and there being innumerable cases wherein we need the assistance of others, which if not afforded we should very soon perish; hence the law of nature requires that we should endeavor to help one another to the utmost of our power in all cases where our assistance is necessary. It is our duty to endeavor always to promote the general good; to do to all as we would be willing to be done by were we in their circumstances; to do justly, to love mercy, and to walk humbly before God. These are some of the laws of nature which every man in the world is bound to observe, and which whoever violates exposes himself to the resentment of mankind, the lashes of his own conscience, and the judgment of Heaven. This plainly shows that the highest state of liberty subjects us to the law of nature and the government of God. The most perfect freedom consists in obeying the dictates of right reason, and submitting to natural law. When a man goes beyond or contrary to the law of nature and reason, he becomes the slave of base passions and vile lusts; he introduces confusion and disorder into society, and brings misery and destruction upon himself. This, therefore, cannot be called a state of freedom, but a state of the vilest slavery and the most dreadful bondage. The servants of sin and corruption are subjected to the worst kind of tyranny in the universe. Hence we conclude that where licentiousness begins, liberty ends.

The law of nature is a perfect standard and measure of action for beings that persevere in a state of moral rectitude; but the case is far different with us, who are in a fallen and degenerate estate. We have a law in our members which is continually warring against the law of the mind, by which we often become enslaved to the basest lusts, and are brought into bondage to the vilest passions. The strong propensities of our animal nature often overcome the sober dictates of reason and conscience, and betray us into actions injurious to the public and destructive of the safety and happiness of society. Men of unbridled lusts, were they not restrained by the power of the civil magistrate, would spread horror and desolation all around them. This makes it absolutely necessary that societies should form themselves into politic bodies, that they may enact laws for the public safety, and appoint particular penalties for the violation of their laws, and invest a suitable number of persons with authority to put in execution and enforce the laws of the state, in order that wicked men may be restrained from doing mischief to their fellow-creatures, that the injured may have their rights restored to them, that the virtuous may be encouraged in doing good, and that every member of society may be protected and secured in the peaceable, quiet possession and enjoyment of all those liberties and privileges which the Deity has bestowed upon him; i.e., that he may safely enjoy and pursue whatever he chooses, that is consistent with the public good. This shows that the end and design of civil government cannot be to deprive men of their liberty or take away their freedom; but, on the contrary, the true design of civil government is to protect men in the enjoyment of liberty.

From hence it follows that tyranny and arbitrary power are utterly inconsistent with and subversive of the very end and design of civil government, and directly contrary to natural law, which is the true foundation of civil government and all politic law. Consequently, the authority of a tyrant is of itself null and void; for as no man can have a right to act contrary to the law of nature, it is impossible that any individual, or even the greatest number of men, can confer a right upon another of which they themselves are not possessed; i.e., no body of men can justly and lawfully authorize any person to tyrannize over and enslave his fellow-creatures, or do anything contrary to equity and goodness. As magistrates have no authority but what they derive from the people, whenever they act contrary to the public good, and pursue measures destructive of the peace and safety of the community, they forfeit their right to govern the people. Civil rulers and magistrates are properly of human creation; they are set up by the people to be the guardians of their rights, and to secure their persons from being injured or oppressed, the safety of the public being the supreme law of the state, by which the magistrates are to be governed, and which they are to consult upon all occasions. The modes of administration may be very different, and the forms of government may vary from each other in different ages and nations; but, under every form, the end of civil government is the same, and cannot vary: it is like the laws of the Medes and Persians—it altereth not.

Though magistrates are to consider themselves as the servants of the people, seeing from them it is that they derive their power and authority, yet they may also be considered as the ministers of God ordained by him for the good of mankind; for, under him, as the Supreme Magistrate of the universe, they are to act: and it is God who has not only declared in his word what are the necessary qualifications of a ruler, but who also raises up and qualifies men for such an important station. The magistrate may also, in a more strict and proper sense, be said to be ordained of God, because reason, which is the voice of God, plainly requires such an order of men to be appointed for the public good. Now, whatever right reason requires as necessary to be done is as much the will and law of God as though it were enjoined us by an immediate revelation from heaven, or commanded in the sacred Scriptures.

From this account of the origin, nature, and design of civil government, we may be very easily led into a thorough knowledge of our duty; we may see the reason why we are bound to obey magistrates, viz., because they are the ministers of God for good unto the people. While, therefore, they rule in the fear of God, and while they promote the welfare of the state, i.e., while they act in the character of magistrates, it is the indispensable duty of all to submit to them and to oppose a turbulent, factious, and libertine spirit, whenever and wherever it discovers itself. When a people have by their free consent conferred upon a number of men a power to rule and govern them they are bound to obey them. Hence disobedience becomes a breach of faith; it is violating a constitution of their own appointing, and breaking a compact for which they ought to have the most sacred regard. Such a conduct discovers so base and disingenuous a temper of mind, that it must expose them to contempt in the judgment of all the sober, thinking part of mankind. Subjects are bound to obey lawful magistrates by every tender tie of human nature, which disposes us to consult the public good, and to seek the good of our brethren, our wives, our children, our friends and acquaintance; for he that opposes lawful authority does really oppose the safety and happiness of his fellow-creatures. A factious, seditious person, that opposes good government, is a monster in nature; for he is an enemy to his own species, and destitute of the sentiments of humanity.

Subjects are also bound to obey magistrates, for conscience' sake, out of regard to the divine authority, and out of obedience to the will of God; for if magistrates are the ministers of God, we cannot disobey them without being disobedient to the law of God; and this extends to all men in authority, from the highest ruler to the lowest officer in the state. To oppose them when in the exercise of lawful authority is an act of disobedience to the Deity, and, as such, will be punished by him. It will, doubtless, be readily granted by every honest man that we ought cheerfully to obey the magistrate, and submit to all such regulations of government as tend to promote the public good; but as this general definition may be liable to be misconstrued, and every man may think himself at liberty to disregard any laws that do not suit his interest, humor, or fancy, I would observe that, in a multitude of cases, many of us, for want of being properly acquainted with affairs of state, may be very improper judges of particular laws whether they are just or not. In such cases it becomes us, as good members of society, peaceably and conscientiously to submit, though we cannot see the reasonableness of every law to which we submit, and that for this plain reason: if any number of men should take it upon themselves to oppose authority for acts, which may be really necessary for the public safety, only because they do not see the reasonableness of them, the direct consequence will be introducing confusion and anarchy into the state.

It is also necessary that the minor part should submit to the major; e.g., when legislators have enacted a set of laws which are highly approved by a large majority of the community as tending to promote the public good, in this case, if a small number of persons are so unhappy as to view the matter in a very different point of light from the public, though they have an undoubted right to show the reasons of their dissent from the judgment of the public, and may lawfully use all proper arguments to convince the public of what they judge to be an error, yet, if they fail in their attempt, and the majority still continue to approve of the laws that are enacted, it is the duty of those few that dissent peaceably and for conscience's sake to submit to the public judgment, unless something is required of them which they judge would be sinful for them to comply with; for in that case they ought to obey the dictates of their own consciences rather than any human authority whatever. Perhaps, also, some cases of intolerable oppression, where compliance would bring on inevitable ruin and destruction, may justly warrant the few to refuse submission to what they judge inconsistent with their peace and safety; for the law of self-preservation will always justify opposing a cruel and tyrannical imposition, except where opposition is attended with greater evils than submission, which is frequently the case where a few are oppressed by a large and powerful majority. Except the above-named cases, the minor ought always to submit to the major; otherwise, there can be no peace nor harmony in society. And, besides, it is the major part of a community that have the sole right of establishing a constitution and authorizing magistrates; and consequently it is only the major part of the community that can claim the right of altering the constitution, and displacing the magistrates; for certainly common sense will tell us that it requires as great an authority to set aside a constitution as there was at first to establish it. The collective body, not a few individuals, ought to constitute the supreme authority of the state.

This shows the reason why the primitive Christians did not oppose the cruel persecutions that were inflicted upon them by the heathen magistrates. They were few compared with the heathen world, and for them to have attempted to resist their enemies by force would have been like a small parcel of sheep endeavoring to oppose a large number of ravening wolves and savage beasts of prey. It would, without a miracle, have brought upon them inevitable ruin and destruction. Hence the wise and prudent advice of our Savior to them is, "When they persecute you in this city, flee ye to another."

The only difficulty remaining is to determine when a people may claim a right of forming themselves into a body politic, and assume the powers of legislation. In order to determine this point, we are to remember that all men being by nature equal, all the members of a community have a natural right to assemble themselves together, and act and vote for such regulations as they judge are necessary for the good of the whole. But when a community is become very numerous, it is very difficult, and in many cases impossible, for all to meet together to regulate the affairs of the state; hence comes the necessity of appointing delegates to represent the people in a general assembly. And this ought to be looked upon as a sacred and inalienable right, of which a people cannot justly divest themselves, and which no human authority can in equity ever take from them, viz., that no one be obliged to submit to any law except such as are made either by himself or by his representative.

If representation and legislation are inseparably connected, it follows, that when great numbers have emigrated into a foreign land, and are so far removed from the parent state that they neither are or can be properly represented by the government from which they have emigrated, that then nature itself points out the necessity of their assuming to themselves the powers of legislation; and they have a right to consider themselves as a separate state from the other, and as such, to form themselves into a body politic.

In the next place, when a people find themselves cruelly oppressed by the parent state, they have an undoubted right to throw off the yoke, and to assert their liberty, if they find good reason to judge that they have sufficient power and strength to maintain their ground in defending their just rights against their oppressors; for, in this case, by the law of self-preservation, which is the first law of nature, they have not only an undoubted right, but it is their indispensable duty, if they cannot be redressed any other way, to renounce all submission to the government that has oppressed them, and set up an independent state of their own, even though they may be vastly inferior in numbers to the state that has oppressed them. When either of the aforesaid cases takes place, and more especially when both concur, no rational man, I imagine, can have any doubt in his own mind whether such a people have a right to form themselves into a body politic, and assume to themselves all the powers of a free state. For, can it be rational to suppose that a people should be subjected to the tyranny of a set of men who are perfect strangers to them, and cannot be supposed to have that fellow-feeling for them that we generally have for those with whom we are connected and acquainted; and, besides, through their unacquaintedness with the circumstances of the people over whom they claim the right of jurisdiction, are utterly unable to judge, in a multitude of cases, which is best for them?

It becomes me not to say what particular form of government is best for a community, whether a pure democracy, aristocracy, monarchy, or a mixture of all the three simple forms. They have all their advantages and disadvantages, and when they are properly administered may, any of them, answer the design of civil government tolerably. Permit me, however, to say, that an unlimited, absolute monarchy, and an aristocracy not subject to the control of the people, are two of the most exceptionable forms of government: firstly, because in neither of them is there a proper representation of the people; and, secondly, because each of them being entirely independent of the people, they are very apt to degenerate into tyranny. However, in this imperfect state, we cannot expect to have government formed upon such a basis but that it may be perverted by bad men to evil purposes. A wise and good man would be very loth to undermine a constitution that was once fixed and established, although he might discover many imperfections in it; and nothing short of the most urgent necessity would ever induce him to consent to it; because the unhinging a people from a form of government to which they had been long accustomed might throw them into such a state of anarchy and confusion as might terminate in their destruction, or perhaps, in the end, subject them to the worst kind of tyranny.

Having thus shown the nature, end, and design of civil government, and pointed out the reasons why subjects are bound to obey magistrates, viz., because in so doing they both consult their own happiness as individuals, and also promote the public good and the safety of the state, I proceed, in the next place, to show that the same principles that oblige us to submit to civil government do also equally oblige us, where we have power and ability, to resist and oppose tyranny; and that where tyranny begins, government ends. For, if magistrates have no authority but what they derive from the people if they are properly of human creation; if the whole end and design of their institution is to promote the general good, and to secure to men their just rights, it will follow, that when they act contrary to the end and design of their creation they cease being magistrates, and the people which gave them their authority have the right to take it from them again. This is a very plain dictate of common sense, which universally obtains in all similar cases; for who is there that, having employed a number of men to do a particular piece of work for him but what would judge that he had a right to dismiss them from his service when he found that they went directly contrary to his orders, and that, instead of accomplishing the business he had set them about, they would infallibly ruin and destroy it? If, then, men, in the common affairs of life, always judge that they have a right to dismiss from their service such persons as counteract their plans and designs, though the damage will affect only a few individuals, much more must the body politic have a right to depose any persons, though appointed to the highest place of power and authority, when they find that they are unfaithful to the trust reposed in them, and that, instead of consulting the general good, they are disturbing the peace of society by making laws cruel and oppressive, and by depriving the subjects of their just rights and privileges. Whoever pretends to deny this proposition must give up all presence of being master of that common sense and reason by which the Deity has distinguished us from the brutal herd.

As our duty of obedience to the magistrate is founded upon our obligation to promote the general good, our readiness to obey lawful authority will always arise in proportion to the love and regard that we have for the welfare of the public; and the same love and regard for the public will inspire us with as strong a zeal to oppose tyranny as we have to obey magistracy. Our obligation to promote the public good extends as much to the opposing every exertion of arbitrary power that is injurious to the state as it does to the submitting to good and wholesome laws. No man, therefore, can be a good member of the community that is not as zealous to oppose tyranny as he is ready to obey magistracy. A slavish submission to tyranny is a proof of a very sordid and base mind. Such a person cannot be under the influence of any generous human sentiments, nor have a tender regard for mankind.

Further: if magistrates are no farther ministers of God than they promote the good of the community, then obedience to them neither is nor can be unlimited; for it would imply a gross absurdity to assert that, when magistrates are ordained by the people solely for the purpose of being beneficial to the state, they must be obeyed when they are seeking to ruin and destroy it. This would imply that men were bound to act against the great law of self-preservation, and to contribute their assistance to their own ruin and destruction, in order that they may please and gratify the greatest monsters in nature, who are violating the laws of God and destroying the rights of mankind. Unlimited submission and obedience is due to none but God alone. He has an absolute right to command; he alone has an uncontrollable sovereignty over us, because he alone is unchangeably good; he never will nor can require of us, consistent with his nature and attributes, anything that is not fit and reasonable; his commands are all just and good; and to suppose that he has given to any particular set of men a power to require obedience to that which is unreasonable, cruel, and unjust, is robbing the Deity of his justice and goodness, in which consists the peculiar glory of the divine character, and it is representing him under the horrid character of a tyrant.

If magistrates are ministers of God only because the law of God and reason points out the necessity of such an institution for the good of mankind, it follows, that whenever they pursue measures directly destructive of the public good they cease being God's ministers, they forfeit their right to obedience from the subject, they become the pests of society, and the community is under the strongest obligation of duty, both to God and to its own members, to resist and oppose them, which will be so far from resisting the ordinance of God that it will be strictly obeying his commands. To suppose otherwise will imply that the Deity requires of us an obedience that is self-contradictory and absurd, and that one part of his law is directly contrary to the other; i.e., while he commands us to pursue virtue and the general good, he does at the same time require us to persecute virtue, and betray the general good, by enjoining us obedience to the wicked commands of tyrannical oppressors. Can any one not lost to the principles of humanity undertake to defend such absurd sentiments as these? As the public safety is the first and grand law of society, so no community can have a right to invest the magistrate with any power or authority that will enable him to act against the welfare of the state and the good of the whole. If men have at any time wickedly and foolishly given up their just rights into the hands of the magistrate, such acts are null and void, of course; to suppose otherwise will imply that we have a right to invest the magistrate with a power to act contrary to the law of God, which is as much as to say that we are not the subjects of divine law and government. What has been said is, I apprehend, abundantly sufficient to show that tyrants are no magistrates, or that whenever magistrates abuse their power and authority to the subverting the public happiness, their authority immediately ceases, and that it not only becomes lawful, but an indispensable duty to oppose them; that the principle of self-preservation, the affection and duty that we owe to our country, and the obedience we owe the Deity, do all require us to oppose tyranny.

If it be asked, Who are the proper judges to determine when rulers are guilty of tyranny and oppression? I answer, the public. Not a few disaffected individuals, but the collective body of the state, must decide this question; for, as it is the collective body that invests rulers with their power and authority, so it is the collective body that has the sole right of judging whether rulers act up to the end of their institution or not. Great regard ought always to be paid to the judgment of the public. It is true the public may be imposed upon by a misrepresentation of facts; but this may be said of the public which cannot always be said of individuals, viz., that the public is always willing to be rightly informed, and when it has proper matter of conviction laid before it its judgment is always right.

This account of the nature and design of civil government, which is so clearly suggested to us by the plain principles of common sense and reason, is abundantly confirmed by the sacred Scriptures, even by those very texts which have been brought by men of slavish principles to establish the absurd doctrine of unlimited passive obedience and non-resistance, as will abundantly appear by examining the two most noted texts that are commonly brought to support the strange doctrine of passive obedience. The first that I shall cite is in 1 Peter 2:13, 14: "Submit yourselves to every ordinance of man," or, rather, as the words ought to be rendered from the Greek, submit yourselves to every human creation, or human constitution, "for the Lord's sake, whether it be to the king as supreme, or unto governors, as unto them that are sent by him for the punishment of evil-doers, and for the praise of them that do well." Here we see that the apostle asserts that magistracy is of human creation or appointment; that is, the magistrates have no power or authority but what they derive from the people; that this power they are to exert for the punishment of evil-doers, and for the praise of them that do well; i.e., the end and design of the appointment of magistrates is to restrain wicked men, by proper penalties, from injuring society, and to encourage and honor the virtuous and obedient. Upon this account Christians are to submit to them for the Lord's sake; which is as if he had said, Though magistrates are of mere human appointment, and can claim no power or authority but what they derive from the people, yet, as they are ordained by men to promote the general good by punishing evil-doers and by rewarding and encouraging the virtuous and obedient, you ought to submit to them out of a sacred regard to the divine authority; for as they, in the faithful discharge of their office, do fulfill the will of God, so ye, by submitting to them, do fulfill the divine command. If the only reason assigned by the apostle why magistrates should be obeyed out of a regard to the divine authority is because they punish the wicked and encourage the good, it follows, that when they punish the virtuous and encourage the vicious we have a right to refuse yielding any submission or obedience to them; i.e., whenever they act contrary to the end and design of their institution, they forfeit their authority to govern the people, and the reason for submitting to them, out of regard to the divine authority, immediately ceases; and they being only of human appointment, the authority which the people gave them, the public have a right to take from them, and to confer it upon those who are more worthy. So far is this text from favoring arbitrary principles, that there is nothing in it but what is consistent with and favorable to the highest liberty that any man can wish to enjoy; for this text requires us to submit to the magistrate no further than he is the encourager and protector of virtue and the punisher of vice; and this is consistent with all that liberty which the Deity has bestowed upon us.

The other text which I shall mention, and which has been made use of by the favorers of arbitrary government as their great sheet-anchor and main support, is in Romans 13, the first six verses: "Let every soul be subject to the higher powers; for there is no power but of God. The powers that be are ordained of God. Whosoever therefore resisteth the power, resisteth the ordinance of God; and they that resist shall receive to themselves damnation; for rulers are not a terror to good works, but to the evil. Wilt thou then not be afraid of the power? Do that which is good, and thou shalt have praise of the same: for he is the minister of God to thee for good. But if thou do that which is evil, be afraid; for he beareth not the sword in vain: for he is the minister of God, a revenger to execute wrath upon him that doeth evil. Wherefore ye must needs be subject not only for wrath, but also for conscience' sake. For, for this cause pay you tribute also; for they are God's ministers, attending continually upon this very thing." A very little attention, I apprehend, will be sufficient to show that this text is so far from favoring arbitrary government, that, on the contrary, it strongly holds forth the principles of true liberty. Subjection to the higher powers is enjoined by the apostle because there is no power but of God; the powers that be are ordained of God; consequently, to resist the power is to resist the ordinance of God: and he repeatedly declares that the ruler is the minister of God. Now, before we can say whether this text makes for or against the doctrine of unlimited passive obedience, we muse find out in what sense the apostle affirms that magistracy is the ordinance of God, and what he intends when he calls the ruler the minister of God.

I can think but of three possible senses in which magistracy can with any propriety be called God's ordinance, or in which rulers can be said to be ordained of God as his ministers. The first is a plain declaration from the word of God that such a one and his descendants are, and shall be, the only true and lawful magistrates: thus we find in Scripture the kingdom of Judah to be settled by divine appointment in the family of David. Or,

Secondly, by an immediate commission from God, ordering and appointing such a one by name to be the ruler over the people: thus Saul and David were immediately appointed by God to be kings over Israel. Or,

Thirdly, magistracy may be called the ordinance of God, and rulers may be called the ministers of God, because the nature and reason of things, which is the law of God, requires such an institution for the preservation and safety of civil society. In the two first senses the apostle cannot be supposed to affirm that magistracy is God's Ordinance, for neither he nor any of the sacred writers have entailed the magistracy to any one particular family under the gospel dispensation. Neither does he nor any of the inspired writers give us the least hint that any person should ever be immediately commissioned from God to bear rule over the people. The third sense, then, is the only sense in which the apostle can be supposed to affirm that the magistrate is the minister of God, and that magistracy is the ordinance of God; viz., that the nature and reason of things require such an institution for the preservation and safety of mankind. Now, if this be the only sense in which the apostle affirms that magistrates are ordained of

God as his ministers, resistance must be criminal only so far forth as they are the ministers of God, i. e., while they act up to the end of their institution, and ceases being criminal when they cease being the ministers of God, i.e., when they act contrary to the general good, and seek to destroy the liberties of the people.

That we have gotten the apostle's sense of magistracy being the ordinance of God, will plainly appear from the text itself; for, after having asserted that to resist the power is to resist the ordinance of God, and they that resist shall receive to themselves damnation, he immediately adds as the reason of this assertion, "For rulers are not a terror to good works, but to the evil. Wilt thou then not be afraid of the power? Do that which is good, and thou shalt have praise of the same: for he is the minister of God to thee for good. But if thou do that which is evil, be afraid; for he beareth not the sword in vain: for he is the minister of God, a revenger to execute wrath upon him that doeth evil." Here is a plain declaration of the sense in which he asserts that the authority of the magistrate is ordained of God, viz., because rulers are not a terror to good works, but to the evil; therefore we ought to dread offending them, for we cannot offend them but by doing evil; and if we do evil we have just reason to fear their power; for they bear not the sword in vain, but in this case the magistrate is a revenger to execute wrath upon him that doeth evil: but if we are found doers of that which is good, we have no reason to fear the authority of the magistrate; for in this case, instead of being punished, we shall be protected and encouraged. The reason why the magistrate is called the minister of God is because he is to protect, encourage, and honor them that do well, and to punish them that do evil; therefore it is our duty to submit to them, not merely for fear of being punished by them, but out of regard to the divine authority, under which they are deputed to execute judgment and to do justice. For this reason, according to the apostle, tribute is to be paid them, because, as the ministers of God, their whole business is to protect every man in the enjoyment of his just rights and privileges, and to punish every evil-doer.

If the apostle, then, asserts that rulers are ordained of God only because they are a terror to evil works and a praise to them that do well; if they are ministers of God only because they encourage virtue and punish vice; if for this reason only they are to be obeyed for conscience' sake; if the sole reason why they have a right to tribute is because they devote themselves wholly to the business of securing to men their just rights, and to the punishing of evil-doers, it follows, by undeniable consequence, that when they become the pests of human society, when they promote and encourage evil-doers, and become a terror to good works, they then cease being the ordinance of God; they are no longer rulers nor ministers of God; they are so far from being the powers that are ordained of God that they become the ministers of the powers of darkness, and it is so far from being a crime to resist them, that in many cases it may be highly criminal in the sight of Heaven to refuse resisting and opposing them to the utmost of our power; or, in other words, that the same reasons that require us to obey the ordinance of God, do equally oblige us, when we have power and opportunity, to oppose and resist the ordinance of Satan.

Hence we see that the apostle Paul, instead of being a friend to tyranny and arbitrary government, turns out to be a strong advocate for the just rights of mankind, and is for our enjoying all that liberty with which God has invested us; for no power (according to the apostle) is ordained of God but what is an encourager of every good and virtuous action, "Do that which is good, and thou shalt have praise of the same." No man need to be afraid of this power which is ordained of God who does nothing but what is agreeable to the law of God; for this power will not restrain us from exercising any liberty which the Deity has granted us; for the minister of God is to restrain us from nothing but the doing of that which is evil, and to this we have no right. To practice evil is not liberty, but licentiousness. Can we conceive of a more perfect, equitable, and generous plan of government than this which the apostle has laid down, viz., to have rulers appointed over us to encourage us to every good and virtuous action, to defend and protect us in our just rights and privileges, and to grant us everything that can tend to promote our true interest and happiness; to restrain every licentious action, and to punish every one that would injure or harm us; to become a terror of evil-doers; to make and execute such just and righteous laws as shall effectually deter and hinder men from the commission of evil, and to attend continually upon this very thing; to make it their constant care and study, day and night, to promote the good and welfare of the community, and to oppose all evil practices? Deservedly may such rulers be called the ministers of God for good. They carry on the same benevolent design towards the community which the great Governor of the universe does towards his whole creation. 'Tis the indispensable duty of a people to pay tribute, and to afford an easy and comfortable subsistence to such rulers, because they are the ministers of God, who are continually laboring and employing their time for the good of the community. He that resists such magistrates does, in a very emphatical sense, resist the ordinance of God; he is an enemy to mankind, odious to God, and justly incurs the sentence of condemnation from the great Judge of quick and dead. Obedience to such magistrates is yielding obedience to the will of God, and, therefore, ought to be performed from a sacred regard to the divine authority.

For any one from hence to infer that the apostle enjoins in this text unlimited obedience to the worst of tyrants, and that he pronounces damnation upon those that resist the arbitrary measures of such pests of society, is just as good sense as if one should affirm, that because the Scripture enjoins us obedience to the laws of God, therefore we may not oppose the power of darkness; or because we are commanded to submit to the ordinance of God, therefore we may not resist the ministers of Satan. Such wild work must be made with the apostle before he can be brought to speak the language of oppression! It is as plain, I think, as words can make it, that, according to this text, no tyrant can be a ruler; for the apostle's definition of a ruler is, that he is not a terror to good works, but to the evil; and that he is one who is to praise and encourage those that do well. Whenever, then, the ruler encourages them that do evil, and is a terror to those that do well, i. e., as soon as he becomes a tyrant, he forfeits his authority to govern, and becomes the minister of Satan, and, as such, ought to be opposed.

I know it is said that the magistrates were, at the time when the apostle wrote, heathens, and that Nero, that monster of tyranny, was then Emperor of Rome; that therefore the apostle, by enjoining submission to the powers that then were, does require unlimited obedience to be yielded to the worst of tyrants. Now, not to insist upon what has been often observed, viz., that this epistle was written most probably about the beginning of Nero's reign, at which time he was a very humane and merciful prince, did everything that was generous and benevolent to the public, and showed every act of mercy and tenderness to particulars, and therefore might at that time justly deserve the character of the minister of God for good to the people, I say, waiving this, we will suppose that this epistle was written after that Nero was become a monster of tyranny and wickedness; it will by no means follow from thence that the apostle meant to enjoin unlimited subjection to such an authority, or that he intended to affirm that such a cruel, despotic authority was the ordinance of God. The plain, obvious sense of his words, as we have already seen, forbids such a construction to be put upon them, for they plainly imply a strong abhorrence and disapprobation of such a character, and clearly prove that Nero, so far forth as he was a tyrant, could not be the minister of God, nor have a right to claim submission from the people; so that this ought, perhaps, rather to be viewed as a severe satire upon Nero, than as enjoining any submission to him.

It is also worthy to be observed that the apostle prudently waived mentioning any particular persons that were then in power, as it might have been construed in an invidious light, and exposed the primitive Christians to the severe resentments of the men that were then in power. He only in general requires submission to the higher powers, because the powers that be are ordained of God. Now, though the emperor might at that time be such a tyrant that he could with no propriety be said to be ordained of God, yet it would be somewhat strange if there were no men in power among the Romans that acted up to the character of good magistrates, and that deserved to be esteemed as the ministers of God for good unto the people. If there were any such, notwithstanding the tyranny of Nero, the apostle might with great propriety enjoin submission to those powers that were ordained of God, and by so particularly pointing out the end and design of magistrates, and giving his definition of a ruler, he might design to show that neither Nero, nor any other tyrant, ought to be esteemed as the minister of God. Or, rather—which appears to me to be the true sense—the apostle meant to speak of magistracy in general, without any reference to the emperor, or any other person in power, that was then at Rome; and the meaning of this passage is as if he had said, It is the duty of every Christian to be a good subject of civil government, for the power and authority of the civil magistrate are from God; for the powers that be are ordained of God; i.e., the authority of the magistrates that are now either at Rome or elsewhere is ordained of the Deity. Wherever you find any lawful magistrates, remember, they are of divine ordination. But that you may understand what I mean when I say that magistrates are of divine ordination, I will show you how you may discern who are lawful magistrates, and ordained of God, from those who are not. Those only are to be esteemed lawful magistrates, and ordained of God, who pursue the public good by honoring and encouraging those that do well and punishing all that do evil. Such, and such only, wherever they are to be found, are the ministers of God for good: to resist such is resisting the ordinance of God, and exposing yourselves to the divine wrath and condemnation.

In either of these senses the text cannot make anything in favor of arbitrary government. Nor could he with any propriety tell them that they need not be afraid of the power so long as they did that which was good, if he meant to recommend an unlimited submission to a tyrannical Nero; for the best characters were the likeliest to fall a sacrifice to his malice. And, besides, such an injunction would be directly contrary to his own practice, and the practice of the primitive Christians, who refused to comply with the sinful commands of men in power; their answer in such cases being this, We ought to obey God rather than men. Hence the apostle Paul himself suffered many cruel persecutions because he would not renounce Christianity, but persisted in opposing the idolatrous worship of the pagan world.

This text, being rescued from the absurd interpretations which the favorers of arbitrary government have put upon it, turns out to be a noble confirmation of that free and generous plan of government which the law of nature and reason points out to us. Nor can we desire a more equitable plan of government than what the apostle has here laid down; for, if we consult our happiness and real good, we can never wish for an unreasonable liberty, viz., a freedom to do evil, which, according to the apostle, is the only thing that the magistrate is to refrain us from. To have a liberty to do whatever is fit, reasonable, or good, is the highest degree of freedom that rational beings can possess. And how honorable a station are those men placed in, by the providence of God, whose business it is to secure to men this rational liberty, and to promote the happiness and welfare of society, by suppressing vice and immorality, and by honoring and encouraging everything that is honorable, virtuous, and praiseworthy! Such magistrates ought to be honored and obeyed as the ministers of God and the servants of the King of Heaven. Can we conceive of a larger and more generous plan of government than this of the apostle? Or can we find words more plainly expressive of a disapprobation of an arbitrary and tyrannical government? I never read this text without admiring the beauty and nervousness of it; and I can hardly conceive how he could express more ideas in so few words than he has done. We see here, in one view, the honor that belongs to the magistrate, because he is ordained of God for the public good. We have his duty pointed out, viz., to honor and encourage the virtuous, to promote the real good of the community, and to punish all wicked and injurious persons. We are taught the duty of the subject, viz., to obey the magistrate for conscience' sake, because he is ordained of God; and that rulers, being continually employed under God for our good, are to be generously maintained by the paying them tribute; and that disobedience to rulers is highly criminal, and will expose us to the divine wrath. The liberty of the subject is also clearly asserted, viz., that subjects are to be allowed to do everything that is in itself just and right, and are only to be restrained from being guilty of wrong actions. It is also strongly implied, that when rulers become oppressive to the subject and injurious to the state, their authority, their respect, their maintenance, and the duty of submitting to them, must immediately cease; they are then to be considered as the ministers of Satan, and, as such, it becomes our indispensable duty to resist and oppose them.

Thus we see that both reason and revelation perfectly agree in pointing out the nature, end, and design of government, viz., that it is to promote the welfare and happiness of the community; and that subjects have a right to do everything that is good, praiseworthy, and consistent with the good of the community, and are only to be restrained when they do evil and are injurious either to individuals or the whole community; and that they ought to submit to every law that is beneficial to the community for conscience' sake, although it may in some measure interfere with their private interest, for every good man will be ready to forego his private interest for the sake of being beneficial to the public. Reason and revelation, we see, do both teach us that our obedience to rulers is not unlimited, but that resistance is not only allowable, but an indispensable duty in the case of intolerable tyranny and oppression. From both reason and revelation we learn that, as the public safety is the supreme law of the state—being the true standard and measure by which we are to judge whether any law or body of laws are just or not—so legislatures have a right to make, and require subjection to, any set of laws that have a tendency to promote the good of the community.

Our governors have a right to take every proper method to form the minds of their subjects so that they may become good members of society. The great difference that we may observe among the several classes of mankind arises chiefly from their education and their laws: hence men become virtuous or vicious, good commonwealthsmen or the contrary, generous, noble, and courageous, or base, mean-spirited, and cowardly, according to the impression that they have received from the government that they are under, together with their education and the methods that have been practiced by their leaders to form their minds in early life. Hence the necessity of good laws to encourage every noble and virtuous sentiment, to suppress vice and immorality, to promote industry, and to punish idleness, that parent of innumerable evils; to promote arts and sciences, and to banish ignorance from among mankind.

And as nothing tends like religion and the fear of God to make men good members of the commonwealth, it is the duty of magistrates to become the patrons and promoters of religion and piety, and to make suitable laws for the maintaining public worship, and decently supporting the teachers of religion. Such laws, I apprehend, are absolutely necessary for the well-being of civil society. Such laws may be made, consistent with all that liberty of conscience which every good member of society ought to be possessed of; for, as there are few, if any, religious societies among us but what profess to believe and practice all the great duties of religion and morality that are necessary for the well-being of society and the safety of the state, let every one be allowed to attend worship in his own society, or in that way that he judges most agreeable to the will of God, and let him be obliged to contribute his assistance to the supporting and defraying the necessary charges of his own meeting. In this case no one can have any right to complain that he is deprived of liberty of conscience, seeing that he has a right to choose and freely attend that worship that appears to him to be most agreeable to the will of God; and it must be very unreasonable for him to object against being obliged to contribute his part towards the support of that worship which he has chosen. Whether some such method as this might not tend, in a very eminent manner, to promote the peace and welfare of society, I must leave to the wisdom of our legislators to determine; be sure it would take off some of the most popular objections against being obliged by law to support public worship while the law restricts that support only to one denomination.

But for the civil authority to pretend to establish particular modes of faith and forms of worship, and to punish all that deviate from the standard which our superiors have set up, is attended with the most pernicious consequences to society. It cramps all free and rational inquiry, fills the world with hypocrites and superstitious bigots—nay, with infidels and skeptics; it exposes men of religion and conscience to the rage and malice of fiery, blind zealots, and dissolves every tender tie of human nature; in short, it introduces confusion and every evil work. And I cannot but look upon it as a peculiar blessing of Heaven that we live in a land where every one can freely deliver his sentiments upon religious subjects, and have the privilege of worshipping God according to the dictates of his own conscience without any molestation or disturbance—a privilege which I hope we shall ever keep up and strenuously maintain. No principles ought ever to be discountenanced by civil authority but such as tend to the subversion of the state. So long as a man is a good member of society, he is accountable to God alone for his religious sentiments; but when men are found disturbers of the public peace, stirring up sedition, or practicing against the state, no presence of religion or conscience ought to screen them from being brought to condign punishment. But then, as the end and design of punishment is either to make restitution to the injured or to restrain men from committing the like crimes for the future, so, when these important ends are answered, the punishment ought to cease; for whatever is inflicted upon a man under the notion of punishment after these important ends are answered, is not a just and lawful punishment, but is properly cruelty and base revenge.

From this account of civil government we learn that the business of magistrates is weighty and important. It requires both wisdom and integrity. When either are wanting, government will be poorly administered; more especially if our governors are men of loose morals and abandoned principles; for if a man is not faithful to God and his own soul, how can we expect that he will be faithful to the public? There was a great deal of propriety in the advice that Jethro gave to Moses to provide able men, men of truth, that feared God, and that hated covetousness, and to appoint them for rulers over the people. For it certainly implies a very gross absurdity to suppose that those who are ordained of God for the public good should have no regard to the laws of God, or that the ministers of God should be despisers of the divine commands. David, the man after God's own heart, makes piety a necessary qualification in a ruler: "He that ruleth over men (says he) must be just, ruling in the fear of God." It is necessary it should be so, for the welfare and happiness of the state; for, to say nothing of the venality and corruption, of the tyranny and oppression, that will take place under unjust rulers, barely their vicious and irregular lives will have a most pernicious effect upon the lives and manners of their subjects: their authority becomes despicable in the opinion of discerning men. And, besides, with what face can they make or execute laws against vices which they practice with greediness? A people that have a right of choosing their magistrates are criminally guilty in the sight of Heaven when they are governed by caprice and humor, or are influenced by bribery to choose magistrates that are irreligious men, who are devoid of sentiment, and of bad morals and base lives. Men cannot be sufficiently sensible what a curse they may bring upon themselves and their posterity by foolishly and wickedly choosing men of abandoned characters and profligate lives for their magistrates and rulers.

We have already seen that magistrates who rule in the fear of God ought not only to be obeyed as the ministers of God, but that they ought also to be handsomely supported, that they may cheerfully and freely attend upon the duties of their station; for it is an area of shame and disgrace to society to see men that serve the public laboring under indigent and needy circumstances; and, besides, it is a maxim of eternal truth that the laborer is worthy of his reward.

It is also a great duty incumbent on people to treat those in authority with all becoming honor and respect, to be very careful of casting any aspersion upon their characters. To despise government, and to speak evil of dignities, is represented in Scripture as one of the worst of characters, and it was an injunction of Moses, "Thou shalt not speak evil of the ruler of thy people." Great mischief may ensue upon reviling the character of good rulers; for the unthinking herd of mankind are very apt to give ear to scandal, and when it falls upon men in power, it brings their authority into contempt, lessens their influence, and disheartens them from doing that service to the community of which they are capable; whereas, when they are properly honored, and treated with that respect which is due to their station, it inspires them with courage and a noble ardor to serve the public: their influence among the people is strengthened, and their authority becomes firmly established. We ought to remember that they are men like to ourselves, liable to the same imperfections and infirmities with the rest of us, and therefore, so long as they aim at the public good their mistakes, misapprehensions, and infirmities, ought to be treated with the utmost humanity and tenderness.

But though I would recommend to all Christians, as a part of the duty that they owe to magistrates, to treat them with proper honor and respect, none can reasonably suppose that I mean that they ought to be flattered in their vices, or honored and caressed while they are seeking to undermine and ruin the state; for this would be wickedly betraying our just rights, and we should be guilty of our own destruction. We ought ever to persevere with firmness and fortitude in maintaining and contending for all that liberty that the Deity has granted us. It is our duty to be ever watchful over our just rights, and not suffer them to be wrested out of our hands by any of the artifices of tyrannical oppressors. But there is a wide difference between being jealous of our rights, when we have the strongest reason to conclude that they are invaded by our rulers, and being unreasonably suspicious of men that are zealously endeavoring to support the constitution, only because we do not thoroughly comprehend all their designs. The first argues a noble and generous mind, the other, a low and base spirit.

Thus have I considered the nature of the duty enjoined in the text, and have endeavored to show that the same principles that require obedience to lawful magistrates do also require us to resist tyrants; this I have confirmed from reason and Scripture.

It was with a particular view to the present unhappy controversy that subsists between us and Great Britain that I chose to discourse upon the nature and design of government, and the rights and duties both of governors and governed, that so, justly understanding our rights and privileges, we may stand firm in our opposition to ministerial tyranny, while at the same time we pay all proper obedience and submission to our lawful magistrates; and that, while we are contending for liberty, we may avoid running into licentiousness; and that we may preserve the due medium between submitting to tyranny and running into anarchy. I acknowledge that I have undertaken a difficult task; but, as it appeared to me, the present state of affairs loudly called for such a discourse; and, therefore, I hope the wise, the generous, and the good, will candidly receive my good intentions to serve the public. I shall now apply this discourse to the grand controversy that at this day subsists between Great Britain and the American colonies.

And here, in the first place, I cannot but take notice how wonderfully Providence has smiled upon us by causing the several colonies to unite so firmly together against the tyranny of Great Britain, though differing from each other in their particular interest, forms of government, modes of worship, and particular customs and manners, besides several animosities that had subsisted among them. That, under these circumstances, such a union should take place as we now behold, was a thing that might rather have been wished than hoped for.

And, in the next place, who could have thought that, when our charter was vacated, when we became destitute of any legislative authority, and when our courts of justice in many parts of the country were stopped, so that we could neither make nor execute laws upon offenders, who, I say, would have thought, that in such a situation the people should behave so peaceably, and maintain such good order and harmony among themselves? This is a plain proof that they, having not the civil law to regulate themselves by, became a law unto themselves; and by their conduct they have shown that they were regulated by the law of God written in their hearts. This is the Lord's doing, and it ought to be marvelous in our eyes.

From what has been said in this discourse, it will appear that we are in the way of our duty in opposing the tyranny of Great Britain; for, if unlimited submission is not due to any human power, if we have an undoubted right to oppose and resist a set of tyrants that are subverting our just rights and privileges, there cannot remain a doubt in any man, that will calmly attend to reason, whether we have a right to resist and oppose the arbitrary measures of the King and Parliament; for it is plain to demonstration, nay, it is in a manner self-evident, that they have been and are endeavoring to deprive us not only of the privileges of Englishmen, and our charter rights, but they have endeavored to deprive us of what is much more sacred, viz., the privileges of men and Christians; i.e., they are robbing us of the inalienable rights that the God of nature has given us as men and rational beings, and has confirmed to us in his written word as Christians and disciples of that Jesus who came to redeem us from the bondage of sin and the tyranny of Satan, and to grant us the most perfect freedom, even the glorious liberty of the sons and children of God; that here they have endeavored to deprive us of the sacred charter of the King of Heaven. But we have this for our consolation: the Lord reigneth; he governs the world in righteousness, and will avenge the cause of the oppressed when they cry unto him. We have made our appeal to Heaven, and we cannot doubt but that the Judge of all the earth will do right.

Need I upon this occasion descend to particulars? Can any one be ignorant what the things are of which we complain? Does not every one know that the King and Parliament have assumed the right to tax us without our consent? And can any one be so lost to the principles of humanity and common sense as not to view their conduct in this affair as a very grievous imposition? Reason and equity require that no one be obliged to pay a tax that he has never consented to, either by himself or by his representative.

But, as Divine Providence has placed us at so great a distance from Great Britain that we neither are nor can be properly represented in the British Parliament, it is a plain proof that the Deity designed that we should have the powers of legislation and taxation among ourselves; for can any suppose it to be reasonable that a set of men that are perfect strangers to us should have the uncontrollable right to lay the most heavy and grievous burdens upon us that they please, purely to gratify their unbounded avarice and luxury? Must we be obliged to perish with cold and hunger to maintain them in idleness, in all kinds of debauchery and dissipation? But if they have the right to take our property from us without our consent, we must be wholly at their mercy for our food and raiment, and we know by sad experience that their tender mercies are cruel.

But because we were not willing to submit to such an unrighteous and cruel decree, though we modestly complained and humbly petitioned for a redress of our grievances, instead of hearing our complaints, and granting our requests, they have gone on to add iniquity to transgression, by making several cruel and unrighteous acts. Who can forget the cruel act to block up the harbor of Boston, whereby thousands of innocent persons must have been inevitably ruined had they not been supported by the continent? Who can forge the act for vacating our charter, together with many other cruel acts which it is needless to mention? But, not being able to accomplish their wicked purposes by mere acts of Parliament, they have proceeded to commence open hostilities against us, and have endeavored to destroy us by fire and sword. Our towns they have burnt, our brethren they have slain, our vessels they have taken, and our goods they have spoiled. And, after all this wanton exertion of arbitrary power, is there the man that has any of the feeling of humanity left who is not fired with a noble indignation against such merciless tyrants, who have not only brought upon us all the horrors of a civil war, but have also added a piece of barbarity unknown to Turks and Mohammedan infidels, yea, such as would be abhorred and detested by the savages of the wilderness, I mean their cruelly forcing our brethren whom they have taken prisoners, without any distinction of Whig or Tory, to serve on board their ships of war, thereby obliging them to take up arms against their own countrymen, and to fight against their brethren, their wives, and their children, and to assist in plundering their own estates! This, my brethren, is done by men who call themselves Christians, against their Christian brethren, against men who till now gloried in the name of Englishmen, and who were ever ready to spend their lives and fortunes in the defense of British rights. Tell it not in Gath, publish it not in the streets of Askelon, lest it cause our enemies to rejoice and our adversaries to triumph! Such a conduct as this brings a great reproach upon the profession of Christianity; nay, it is a great scandal even to human nature itself.

It would be highly criminal not to feel a due resentment against such tyrannical monsters. It is an indispensable duty, my brethren, which we owe to God and our country, to rouse up and bestir ourselves, and, being animated with a noble zeal for the sacred cause of liberty, to defend our lives and fortunes, even to the shedding the last drop of blood. The love of our country, the tender affection that we have for our wives and children, the regard we ought to have for unborn posterity, yea, everything that is dear and sacred, do now loudly call upon us to use our best endeavors to save our country. We must beat our ploughshares into swords, and our pruning-hooks into spears, and learn the art of self-defense against our enemies. To be careless and remiss, or to neglect the cause of our country through the base motives of avarice and self-interest, will expose us not only to the resentments of our fellow-creatures, but to the displeasure of God Almighty; for to such base wretches, in such a time as this, we may apply with the utmost propriety that passage in Jeremiah 48:10: "Cursed be he that doeth the work of the Lord deceitfully, and cursed be he that keepeth back his sword from blood." To save our country from the hands of our oppressors ought to be dearer to us even than our own lives, and, next to the eternal salvation of our own souls, is the thing of the greatest importance,—a duty so sacred that it cannot justly be dispensed with for the sake of our secular concerns. Doubtless for this reason God has been pleased to manifest his anger against those who have refused to assist their country against its cruel oppressors. Hence, in a case similar to ours, when the Israelites were struggling to deliver themselves from the tyranny of Jabin, the King of Canaan, we find a most bitter curse denounced against those who refused to grant their assistance in the common cause; see Judges 5:23: "Curse ye Meroz, said the angel of the Lord, curse ye bitterly the inhabitants thereof; because they came not to the help of the Lord, to the help of the Lord against the mighty."

Now, if such a bitter curse is denounced against those who refused to assist their country against its oppressors, what a dreadful doom are those exposed to who have not only refused to assist their country in this time of distress, but have, through motives of interest or ambition, shown themselves enemies to their country by opposing us in the measures that we have taken, and by openly favoring the British Parliament! He that is so lost to humanity as to be willing to sacrifice his country for the sake of avarice or ambition, has arrived to the highest stage of wickedness that human nature is capable of, and deserves a much worse name than I at present care to give him. But I think I may with propriety say that such a person has forfeited his right to human society, and that he ought to take up his abode, not among the savage men, but among the savage beasts of the wilderness.

Nor can I wholly excuse from blame those timid persons who, through their own cowardice, have been induced to favor our enemies, and have refused to act in defense of their country; for a due sense of the ruin and destruction that our enemies are bringing upon us is enough to raise such a resentment in the human breast that would, I should think, be sufficient to banish fear from the most timid male. And, besides, to indulge cowardice in such a cause argues a want of faith in God; for can he that firmly believes and relies upon the providence of God doubt whether he will avenge the cause of the injured when they apply to him for help? For my own part, when I consider the dispensations of Providence towards this land ever since our fathers first settled in Plymouth, I find abundant reason to conclude that the great Sovereign of the universe has planted a vine in this American wilderness which he has caused to take deep root, and it has filled the land, and that he will never suffer it to be plucked up or destroyed.

Our fathers fled from the rage of prelatical tyranny and persecution, and came into this land in order to enjoy liberty of conscience, and they have increased to a great people. Many have been the interpositions of Divine Providence on our behalf, both in our fathers' days and ours; and, though we are now engaged in a war with Great Britain, yet we have been prospered in a most wonderful manner. And can we think that he who has thus far helped us will give us up into the hands of our enemies? Certainly he that has begun to deliver us will continue to show his mercy towards us, in saving us from the hands of our enemies: he will not forsake us if we do not forsake him. Our cause is so just and good that nothing can prevent our success but only our sins. Could I see a spirit of repentance and reformation prevail through the land, I should not have the least apprehension or fear of being brought under the iron rod of slavery, even though all the powers of the globe were combined against us. And though I confess that the irreligion and profaneness which are so common among us gives something of a damp to my spirits, yet I cannot help hoping, and even believing, that Providence has designed this continent for to be the asylum of liberty and true religion; for can we suppose that the God who created us free agents, and designed that we should glorify and serve him in this world that we might enjoy him forever hereafter, will suffer liberty and true religion to be banished from off the face of the earth? But do we not find that both religion and liberty seem to be expiring and gasping for life in the other continent—where, then, can they find a harbor or place of refuge but in this?

There are some who pretend that it is against their consciences to take up arms in defense of their country; but can any rational being suppose that the Deity can require us to contradict the law of nature which he has written in our hearts, a part of which I am sure is the principle of self-defense, which strongly prompts us all to oppose any power that would take away our lives, or the lives of our friends? Now, for men to take pains to destroy the tender feelings of human nature, and to eradicate the principles of self-preservation, and then to persuade themselves that in so doing they submit to and obey the will of God, is a plain proof how easily men may be led to pervert the very first and plainest principles of reason and common sense, and argues a gross corruption of the human mind. We find such persons are very inconsistent with themselves; for no men are more zealous to defend their property, and to secure their estates from the encroachments of others, while they refuse to defend their persons, their wives, their children, and their country, against the assaults of the enemy. We see to what unaccountable lengths men will run when once they leave the plain road of common sense, and violate the law which God has written in the heart. Thus some have thought they did God service when they unmercifully butchered and destroyed the lives of the servants of God; while others, upon the contrary extreme, believe that they please God while they sit still and quietly behold their friends and brethren killed by their unmerciful enemies, without endeavoring to defend or rescue them. The one is a sin of omission, and the other is a sin of commission, and it may perhaps be difficult to say, under certain circumstances, which is the most criminal in the sight of Heaven. Of this I am sure, that they are, both of them, great violations of the law of God.

Having thus endeavored to show the lawfulness and necessity of defending ourselves against the tyranny of Great Britain, I would observe that Providence seems plainly to point to us the expediency, and even necessity, of our considering ourselves as an independent state. For, not to consider the absurdity implied in making war against a power to which we profess to own subjection, to pass by the impracticability of our ever coming under subjection to Great Britain upon fair and equitable terms, we may observe that the British Parliament has virtually declared us an independent state by authorizing their ships of war to seize all American property, wherever they can find it, without making any distinction between the friends of administration and those that have appeared in opposition to the acts of Parliament. This is making us a distinct nation from themselves. They can have no right any longer to style us rebels; for rebellion implies a particular faction risen up in opposition to lawful authority, and, as such, the factious party ought to be punished, while those that remain loyal are to be protected. But when war is declared against a whole community without distinction, and the property of each party is declared to be seizable, this, if anything can be, is treating us as an independent state. Now, if they are pleased to consider us as in a state of independency, who can object against our considering ourselves so too?

But while we are nobly opposing with our lives and estates the tyranny of the British Parliament, let us not forget the duty which we owe to our lawful magistrates; let us never mistake licentiousness for liberty. The more we understand the principles of liberty, the more readily shall we yield obedience to lawful authority; for no man can oppose good government but he that is a stranger to true liberty. Let us ever check and restrain the factious disturbers of the peace; whenever we meet with persons that are loth to submit to lawful authority, let us treat them with the contempt which they deserve, and even esteem them as the enemies of their country and the pests of society. It is with peculiar pleasure that I reflect upon the peaceable behavior of my countrymen at a time when the courts of justice were stopped and the execution of laws suspended. It will certainly be expected of a people that could behave so well when they had nothing to restrain them but the laws written in their hearts, that they will yield all ready and cheerful obedience to lawful authority. There is at present the utmost need of guarding ourselves against a seditious and factious temper; for when we are engaged with so powerful an enemy from without, our political salvation, under God, does, in an eminent manner, depend upon our being firmly united together in the bonds of love to one another, and of due submission to lawful authority. I hope we shall never give any just occasion to our adversaries to reproach us as being men of turbulent dispositions and licentious principles, that cannot bear to be restrained by good and wholesome laws, even though they are of our own making, nor submit to rulers of our own choosing. But I have reason to hope much better things of my countrymen, though I thus speak. However, in this time of difficulty and distress, we cannot be too much guarded against the least approaches to discord and faction. Let us, while we are jealous of our rights, take heed of unreasonable suspicions and evil surmises which have no proper foundation; let us take heed lest we hurt the cause of liberty by speaking evil of the ruler of the people.

Let us treat our rulers with all that honor and respect which the dignity of their station requires; but let it be such an honor and respect as is worthy of the sons of freedom to give. Let us ever abhor the base arts that are used by fawning parasites and cringing courtiers, who by their low artifices and base flatteries obtain offices and posts which they are unqualified to sustain, and honors of which they are unworthy, and oftentimes have a greater number of places assigned them than any one person of the greatest abilities can ever properly fill, by means of which the community becomes greatly injured, for this reason, that many an important trust remains undischarged, and many an honest and worthy member of society is deprived of those honors and privileges to which he has a just right, whilst the most despicable, worthless courtier is loaded with honorable and profitable commissions. In order to avoid this evil, I hope our legislators will always despise flattery as something below the dignity of a rational mind, and that they will ever scorn the man that will be corrupted or take a bribe. And let us all resolve with ourselves that no motives of interest, nor hopes of preferment shall ever induce us to act the part of fawning courtiers towards men in power. Let the honor and respect which we show our superiors be true and genuine, flowing from a sincere and upright heart.

The honors that have been paid to arbitrary princes have often been very hypocritical and insincere. Tyrants have been flattered in their vices, and have often had an idolatrous reverence paid them. The worst princes have been the most flattered and adored; and many such, in the pagan world, assumed the title of gods, and had divine honors paid them. This idolatrous reverence has ever been the inseparable concomitant of arbitrary power and tyrannical government; for even Christian princes, if they have not been adored under the character of gods, yet the titles given them strongly savor of blasphemy, and the reverence paid them is really idolatrous. What right has a poor sinful worm of the dust to claim the title of his most sacred Majesty? Most sacred certainly belongs only to God alone—for there is none holy as the Lord—yet how common is it to see this title given to kings! And how often have we been told that the king can do no wrong! Even though he should be so foolish and wicked as hardly to be capable of ever being in the right, yet still it must be asserted and maintained that it is impossible for him to do wrong!

The cruel, savage disposition of tyrants, and the idolatrous reverence that is paid them, are both most beautifully exhibited to view by the apostle John in the Revelation, thirteenth chapter, from the first to the tenth verse, where the apostle gives a description of a horrible wild beast which he saw rise out of the sea, having seven heads and ten horns, and upon his heads the names of blasphemy. By heads are to be understood forms of government, and by blasphemy, idolatry; so that it seems implied that there will be a degree of idolatry in every form of tyrannical government. This beast is represented as having the body of a leopard, the feet of a bear, and the mouth of a lion; i.e., a horrible monster, possessed of the rage and fury of the lion, the fierceness of the bear, and the swiftness of the leopard to seize and devour its prey. Can words more strongly point out, or exhibit in more lively colors, the exceeding rage, fury, and impetuosity of tyrants, in their destroying and making havoc of mankind? To this beast we find the dragon gave his power, seat, and great authority; i.e., the devil constituted him to be his viceregent on earth; this is to denote that tyrants are the ministers of Satan, ordained by him for the destruction of mankind.

By the beast with seven heads and ten horns I understand the tyranny of arbitrary princes, viz., the emperors and kings of the Eastern and Western Roman Empire, and not the tyranny of the Pope and clergy; for the description of every part of this beast will answer better to be understood of political than of ecclesiastical tyrants. Thus the seven heads are generally interpreted to denote the several forms of Roman government; the ten horns are understood to be ten kingdoms that were set up in the

Western Empire; and by the body of the beast it seems most natural to understand the Eastern, or Greek Empire, for it is said to be like a leopard. This image is taken from Daniel 7:6, where the third beast is said to be like a leopard. Now, by the third beast in Daniel is understood, by the best interpreters, the Grecian Monarchy. It is well known that John frequently borrows his images from Daniel, and I believe it will be found, upon a critical examination of the matter, that whenever he does so he means the same thing with Daniel; if this be true (as I am fully persuaded it is), then, by the body of this beast being like a leopard in the Revelation of John, is to be understood the Eastern, or Greek Empire, which was that part of the old Roman Empire that remained whole for several ages after the Western Empire was broken into ten kingdoms. Further: after the beast was risen it is said that the dragon gave him his seat. Now, by the dragon is meant the devil, who is represented as presiding over the Roman Empire in its pagan state; but the seat of the Roman Empire in its pagan state was Rome. Here, then, is a prophecy that the emperor of the East should become possessed of Rome, which exactly agrees with what we know from history to be fact; for the Emperor Justinian's generals having expelled the Goths out of Italy, Rome was brought into subjection to the emperor of the East, and was for a long time governed by the emperor's lieutenant, who resided at Ravenna. These considerations convince me that the Greek Empire, and not the Pope and his clergy, is to be understood by the body of the beast, which was like a leopard. And what further confirms me in this belief is, that it appears to me that the Pope and the papal clergy are to be understood by the second beast which we read of in Revelation 13:11-17, for of him it is said that "he had two horns like a lamb." A lamb, we know, is the figure by which Jesus Christ is signified in the Revelation and many other parts of the New Testament. The Pope claims both a temporal and spiritual sovereignty denoted by the two horns, under the character of the vicar of Jesus Christ, and yet, under this high presence of being the vicar of Jesus Christ, he speaks like a dragon; i.e., he promotes idolatry in the Christian Church, in like manner as the dragon did in the heathen world. To distinguish him from the first beast he is called (Revelation 19) "the false prophet that wrought miracles;" i.e., like Mahomet, he pretends to be a lawgiver, and claims infallibility, and his emissaries endeavor to confirm this doctrine by pretended miracles. How wonderfully do all these characters agree to the Pope! Wherefore I conclude that the second, and not the first beast, denotes the tyranny of the Pope and his clergy.

Such a horrible monster, we should have thought, would have been abhorred and detested of all mankind, and that all nations would have joined their powers and forces together to oppose and utterly destroy him from off the face of the earth; but, so far are they from doing this, that, on the contrary, they are represented as worshipping him (verse 8): "And all that dwell on the earth shall worship him," viz., all those "whose names are not written in the Lamb's book of life;" i.e., the wicked world shall pay him an idolatrous reverence, and worship him with a godlike adoration. What can in a more lively manner show the gross stupidity and wickedness of mankind, in thus tamely giving up their just rights into the hands of tyrannical monsters, and in so readily paying them such an unlimited obedience as is due to God alone?

We may observe, further, that these men are said (verse 4) to "worship the dragon;"—not that it is to be supposed that they, in direct terms, paid divine homage to Satan, but that the adoration paid to the beast, who was Satan's viceregent, did ultimately center in him. Hence we learn that those who pay an undue and sinful veneration to tyrants are properly the servants of the devil; they are worshippers of the prince of darkness, for in him all that undue homage and adoration centers that is given to his ministers. Hence that terrible denunciation of divine wrath against the worshippers of the beast and his image: "If any man worship the beast and his image, and receive his mark in his forehead, or in his hand, the same shall drink of the wine of the wrath of God which is poured out without mixture into the cup of his indignation, and he shall be tormented with fire and brimstone in the presence of the holy angels, and in the presence of the Lamb; and the smoke of their torment ascendeth for ever and ever: and they have no rest day nor night, who worship the beast and his image, and who receive the mark of his name." We have here set forth in the clearest manner, by the inspired apostle, God's abhorrence of tyranny and tyrants, together with the idolatrous reverence that their wretched subjects are wont to pay them, and the awful denunciation of divine wrath against those who are guilty of this undue obedience to tyrants.

Does it not, then, highly concern us all to stand fast in the liberty wherewith Heaven hath made us free, and to strive to get the victory over the beast and his image—over every species of tyranny? Let us look upon a freedom from the power of tyrants as a blessing that cannot be purchased too dear, and let us bless God that he has so far delivered us from that idolatrous reverence which men are so very apt to pay to arbitrary tyrants; and let us pray that he would be pleased graciously to perfect the mercy he has begun to show us by confounding the devices of our enemies and bringing their counsels to naught, and by establishing our just rights and privileges upon such a firm and lasting basis that the powers of earth and hell shall not prevail against it.

Under God, every person in the community ought to contribute his assistance to the bringing about of so glorious and important an event; but in a more eminent manner does this important business belong to the gentlemen that are chosen to represent the people in this General Assembly, including those that have been appointed members of the Honorable Council Board.

Honored fathers, we look up to you, in this day of calamity and distress, as the guardians of our invaded rights, and the defenders of our liberties against British tyranny. You are called, in Providence, to save your country from ruin. A trust is reposed in you of the highest importance to the community that can be conceived of, its business the most noble and grand, and a task the most arduous and difficult to accomplish that ever engaged the human mind—I mean as to things of the present life. But as you are engaged in the defense of a just and righteous cause, you may with firmness of mind commit your cause to God, and depend on his kind providence for direction and assistance. You will have the fervent wishes and prayers of all good men that God would crown all your labors with success, and direct you into such measures as shall tend to promote the welfare and happiness of the community, and afford you all that wisdom and prudence which is necessary to regulate the affairs of state at this critical period.

Honored fathers of the House of Representatives: We trust to your wisdom and goodness that you will be led to appoint such men to be in council whom you know to be men of real principle, and who are of unblemished lives; that have shown themselves zealous and hearty friends to the liberties of America; and men that have the fear of God before their eyes; for such only are men that can be depended upon uniformly to pursue the general good.

My reverend fathers and brethren in the ministry will remember that, according to our text, it is part of the work and business of a gospel minister to teach his hearers the duty they owe to magistrates. Let us, then, endeavor to explain the nature of their duty faithfully, and show them the difference between liberty and licentiousness; and, while we are animating them to oppose tyranny and arbitrary power, let us inculcate upon them the duty of yielding due obedience to lawful authority. In order to the right and faithful discharge of this part of our ministry, it is necessary that we should thoroughly study the law of nature, the rights of mankind, and the reciprocal duties of governors and governed. By this means we shall be able to guard them against the extremes of slavish submission to tyrants on one hand and of sedition and licentiousness on the other. We may, I apprehend, attain a thorough acquaintance with the law of nature and the rights of mankind, while we remain ignorant of many technical terms of law, and are utterly unacquainted with the obscure and barbarous Latin that was so much used in the ages of popish darkness and superstition.

To conclude: While we are fighting for liberty, and striving against tyranny, let us remember to fight the good fight of faith and earnestly seek to be delivered from that bondage of corruption which we are brought into by sin, and that we may be made partakers of the glorious liberty of the sons and children of God: which may the Father of Mercies grant us all, through Jesus Christ. Amen.

LEXINGTON

By John Greenleaf Whittier

As the Revolutionary War began, the ragtag American militia fought with extraordinary courage and distinction. The first of the battles was little more than a skirmish, yet it inspired a "shot heard 'round the world" sense of national pride. In this verse another of America's greatest historical poets re-creates the epic scene.

No Berserk thirst of blood had they,
No battle-joy was theirs, who set
Against the alien bayonet
Their homespun breasts in that old day.

Their feet had trodden peaceful ways;
They loved not strife, they dreaded pain;
They saw not, what to us is plain,
That God would make man's wrath His praise.

No seers were they, but simple men;
Its vast results the future hid:
The meaning of the work they did
Was strange and dark and doubtful then.

Swift as their summons came they left
The plow mid-furrow standing still,
The half-ground corn grist in the mill,
The spade in earth, the axe in cleft.

They went where duty seemed to call,
They scarcely asked the reason why;

They only knew they could but die,
And death was not the worst of all!

Of man for man the sacrifice,
All that was theirs to give, they gave.
The flowers that blossomed from their grave
Have sown themselves beneath all skies.

Their death-shot shook the feudal tower,
And shattered slavery's chain as well
On the sky's dome, as on a bell,
Its echo struck the world's great hour.

That fateful echo is not dumb:
The nations listening to its sound
Wait, from a century's vantage-ground,
The holier triumphs yet to come.

The bridal time of Law and Love,
The gladness of the world's release,
When, war-sick, at the feet of Peace
The hawk shall nestle with the dove!

The golden age of brotherhood
Unknown to other rivalries
Than of the mild humanities,
And gracious interchange of good,

When closer strand shall lean to strand,
Till meet, beneath saluting flags,
The eagle of our mountain-crags,
The lion of our Motherland!

NATHAN HALE

By Francis Miles Finch

In addition to the feats of courage displayed by communities, militias, and armies, the coming of the revolutionary conflict highlighted numerous instances of individual valor. In this retelling of the famous story of a patriot who gave his life for the cause of freedom, the tension of war is conjured in a compelling fashion.

To drum-beat and heart-beat,
A soldier marches by;
There is color in his cheek,
There is courage in his eye,
Yet to drum-beat and heart-beat
In a moment he must die.

By the starlight and moonlight,
He seeks the Briton's camp;
He hears the rustling flag
And the armed sentry's tramp;
And the starlight and moonlight
His silent wanderings lamp.

With slow tread and still tread,
He scans the tented line;
And he counts the battery guns,
By the gaunt and shadowy pine;
And his slow tread and still tread
Gives no warning sign.

The dark wave, the plumed wave,
It meets his eager glance;
And it sparkles 'neath the stars,
Like the glimmer of a lance
A dark wave, a plumed wave,
On an emerald expanse.

A sharp clang, a still clang,
And terror in the sound!
For the sentry, falcon-eyed,
In the camp a spy hath found;
With a sharp clang, a steel clang,
The patriot is bound.

With calm brow, and steady brow,
He listens to his doom;
In his look there is no fear,
Nor a shadow-trace of gloom;
But with calm brow and steady brow,
He robes him for the tomb.

In the long night, the still night,
He kneels upon the sod;
and the brutal guards withhold
E'en the solemn word of God!
In the long night, the still night,
He walks where Christ hath trod.

'Neath the blue morn, the sunny morn,
He dies upon the tree;
And he mourns that he can lose
But one life for Liberty;
And in the blue morn, the sunny morn,
His spirit wings are free.

But his last words, his message-words,
They burn, lest friendly eye
Should read how proud and calm
A patriot could die,
With his last words, his dying words,
A soldier's battle-cry.

From Fame-leaf and Angel-leaf,
From monument and urn,
The sad of earth, the glad of heaven
His tragic fate shall learn;
But on Fame-leaf and Angel-leaf
The name of Hale shall burn!

VALLEY FORGE

By Thomas Buchanan Read

After a series of discouraging defeats, the ill-equipped Continental Army spent the bitterly cold winter of 1777 camped at Valley Forge, Pennsylvania. Despite the hardships, the resolve demonstrated by the officer corps—and particularly the resolve of General George Washington—enabled the soldiers to endure so they might fight another day. This well-known verse celebrates that resolve and the cause that lay behind it.

O'er town and cottage, vale and height,
Down came Winter, fierce and white,
And shuddering wildly, as distraught
At horrors his own hand had wrought.

His child, the young Year, newly born,
Cheerless, cowering, and affrighted,
Wailed with a shivering voice forlorn,
As on a frozen heath benighted.
In vain the hearths were set aglow,
In vain the evening lamps were lighted,
To cheer the dreary realm of snow:
Old Winter's brow would not be smoothed,
Nor the young Year's wailing soothed.

How sad the wretch at morn or eve
Compelled his starving home to leave,
Who, plunged breast-deep from drift to drift,
Toils slowly on from rift to rift,
Still hearing in his aching ear
The cry his fancy whispers near,
Of little ones who weep for bread
Within an ill-provided shed!

But wilder, fiercer, sadder still,
Freezing the tear it caused to start,
Was the inevitable chill
Which pierced a nation's agued heart

A nation with its naked breast
Against the frozen barriers prest,
Heaving its tedious way and slow
Through shifting gulfs and drifts of woe,
Where every blast that whistled by
Was bitter with its children's cry.

Such was the winter's awful sight
for many a dreary day and night,
What time our country's hope forlorn,
Of every needed comfort shorn,
Lay housed within a hurried tent,
Where every keen blast found a rent,
And oft the snow was seen to sift
Along the floor it piling drift,
Or, mocking the scant blanket's fold,
Across the night-crouch frequent rolled;
Where every path by a soldier beat,
Or every track where a sentinel stood,
Still held the print of naked feet,
And oft the crimson stains of blood;
Where Famine held her spectral court,
And joined by all her fierce allies:
She ever loved a camp or fort
Beleaguered by the wintry skies
But chiefly when Disease is by,
To sink the frame and dim the eye,
Until, with reeking forehead bent,
In martial garments cold and damp,
Pale Death patrols from tent to tent,
To count the charnels of the camp.

Such was the winter that prevailed
Within the crowded, frozen gorge;
Such were the horrors that assailed
The patriot at Valley Forge.
It was a midnight storm of woes
To clear the sky for Freedom's morn;
And such must ever be the throes
The hour when Liberty is born.

THE ARTICLES OF CONFEDERATION

The first constitution of our new nation was finally ratified and adopted on March 1, 1781. Throughout the Revolutionary War the federal union had been held together by a provisional government, and both the nascent presidency and the assembled Congress had only such powers as the states afforded them by proxy. This new constitution enumerated the powers of both the federation and the individual states and was heralded as a great leap forward in republicanism.

To all to whom these presents shall come, we the undersigned delegates of the states affixed to our names send greeting. Whereas, The delegates of the United States of America in Congress assembled did on the fifteenth day of November in the year of Our Lord one thousand seven hundred and seventy-seven, and in the second year of the independence of America, agree to certain articles of confederation and perpetual union between the states of New Hampshire, Massachusetts Bay, Rhode Island and Providence Plantations, Connecticut, New York, New Jersey, Pennsylvania, Delaware, Maryland, Virginia, North Carolina, South Carolina, and Georgia in the words following, viz:

"Articles of Confederation and perpetual union between the states of New Hampshire, Massachusetts Bay, Rhode Island and Providence Plantations, Connecticut, New York, New Jersey, Pennsylvania, Delaware, Maryland, Virginia, North Carolina, South Carolina, and Georgia."

ARTICLE I

The style of this confederacy shall be "The United States of America."

ARTICLE II

Each state retains its sovereignty, freedom, and independence, and every power, jurisdiction, and right, which is not by this confederation expressly delegated to the United States, in Congress assembled.

ARTICLE III

The said states hereby severally enter into a firm league of friendship with each other for their common defense, the security of their liberties, and their mutual and general welfare, binding themselves to assist each other against all force offered to, or attacks made upon them, or any of them, on account of religion, sovereignty, trade, or any other pretense whatever.

ARTICLE IV

The better to secure and perpetuate mutual friendship and intercourse among the people of the different states in this union, the free inhabitants of each of these states—paupers, vagabonds, and fugitives from justice excepted—shall be entitled to all privileges and immunities of free citizens in the several states; and the people of each state shall have free ingress and regress to and from any other state, and shall enjoy therein all the privileges of trade and commerce, subject to the same duties, impositions, and restrictions as the inhabitants thereof respectively, provided that such restrictions shall not extend so far as to prevent the removal of property imported into any state, to any other state of which the owner is an inhabitant; provided also that no imposition, duties, or restriction shall be laid by any state on the property of the United States, or either of them.

If any person guilty of, or charged with treason, felony, or other high misdemeanor in any state shall flee from justice, and be found in any of the United States, he shall upon demand of the governor or executive power of the state from which he fled be delivered up and removed to the state having jurisdiction of his offense.

Full faith and credit shall be given in each of these states to the records, acts, and judicial proceedings of the courts and magistrates of every other state.

ARTICLE V

For the more convenient management of the general interests of the United States, delegates shall be annually appointed in such manner as the legislature of each state shall direct, to meet in Congress on the first Monday in November, in every year, with a power reserved to each state to recall its delegates, or any of them, at any time within the year, and to send others in their stead for the remainder of the year.

No state shall be represented in Congress by less than two, nor by more than seven members; and no person shall be capable of being a delegate for more than three years in any term of six years; nor shall any person, being a delegate, be capable of holding any office under the United States for which he, or another for his benefit, receives any salary, fees, or emolument of any kind.

Each state shall maintain its own delegates in a meeting of the states, and while they act as members of the committee of the states.

In determining questions in the United States in Congress assembled, each state shall have one vote.

Freedom of speech and debate in Congress shall not be impeached or questioned in any court, or place out of Congress, and the members of Congress shall be protected in their persons from arrests and imprisonments during the time of their going to and from, and attendance on Congress, except for treason, felony, or breach of the peace.

ARTICLE VI

No state without the consent of the United States in Congress assembled shall send any embassy to, or receive any embassy from, or enter into any conference, agreement, or alliance or treaty with any king, prince, or state; nor shall any person holding any office of profit or trust under the United States, or any of them, accept of any present, emolument, office, or title of any kind whatever from any king, prince, or foreign state; nor shall the United States in Congress assembled, or any of them, grant any title of nobility.

No two or more states shall enter into any treaty, confederation, or alliance whatever between them without the consent of the United States in Congress assembled, specifying accurately the purposes for which the same is to be entered into, and how long it shall continue.

No state shall lay any imposts or duties which may interfere with any stipulations in treaties entered into by the United States in Congress assembled, with any king, prince, or state, in pursuance of any treaties already proposed by Congress to the courts of France and Spain.

No vessels of war shall be kept up in time of peace by any state, except such number only as shall be deemed necessary by the United States in Congress assembled, for the defense of such state, or its trade; nor shall any body of forces be kept up by any state in time of peace, except such number only as in the judgment of the United States, in Congress assembled, shall be deemed requisite to garrison the forts necessary for the defense of such state; but every state shall always keep up a well-regulated and disciplined militia, sufficiently armed and accoutered, and shall provide and constantly have ready for use, in public stores, a due number of field pieces and tents, and a proper quantity of arms, ammunition, and camp equipage.

No state shall engage in any war without the consent of the United States in Congress assembled, unless such state be actually invaded by enemies, or shall have received certain advice of a resolution being formed by some nation of Indians to invade such state, and the danger is so imminent as not to admit of a delay till the United States in Congress assembled can be consulted.

ARTICLE VII

When land forces are raised by any state for the common defense, all officers of or under the rank of colonel shall be appointed by the legislature of each state respectively by whom such forces shall be raised, or in such manner as such state shall direct, and all vacancies shall be filled up by the state which first made the appointment.

ARTICLE VIII

All charges of war, and all other expenses that shall be incurred for the common defense or general welfare, and allowed by the United States in Congress assembled, shall be defrayed out of a common treasury, which shall be supplied by the several states in proportion to the value of all land within each state, granted to or surveyed for any person, as such land and the buildings and improvements thereon shall be estimated according to such mode as the United States in Congress assembled shall from time to time direct and appoint.

ARTICLE IX

The United States in Congress assembled shall have the sole and exclusive right and power of determining on peace and war, except in the cases mentioned in the sixth article—of sending and receiving ambassadors—entering into treaties and alliances, provided that no treaty of commerce shall be made whereby the legislative power of the respective states shall be restrained from imposing such imposts and duties on foreigners, as their own people are subjected to, or from prohibiting the exportation or importation of any species of goods or commodities whatsoever—of establishing rules for deciding in all cases, what captures on land or water shall be legal, and in what manner prizes taken by land or naval forces in the service of the United States shall be divided or appropriated—of granting letters of marque and reprisal in times of peace—appointing courts for the trial of piracies and felonies committed on the high seas and establishing courts for receiving and determining finally appeals in all cases of captures, provided that no member of Congress shall be appointed a judge of any of the said courts.

The United States in Congress assembled shall also be the last resort on appeal in all disputes and differences now subsisting or that hereafter may arise between two or more states concerning boundary, jurisdiction, or any other cause whatever....

All controversies concerning the private right of soil claimed under different grants of two or more states, whose jurisdiction as they may respect such lands, and the states which passed such grants are adjusted, the said grants of either of them being at the same time claimed to have originated antecedent to such settlement of jurisdiction, shall on the petition of either party to the Congress of the United States be finally determined as near as may be in the same manner as is before prescribed for deciding disputes respecting territorial jurisdiction between different states.

The United States in Congress assembled shall also have the sole and exclusive right and power of regulating the alloy and value of coin struck by their own authority, or by that of the respective states—fixing the standard of weights and measures throughout the United States—regulating the trade and managing all affairs with the Indians, not members of any of the states, provided that the legislative right of any state within its own limits be not infringed or violated—establishing and regulating post offices from one state to another throughout all the United States, and exacting such postage on the papers passing through the same as may be requisite to defray the expenses of the said office—appointing all officers of the land forces in the service of the United States, excepting regimental officers—appointing all the officers of the naval forces, and commissioning all officers whatever in the service of the United States—making rules for the government and regulation of the said land and naval forces, and directing their operations.

The United States in Congress assembled shall have authority to appoint a committee to sit in the recess of Congress, to be denominated a Committee of the States, and to consist of one delegate from each state; and to appoint such other committees and civil officers as may be necessary for managing the general affairs of the United States under their direction—to appoint one of their number to preside, provided that no person be allowed to serve in the office of president more than one year in any term of three years; to ascertain the necessary sums of money to be raised for the service of the United States, and to appropriate and apply the same for defraying the public expenses—to borrow money or emit bills on the credit of the United States, transmitting every half-year to the respective states an account of the sums of money so borrowed or emitted—to build and equip a navy—to agree upon the number of land forces, and to make requisitions from each state for its quota in proportion to the number of white inhabitants in each state; which requisition shall be binding, and thereupon the legislature of each state shall appoint the regimental officers, raise the men, and clothe, arm, and equip them in a soldierlike manner at the expense of the United States, and the officers and men so clothed, armed, and equipped shall march to the place appointed, and within the time agreed on by the United States in Congress assembled.

The United States in Congress assembled shall never engage in a war, nor grant letters of marque and reprisal in time of peace, nor enter into any treaties or alliances, nor coin money, nor regulate the value thereof, nor ascertain the sums and expenses necessary for the defense and welfare of the United States, or any of them, nor emit bills, nor borrow money on the credit of the United States, nor appropriate money, nor agree upon the number of vessels of war to be built or purchased, nor the number of land or sea forces to be raised, nor appoint a commander in chief of the army or navy, unless nine states assent to the same: nor shall a question on any other point, except for adjourning from day to day, be determined unless by the votes of a majority of the United States in Congress assembled.

The Congress of the United States shall have power to adjourn to any time within the year, and to any place within the United States, so that no period of adjournment be for a longer duration than the space of six months, and shall publish the journal of their proceedings monthly, except such parts thereof relating to treaties, alliances, or military operations, as in their judgment require secrecy; and the yeas and nays of the delegates of each state on any question shall be entered on the journal when it is desired by any delegate; and the delegates of a state, or any of them, at his or their request shall be furnished with a transcript of the said journal, except such parts as are above excepted, to lay before the legislatures of the several states.

ARTICLE X

The Committee of the States, or any nine of them, shall be authorized to execute, in the recess of Congress, such of the powers of Congress as the United States in Congress assembled, by the consent of nine states, shall from time to time think expedient to vest them with; provided that no power be delegated to the said committee for the exercise of which, by the Articles of Confederation, the voice of nine states in the Congress of the United States assembled is requisite.

ARTICLE XI

Canada acceding to this confederation, and joining in the measures of the United States, shall be admitted into, and entitled to all the advantages of this union: but no other colony shall be admitted into the same unless such admission be agreed to by nine states.

ARTICLE XII

All bills of credit emitted, monies borrowed, and debts contracted by, or under the authority of Congress, before the assembling of the United States in pursuance of the present confederation, shall be deemed and considered as a charge against the United States, for payment and satisfaction whereof the said United States and the public faith are hereby solemnly pledged.

ARTICLE XIII

Every state shall abide by the determinations of the United States in Congress assembled on all questions which, by this confederation, are submitted to them. And the articles of this confederation shall be inviolably observed by every state, and the union shall be perpetual; nor shall any alteration at any time hereafter be made in any of them, unless such alteration be agreed to in a Congress of the United States, and be afterward confirmed by the legislatures of every state.

And Whereas, It hath pleased the Great Governor of the World to incline the hearts of the legislatures we respectively represent in Congress to approve of, and to authorize us to ratify, the said Articles of Confederation and perpetual union: Know Ye, That we the undersigned delegates, by virtue of the power and authority to us given for that purpose, do by these presents, in the name and in behalf of our respective constituents, fully and entirely ratify and confirm each and every of the said Articles of Confederation and perpetual union, and all and singular the matters and things therein contained: and we do further solemnly plight and engage the faith of our respective constituents, that they shall abide by the determinations of the United States in Congress assembled on all questions which, by the said confederation, are submitted to them. And that the articles thereof shall be inviolably observed by the states we respectively represent, and that the union shall be perpetual. In witness whereof we have hereunto set our hands in Congress.

Done at Philadelphia in the state of Pennsylvania the ninth day of July in the year of Our Lord one thousand seven hundred and seventy-eight, and in the third year of the independence of America.

THE VOW OF WASHINGTON

By John Greenleaf Whittier

Following his successful campaign to ensure the independence of his new nation, General George Washington surrendered his commission to President Thomas Mifflin and the assembled Congress of the United States on December 23, 1783. Though his troops were ready to declare him king, he had not fought the war only to see another monarch established in America; and he desired to honor the federal government as it was then constituted. He retired to private life at Mount Vernon, his home on the Potomac River. It would only be a short retirement, however; the controversy over a new form of federalism brought him back into public life and ultimately to the presidency itself. This verse celebrates his extraordinary commitment and submission to authority.

The sword was sheathed: In April's sun
Lay green the fields by Freedom won;
And severed sections, weary of debates,
Joined hands at last and were United States.

O City sitting by the Sea!
How proud the day that dawned on thee,
When the new era, long desired, began,
And, in its need, the hour had found the man!

One thought the cannon salvos spoke,
The resonant bell-tower's vibrant stroke,
The voiceful streets, the plaudit-echoing halls,
And prayer and hymn borne heavenward from Saint Paul's!

How felt the land in every part
The strong throb of a nation's heart,
As its great leader gave, with reverent awe,
His pledge to Union, Liberty, and Law!

That pledge the heavens above him heard,
That vow the sleep of centuries stirred;
In world-wide wonder listening peoples bent
Their gaze on Freedom's great experiment.
Could it succeed? Of honor sold
And hopes deceived all history told.
Above the wrecks that strewed the mournful past,
Was the long dream of ages true at last?

Thank God! The people's choice was just,
The one man equal to his trust,
Wise beyond lore, and without weakness good,
Calm in the strength of flawless rectitude!

His rule of justice, order, peace,
Made possible the world's release;
Taught prince and serf that power is but a trust,
And rule alone, which serves the ruled, is just.

That Freedom generous is, but strong
In hate of fraud and selfish wrong,

Pretence that turns her holy truth to lies,
And lawless license masking in her guise.

Land of his love! With one glad voice
Let thy great sisterhood rejoice;
A century's suns o'er thee have risen and set,
And, God be praised, we are one nation yet.

And still we trust the years to be
Shall prove his hope was destiny,
Leaving our flag, with all its added stars,
Unrent by faction and unstained by wars.

Lo! Where with patient toil he nursed
And trained the new-set plant at first,
The widening branches of a stately tree
Stretch from the sunrise to the sunset sea.

And in its broad and sheltering shade,
Sitting with none to make afraid,
Were we now silent, through each mighty limb,
The winds of heaven would sing the praise of him.

THE NORTHWEST ORDINANCE

Written under the authority of the new national federation, this document was an ordinance for the government of the once-disputed American territories northwest of the Ohio River. After successfully convincing the individual states to give up their competing claims in the region, the federal government initiated a pattern for annexation that would be followed throughout the nation's rapid conquest of much of the rest of the North American continent. In addition, the ordinance sheds light on the original intentions of the Founders concerning the role and function of government in society. It was ratified on July 13, 1787.

B e it ordained by the United States in Congress assembled, that the said territory, for the purposes of temporary government, be one district, subject, however, to be divided into two districts as future circumstances may, in the opinion of Congress, make it expedient.

Be it ordained by the authority aforesaid, that the estates, both of resident and nonresident proprietors in the said territory, dying intestate, shall descend to, and be distributed among, their children and the descendants of a deceased child in equal parts; the descendants of a deceased child or grandchild to take the share of their deceased parent in equal parts among them; and where there shall be no children or descendants, then in equal parts to the next of kin in equal degree; and among collaterals, the children of a deceased brother or sister of the intestate shall have, in equal parts among them, their deceased parents' share; and there shall in no case be a distinction between kindred of the whole and half-blood; saving, in all cases, to the widow of the intestate her third part of the real estate for life, and one-third part of the personal estate; and this law relative to descents and dower shall remain in full force until altered by the legislature of the district.

And until the governor and judges shall adopt laws as hereinafter mentioned, estates in the said territory may be devised or bequeathed by wills in writing, signed and sealed by him or her in whom the estate may be (being of full age) and attested by three witnesses; and real estates may be conveyed by lease and release, or bargain and sale, signed, sealed, and delivered by the person, being of full age, in whom the estate may be, and attested by two witnesses.

Be it ordained by the authority aforesaid, that there shall be appointed, from time to time, by Congress, a governor, whose commission shall continue in force for the term of three years, unless sooner revoked by Congress; he shall reside in the district, and have a freehold estate therein, in one thousand acres of land while in the exercise of his office.

There shall be appointed from time to time, by Congress, a secretary, whose commission shall continue in force for four years unless sooner revoked; he shall reside in the district, and have a freehold estate therein, in five hundred acres of land while in the exercise of his office. It shall be his duty to keep and preserve the acts and laws passed by the legislature, and the public records of the district, and the proceedings of the governor in his executive department, and transmit authentic copies of such acts and proceedings every six months to the secretary of Congress. There shall also be appointed a court, to consist of three judges, any two of whom to form a court, who shall have a common law jurisdiction, and reside in the district, and have each therein a freehold estate in five hundred acres of land while in the exercise of their offices; and their commissions shall continue in force during good behavior.

The governor and judges, or a majority of them, shall adopt and publish in the district such laws of the original states, criminal and civil, as may be necessary and best suited to the circumstances of the district, and report them to Congress from time to time; which laws shall be in force in the district until the organization of the general assembly therein, unless disapproved of by Congress; but afterward the legislature shall have authority to alter them as they shall think fit.

The governor, for the time being, shall be commander in chief of the militia, appoint and commission all officers in the same below the rank of general officers; all general officers shall be appointed and commissioned by Congress.

Previous to the organization of the general assembly, the governor shall appoint such magistrates and other civil officers in each county or township as he shall find necessary for the preservation of the peace and good order in the same. After the general assembly shall be organized, the powers and duties of the magistrates and other civil officers shall be regulated and defined by the said assembly; but all magistrates and other civil officers not herein otherwise directed shall, during the continuance of this temporary government, be appointed by the governor.

For the prevention of crimes and injuries, the laws to be adopted or made shall have force in all parts of the district, and for the execution of process, criminal and civil, the governor shall make proper divisions thereof; and he shall proceed from time to time, as circumstances may require, to lay out the parts of the district in which the Indian titles shall have been extinguished, into counties and townships, subject, however, to such alterations as may thereafter be made by the legislature.

So soon as there shall be five thousand free male inhabitants of full age in the district, upon giving proof thereof to the governor, they shall receive authority, with time and place, to elect representatives from their counties or townships to represent them in the general assembly:

Provided, that, for every five hundred free male inhabitants, there shall be one representative, and so on, progressively, with the number of free male inhabitants, shall the right of representation increase, until the number of representatives shall amount to twenty-five; after which, the number and proportion of representatives shall be regulated by the legislature:

Provided, that no person be eligible or qualified to act as a representative unless he shall have been a citizen of one of the United States three years, and be a resident in the district, or unless he shall have resided in the district three years; and, in either case, shall likewise hold in his own right, in fee simple, two hundred acres of land within the same:

Provided, also, that a freehold in fifty acres of land in the district, having been a citizen of one of the states, and being resident in the district, or the like freehold and two years' residence in the district, shall be necessary to qualify a man as an elector of a representative.

The representatives thus elected shall serve for the term of two years; and in case of the death of a representative, or removal from office, the governor shall issue a writ to the county or township for which he was a member, to elect another in his stead to serve for the residue of the term.

The general assembly or legislature shall consist of the governor, legislative council, and a house of representatives. The legislative council shall consist of five members, to continue in office five years unless sooner removed by Congress; any three of whom to be a quorum: and the members of the council shall be nominated and appointed in the following manner, to wit:

As soon as representatives shall be elected, the governor shall appoint a time and place for them to meet together; and, when met, they shall nominate ten persons, residents in the district and each possessed of a freehold in five hundred acres of land, and return their names to Congress; five of whom Congress shall appoint and commission to serve as aforesaid; and, whenever a vacancy shall happen in the council, by death or removal from office, the house of representatives shall nominate two persons, qualified as aforesaid, for each vacancy, and return their names to Congress; one of whom Congress shall appoint and commission for the residue of the term.

And the governor, legislative council, and house of representatives shall have authority to make laws, in all cases, for the good government of the district, not repugnant to the principles and articles in this ordinance established and declared. And all bills, having passed by a majority in the house, and by a majority in the council, shall be referred to the governor for his assent.

And, for extending the fundamental principles of civil and religious liberty, which form the basis whereon these republics, their laws, and constitutions are erected; to fix and establish those principles as the basis of all laws, constitutions, and governments, which forever hereafter shall be formed in the said territory; to provide also for the establishment of states, and permanent government therein, and for their admission to a share in the federal councils on an equal footing with the original states, at as early periods as may be consistent with the general interest:

It is hereby ordained and declared by the authority aforesaid, that the following articles shall be considered as articles of compact between the original states and the people and states in the said territory, and forever remain unalterable, unless by common consent, to wit:

ARTICLE I

No person, demeaning himself in a peaceable and orderly manner, shall ever be molested on account of his mode of worship or religious sentiments in the said territory.

ARTICLE II

The inhabitants of the said territory shall always be entitled to the benefits of the writ of habeas corpus and of the trial by jury; of a proportionate representation of the people in the legislature; and of judicial proceedings according to the course of the common law. All persons shall be bailable, unless for capital offenses, where the proof shall be evident, or the presumption great. All fines shall be moderate; and no cruel or unusual punishments shall be inflicted. No man shall be deprived of his liberty or property, but by the judgment of his peers or the law of the land.

ARTICLE III

Religion, morality, and knowledge being necessary to good government and the happiness of mankind, schools and the means of education shall forever be encouraged. The utmost good faith shall always be observed toward the Indians; their lands and property shall never be taken from them without their consent; and in their property, rights, and liberty they shall never be invaded or disturbed unless in just and lawful wars authorized by Congress; but laws founded in justice and humanity shall from time to time be made for preventing wrongs being done to them, and for preserving peace and friendship with them.

ARTICLE IV

The said territory, and the states which may be formed therein, shall forever remain a part of this confederacy of the United States of America, subject to the Articles of Confederation, and to such alterations therein as shall be constitutionally made; and to all the acts and ordinances of the United States in Congress assembled, conformable thereto.

The inhabitants and settlers in the said territory shall be subject to pay a part of the federal debts contracted, or to be contracted, and a proportional part of the expenses of government to be apportioned on them by Congress, according to the same common rule and measure by which apportionments thereof shall be made on other states; and the taxes for paying their proportion shall be laid and levied by the authority and direction of the legislatures of the district or districts, or new states, as in the original states, within the time agreed upon by the United States in Congress assembled.

The navigable waters leading into the Mississippi and St. Lawrence, and the carrying places between the same, shall be common highways and forever free, as well to the inhabitants of the said territory as to the citizens of the United States, and those of any other states that may be admitted into the confederacy, without any tax, impost, or duty therefore.

ARTICLE V

There shall be formed in the said territory not less than three nor more than five states; and the boundaries of the states, as soon as Virginia shall alter her act of cession and consent to the same, shall become fixed and established as follows, to wit: The western state, in the said territory, shall be bounded by the Mississippi, the Ohio, and Wabash rivers; a direct line drawn from the Wabash and Post Vincents due north to the territorial line between the United States and Canada; and, by the said territorial line, to the Lake of the Woods and Mississippi. The middle state shall be bounded by the said direct line, the Wabash from Post Vincents to the Ohio, by the Ohio, by a direct line drawn due north from the mouth of the Great Miami to the said territorial line, and by the said territorial line. The eastern state shall be bounded by the last mentioned direct line, the Ohio, Pennsylvania, and the said territorial line.

Provided, however, and it is further understood and declared that the boundaries of these three states shall be subject so far to be altered, that, if Congress shall hereafter find it expedient, they shall have authority to form one or two states in that part of the said territory which lies north of an east-and-west line drawn through the southerly bend or extreme of Lake Michigan. And whenever any of the said states shall have sixty thousand free inhabitants therein, such state shall be admitted, by its delegates, into the Congress of the United States on an equal footing with the original states, in all respects whatever; and shall be at liberty to form a permanent constitution and state government:

Provided, the constitution and government so to be formed shall be republican, and in conformity to the principles contained in these articles; and, so far as it can be consistent with the general interest of the confederacy, such admission shall be allowed at an earlier period, and when there may be a less number of free inhabitants in the state than sixty thousand.

ARTICLE VI

There shall be neither slavery nor involuntary servitude in the said territory, otherwise than in punishment of crimes whereof the party shall have been duly convicted: Provided, always, that any person escaping into the same, from whom labor or service is lawfully claimed in any one of the original states, such fugitive may be lawfully reclaimed, and conveyed to the person claiming his or her labor or services as aforesaid.

Be it ordained by the authority aforesaid, that the resolutions of the twenty-third of April 1784, relative to the subject of this ordinance, be, and the same are hereby repealed and declared null and void.

IN FAVOR OF THE FEDERAL CONSTITUTION

By James Madison

This speech was delivered on June 6, 1788, as a rebuttal to an earlier oration from Patrick Henry. The anti-Federalists—led by Henry—believed that the newly proposed constitution gave too much power to the central government, was too vague, and was not explicitly Christian. They believed that the Articles of Confederation, which had served the nation well in its conflict against the world's greatest military and commercial power, needed merely to be amended, not scrapped altogether. They feared a day when the federal system would become gigantic, intrusive, and spendthrifty. The Federalists believed that such fears were ridiculous and that a stronger central government was necessary. This speech proved to be instrumental in reversing opinion against the new federal constitution.

We ought, sir, to examine the Constitution on its own merits solely. We are to inquire whether it will promote the public happiness; its aptitude to produce this desirable object ought to be the exclusive subject of our present researches. In this pursuit, we ought not to address our arguments to the feelings and passions but to those understandings and judgments which were selected by the people of this country, to decide this great question by a calm and rational investigation.

I hope that gentlemen, in displaying their abilities on this occasion, instead of giving opinions and making assertions, will condescend to prove and demonstrate by a fair and regular discussion. It gives me pain to hear gentlemen continually distorting the natural construction of language; for it is sufficient if any human production can stand a fair discussion. Before I proceed to make some additions to the reasons which have been adduced by my honorable friend over the way, I must take the liberty to make some observations on what was said by another gentleman.

He told us that this Constitution ought to be rejected because it endangered the public liberty, in his opinion, in many instances. Give me leave to make answer to that observation. Let the dangers which this system is supposed to be replete with be clearly pointed out. If any dangerous and unnecessary powers be given to the general legislature, let them be plainly demonstrated; and let us not rest satisfied with general assertions of danger, without examination. If powers be necessary, apparent danger is not a sufficient reason against conceding them. He has suggested that licentiousness has seldom produced the loss of liberty, but that the tyranny of rulers has almost always affected it. Since the general civilization of mankind I believe there are more instances of the abridgment of the freedom of the people by gradual and silent encroachments of those in power than by violent and sudden usurpations; but, on a candid examination of history, we shall find that turbulence, violence, and abuse of power, by the majority trampling on the rights of the minority, have produced factions and commotions which, in republics, have more frequently than any other cause, produced despotism. If we go over the whole history of ancient and modern republics we shall find their destruction to have generally resulted from those causes. If we consider the peculiar situation of the United States, and what are the sources of that diversity of sentiment which pervades its inhabitants, we shall find great danger to fear that the same causes may terminate here in the same fatal effects which they produced in those republics. This danger ought to be wisely guarded against...

I must confess I have not been able to find his usual consistency in the gentleman's argument on this occasion. He informs us that the people of the country are at perfect repose; that is, every man enjoys the fruits of his labor peaceably and securely, and that everything is in perfect tranquility and safety. I wish sincerely that this were true. If this be their happy situation, why has every state acknowledged the contrary? Why were deputies from all the states sent to the general convention? Why have complaints of national and individual distresses been echoed and reechoed throughout the continent? Why has our general government been so shamefully disgraced and our Constitution violated? Wherefore have laws been made to authorize a change, and wherefore are we now assembled here? A federal government is formed for the protection of its individual members. Ours has attacked itself with impunity. Its authority has been disobeyed and despised.

I think I perceive a glaring inconsistency in another of his arguments. He complains of this Constitution because it requires the consent of at least three-fourths of the states to introduce amendments which shall be necessary for the happiness of the people....In the first case, he asserts that a majority ought to have the power of altering the government when found to be inadequate to the security of public happiness. In the last case, he affirms that even three-fourths of the community have not a right to alter a government which experience has proved to be subversive of national felicity! nay, that the most necessary and urgent alterations cannot be made without the absolute unanimity of all the states! Does not the thirteenth article of the Confederation expressly require that no alteration shall be made without the unanimous consent of all the states? Could anything in theory be more perniciously improvident and injudicious than this submission of the will of the majority to the most trifling minority? Have not experience and practice actually manifested this theoretical inconvenience to be extremely impolitic?

The power of raising and supporting armies is exclaimed against as dangerous and unnecessary. I wish there were no necessity of vesting this power in the general government. But suppose a foreign nation were to declare war against the United States; must not the general legislature have the power of defending the United States? Ought it to be known to foreign nations that the general government of the United States of America has no power to raise and support an army, even in the utmost danger, when attacked by external enemies? Would not their knowledge of such a circumstance stimulate them to fall upon us? If, sir, Congress be not invested with this power, any powerful nation, prompted by ambition or avarice, will be invited by our weakness to attack us; and such an attack by disciplined veterans would certainly be attended with success, when only opposed by irregular, undisciplined militia.

Give me leave to say something of the nature of the government and to show that it is safe and just to vest it with the power of taxation. There are a number of opinions, but the principal question is whether it be a federal or a consolidated government. In order to judge properly of the question before us, we must consider it minutely in its principal parts. I conceive myself that it is of a mixed nature; it is in a manner unprecedented; we cannot find one express example in the experience of the world. It stands by itself. In some respects it is a government of a federal nature; in others, it is of a consolidated nature. Even if we attend to the manner in which the Constitution is investigated, ratified, and made the act of the people of America, I can say, notwithstanding what the honorable gentleman has alleged, that this government is not completely consolidated, nor is it entirely federal. Who are parties to it? The people—but not the people as composing one great body, but the people as composing thirteen sovereignties. Were it, as the gentleman asserts, a consolidated government, the assent of a majority of the people would be sufficient for its establishment; and, as a majority have adopted it already, the remaining states would be bound by the act of the majority, even if they unanimously rejected it. Were it such a government as is suggested it would be now binding on the people of this state without their having had the privilege of deliberating on it. But, sir, no state is bound by it, as it is, without its own consent. Should all the states adopt it, it will be then a government established by the thirteen states of America, not through the intervention of the legislatures, but by the people at large. In this particular respect the distinction between the existing and the proposed governments is very material. The existing system has been derived from the dependent derivative authority of the legislatures of the states; whereas, this is derived from the superior power of the people.

If we look at the manner in which alterations are to be made in it, the same idea is, in some degree, attended to. By the new system a majority of the states cannot introduce amendments, nor are all the states required for that purpose; three-fourths of them must concur in alterations. In this there is a departure from the federal idea. The members of the national House of Representatives are to be chosen by the people at large, in proportion to the numbers in the respective districts. When we come to the Senate, its members are elected by the states in their equal and political capacity. But had the government been completely consolidated, the Senate would have been chosen by the people in their individual capacity, in the same manner as the members of the other house. Thus it is of a complicated nature; and this complication, I trust, will be found to exclude the evils of absolute consolidation, as well as of a mere confederacy.

Those who wish to become federal representatives must depend on their credit with that class of men who will be the most popular in their counties, who generally represent the people in the state governments; they can, therefore, never succeed in any measure contrary to the wishes of those on whom they depend. It is almost certain, therefore, that the deliberations of the members of the federal House of Representatives will be directed to the interests of the people of America. As to the other branch, the senators will be appointed by the legislatures; and, though elected for six years, I do not conceive they will so soon forget the source from whence they derive their political existence. This election of one branch of the federal by the state legislatures secures an absolute dependence of the former on the latter. The biennial exclusion of one-third will lessen the facility of a combination and may put a stop to intrigues. I appeal to our past experience whether they will attend to the interests of their constituent states. Have not those gentlemen who have been honored with seats in Congress, often signalized themselves by their attachment to their seats?

I wish this government may answer the expectation of its friends and foil the apprehension of its enemies. I hope the patriotism of the people will continue and be a sufficient guard to their liberties. I believe its tendency will be that the state governments will counteract the general interest and ultimately prevail. The number of the representatives is yet sufficient for our safety and will gradually increase; and, if we consider their different sources of information, the number will not appear too small.

THE FEDERALIST: NUMBER 30

By Alexander Hamilton

The Federalist Papers are among the most important documents in American political history. They were originally composed as newspaper articles by three men: Alexander Hamilton, James Madison, and John Jay. Strong Federalists, they desired to see the states ratify the new constitution that had been drafted at a secret—and unauthorized—meeting of influential leaders in Philadelphia. This essay was written by the future secretary of the treasury to discuss the taxing authority of the envisioned federal state.

It has been already observed that the federal government ought to possess the power of providing for the support of the national forces; in which proposition was intended to be included the expense of raising troops, of building and equipping fleets, and all other expenses in any wise connected with military arrangements and operations. But these are not the only objects to which the jurisdiction of the Union in respect to revenue must necessarily be empowered to extend. It must embrace a provision for the support of the national civil list; for the payment of the national debts contracted, or that may be contracted; and, in general, for all those matters which will call for disbursements out of the national treasury. The conclusion is that there must be interwoven in the frame of the government a general power of taxation, in one shape or another.

Money is, with propriety, considered as the vital principle of the body politic; as that which sustains its life and motion and enables it to perform its most essential functions. A complete power, therefore, to procure a regular and adequate supply of revenue, as far as the resources of the community will permit, may be regarded as an indispensable ingredient in every constitution. From a deficiency in this particular, one of two evils must ensue: either the people must be subjected to continual plunder, as a substitute for a more eligible mode of supplying the public wants, or the government must sink into a fatal atrophy, and, in a short course of time, perish.

In the Ottoman or Turkish empire the sovereign, though in other respects absolute master of the lives and fortunes of his subjects, has no right to impose a new tax. The consequence is that he permits the bashaws or governors of provinces to pillage the people at discretion, and, in turn, squeezes out of them the sums of which he stands in need to satisfy his own exigencies and those of the state. In America, from a like cause, the government of the Union has gradually dwindled into a state of decay, approaching nearly to annihilation. Who can doubt that the happiness of the people in both countries would be promoted by competent authorities in the proper hands to provide the revenues which the necessities of the public might require?

The present Confederation, feeble as it is, intended to repose in the United States an unlimited power of providing for the pecuniary wants of the Union. But proceeding upon an erroneous principle, it has been done in such a manner as entirely to have frustrated the intention. Congress, by the articles which compose that compact (as has already been stated), are authorized to ascertain and call for any sums of money necessary in their judgment to the service of the United States; and their requisitions, if conformable to the rule of apportionment, are in every constitutional sense obligatory upon the States. These have no right to question the propriety of the demand; no discretion beyond that of devising the ways and means of furnishing the sums demanded. But though this be strictly and truly the case; though the assumption of such a right would be an infringement of the articles of Union; though it may seldom or never have been avowedly claimed, yet in practice it has been constantly exercised and would continue to be so, as long as the revenues of the Confederacy should remain dependent on the intermediate agency of its members. What the consequences of this system have been is within the knowledge of every man the least conversant in our public affairs, and has been abundantly unfolded in different parts of these inquiries. It is this which affords ample cause of mortification to ourselves, and of triumph to our enemies.

What remedy can there be for this situation, but in a change of the system which has produced it—in a change of the fallacious and delusive system of quotas and requisitions? What substitute can there be imagined for this ignis fatuus in finance, but that of permitting the national government to raise its own revenues by the ordinary methods of taxation authorized in every well-ordered constitution of civil government? Ingenious men may declaim with plausibility on any subject; but no human ingenuity can point out any other expedient to rescue us from the inconveniences and embarrassments naturally resulting from defective supplies of the public treasury.

The more intelligent adversaries of the new Constitution admit the force of this reasoning; but they qualify their admission by a distinction between what they call internal and external taxation. The former they would reserve to the State governments; the latter, which they explain into commercial imposts, or rather duties on imported articles, they declare themselves willing to concede to the federal head. This distinction, however, would violate that fundamental maxim of good sense and sound policy, which dictates that every Power ought to be proportionate to its Object; and would still leave the general government in a kind of tutelage to the State governments, inconsistent with every idea of vigor or efficiency. Who can pretend that commercial imposts are, or would be, alone equal to the present and future exigencies of the Union? Taking into the account the existing debt, foreign and domestic, upon any plan of extinguishment which a man moderately impressed with the importance of public justice and public credit could approve, in addition to the establishments which all parties will acknowledge to be necessary, we could not reasonably flatter ourselves that this resource alone, upon the most improved scale, would ever suffice for its present necessities. Its future necessities admit not of calculation or limitation; and upon the principle more than once adverted to the power of making provision for them as they arise ought to be equally unconfined. I believe it may be regarded as a position warranted by the history of mankind that, in the usual progress of things, the necessities of a nation, in every stage of its existence, will be found at least equal to its resources.

To say that deficiencies may be provided for by requisitions upon the States is on the one hand to acknowledge that this system cannot be depended upon, and on the other hand to depend upon it for every thing beyond a certain limit. Those who have carefully attended to its vices and deformities as they have been exhibited by experience or delineated in the course of these papers must feel an invincible repugnancy to trusting the national interests in any degree to its operation. Its inevitable tendency, whenever it is brought into activity, must be to enfeeble the Union, and sow the seeds of discord and contention between the federal head and its members, and between the members themselves. Can it be expected that the deficiencies would be better supplied in this mode than the total wants of the Union have heretofore been supplied in the same mode? It ought to be recollected that if less will be required from the States, they will have proportionately less means to answer the demand. If the opinions of those who contend for the distinction which has been mentioned were to be received as evidence of truth, one would be led to conclude that there was some known point in the economy of national affairs at which it would be safe to stop and to say: Thus far the ends of public happiness will be promoted by supplying the wants of government, and all beyond this is unworthy of our care or anxiety. How is it possible that a government half supplied and always necessitous can fulfil the purposes of its institution, can provide for the security, advance the prosperity, or support the reputation of the commonwealth? How can it ever possess either energy or stability, dignity or credit, confidence at home or respectability abroad? How can its administration be anything else than a succession of expedients temporizing, impotent, disgraceful? How will it be able to avoid a frequent sacrifice of its engagements to immediate necessity? How can it undertake or execute any liberal or enlarged plans of public good?

Let us attend to what would be the effects of this situation in the very first war in which we should happen to be engaged. We will presume, for argument's sake, that the revenue arising from the impost duties answers the purposes of a provision for the public debt and of a peace establishment for the Union. Thus circumstanced, a war breaks out. What would be the probable conduct of the government in such an emergency? Taught by experience that proper dependence could not be placed on the success of requisitions, unable by its own authority to lay hold of fresh resources, and urged by considerations of national danger, would it not be driven to the expedient of diverting the funds already appropriated from their proper objects to the defense of the State? It is not easy to see how a step of this kind could be avoided; and if it should be taken, it is evident that it would prove the destruction of public credit at the very moment that it was becoming essential to the public safety. To imagine that at such a crisis credit might be dispensed with would be the extreme of infatuation. In the modern system of war, nations the most wealthy are obliged to have recourse to large loans. A country so little opulent as ours must feel this necessity in a much stronger degree. But who would lend to a government that prefaced its overtures for borrowing by an act which demonstrated that no reliance could be placed on the steadiness of its measures for paying? The loans it might be able to procure would be as limited in their extent as burdensome in their conditions. They would be made upon the same principles that usurers commonly lend to bankrupt and fraudulent debtors—with a sparing hand and at enormous premiums.

It may perhaps be imagined that from the scantiness of the resources of the country the necessity of diverting the established funds in the case supposed would exist, though the national government should possess an unrestrained power of taxation. But two considerations will serve to quiet all apprehension on this head: one is that we are sure the resources of the community, in their full extent, will be brought into activity for the benefit of the Union; the other is that whatever deficiencies there may be can without difficulty be supplied by loans.

The power of creating new funds upon new objects of taxation by its own authority would enable the national government to borrow as far as its necessities might require. Foreigners, as well as the citizens of America, could then reasonably repose confidence in its engagements; but to depend upon a government that must itself depend upon thirteen other governments for the means of fulfilling its contracts, when once its situation is clearly understood, would require a degree of credulity not often to be met with in the pecuniary transactions of mankind, and little reconcilable with the usual sharp-sightedness of avarice.

Reflections of this kind may have trifling weight with men who hope to see realized in America the halcyon scenes of the poetic or fabulous age; but to those who believe we are likely to experience a common portion of the vicissitudes and calamities which have fallen to the lot of other nations, they must appear entitled to serious attention. Such men must behold the actual situation of their country with painful solicitude, and deprecate the evils which ambition or revenge might, with too much facility, inflict upon it.

THE FEDERALIST: NUMBER 47

By James Madison

In this closely argued essay the constitutional idea of the separation of powers is discussed. By holding one another in check, the Federalists felt that the executive, legislative, and judicial powers could not create the kind of intrusive governmental tyranny the anti-Federalists so greatly feared.

Having reviewed the general form of the proposed government and the general mass of power allotted to it, I proceed to examine the particular structure of this government, and the distribution of this mass of power among its constituent parts.

One of the principal objections inculcated by the more respectable adversaries to the Constitution is its supposed violation of the political maxim that the legislative, executive, and judiciary departments ought to be separate and distinct. In the structure of the federal government no regard, it is said, seems to have been paid to this essential precaution in favor of liberty. The several departments of power are distributed and blended in such a manner as at once to destroy all symmetry and beauty of form, and to expose some of the essential parts of the edifice to the danger of being crushed by the disproportionate weight of other parts.

No political truth is certainly of greater intrinsic value, or is stamped with the authority of more enlightened patrons of liberty than that on which the objection is founded. The accumulation of all powers, legislative, executive, and judiciary, in the same hands, whether of one, a few, or many, and whether hereditary, self-appointed, or elective, may justly be pronounced the very definition of tyranny. Were the federal Constitution, therefore, really chargeable with this accumulation of power, or with a mixture of powers, having a dangerous tendency to such an accumulation, no further arguments would be necessary to inspire a universal reprobation of the system. I persuade myself, however, that it will be made apparent to everyone that the charge cannot be supported, and that the maxim on which it relies has been totally misconceived and misapplied. In order to form correct ideas on this important subject it will be proper to investigate the sense in which the preservation of liberty requires that the three great departments of power should be separate and distinct.

The oracle who is always consulted and cited on this subject is the celebrated Montesquieu. If he be not the author of this invaluable precept in the science of politics, he has the merit at least of displaying and recommending it most effectually to the attention of mankind. Let us endeavor, in the first place, to ascertain his meaning on this point.

The British Constitution was to Montesquieu what Homer has been to the didactic writers on epic poetry. As the latter have considered the work of the immortal bard as the perfect model from which the principles and rules of the epic art were to be drawn, and by which all similar works were to be judged, so this great political critic appears to have viewed the Constitution of England as the standard, or to use his own expression, as the mirror of political liberty; and to have delivered, in the form of elementary truths, the several characteristic principles of that particular system. That we may be sure, then, not to mistake his meaning in this case, let us recur to the source from which the maxim was drawn.

On the slightest view of the British Constitution, we must perceive that the legislative, executive, and judiciary departments are by no means totally separate and distinct from each other. The executive magistrate forms an integral part of the legislative authority. He alone has the prerogative of making treaties with foreign sovereigns which, when made, have, under certain limitations, the force of legislative acts. All the members of the judiciary department are appointed by him, can be removed by him on the address of the two Houses of Parliament, and form, when he pleases to consult them, one of his constitutional councils. One branch of the legislative department forms also a great constitutional council to the executive chief, as, on another hand, it is the sole depository of judicial power in cases of impeachment, and is invested with the supreme appellate jurisdiction in all other cases. The judges, again, are so far connected with the legislative department as often to attend and participate in its deliberations, though not admitted to a legislative vote.

From these facts, by which Montesquieu was guided, it may clearly be inferred that in saying "There can be no liberty where the legislative and executive powers are united in the same person, or body of magistrates," or, "if the power of judging be not separated from the legislative and executive powers," he did not mean that these departments ought to have no partial agency in, or no control over, the acts of each other. His meaning, as his own words import, and still more conclusively as illustrated by the example in his eye, can amount to no more than this, that where the whole power of one department is exercised by the same hands which possess the whole power of another department, the fundamental principles of a free constitution are subverted. This would have been the case in the constitution examined by him, if the king, who is the sole executive magistrate, had possessed also the complete legislative power, or the supreme administration of justice; or if the entire legislative body had possessed the supreme judiciary, or the supreme executive authority. This, however, is not among the vices of that constitution. The magistrate in whom the whole executive power resides cannot of himself make a law, though he can put a negative on every law; nor administer justice in person, though he has the appointment of those who do administer it. The judges can exercise no executive prerogative, though they are shoots from the executive stock; nor any legislative function, though they may be advised by the legislative councils. The entire legislature can perform no judiciary act, though by the joint act of two of its branches the judges may be removed from their offices, and though one of its branches is possessed of the judicial power in the last resort. The entire legislature, again, can exercise no executive prerogative, though one of its branches constitutes the supreme executive magistracy, and another, on the impeachment of a third, can try and condemn all the subordinate officers in the executive department.

The reasons on which Montesquieu grounds his maxim are a further demonstration of his meaning. "When the legislative and executive powers are united in the same person or body," says he, "there can be no liberty, because apprehensions may arise lest the same monarch or senate should enact tyrannical laws to execute them in a tyrannical manner." Again: "Were the power of judging joined with the legislative, the life and liberty of the subject would be exposed to arbitrary control, for the judge would then be the legislator. Were it joined to the executive power, the judge might behave with all the violence of an oppressor." Some of these reasons are more fully explained in other passages; but briefly stated as they are here they sufficiently establish the meaning which we have put on this celebrated maxim of this celebrated author.

If we look into the constitutions of the several States we find that, notwithstanding the emphatical and, in some instances, the unqualified terms in which this axiom has been laid down, there is not a single instance in which the several departments of power have been kept absolutely separate and distinct. New Hampshire, whose constitution was the last formed, seems to have been fully aware of the impossibility and inexpediency of avoiding any mixture whatever of these departments, and has qualified the doctrine by declaring "that the legislative, executive, and judiciary powers ought to be kept as separate from, and independent of, each other as the nature of a free government will admit; or as is consistent with that chain of connection that binds the whole fabric of the constitution in one indissoluble bond of unity and amity." Her constitution accordingly mixes these departments in several respects. The Senate, which is a branch of the legislative department, is also a judicial tribunal for the trial of impeachments. The President, who is the head of the executive department, is the presiding member also of the Senate; and, besides an equal vote in all cases, has a casting vote in case of a tie. The executive head is himself eventually elective every year by the legislative department, and his council is every year chosen by and from the members of the same department. Several of the officers of state are also appointed by the legislature. And the members of the judiciary department are appointed by the executive department.

The constitution of Massachusetts has observed a sufficient though less pointed caution in expressing this fundamental article of liberty. It declares "that the legislative department shall never exercise the executive and judicial powers, or either of them; the executive shall never exercise the legislative and judicial powers, or either of them; the judicial shall never exercise the legislative and executive powers, or either of them." This declaration corresponds precisely with the doctrine of Montesquieu, as it has been explained, and is not in a single point violated by the plan of the convention. It goes no farther than to prohibit any one of the entire departments from exercising the powers of another department. In the very Constitution to which it is prefixed, a partial mixture of powers has been admitted. The executive magistrate has a qualified negative on the legislative body, and the Senate, which is a part of the legislature, is a court of impeachment for members both of the executive and judiciary departments. The members of the judiciary department, again, are appointable by the executive department, and removable by the same authority on the address of the two legislative branches. Lastly, a number of the officers of government are annually appointed by the legislative department. As the appointment to offices, particularly executive offices, is in its nature an executive function, the compilers of the Constitution have, in this last point at least, violated the rule established by themselves.

I pass over the constitutions of Rhode Island and Connecticut, because they were formed prior to the Revolution and even before the principle under examination had become an object of political attention.

The constitution of New York contains no declaration on this subject, but appears very clearly to have been framed with an eye to the danger of improperly blending the different departments. It gives, nevertheless, to the executive magistrate, a partial control over the legislative department; and, what is more, gives a like control to the judiciary department; and even blends the executive and judiciary departments in the exercise of this control. In its council of appointment members of the legislative are associated with the executive authority, in the appointment of officers, both executive and judiciary. And its court for the trial of impeachments and correction of errors is to consist of one branch of the legislature and the principal members of the judiciary department.

The constitution of New Jersey has blended the different powers of government more than any of the preceding. The governor, who is the executive magistrate, is appointed by the legislature; is chancellor and ordinary, or surrogate of the State; is a member of the Supreme Court of Appeals, and president, with a casting vote, of one of the legislative branches. The same legislative branch acts again as executive council to the governor, and with him constitutes the Court of Appeal. The members of the judiciary department are appointed by the legislative department, and removable by one branch of it, on the impeachment of the other.

According to the constitution of Pennsylvania, the president, who is the head of the executive department, is annually elected by a vote in which the legislative department predominates. In conjunction with an executive council, he appoints the members of the judiciary department and forces a court of impeachment for trial of all officers, judiciary as well as executive. The judges of the Supreme Court and justices of the peace seem also to be removable by the legislature; and the executive power of pardoning, in certain cases, to be referred to the same department. The members of the executive council are made Ex Officio justices of peace throughout the State.

In Delaware, the chief executive magistrate is annually elected by the legislative department. The speakers of the two legislative branches are vice-presidents in the executive department. The executive chief, with six others appointed, three by each of the legislative branches, constitutes the Supreme Court of Appeals; he is joined with the legislative department in the appointment of the other judges. Throughout the States it appears that the members of the legislature may at the same time be justices of the peace; in this State, the members of one branch of it are Ex Officio justices of the peace; as are also the members of the executive council. The principal officers of the executive department are appointed by the legislative; and one branch of the latter forms a court of impeachments. All officers may be removed on address of the legislature.

Maryland has adopted the maxim in the most unqualified terms; declaring that the legislative, executive, and judicial powers of government ought to be forever separate and distinct from each other. Her constitution, notwithstanding, makes the executive magistrate appointable by the legislative department; and the members of the judiciary by the executive department.

The language of Virginia is still more pointed on this subject. Her constitution declares "that the legislative, executive, and judiciary departments shall be separate and distinct; so that neither exercises the powers properly belonging to the other, nor shall any person exercise the powers of more than one of them at the same time, except that the justices of county courts shall be eligible to either House of Assembly." Yet we find not only this express exception with respect to the members of the inferior courts, but that the chief magistrate with his executive council, are appointable by the legislature; that two members of the latter are triennially displaced at the pleasure of the legislature; and that all the principal offices, both executive and judiciary, are filled by the same department. The executive perogative of pardon, also, is in one case vested in the legislative department.

The constitution of North Carolina, which declares "that the legislative, executive, and supreme judicial powers of government ought to be forever separate and distinct from each other," refers, at the same time, to the legislative department, the appointments not only of the executive chief but all the principal officers within both that and the judiciary department.

In South Carolina, the constitution makes the executive magistracy eligible by the legislative department. It gives to the latter also, the appointment of the members of the judiciary department, including even justices of the peace and sheriffs; and the appointment of officers in the executive department, down to captains in the army and navy of the State.

In the constitution of Georgia where it is declared "that the legislative, executive, and judiciary departments shall be separate and distinct, so that neither exercise the powers properly belonging to the other," we find that the executive department is to be filled by appointments of the legislature;

and the executive perogative of pardon to be finally exercised by the same authority. Even justices of the peace are to be appointed by the legislature.

In citing these cases, in which the legislative, executive, and judiciary departments have not been kept totally separate and distinct, I wish not to be regarded as an advocate for the particular organizations of the several State governments. I am fully aware that among the many excellent principles which they exemplify they carry strong marks of the haste, and still stronger of the inexperience, under which they were framed. It is but too obvious that in some instances the fundamental principle under consideration has been violated by too great a mixture, and even an actual consolidation of the different powers; and that in no instance has a competent provision been made for maintaining in practice the separation delineated on paper. What I have wished to evince is that the charge brought against the proposed Constitution of violating the sacred maxim of free government is warranted neither by the real meaning annexed to that maxim by its author, nor by the sense in which it has hitherto been understood in America. This interesting subject will be resumed in the ensuing paper.

THE CONSTITUTION

On May 25, 1787, a Constitutional Convention met in Philadelphia with representatives from seven states. Their purpose was to draft amendments to the Articles of Confederation. Eventually, however, they determined that in order to achieve their ends they would have to create an entirely new document. By September 17, 1787, twelve state delegations had contributed to an acceptable draft of the new document. Requiring the ratification of only nine states to take effect, the document met stiff opposition and failed to become official until June 21, 1788. It took until May 29, 1790, before all of the thirteen original states would actually ratify the document.

W e the people of the United States, in order to form a more perfect union, establish justice, insure domestic tranquillity, provide for the common defense, promote the general welfare, and secure the blessings of liberty to ourselves and our posterity, do ordain and establish this Constitution for the United States of America.

ARTICLE I

Section 1: All legislative powers herein granted shall be vested in a Congress of the United States, which shall consist of a Senate and House of Representatives.

Section 2: The House of Representatives shall be composed of members chosen every second year by the people of the several states, and the electors in each state shall have the qualifications requisite for electors of the most numerous branch of the state legislature.

No person shall be a representative who shall not have attained to the age of twenty-five years, and been seven years a citizen of the United States, and who shall not, when elected, be an inhabitant of that state in which he shall be chosen.

Representatives and direct taxes shall be apportioned among the several states which may be included within this Union, according to their respective numbers, which shall be determined by adding to the whole number of free persons, including those bound to service for a term of years, and excluding Indians not taxed, three-fifths of all other persons. The actual enumeration shall be made within three years after the first meeting of the Congress of the United States, and within every subsequent term of ten years, in such manner as they shall by law direct. The number of representatives shall not exceed one for every thirty thousand, but each state shall have at least one representative; and until such enumeration shall be made, the state of New Hampshire shall be entitled to choose three, Massachusetts eight, Rhode Island and Providence Plantations one, Connecticut five, New York six, New Jersey four, Pennsylvania eight, Delaware one, Maryland six, Virginia ten, North Carolina five, South Carolina five, and Georgia three.

When vacancies happen in the representation from any state, the executive authority thereof shall issue writs of election to fill such vacancies.

The House of Representatives shall choose their speaker and other officers; and shall have the sole power of impeachment.

Section 3: The Senate of the United States shall be composed of two senators from each state, chosen by the legislature thereof, for six years; and each senator shall have one vote.

Immediately after they shall be assembled in consequence of the first election, they shall be divided as equally as may be into three classes. The seats of the senators of the first class shall be vacated at the expiration of the second year, of the second class at the expiration of the fourth year, and of the third class at the expiration of the sixth year, so that one third may be chosen every second year; and if vacancies happen by resignation, or otherwise, during the recess of the legislature of any state, the executive thereof may make temporary appointments until the next meeting of the legislature, which shall then fill such vacancies.

No person shall be a senator who shall not have attained to the age of thirty years, and been nine years a citizen of the United States, and who shall not, when elected, be an inhabitant of that state for which he shall be chosen.

The vice president of the United States shall be president of the Senate, but shall have no vote, unless they be equally divided.

The Senate shall choose their other officers, and also a president pro tempore, in the absence of the vice president, or when he shall exercise the office of president of the United States.

The Senate shall have the sole power to try all impeachments. When sitting for that purpose, they shall be on oath or affirmation. When the president of the United States is tried, the chief justice shall preside: and no person shall be convicted without the concurrence of two-thirds of the members present.

Judgment in cases of impeachment shall not extend further than to removal from office, and disqualification to hold and enjoy any office of honor, trust or profit under the United States: but the party convicted shall nevertheless be liable and subject to indictment, trial, judgment, and punishment, according to law

Section 4: The times, places, and manner of holding elections for senators and representatives shall be prescribed in each state by the legislature thereof; but the Congress may at any time by law make or alter such regulations, except as to the places of choosing senators.

The Congress shall assemble at least once in every year, and such meeting shall be on the first Monday in December, unless they shall by law appoint a different day.

Section 5: Each House shall be the judge of the elections, returns, and qualifications of its own members, and a majority of each shall constitute a quorum to do business; but a smaller number may adjourn from day to day, and may be authorized to compel the attendance of absent members, in such manner, and under such penalties as each House may provide.

Each House may determine the rules of its proceedings, punish its members for disorderly behavior, and, with the concurrence of two-thirds, expel a member.

Each House shall keep a journal of its proceedings, and from time to time publish the same, excepting such parts as may in their judgment require secrecy; and the yeas and nays of the members of either House on any question shall, at the desire of one-fifth of those present, be entered on the journal.

Neither House, during the session of Congress, shall, without the consent of the other, adjourn for more than three days, nor to any other place than that in which the two Houses shall be sitting.

Section 6: The senators and representatives shall receive a compensation for their services, to be ascertained by law, and paid out of the Treasury of the United States. They shall in all cases, except treason, felony, and breach of the peace, be privileged from arrest during their attendance at the session of their respective Houses, and in going to and returning from the same; and for any speech or debate in either House, they shall not be questioned in any other place.

No senator or representative shall, during the time for which he was elected, be appointed to any civil office under the authority of the United States, which shall have been created, or the emoluments whereof shall have been increased during such time; and no person holding any office under the United States shall be a member of either House during his continuance in office.

Section 7: All bills for raising revenue shall originate in the House of Representatives; but the Senate may propose or concur with amendments as on other bills.

Every bill which shall have passed the House of Representatives and the Senate, shall, before it become a law, be presented to the president of the United States; if he approve he shall sign it, but if not he shall return it, with his objections to that House in which it shall have originated, who shall enter the objections at large on their journal, and proceed to reconsider it. If after such reconsideration two-thirds of that House shall agree to pass the bill, it shall be sent, together with the objections, to the other House, by which it shall likewise be reconsidered, and if approved by two-thirds of that House, it shall become a law. But in all such cases the votes of both Houses shall be determined by yeas and nays, and the names of the persons voting for and against the bill shall be entered on the journal of each House respectively. If any bill shall not be returned by the president within ten days (Sundays excepted) after it shall have been presented to him, the same shall be a law, in like manner as if he had signed it, unless the Congress by their adjournment prevent its return, in which case it shall not be a law.

Every order, resolution, or vote to which the concurrence of the Senate and House of Representatives may be necessary (except on a question of adjournment) shall be presented to the president of the United States; and before the same shall take effect, shall be approved by him, or being disapproved by him, shall be re-passed by two-thirds of the Senate and House of Representatives, according to the rules and limitations prescribed in the case of a bill.

Section 8: The Congress shall have power to lay and collect taxes, duties, imposts, and excises, to pay the debts and provide for the common defense and general welfare of the United States; but all duties, imposts, and excises shall be uniform throughout the United States;

To borrow money on the credit of the United States;

To regulate commerce with foreign nations, and among the several states, and with the Indian tribes;

To establish an uniform rule of naturalization, and uniform laws on the subject of bankruptcies throughout the United States;

To coin money, regulate the value thereof, and of foreign coin, and fix the standard of weights and measures;

To provide for the punishment of counterfeiting the securities and current coin of the United States;

To establish post offices and post roads;

To promote the progress of science and useful arts, by securing for limited times to authors and inventors the exclusive right to their respective writings and discoveries;

To constitute tribunals inferior to the Supreme Court;

To define and punish piracies and felonies committed on the high seas, and offenses against the law of nations;

To declare war, grant letters of marque and reprisal, and make rules concerning captures on land and water;

To raise and support armies, but no appropriation of money to that use shall be for a longer term than two years;

To provide and maintain a navy;

To make rules for the government and regulation of the land and naval forces;

To provide for calling forth the militia to execute the laws of the Union, suppress insurrections, and repel invasions;

To provide for organizing, arming, and disciplining the militia, and for governing such part of them as may be employed in the service of the United States, reserving to the states respectively, the appointment of the officers, and the authority of training the militia according to the discipline prescribed by Congress;

To exercise exclusive legislation in all cases whatsoever, over such district (not exceeding ten miles square) as may, by cession of particular states, and the acceptance of Congress, become the seat of the government of the United States, and to exercise like authority over all places purchased by the consent of the legislature of the state in which the same shall be, for the erection of forts, magazines, arsenals, dockyards, and other needful buildings; and,

To make all laws which shall be necessary and proper for carrying into execution the foregoing powers, and all other powers vested by this Constitution in the government of the United States, or in any department or officer thereof.

Section 9: The migration or importation of such persons as any of the states now existing shall think proper to admit, shall not be prohibited by the Congress prior to the year one thousand eight hundred and eight, but a tax or duty may be imposed on such importation, not exceeding ten dollars for each person.

The privilege of the writ of habeas corpus shall not be suspended, unless when in cases of rebellion or invasion the public safety may require it.

No bill of attainder or ex post facto law shall be passed.

No capitation, or other direct, tax shall be laid, unless in proportion to the census or enumeration herein before directed to be taken.

No tax or duty shall be laid on articles exported from any state.

No preference shall be given by any regulation of commerce or revenue to the ports of one state over those of another; nor shall vessels bound to, or from, one state, be obliged to enter, clear, or pay duties in another.

No money shall be drawn from the Treasury, but in consequence of appropriations made by law; and a regular statement and account of the receipts and expenditures of all public money shall be published from time to time.

No title of nobility shall be granted by the United States: and no person holding any office of profit or trust under them, shall, without the consent of the Congress, accept of any present, emolument, office, or title, of any kind whatever, from any king, prince, or foreign state.

Section 10: No state shall enter into any treaty, alliance, or confederation; grant letters of marque and reprisal; coin money; emit bills of credit; make anything but gold and silver coin a tender in payment of debts; pass any bill of attainder, ex post facto law, or law impairing the obligation of contracts; or grant any title of nobility.

No state shall, without the consent of the Congress, lay any imposts or duties on imports or exports, except what may be absolutely necessary for executing its inspection laws: and the net produce of all duties and imposts, laid by any state on imports or exports, shall be for the use of the Treasury of the United States; and all such laws shall be subject to the revision and control of the Congress.

No state shall, without the consent of Congress, lay any duty of tonnage, keep troops or ships of war in time of peace, enter into any agreement or compact with another state or with a foreign power, or engage in war, unless actually invaded, or in such imminent danger as will not admit of delay.

ARTICLE II

Section 1: The executive power shall be vested in a president of the United States of America. He shall hold his office during the term of four years, and, together with the vice president, chosen for the same term, be elected, as follows.

Each state shall appoint, in such manner as the legislature thereof may direct, a number of electors, equal to the whole number of senators and representatives to which the state may be entitled in the Congress: but no senator or representative, or person holding an office of trust or profit under the United States, shall be appointed an elector.

The electors shall meet in their respective states, and vote by ballot for two persons, of whom one at least shall not be an inhabitant of the same state with themselves. And they shall make a list of all the persons voted for, and of the number of votes for each; which list they shall sign and certify, and transmit sealed to the seat of the government of the United States, directed to the president of the Senate. The president of the Senate shall, in the presence of the Senate and House of Representatives, open all the certificates, and the votes shall then be counted. The person having the greatest number of votes shall be the president, if such number be a majority of the whole number of electors appointed; and if there be more than one who have such majority, and have an equal number of votes, then the House of Representatives shall immediately choose by ballot one of them for president; and if no person have a majority, then from the five highest on the list the said House shall in like manner choose the president. But in choosing the president, the votes shall be taken by states, the representation from each state having one vote; a quorum for this purpose shall consist of a member or members from two-thirds of the states, and a majority of all the states shall be necessary to a choice. In every case, after the choice of the president, the person having the greatest number of votes of the electors shall be the vice president. But if there should remain two or more who have equal votes, the Senate shall choose from them by ballot the vice president.

The Congress may determine the time of choosing the electors, and the day on which they shall give their votes; which day shall be the same throughout the United States.

No person except a natural-born citizen, or a citizen of the United States at the time of the adoption of this Constitution, shall be eligible to the office of president; neither shall any person be eligible to that office who shall not have attained to the age of thirty-five years, and been fourteen years a resident within the United States.

In case of the removal of the president from office, or of his death, resignation, or inability to discharge the powers and duties of the said office, the same shall devolve on the vice president, and the Congress may by law provide for the case of removal, death, resignation, or inability, both of the president and vice president, declaring what officer shall then act as president, and such officer shall act accordingly, until the disability be removed, or a president shall be elected.

The president shall, at stated times, receive for his services, a compensation, which shall neither be increased nor diminished during the period for which he shall have been elected, and he shall not receive within that period any other emolument from the United States, or any of them.

Before he enter on the execution of his office, he shall take the following oath or affirmation: "I do solemnly swear (or affirm) that I will faithfully execute the office of president of the United States, and will to the best of my ability, preserve, protect, and defend the Constitution of the United States."

Section 2: The president shall be commander in chief of the army and navy of the United States, and of the militia of the several states, when called into the actual service of the United States; he may require the opinion, in writing, of the principal officer in each of the executive departments, upon any subject relating to the duties of their respective offices, and he shall have power to grant reprieves and pardons for offenses against the United States, except in cases of impeachment.

He shall have power, by and with the advice and consent of the Senate, to make treaties, provided two-thirds of the senators present concur; and he shall nominate, and by and with the advice and consent of the Senate, shall appoint ambassadors, other public ministers and consuls, judges of the Supreme Court, and all other officers of the United States, whose appointments are not herein otherwise provided for, and which shall be established by law: but the Congress may by law vest the appointment of such inferior officers, as they think proper, in the president alone, in the courts of law, or in the heads of departments.

The president shall have power to fill up all vacancies that may happen during the recess of the Senate, by granting commissions which shall expire at the end of their next session.

Section 3: He shall from time to time give to the Congress information of the state of the Union, and recommend to their consideration such measures as he shall judge necessary and expedient; he may, on extraordinary occasions, convene both Houses, or either of them, and in case of disagreement between them, with respect to the time of adjournment, he may adjourn them to such time as he shall think proper; he shall receive ambassadors and other public ministers; he shall take care that the laws be faithfully executed, and shall commission all the officers of the United States.

Section 4: The president, vice president, and all civil officers of the United States shall be removed from office on impeachment for, and conviction of, treason, bribery, or other high crimes and misdemeanors.

ARTICLE III

Section 1: The judicial power of the United States shall be vested in one Supreme Court, and in such inferior courts as the Congress may from time to time ordain and establish. The judges, both of the supreme and inferior courts, shall hold their offices during good behavior, and shall, at stated times, receive for their services, a compensation, which shall not be diminished during their continuance in office.

Section 2: The judicial power shall extend to all cases, in law and equity, arising under this Constitution, the laws of the United States, and treaties made, or which shall be made, under their authority; to all cases affecting ambassadors, other public ministers and consuls; to all cases of admiralty and maritime jurisdiction; to controversies to which the United States shall be a party; controversies between two or more states—between a state and citizens of another state—between citizens of different states—between citizens of the same state claiming lands under grants of different states, and between a state, or the citizens thereof, and foreign states, citizens, or subjects.

In all cases affecting ambassadors, other public ministers and consuls, and those in which a state shall be party, the Supreme Court shall have original jurisdiction. In all the other cases before mentioned, the Supreme Court shall have appellate jurisdiction, both as to law and fact, with such exceptions, and under such regulations as the Congress shall make.

The trial of all crimes, except in cases of impeachment, shall be by jury; and such trial shall be held in the state where the said crimes shall have been committed; but when not committed within any state, the trial shall be at such place or places as the Congress may by law have directed.

Section 3: Treason against the United States shall consist only in levying war against them, or in adhering to their enemies, giving them aid and comfort. No person shall be convicted of treason unless on the testimony of two witnesses to the same overt act, or on confession in open court.

The Congress shall have power to declare the punishment of treason, but no attainder of treason shall work corruption of blood, or forfeiture except during the life of the person attainted.

ARTICLE IV

Section 1: Full faith and credit shall be given in each state to the public acts, records, and judicial proceedings of every other state. And the Congress may by general laws prescribe the manner in which such acts, records, and proceedings shall be proved, and the effect thereof.

Section 2: The citizens of each state shall be entitled to all privileges and immunities of citizens in the several states.

A person charged in any state with treason, felony, or other crime, who shall flee from justice, and be found in another state, shall on demand of the executive authority of the state from which he fled, be delivered up, to be removed to the state having jurisdiction of the crime.

No person held to service or labor in one state, under the laws thereof, escaping into another, shall, in consequence of any law or regulation therein, be discharged from such service or labor, but shall be delivered up on claim of the party to whom such service or labor may be due.

Section 3: New states may be admitted by the Congress into this Union; but no new state shall be formed or erected within the jurisdiction of any other state; nor any state be formed by the junction of two or more states, or parts of states, without the consent of the legislatures of the states concerned as well as of the Congress.

The Congress shall have power to dispose of and make all needful rules and regulations respecting the territory or other property belonging to the United States; and nothing in this Constitution shall be so construed as to prejudice any claims of the United States, or of any particular state.

Section 4: The United States shall guarantee to every state in this Union a republican form of government, and shall protect each of them against invasion; and on application of the legislature, or of the executive (when the legislature cannot be convened) against domestic violence.

ARTICLE V

The Congress, whenever two-thirds of both Houses shall deem it necessary, shall propose amendments to this Constitution, or, on the application of the legislatures of two-thirds of the several states, shall call a convention for proposing amendments, which, in either case, shall be valid to all intents and purposes, as part of this Constitution, when ratified by the legislatures of three-fourths of the several states, or by conventions in three-fourths thereof, as the one or the other mode of ratification may be proposed by the Congress; provided that no amendment which may be made prior to the year one thousand eight hundred and eight shall in any manner affect the first and fourth clauses in the ninth section of the first article; and that no state, without its consent, shall be deprived of its equal suffrage in the Senate.

ARTICLE VI

All debts contracted and engagements entered into, before the adoption of this Constitution, shall be as valid against the United States under this Constitution, as under the Confederation.

This Constitution, and the laws of the United States which shall be made in pursuance thereof, and all treaties made, or which shall be made, under the authority of the United States, shall be the supreme law of the land; and the judges in every state shall be bound thereby, anything in the constitution or laws of any state to the contrary notwithstanding.

The senators and representatives before mentioned, and the members of the several state legislatures, and all executive and judicial officers, both of the United States and of the several states, shall be bound by oath or affirmation, to support this Constitution; but no religious test shall ever be required as a qualification to any office or public trust under the United States.

ARTICLE VII

The ratification of the conventions of nine states shall be sufficient for the establishment of this Constitution between the states so ratifying the same.

Done in convention by the unanimous consent of the states present the seventeenth day of September in the year of Our Lord one thousand seven hundred and eighty-seven and of the Independence of the United States of America the twelfth. In witness whereof we have hereunto subscribed our names.

THE BILL OF RIGHTS

Because of the opposition to the adoption of the Constitution by the anti-Federalists, several states proposed amending the document to better protect the states, as well as individuals, from the incursions of the centralized federal government. Thus these ten new planks were drafted, debated, and eventually adopted. They became the first ten amendments to the Constitution—finally ratified on December 15, 1791.

The conventions of a number of states having at the time of their adopting the Constitution, expressed a desire, in order to prevent misconstruction or abuse of its powers, that further declaratory and restrictive clauses should be added: and as extending the ground of public confidence in the government, will best insure the beneficent ends of its institution.

ARTICLE I

Congress shall make no law respecting an establishment of religion, or prohibiting the free exercise thereof; or abridging the freedom of speech, or of the press; or the right of the people peaceably to assemble, and to petition the government for a redress of grievances.

ARTICLE II

A well-regulated militia, being necessary to the security of a free state, the right of the people to keep and bear arms, shall not be infringed.

ARTICLE III

No soldier shall, in time of peace be quartered in any house, without the consent of the owner, nor in time of war, but in a manner to be prescribed by law.

ARTICLE IV

The right of the people to be secure in their persons, houses, papers, and effects, against unreasonable searches and seizures, shall not be violated, and no warrants shall issue, but upon probable cause, supported by oath or affirmation, and particularly describing the place to be searched, and the persons or things to be seized.

Article V

No person shall be held to answer for a capital, or otherwise infamous crime, unless on a presentment or indictment of a grand jury, except in cases arising in the land or naval forces, or in the militia, when in actual service in time of war or public danger; nor shall any person be subject for the same offense to be twice put in jeopardy of life or limb; nor shall be compelled in any criminal case to be a witness against himself, nor be deprived of life, liberty, or property, without due process of law; nor shall private property be taken for public use, without just compensation.

ARTICLE VI

In all criminal prosecutions, the accused shall enjoy the right to a speedy and public trial, by an impartial jury of the state and district wherein the crime shall have been committed, which district shall have been previously ascertained by law, and to be informed of the nature and cause of the accusation; to be confronted with the witnesses against him; to have compulsory process for obtaining witnesses in his favor, and to have the assistance of counsel for his defense.

ARTICLE VII

In suits at common law, where the value in controversy shall exceed twenty dollars, the right of trial by jury shall be preserved, and no fact tried by a jury shall be otherwise reexamined in any court of the United States, than according to the rules of the common law.

ARTICLE VIII

Excessive bail shall not be required, nor excessive fines imposed, nor cruel and unusual punishments inflicted.

ARTICLE IX

The enumeration in the Constitution, of certain rights, shall not be construed to deny or disparage others retained by the people.

ARTICLE X

The powers not delegated to the United States by the Constitution, nor prohibited by it to the states, are reserved to the states respectively, or to the people.

WASHINGTON'S INAUGURAL

By George Washington

This inaugural address was delivered by the unanimously elected chief executive in the Senate Chamber of Federal Hall in New York City on April 30, 1789. In close collaboration with James Madison, the new president essentially wanted to remind his fellow citizens that the event of his accession of power was not of his own choosing. He also wished to beg their representatives not to embarrass him with financial compensation for doing his duty, to invoke the blessings of heaven, to reflect upon God's good providence, to take a few jabs at the anti-Federalists, to celebrate the moral foundations of liberty, and to put the American experiment in free government into some sort of historical perspective.

Fellow citizens of the Senate and of the House of Representatives: Among the vicissitudes incident to life, no event could have filled me with greater anxieties than that of which the notification was transmitted by your order, and received on the fourteenth day of the present month: On the one hand, I was summoned by my country, whose voice I can never hear but with veneration and love, from a retreat which I had chosen with the fondest predilection, and, in my flattering hopes, with an immutable decision, as the asylum of my declining years: a retreat which was rendered every day more necessary as well as more dear to me, by the addition of habit to inclination, and of frequent interruptions in my health to the gradual waste committed on it by time. On the other hand, the magnitude and difficulty of the trust to which the voice of my country called me, being sufficient to awaken in the wisest and most experienced of her citizens, a distrustful scrutiny into his qualifications, could not but overwhelm with despondence, one, who, inheriting inferior endowments from nature and unpracticed in the duties of civil administration, ought to be peculiarly conscious of his own deficiencies. In this conflict of emotions, all I dare aver, is, that it has been my faithful study to collect my duty from a just appreciation of every circumstance, by which it might be affected. All I dare hope, is, that, if in executing this task I have been too much swayed by a grateful remembrance of former instances, or by an affectionate sensibility to this transcendent proof, of the confidence of my fellow-citizens; and have thence too little consulted my incapacity as well as disinclination for the weighty and untried cares before me; my error will be palliated by the motives which misled me, and its consequences be judged by my Country, with some share of the partiality in which they originated.

Such being the impressions under which I have, in obedience to the public summons, repaired to the present station; it would be peculiarly improper to omit in this first official act, my fervent supplications to that Almighty Being who rules over the universe, who presides in the councils of nations, and whose providential aids can supply every human defect, that His benediction may consecrate to the liberties and happiness of the people of the United States, a government instituted by themselves for these essential purposes: and may enable every instrument employed in its administration to execute with success, the functions allotted to His charge. In tendering this homage to the Great Author of every public and private good, I assure myself that it expresses your sentiments not less than my own; nor those of my fellow-citizens at large, less than either. No people can be bound to acknowledge and adore the invisible hand, which conducts the affairs of men more than the people of the United States. Every step, by which they have advanced to the character of an independent nation, seems to have been distinguished by some token of providential agency. And in the important revolution just accomplished in the system of their united government; the tranquil deliberations and voluntary consent of so many distinct communities, from which the event has resulted, cannot be compared with the means by which most governments have been established, without some return of pious gratitude along with an humble anticipation of the future blessings which the past seem to presage. These reflections, arising out of the present crisis, have forced themselves too strongly on my mind to be suppressed. You will join with me I trust in thinking, that there are none under the influence of which, the proceedings of a new and free Government can more auspiciously commence.

By the article establishing the executive department, it is made the duty of the president "to recommend to your consideration, such measures as he shall judge necessary and expedient. The circumstances under which I now meet you, will acquit me from entering into that subject, farther than to refer to the great constitutional charter under which you are assembled; and which, in defining your powers, designates the objects to which your attention is to be given. It will be more consistent with those circumstances, and far more congenial with the feelings which actuate me, to substitute, in place of a recommendation of particular measures, the tribute that is due to the talents, the rectitude, and the patriotism which adorn the characters selected to devise and adopt them. In these honorable qualifications, I behold the surest pledges, that as on one side, no local prejudices, or attachments; no separate views, nor party animosities, will misdirect the comprehensive and equal eye which ought to watch over this great assemblage of communities and interests: so, on another, that the foundations of our national policy will be laid in the pure and immutable principles of private morality; and the pre-eminence of free government, be exemplified by all the attributes which can win the affections of its citizens, and command the respect of the world. I dwell on this prospect with every satisfaction which an ardent love for my country can inspire: since there is no truth more thoroughly established, than that there exists in the economy and course of nature, an indissoluble union between virtue and happiness, between duty and advantage, between the genuine maxims of an honest and magnanimous policy, and the solid rewards of public prosperity and felicity: since we ought to be no less persuaded that the propitious smiles of Heaven, can never be expected on a nation that disregards the eternal rules of order and right, which Heaven itself has ordained: and since the preservation of the sacred fire of liberty, and the destiny of the Republican model of Government, are justly considered as deeply, perhaps as finally staked, on the experiment entrusted to the hands of the American people.

Besides the ordinary objects submitted to your care, it will remain with your judgment to decide, how far an exercise of the occasional power delegated by the Fifth article of the Constitution is rendered expedient at the present juncture by the nature of objections which have been urged against the system, or by the degree of inquietude which has given birth to them.—Instead of undertaking particular recommendations on this subject, in which I could be guided by no lights derived from official opportunities, I shall again give way to my entire confidence in your discernment and pursuit of the public good: For I assure myself that whilst you carefully avoid every alteration which might endanger the benefits of an united and effective government, or which ought to await the future lessons of experience; a reverence for the characteristic rights of freemen, and a regard for the public harmony, will sufficiently influence your deliberations on the question how far the former can be more impregnably fortified, or the latter be safely and advantageously promoted.

To the preceding observations I have one to add, which will be most properly addressed to the House of Representatives. It concerns myself, and will therefore be as brief as possible. When I was first honored with a call into the service of my country, then on the eve of an arduous struggle for its liberties, the light in which I contemplated my duty required that I should renounce every pecuniary compensation. From this resolution I have in no instance departed. And being still under the impressions which produced it, I must decline as inapplicable to myself, any share in the personal emoluments, which may be indispensably included in a permanent provision for the Executive Department; and must accordingly pray that the pecuniary estimates for the station in which I am placed, may, during my continuance in it, be limited to such actual expenditures as the public good may be thought to require.

Having thus imparted to you my sentiments, as they have been awakened by the occasion which brings us together, I shall take my present leave; but not without resorting once more to the benign parent of the human race, in humble supplication that since he has been pleased to favor the American people with opportunities for deliberating in perfect tranquility, and dispositions for deciding with unparalleled unanimity on a form of government, for the security of their union, and the advancement of their happiness, so this divine blessing may be equally conspicuous in the enlarged views, the temperate consultations and the wise measures on which the success of this government must depend.

FAREWELL ADDRESS

By George Washington

By September 17, 1796, when this address was delivered to his cabinet in Philadelphia, the president had already served two terms and did not wish to serve a third. His immense popularity had dwindled dramatically due to his fierce federalism and his opposition to the formation of political parties that were emerging. In addition, he was tired of being lampooned in the political press. He considered this message so important that he had the full text published in newspapers around the country two days later so it would reach a much wider audience. The address warned against foreign involvements, political factions, and sectionalism and promoted religion, morality, and education.

Friends and fellow citizens: The period for a new election of a citizen to administer the executive government of the United States being not far distant, and the time actually arrived when your thoughts must be employed in designating the person who is to be clothed with that important trust, it appears to me proper, especially as it may conduce to a more distinct expression of the public voice, that I should now apprise you of the resolution I have formed to decline being considered among the number of those out of whom a choice is to be made.

In looking forward to the moment which is intended to terminate the career of my political life, my feelings do not permit me to suspend the deep acknowledgment of that debt of gratitude which I owe to my beloved country for the many honors it has conferred upon me; still more for the steadfast confidence with which it has supported me, and for the opportunities I have thence enjoyed of manifesting my inviolable attachment by services faithful and persevering, though in usefulness unequal to my zeal.

Here, perhaps, I ought to stop. But a solicitude for your welfare, which cannot end but with my life, and the apprehension of danger natural to that solicitude urge me on an occasion like the present to offer to your solemn contemplation and to recommend to your frequent review some sentiments which are the result of much reflection, of no inconsiderable observation, and which appear to me all important to the permanency of your felicity as a people.

The unity of government which constitutes you one people is also now dear to you. It is justly so, for it is a main pillar in the edifice of your real independence, the support of your tranquillity at home, your peace abroad, of your safety, of your prosperity, of that very liberty which you so highly prize.

But as it is easy to foresee that from different causes and from different quarters much pains will be taken, many artifices employed, to weaken in your minds the conviction of this truth, as this is the point in your political fortress against which the batteries of internal and external enemies will be most constantly and actively (though often covertly and insidiously) directed, it is of infinite moment that you should properly estimate the immense value of your national union to your collective and individual happiness.

The name of American, which belongs to you in your national capacity, must always exalt the just pride of patriotism more than any appellation derived from local discriminations. With slight shades of difference, you have the same religion, manners, habits, and political principles. You have in a common cause fought and triumphed together. The independence and liberty you possess are the work of joint councils and joint efforts, of common dangers, sufferings, and successes.

But these considerations, however powerfully they address themselves to your sensibility, are greatly outweighed by those which apply more immediately to your interest. Here every portion of our country finds the most commanding motives for carefully guarding and preserving the union of the whole.

In contemplating the causes which may disturb our Union, it occurs as matter of serious concern that any ground should have been furnished for characterizing parties by geographical discriminations—Northern and Southern, Atlantic and Western—whence designing men may endeavor to excite a belief that there is a real difference of local interests and views. One of the expedients of party to acquire influence within particular districts is to misrepresent the opinions and aims of other districts. You cannot shield yourselves too much against the jealousies and heartburnings which spring from these misrepresentations. They tend to render alien to each other those who ought to be bound together by fraternal affection.

To the efficacy and permanency of your Union a government for the whole is indispensable. No alliances, however strict, between the parts can be an adequate substitute. They must inevitably experience the infractions and interruptions which all alliances in all times have experienced. Sensible of this momentous truth, you have improved upon your first essay by the adoption of a constitution of government better calculated than your former for an intimate union, and for the efficacious management of your common concerns.

Toward the preservation of your government and the permanency of your present happy state, it is requisite not only that you steadily discountenance irregular oppositions to its acknowledged authority, but also that you resist with care the spirit of innovation upon its principles, however specious the pretexts. One method of assault may be to effect in the forms of the Constitution alterations which will impair the energy of the system, and thus to undermine what cannot be directly overthrown.

I have already intimated to you the danger of parties in the state, with particular reference to the founding of them on geographical discriminations. Let me now take a more comprehensive view and warn you in the most solemn manner against the baneful effects of the spirit of party generally.

The alternate domination of one faction over another, sharpened by the spirit of revenge natural to party dissension, which in different ages and countries has perpetrated the most horrid enormities, is itself a frightful despotism. But this leads at length to a more formal and permanent despotism. The disorders and miseries which result gradually incline the minds of men to seek security and repose in the absolute power of an individual, and sooner or later the chief of some prevailing faction, more able or more fortunate than his competitors, turns this disposition to the purposes of his own elevation on the ruins of public liberty.

Of all the dispositions and habits which lead to political prosperity, religion and morality are indispensable supports. In vain would that man claim the tribute of patriotism who should labor to subvert these great pillars of human happiness, these firmest props of the duties of men and citizens. The mere politician, equally with the pious man, ought to respect and to cherish them. A volume could not trace all their connections with private and public felicity. Let it simply be asked: Where is the security for property, for reputation, for life, if the sense of religious obligation desert the oaths which are the instruments of investigation in courts of justice?

And let us with caution indulge the supposition that morality can be maintained without religion. Whatever may be conceded to the influence of refined education on minds of peculiar structure, reason and experience both forbid us to expect that national morality can prevail in exclusion of religious principle.

'Tis substantially true that virtue or morality is a necessary spring of popular government. The rule indeed extends with more or less force to every species of free government. Who that is a sincere friend to it can look with indifference upon attempts to shake the foundation of the fabric? Promote, then, as an object of primary importance, institutions for the general diffusion of knowledge. In proportion as the structure of a government gives force to public opinion, it is essential that public opinion should be enlightened.

Observe good faith and justice toward all nations. Cultivate peace and harmony with all. Religion and morality enjoin this conduct; and can it be that good policy does not equally enjoin it? It will be worthy of a free, enlightened, and at no distant period, a great nation, to give to mankind the magnanimous and too novel example of a people always guided by an exalted justice and benevolence. Who can doubt that in the course of time and things the fruits of such a plan would richly repay any temporary advantages which might be lost by a steady adherence to it? Can it be that Providence has not connected the permanent felicity of a nation with its virtues? The experiment, at least, is recommended by every sentiment which ennobles human nature. Alas! is it rendered impossible by its vices?

In the execution of such a plan nothing is more essential than that permanent, inveterate antipathies against particular nations and passionate attachments for others should be excluded, and that in place of them just and amicable feelings toward all should be cultivated.

Harmony, liberal intercourse with all nations are recommended by policy, humanity, and interest. But even our commercial policy should hold an equal and impartial hand, neither seeking nor granting exclusive favors or preferences. There can be no greater error than to expect or calculate upon real favors from nation to nation. 'Tis an illusion which experience must cure, which a just pride ought to discard.

In offering to you, my countrymen, these counsels of an old and affectionate friend, I dare not hope they will make the strong and lasting impression I could wish, that they will control the usual current of the passions or prevent our nation from running the course which has hitherto marked the destiny of nations. But if I may even flatter myself that they may be productive of some partial benefit, some occasional good—that they may now and then recur to moderate the fury of party spirit, to warn against the mischiefs of foreign intrigue, to guard against the impostures of pretended patriotism—this hope will be a full recompense for the solicitude for your welfare by which they have been dictated.

Though in reviewing the incidents of my administration I am unconscious of intentional error, I am nevertheless too sensible of my defects not to think it probable that I may have committed many errors. Whatever they may be, I fervently beseech the Almighty to avert or mitigate the evils to which they may tend. I shall also carry with me the hope that my country will never cease to view them with indulgence, and that after forty-five years of my life dedicated to its service, with an upright zeal, the faults of incompetent abilities will be consigned to oblivion, as myself must soon be to the mansions of rest.

Relying on its kindness in this as in other things, and actuated by that fervent love toward it which is so natural to a man who views in it the native soil of himself and his progenitors for several generations, I anticipate with pleasing expectation that retreat in which I promise myself to realize, without alloy, the sweet enjoyment of partaking, in the midst of my fellow citizens, the benign influence of good laws under a free government—the ever favorite object of my heart and the happy reward, as I trust, of our mutual cares, labors, and dangers.

THE BUNKER HILL ORATION

By Daniel Webster

In 1825, to commemorate the fiftieth anniversary of the great Battle of Bunker Hill in Boston, as well as to dedicate the site of a new monument, Daniel Webster, the venerable senator from New Hampshire, delivered one of the most eloquent orations in American political history. Long studied both for its rhetorical brilliance and its civic perspective, the speech outlines the basic principles and precepts of the nation's extraordinary experiment in liberty.

This uncounted multitude before me and around me proves the feeling which the occasion has excited. These thousands of human faces, glowing with sympathy and joy, and from the impulses of a common gratitude turned reverently to heaven in this spacious temple of the firmament, proclaim that the day, the place, and the purpose of our assembling have made a ,deep impression on our hearts.

If, indeed, there be anything in local association fit to affect the mind of man, we need not strive to repress the emotions which agitate us here. We are among the sepulchers of our fathers. We are on ground distinguished by their valor, their constancy, and the shedding of their blood. We are here, not to fix an uncertain date in our annals, nor to draw into notice an obscure and unknown spot. If our humble purpose had never been conceived, if we ourselves had never been born, the 17th of June 1775, would have been a day on which all subsequent history would have poured its light, and the eminence where we stand a point of attraction to the eyes of successive generations. But we are Americans. We live in what may be called the early age of this great continent; and we know that our posterity, through all time, are here to enjoy and suffer the allotments of humanity. We see before us a probable train of great events; we know that our own fortunes have been happily cast; and it is natural, therefore, that we should be moved by the contemplation of occurrences which have guided our destiny before many of us were born, and settled the condition in which we should pass that portion of our existence which God allows to men on earth.

We do not read even of the discovery of this continent, without feeling something of a personal interest in the event; without being reminded how much it has affected our own fortunes and our own existence. It would be still more unnatural for us, therefore, than for others, to contemplate with unaffected minds that interesting, I may say that most touching and pathetic scene, when the great discoverer of America stood on the deck of his shattered bark, the shades of night falling on the sea, yet no man sleeping; tossed on the billows of an unknown ocean, yet the stronger billows of alternate hope and despair tossing his own troubled thoughts; extending forward his harassed frame, straining westward his anxious and eager eyes, till Heaven at last granted him a moment of rapture and ecstasy, in blessing his vision with the sight of the unknown world.

Nearer to our times, more closely connected with our fates, and therefore still more interesting to our feelings and affections, is the settlement of our own country by colonists from England. We cherish every memorial of these worthy ancestors; we celebrate their patience and fortitude; we admire their daring enterprise; we teach our children to venerate their piety; and we are justly proud of being descended from men who have set the world an example of founding civil institutions on the great and united principles of human freedom and human knowledge. To us, their children, the story of their labors and sufferings can never be without interest. We shall not stand unmoved on the shore of Plymouth, while the sea continues to wash it; nor will our brethren in another early and ancient Colony forget the place of its first establishment, till their river shall cease to flow by it. No vigor of youth, no maturity of manhood, will lead the nation to forget the spots where its infancy was cradled and defended.

But the great event in the history of the continent, which we are now met here to commemorate, that prodigy of modern times, at once the wonder and the blessing of the world, is the American Revolution. In a day of extraordinary prosperity and happiness, of high national honor, distinction, and power, we are brought together, in this place, by our love of country, by our admiration of exalted character, by our gratitude for signal services and patriotic devotion.

The Society whose organ I am was formed for the purpose of rearing some honorable and durable monument to the memory of the early friends of American Independence. They have thought that for this object no time could be more propitious than the present prosperous and peaceful period; that no place could claim preference over this memorable spot; and that no day could be more auspicious to the undertaking, than the anniversary of the battle which was here fought. The foundation of that monument we have now laid. With solemnities suited to the occasion, with prayers to Almighty God for his blessing, and in the midst of this cloud of witnesses, we have begun the work. We trust it will be prosecuted, and that, springing from a broad foundation, rising high in massive solidity and unadorned grandeur, it may remain as long as Heaven permits the works of man to last, a fit emblem, both of the events in memory of which it is raised, and of the gratitude of those who have reared it.

We know, indeed, that the record of illustrious actions is most safely deposited in the universal remembrance of mankind. We know, that if we could cause this structure to ascend, not only till it reached the skies, but till it pierced them, its broad surfaces could still contain but part of that which, in an age of knowledge, hath already been spread over the earth, and which history charges itself with making known to all future times. We know that no inscription on entablatures less broad than the earth itself can carry information of the events we commemorate where it has not already gone; and that no structure, which shall not outlive the duration of letters and knowledge among men, can prolong the memorial. But our object is, by this edifice, to show our own deep sense of the value and importance of the achievements of our ancestors; and, by presenting this work of gratitude to the eye, to keep alive similar sentiments, and to foster a constant regard for the principals of the Revolution. Human beings are composed, not of reason only, but of imagination also, and sentiment; and that is neither wasted nor misapplied which is appropriated to the purpose of giving right direction to sentiments, and opening proper springs of feeling in the heart. Let it not be supposed that our object is to perpetuate national hostility, or even to cherish a mere military spirit. It is higher, purer, nobler. We consecrate our work to the spirit of national independence, and we wish that the light of peace may rest upon it for ever. We rear a memorial of our conviction of that unmeasured benefit which has been conferred on our own land, and of the happy influences which have been produced, by the same events, on the general interests of mankind. We come, as Americans, to mark a spot which must for ever be dear to us and our posterity. We wish that whosoever, in all coming time, shall turn his eye hither, may behold that the place is not undistinguished, where the first great battle of the Revolution was fought. We wish that this structure may proclaim the magnitude and importance of that event to every class and every age. We wish that infancy may learn the purpose of its erection from maternal lips, and that weary and withered age may behold it, and be solaced by the recollections which it suggests. We wish that labor may look up here, and be proud, in the midst of its toil. We wish that, in those days of disaster, which, as they come upon all nations, must be expected to come upon us also, desponding patriotism may turn its eyes hitherward, and be assured that the foundations of our national power are still strong. We wish that this column, rising towards heaven among the pointed spires of so many temples dedicated to God, may contribute also to produce, in all minds, a pious feeling of dependence and gratitude. We wish, finally, that the last object to the sight of him who leaves his native shore, and the first to gladden him who revisits it, may be something which shall remind him of the liberty and the glory of his country. Let it rise! let it rise, till it meet the sun in his coming; let the earliest light of the morning gild it, and parting day linger and play on its summit.

We live in a most extraordinary age. Events so various and so important that they might crowd and distinguish centuries, are, in our times, compressed within the compass of a single life. When has it happened that history has had so much to record, in the same term of years, as since the 17th of June 1775? Our own Revolution, which, under other circumstances, might itself have been expected to occasion a war of half a century, has been achieved twenty-four sovereign and independent States erected; and a general government established over them, so safe, so wise, so free, so practical, that we might well wonder its establishment should have been accomplished so soon, were it not for the greater wonder that it should have been established at all. Two or three millions of people have been augmented to twelve, the great forests of the West prostrated beneath the arm of successful industry, and the dwellers on the banks of the Ohio and the Mississippi become the fellow-citizens and neighbors of those who cultivate the hills of New England. We have a commerce that leaves no sea unexplored; navies, which take no law from superior force; revenues, adequate to all the exigencies of government, almost without taxation; and peace with all nations, founded on equal rights and mutual respect.

Europe, within the same period, has been agitated by a mighty revolution, which, while it has been felt in the individual condition and happiness of almost every man, has shaken to the center her political fabric, and dashed against one another thrones which had stood tranquil for ages. On this, our continent, our own example has been followed, and colonies have sprung up to be nations. Unaccustomed sounds of liberty and free government have reached us from beyond the track of the sun; and at this moment the dominion of European power in this continent, from the place where we stand to the south pole, is annihilated for ever.

In the meantime, both in Europe and America, such has been the general progress of knowledge, such the improvement in legislation, in commerce, in the arts, in letters, and, above all, in liberal ideas and the general spirit of the age, that the whole world seems changed.

Yet, notwithstanding that this is but a faint abstract of the things which have happened since the day of the battle of Bunker Hill, we are but fifty years removed from it; and we now stand here to enjoy all the blessings of our own condition, and to look abroad on the brightened prospects of the world, while we still have among us some of those who were active agents in the scenes of 1775, and who are now here, from every quarter of New England, to visit once more, and under circumstances so affecting, I had almost said so overwhelming, this renowned theater of their courage and patriotism.

Venerable men! you have come down to us from a former generation. Heaven has bounteously lengthened out your lives, that you might behold this joyous day. You are now where you stood fifty years ago this very hour, with your brothers and your neighbors, shoulder to shoulder, in the strife for your country. Behold, how altered! The same heavens are indeed over your heads; the same ocean rolls at your feet but all else how changed! You hear now no roar of hostile cannon, you see no mixed volumes of smoke and flame rising from burning Charlestown. The ground strewed with the dead and the dying; the impetuous charge; the steady and successful repulse; the loud call to repeated assault; the summoning of all that is manly to repeated resistance; a thousand bosoms freely and fearlessly bared in an instant to whatever of terror there may be in war and death— all these you have witnessed, but you witness them no more. All is peace. The heights of yonder metropolis, its towers and roofs, which you then saw filled with wives and children and countrymen in distress and terror, and looking with unutterable emotions for the issue of the combat, have presented you to-day with the sight of its whole happy population, come out to welcome and greet you with a universal jubilee. Yonder proud ships, by a felicity of position appropriately lying at the foot of this mount, and seeming fondly to cling around it, are not means of annoyance to you, but your country's own means of distinction and defense. All is peace; and God has granted you this sight of your country's happiness, ere you slumber in the grave. He has allowed you to behold and to partake the reward of your patriotic toils; and he has allowed us, your sons and countrymen, to meet you here, and in the name of the present generation, in the name of your country, in the name of liberty, to thank you!

But, alas! you are not all here! Time and the sword have thinned your ranks. Prescott, Putnam, Stark, Brooks, Reed, Pomeroy, Bridge! our eyes seek for you in vain amid this broken band. You are gathered to your fathers, and live only to your country in her grateful remembrance and your own bright example. But let us not too much grieve, that you have met the common fate of men. You lived at least long enough to know that your work had been nobly and successfully accomplished. You lived to see your country's independence established, and to sheathe your swords from war. On the light of Liberty you saw arise the light of Peace, like:
"Another morn,
Risen on mid-noon";
and the sky on which you closed your eyes was cloudless.

But, ah! Him! the first great martyr in this great cause! Him! the premature victim of his own self-devoting heart! Him! the head of our civil councils, and the destined leader of our military bands, whom nothing brought hither but the unquenchable fire of his own spirit! Him! cut off by Providence in the hour of overwhelming anxiety and thick gloom; falling ere he saw the star of his country rise; pouring out his generous blood like water, before he knew whether it would fertilize a land of freedom or of bondage!—how shall I struggle with the emotions that stifle the utterance of thy name! Our poor work may perish; but thine shall endure! This monument may moulder away; the solid ground it rests upon may sink down to a level with the sea; but thy memory shall not fail! Wheresoever among men a heart shall be found that beats to the transports of patriotism and liberty, its aspirations shall be to claim kindred with thy spirit.

But the scene amidst which we stand does not permit us to confine our thoughts or our sympathies to those fearless spirits who hazarded or lost their lives on this consecrated spot. We have the happiness to rejoice here in the presence of a most worthy representation of the survivors of the whole Revolutionary army.

Veterans! you are the remnant of many a well-fought field. You bring with you marks of honor from Trenton and Monmouth, from Yorktown, Camden, Bennington, and Saratoga. Veterans of half a century! When in your youthful days you put everything at hazard in your country's cause, good as that cause was, and sanguine as youth is, still your fondest hopes did not stretch onward to an hour like this! At a period to which you could not reasonably have expected to arrive, at a moment of national prosperity such as you could never have foreseen, you are now met here to enjoy the fellowship of old soldiers and to receive the overflowings of a universal gratitude.

But your agitated countenances and your heaving breasts inform me that even this is not an unmixed joy. I perceive that a tumult of contending feelings rushes upon you. The images of the dead, as well as the persons of the living, present themselves before you. The scene overwhelms you, and I turn from it. May the Father of all mercies smile upon your declining years, and bless them! And when you shall here have exchanged your embraces, when you shall once more have pressed the hands which have been so often extended to give succor in adversity, or grasped in the exultation of victory, then look abroad upon this lovely land which your young valor defended, and mark the happiness with which it is filled; yea, look abroad upon the whole earth, and see what a name you have contributed to give to your country, and what a praise you have added to freedom, and then rejoice in the sympathy and gratitude which beam upon your last days from the improved condition of mankind!

The occasion does not require of me any particular account of the battle of the 17th of June, 1775, nor any detailed narrative of the events which immediately preceded it. These are familiarly known to all. In the progress of the great and interesting controversy, Massachusetts and the town of Boston had become early and marked objects of the displeasure of the British Parliament. This had been manifested in the act for altering the government of the Province, and in that for shutting up the port of Boston. Nothing sheds more honor on our early history, and nothing better shows how little the feelings and sentiments of the Colonies were known or regarded in England, than the impression which these measures everywhere produced in America. It had been anticipated, that while the Colonies in general would be terrified by the severity of the punishment inflicted on Massachusetts, the other seaports would be governed by a mere spirit of gain; and that, as Boston was now cut off from all commerce, the unexpected advantage which this blow on her was calculated to confer on other towns would be greedily enjoyed. How miserably such reasoners deceived themselves! How little they knew of the depth, and the strength, and the intenseness of that feeling of resistance to illegal acts of power, which possessed the whole American people! Everywhere the unworthy boon was rejected with scorn. The fortunate occasion was seized, everywhere, to show to the whole world that the Colonies were swayed by no local interest, no partial interest, no selfish interest. The temptation to profit by the punishment of Boston was strongest to our neighbors of Salem. Yet Salem was precisely the place where this miserable proffer was spurned, in a tone of the most lofty self-respect and the most indignant patriotism. "We are deeply affected." said its inhabitants, "with the sense of our public calamities; but the miseries that are now rapidly hastening on our brethren in the capital of the Province greatly excite our commiseration.

"By shutting up the port of Boston some imagine that the course of trade might be turned hither and to our benefit; but we must be dead to every idea of justice, lost to all feelings of humanity, could we indulge a thought to seize on wealth and raise our fortunes on the ruin of our suffering neighbors." These noble sentiments were not confined to our immediate vicinity. In that day of general affection and brotherhood, the blow given to Boston smote on every patriotic heart from one end of the country to the other. Virginia and the Carolinas, as well as Connecticut and New Hampshire, felt and proclaimed the cause to be their own. The Continental Congress, then holding its first session in Philadelphia, expressed its sympathy for the suffering inhabitants of Boston, and addresses were received from all quarters, assuring them that the cause was a common one, and should be met by common efforts and common sacrifices. The Congress of Massachusetts responded to these assurances; and in an address to the Congress at Philadelphia, bearing the official signature, perhaps among the last, of the immortal Warren, notwithstanding the severity of its suffering and the magnitude of the dangers which threatened it, it was declared, that this Colony "is ready at all times, to spend and to be spent in the cause of America."

But the hour drew nigh which was to put professions to the proof, and to determine whether the authors of these mutual pledges were ready to seal them in blood. The tidings of Lexington and Concord had no sooner spread, than it was universally felt that the time was at last come for action. A spirit pervaded all ranks, not transient, not boisterous, but deep, solemn, determined:

> *"Totamque infuse per artus*
> *Mens agitat molem, et magno*
> *Se corpore miscet."*

War on their own soil and at their own doors was, indeed, a strange work to the yeomanry of New England; but their consciences were convinced of its necessity, their country called them to it, and they did not withhold themselves from the perilous trial. The ordinary occupations of life were abandoned; the plough was stayed in the unfinished furrow; wives gave up their husbands, and mothers gave up their sons, to the battles of the civil war. Death might come in honor, on the field; it might come in disgrace, on the scaffold. For either and for both they were prepared. The sentiment of Quincy was full in their hearts. "Blandishments," said that distinguished son of genius and patriotism, "will not fascinate us nor will threats of a halter intimidate; for, under God, we are determined, that, wheresoever, whensoever, or howsoever, we shall be called to make our exit, we will die free men."

The seventeenth of June saw the four New England Colonies standing here, side by side, to triumph or to fall together; and there was with them from that moment to the end of the war, what I hope will remain with them for ever, one cause, one country, one heart.

The battle of Bunker Hill was attended with the most important effects beyond its immediate results as a military engagement. It created at once a state of open, public war. There could now be no longer a question of proceeding against individuals, as guilty of treason or rebellion. That fearful crisis was past. The appeal lay to the sword, and the only question was, whether the spirit and the resources of the people would hold out, till the object should be accomplished. Nor were its general consequences confined to our own country. The previous proceedings of the Colonies, their appeals, resolutions, and addresses, had made their cause known to Europe. Without boasting, we may say, that in no age or country has the public cause been maintained with more force of argument, more power of illustration, or more of that persuasion which excited feeling and elevated principle can alone bestow, than the Revolutionary state papers exhibit. These papers will for ever deserve to be studied, not only for the spirit which they breathe, but for the ability with which they were written.

To this able vindication of their cause, the Colonies had now added a practical and severe proof of their own true devotion to it, and given evidence also of the power which they could bring to its support. All now saw, that if America fell, she would not fall without a struggle. Men felt sympathy and regard, as well as surprise, when they beheld these infant states, remote, unknown, unaided, encounter the power of England, and, in the first considerable battle, leave more of their enemies dead on the field, in proportion to the number of combatants, than had been recently known to fall in the wars of Europe.

Information of these events, circulating throughout the world, at length reached the ears of one who now hears me. He has not forgotten the emotion which the fame of Bunker Hill, and the name of Warren, excited in his youthful breast.

Sir, we are assembled to commemorate the establishment of great public principles of liberty, and to do honor to the distinguished dead. The occasion is too severe for eulogy of the living. But, Sir, your interesting relation to this country, the peculiar circumstances which surround you and surround us, call on me to express the happiness which we derive from your presence and aid in this solemn commemoration.

Fortunate, fortunate man! with what measure of devotion will you not thank God for the circumstances of your extraordinary life! You are connected with both hemispheres and with two generations. Heaven saw fit to ordain that the electric spark of liberty should be conducted, through you, from the New World to the Old; and we, who are now here to perform this duty of patriotism, have all of us long ago received it in charge from our fathers to cherish your name and your virtues. You will account it an instance of your good fortune, Sir, that you crossed the seas to visit us at a time which enables you to be present at this solemnity. You now behold the field, the renown of which reached you in the heart of France, and caused a thrill in your ardent bosom. You see the lines of the little redoubt thrown up by the incredible diligence of Prescott; defended, to the last extremity by his lion-hearted valor; and with which the corner-stone of our monument has now taken its position You see where Warren fell, and where Parker, Gardner, McClary, Moore, and other early patriots fell with him. Those who survived that day, and whose lives have been prolonged to the present hour, are now around you. Some of them you have known in the trying scenes of the war. Behold! they now stretch forth their feeble arms to embrace you. Behold! they raise their trembling voices to invoke the blessing of God on you and yours for ever.

Sir, you have assisted us in laying the foundation of this structure. You have heard us rehearse with our feeble commendation, the names of departed patriots. Monuments and eulogy belong to the dead. We give them this day to Warren and his associates. On other occasions they have been given to your more immediate companions in arms, to Washington, to Greene, to Gates, to Sullivan, and to Lincoln. We have become reluctant to grant these, our highest and last honors, further. We would gladly hold them yet back from the little remnant of that immortal band.

"Serus in coelum redeas."

Illustrious as are your merits, yet far, O, very far distant be the day, when any inscription shall bear your name, or any tongue pronounce its eulogy!

The leading reflection to which this occasion seems to invite us, respects the great changes which have happened in the fifty years since the battle of Bunker Hill was fought. And it peculiarly marks the character of the present age, that, in looking at these changes, and in estimating their effect on our condition, we are obliged to consider, not what has been done in our country only, but in others also. In these interesting times, while nations are making separate and individual advances in improvement, they make, too, a common progress; like vessels on a common tide, propelled by the gales at different rates, according to their several structure and management, but all moved forward by one mighty current, strong enough to bear onward whatever does not sink beneath it.

A chief distinction of the present day is a community of opinions and knowledge amongst men in different nations, existing in a degree heretofore unknown. Knowledge has, in our time, triumphed, and is triumphing, over distance, over difference of language, over diversity of habits, over prejudice, and over bigotry. The civilized and Christian world is fast learning the great lesson, that difference of nation does not imply necessary hostility, and that all contact need not be war. The whole world is becoming a common field for intellect to act in. Energy of mind, genius, power, wheresoever it exists, may speak out in any tongue, and the world will hear it. A great chord of sentiment and feeling runs through two continents, and vibrates over both. Every breeze wafts intelligence from country to country; every wave rolls it; all give it forth, and all in turn receive it. There is a vast commerce of ideas; there are marts and exchanges for intellectual discoveries, and a wonderful fellowship of those individual intelligences which make up the mind and opinion of the age. Mind is the great lever of all things; human thought is the process by which human ends are ultimately answered; and the diffusion of knowledge, so astonishing in the last half-century, has rendered innumerable minds, variously gifted by nature, competent to be competitors or fellow-workers on the theater of intellectual operation.

From these causes important improvements have taken place in the personal condition of individuals. Generally speaking, mankind are not only better fed and better clothed, but they are able also to enjoy more leisure; they possess more refinement and more self-respect. A superior tone of education, manners, and habits prevails. This remark, most true in its application to our own country, is also partly true when applied elsewhere. It is proved by the vastly augmented consumption of those articles of manufacture and of commerce which contribute to the comforts and the decencies of life; an augmentation which has far outrun the progress of population. And while the unexampled and almost incredible use of machinery would seem to supply the place of labor, labor still finds its occupation and its reward; so wisely has Providence adjusted men's wants and desires to their condition and their capacity.

Any adequate survey, however, of the progress made during the last half-century in the polite and the mechanic arts, in machinery and manufactures, in commerce and agriculture, in letters and in science, would require volumes. I must abstain wholly from these subjects, and turn for a moment to the contemplation of what has been done on the great question of politics and government. This is the master topic of the age;

and during the whole fifty years it has intensely occupied the thoughts of men. The nature of civil government, its ends and uses, have been canvassed and investigated; ancient opinions attacked and defended; new ideas recommended and resisted, by whatever power the mind of man could bring to the controversy. From the closet and the public halls the debate has been transferred to the field; and the world has been shaken by wars of unexampled magnitude, and the greatest variety of fortune. A day of peace has at length succeeded; and now that the strife has subsided, and the smoke cleared away, we may begin to see what has actually been done, permanently changing the state and condition of human society. And, without dwelling on particular circumstances, it is most apparent, that, from the before-mentioned causes of augmented knowledge and improved individual condition, a real, substantial, and important change has taken place and is taking place, highly favorable, on the whole, to human liberty and human happiness.

The great wheel of political revolution began to move in America. Here its rotation was guarded, regular, and safe. Transferred to the other continent, from unfortunate but natural causes, it received an irregular and violent impulse; it whirled along with a fearful celerity; till at length, like the chariot wheels in the races of antiquity, it took fire from the rapidity of its own motion, and blazed onward, spreading conflagration and terror around.

We learn from the result of this experiment, how fortunate was our own condition; and how admirably the character of our people was calculated for setting the great example of popular governments. The possession of power did not turn the heads of the American people, for they had long been in the habit of exercising a great degree of self-control. Although the paramount authority of the parent state existed over them, yet a large field of legislation had always been open to our Colonial assemblies. They were accustomed to representative bodies and the forms of free government; they understood the doctrine of the division of power among different branches, and the necessity of checks on each. The character of our countrymen, moreover, was sober, moral, and religious; and there was little in the change to shock their feelings of justice and humanity, or even to disturb an honest prejudice. We had no domestic throne to overturn, no privileged orders to cast down, no violent changes of property to encounter. In the American Revolution, no man sought or wished for more than to defend and enjoy his own. None hoped for plunder or for spoil. Rapacity was unknown to it; the axe was not among the instruments of its accomplishment; and we all know that it could not have lived a single day under any well-founded imputation of possessing a tendency adverse to the Christian religion.

It need not surprise us, that, under circumstances less auspicious, political revolutions elsewhere, even when well intended, have terminated differently. It is, indeed, a great achievement, it is the master-work of the world, to establish governments entirely popular on lasting foundations; nor is it easy, indeed, to introduce the popular principle at all into governments to which it has been altogether a stranger. It cannot be doubted, however, that Europe has come out of the contest, in which she has been so long engaged, with greatly superior knowledge, and, in many respects, in a highly improved condition. Whatever benefit has been acquired is likely to be retained, for it consists mainly in the acquisition of more enlightened ideas. And although kingdoms and provinces may be wrested from the hands that hold them, in the same manner they were obtained; although ordinary and vulgar power may, in human affairs, be lost as it has been won; yet it is the glorious prerogative of the empire of knowledge, that what it gains it never loses. On the contrary, it increases by the multiple of its own power; all its ends become means; all its attainments, helps to new conquests. Its whole abundant harvest is but so much seed wheat, and nothing has limited, and nothing can limit, the amount of ultimate product.

Under the influence of this rapidly increasing knowledge, the people have begun, in all forms of government, to think, and to reason, on affairs of state. Regarding government as an institution for the public good, they demand a knowledge of its operations, and participation in its exercise. A call for the representative system, wherever it is not enjoyed, and where there is already intelligence enough to estimate its value, is perseveringly made. Where men may speak out, they demand it; where the bayonet is at their throats, they pray for it.

When Louis the Fourteenth said, "I am the state," he expressed the essence of the doctrine of unlimited power. By the rules of that system, the people are disconnected from the state; they are its subjects, it is their lord. These ideas, founded in the love of power, and long supported by the excess and the abuse of it, are yielding, in our age, to other opinions; and the civilized world seems at last to be proceeding to the conviction of that fundamental and manifest truth, that the powers of government are but a trust, and that they cannot be lawfully exercised but for the good of the community. As knowledge is more and more extended, this conviction becomes more and more general. Knowledge, in truth, is the great sun in the firmament. Life and power are scattered with all its beams. The prayer of the Grecian champion, when enveloped in unnatural clouds of darkness, is the appropriate political supplication for the people of every country not yet blessed with free institutions:

"Dispel this cloud, the light of heaven restore,
Give me to see—and Ajax asks no more."

We may hope that the growing influence of enlightened sentiment will promote the permanent peace of the world. Wars to maintain family alliances, to uphold or to cast down dynasties, and to regulate successions to thrones, which have occupied so much room in the history of modern times, if not less likely to happen at all, will be less likely to become general and involve many nations, as the great principle shall be more and more established, that the interest of the world is peace, and its first great statute, that every nation possesses the power of establishing a government for itself. But public opinion has attained also an influence over governments which do not admit the popular principle into their organization. A necessary respect for the judgment of the world operates, in some measure, as a control over the most unlimited forms of authority. It is owing, perhaps, to this truth, that the interesting struggle of the Greeks has been suffered to go on so long, without a direct interference, either to wrest that country from its present masters, or to execute the system of pacification by force, and, with united strength, lay the neck of Christian and civilized Greek at the foot of the barbarian Turk. Let us thank God that we live in an age when something has influence besides the bayonet, and when the sternest authority does not venture to encounter the scorching power of public reproach. Any attempt of the kind I have mentioned should be met by one universal burst of indignation; the air of the civilized world ought to be made too warm to be comfortably breathed by any one who would hazard it.

It is, indeed, a touching reflection, that, while in the fullness of our country's happiness, we rear this monument to her honor, we look for instruction in our undertaking to a country which is now in fearful contest, not for works of art or memorials of glory, but for her own existence. Let her be assured, that she is not forgotten in the world; that her efforts are applauded, and that constant prayers ascend for her success. And let us cherish a confident hope for her final triumph. If the true spark of religious and civil liberty be kindled, it will burn. Human agency cannot extinguish it. Like the earth's central fire, it may be smothered for a time; the ocean may overwhelm it; mountains may press it down; but its inherent and unconquerable force will heave both the ocean and the land, and at some time or other, in some place or other, the volcano will break out and flame up to heaven.

Among the great events of the half-century, we must reckon, certainly, the revolution of South America; and we are not likely to overrate the importance of that revolution, either to the people of the country itself or to the rest of the world. The late Spanish colonies, now independent states, under circumstances less favorable, doubtless, than attended our own revolution, have yet successfully commenced their national existence.

They have accomplished the great object of establishing their independence; they are known and acknowledged in the world; and although in regard to their systems of government, their sentiments on religious toleration, and their provision for public instruction, they may have yet much to learn, it must be admitted that they have risen to the condition of settled and established states more rapidly than could have been reasonably anticipated. They already furnish an exhilarating example of the difference between free governments and despotic misrule. Their commerce, at this moment, creates a new activity in all the great marts of the world. They show themselves able, by an exchange of commodities, to bear a useful part in the intercourse of nations.

A new spirit of enterprise and industry begins to prevail; all the great interests of society receive a salutary impulse; and the progress of information not only testifies to an improved condition, but itself constitutes the highest and most essential improvement.

When the battle of Bunker Hill was fought, the existence of South America was scarcely felt in the civilized world. The thirteen little colonies of North America habitually called themselves the "continent." Borne down by colonial subjugation, monopoly, and bigotry, these vast regions of the South were hardly visible above the horizon. But in our day, there has been, as it were, a new creation. The southern hemisphere emerges from the sea. Its lofty mountains begin to lift themselves into the light of heaven; its broad and fertile plains stretch out, in beauty, to the eye of civilized man, and at the mighty bidding of the voice of political liberty the waters of darkness retire.

And now, let us indulge an honest exultation in the conviction of the benefit which the example of our country has produced, and is likely to produce, on human freedom and human happiness. Let us endeavor to comprehend in all its magnitude, and to feel in all its importance, the part assigned to us in the great drama of human affairs. We are placed at the head of the system of representative and popular governments. Thus far our example shows that such governments are compatible, not only with respectability and power, but with repose, with peace, with security of personal rights, with good laws, and a just administration.

We are not propagandists. Wherever other systems are preferred, either as being thought better in themselves, or as better suited to existing conditions, we leave the preference to be enjoyed. Our history hitherto proves, however, that the popular form is practicable, that with wisdom and knowledge men may govern themselves; and the duty incumbent on us is to preserve the consistency of this cheering example, and take care that nothing may weaken its authority with the world. If, in our case, the representative system ultimately fail, popular governments must be pronounced impossible. No combination of circumstances more favorable to the experiment can ever be expected to occur. The last hopes of mankind, therefore, rest with us; and if it should be proclaimed, that our example had become an argument against the experiment, the knell of popular liberty would be sounded throughout the earth.

These are excitements to duty; but they are not suggestions of doubt. Our history and our condition, all that is gone before us, and all that surrounds us, authorize the belief, that popular governments, though subject to occasional variations, in form perhaps not always for the better, may yet, in their general character, be as durable and permanent as other systems. We know, indeed, that in our country any other is impossible. The principle of free governments adheres to the American soil. It is bedded in it, immovable as its mountains.

And let the sacred obligations which have developed on this generation, and on us, sink deep in our hearts. Those who established our liberty and our government are daily dropping from among us. The great trust now descends to new hands. Let us apply ourselves to that which is presented to us, as our appropriate object. We can win no laurels in a war for independence. Earlier and worthier hands have gathered them all. Nor are there places for us by the side of Solon, and Alfred, and other founders of states. Our fathers have filled them. But there remains to us a great duty of defense and preservation; and there is opened to us, also, a noble pursuit, to which the spirit of the times strongly invites us. Our proper business is improvement.

Let our age be the age of improvement. In a day of peace, let us advance the arts of peace and the works of peace. Let us develop the resources of our land, call forth its powers, build up its institutions, promote all its great interests, and see whether we also, in our day and generation, may not perform something worthy to be remembered. Let us cultivate a true spirit of union and harmony. In pursuing the great objects, which our condition points out to us, let us act under a settled conviction, and an habitual feeling, that these twenty-four States are one country. Let our conceptions be enlarged to the circle of our duties. Let us extend our ideas over the whole of the vast field in which we are called to act. Let our object be, *Our Country, Our Whole Country, And Nothing But Our Country.* And, by the blessing of God, may that country itself become a vast and splendid monument, not of oppression and terror, but of Wisdom, of Peace, and of Liberty, upon which the world may gaze with admiration for ever.

SIGNERS OF THE DECLARATION

The men who signed the Declaration of Independence and the Constitution risked their lives, their fortunes, and their sacred honor for a very risky proposition indeed. In so doing they established a precedent for a courageous defense of principle that has been a hallmark of American civilization ever since.

NEW HAMPSHIRE
Josiah Bartlett
William Whipple
Matthew Thornton

MASSACHUSETTS
Samuel Adams
John Adams
Robert Treat Pain
Elbridge Gerry
John Hancock

NEW YORK
William Floyd
Phillip Livingston
Francis Lewis
Lewis Morris

NORTH CAROLINA
William Hooper
Joseph Hewes
John Penn

SOUTH CAROLINA
Edward Rutledge
Thomas Heyward, Jr.
Thomas Lynch, Jr.
Arthur Middleton

NEW JERSEY
Richard Stockton
John Witherspoon
Francis Hopkinson
John Hart
Abraham Clark

RHODE ISLAND
Stephen Hopkins
William Ellery

DELAWARE
Caesar Rodney
George Read
Tho. McKean

MARYLAND
Samuel Chase
William Paca
Thomas Stone
Charles Carroll

CONNECTICUT
Roger Sherman
Samuel Huntington
William Williams
Oliver Wolcott

GEORGIA
Button Gwinnett
Lyman Hall
George Walton

PENNSYLVANIA
Robert Morris
Benjamin Rush
Benjamin Franklin
John Morton
George Clymer
Jas. Smith
George Taylor
James Wilson
George Ross

VIRGINIA
George Wythe
Richard Henry Lee
Thomas Jefferson
Benjamin Harrison
Thomas Nelson, Jr.
Francis Lightfoot Lee
Carter Braxton

SIGNERS OF THE CONSTITUTION

Though their meetings were not authorized, their sessions were held in secret, and their determinations were contrary to popular opinion, the constitutional framers eventually won over their skeptical peers. And the lasting import of their work has gained them great historical significance.

NEW HAMPSHIRE
Nicholas Gilman
John Langdon

MASSACHUSETTS
Nathaniel Gorham
Rufus King

CONNECTICUT
William Samuel Johnson
Roger Sherman

NEW YORK
Alexander Hamilton

NEW JERSEY
William Livinston
David Brearley
William Paterson
Jonathan Dayton

PENNSYLVANIA
Benjamin Franklin
Thomas Mifflin
Robert Morris
George Clymer
Thomas Fitzsimons
Jared Ingersoll
James Wilson
Gouverneur Morris

DELAWARE
George Reed
Gunning Bedford, Jr.
John Dickinson
Richard Bassett
Jacob Broom

MARYLAND
James McHenry
Daniel St. Thomas Jenifer
Daniel Carrol

VIRGINIA
John Blair
James Madison, Jr.

NORTH CAROLINA
William Blount
Richard Dobbs Spaight
Hugh Williamson

SOUTH CAROLINA
John Rutledge
Charles Cotesworth Pinckney
Charles Pinckney
Pierce Butler

GEORGIA
William Few
Abraham Baldwin

THE FORGOTTEN PRESIDENTS

Who was the first president of the United States? Ask any schoolchild and they will readily tell you "George Washington." And of course they would be wrong— at least technically. Washington was not inaugurated until April 30, 1789. And yet the United States continually had functioning governments from as early as September 5, 1774, and operated as a confederated nation from as early as July 4, 1776. During that nearly fifteen-year interval, Congress—first the Continental Congress and then the Confederation Congress—was always moderated by a duly elected president. As the chief executive officer of the government of the United States, the president was recognized as the head of state. Washington was thus the fifteenth in a long line of distinguished presidents; he just happened to be the first under the current constitution. So who were the luminaries who preceded him? The following brief biographies profile these "forgotten presidents."

PEYTON RANDOLPH OF VIRGINIA (1723-1775)

When delegates gathered in Philadelphia for the first Continental Congress, they promptly elected the former King's Attorney of Virginia as the moderator and president of their convocation. He was a propitious choice—a legal prodigy who studied at the Inner Temple in London, served as his native colony's Attorney General, and tutored many of the most able men of the South at William and Mary College, including the young Patrick Henry. His home in Williamsburg was the gathering place for Virginia's legal and political gentry, and it remains a popular attraction in the restored colonial capital. He had served as a delegate in the Virginia House of Burgesses, and had been a commander under William Byrd in the colonial militia. He was a scholar of some renown—having begun a self-guided reading of the classics when he was thirteen. Despite suffering poor health, he twice served as president in the Continental Congress, in 1774 from September 5 to October 21, and then again for a few days in 1775 from May 10 to May 23. He never lived to see independence, yet was numbered among the nation's most revered founders.

HENRY MIDDLETON (1717-1784)

America's second elected president was one of the wealthiest planters in the South and the patriarch of one of the most powerful families anywhere in the nation. His public spirit was evident from an early age. He was a member of his state's Common House from 1744-1747; during the last two years he served as the speaker. During 1755 he was the King's Commissioner of Indian Affairs. He was a member of the South Carolina

Council from 1755-1770, and his valor in the war with the Cherokees during 1760-1761 demonstrated his cool leadership abilities while under pressure and earned him wide recognition throughout the colonies. He was elected as a delegate to the first session of the Continental Congress, and when Peyton Randolph was forced to resign the presidency, his peers immediately turned to Middleton to complete the term. He served as the fledgling coalition's president from October 22, 1774, until Randolph was able to briefly resume his duties on May 10, 1775. Afterward he was a member of the Congressional Council of Safety and helped to establish the young nation's policy toward the encouragement and support of education. In February 1776 he resigned his political involvements in order to prepare his family and lands for what he believed was inevitable war. He was replaced by his son Arthur, who eventually became a signer of both the Declaration of Independence and the Articles of Confederation, served time as an English prisoner of war, and was twice elected Governor of his state.

JOHN HANCOCK (1737-1793)

The third president was a patriot, rebel leader, and merchant who with giant strokes signed his name into immortality on the Declaration of Independence. The boldness of his signature has lived in American minds as a perfect expression of the strength and freedom—and defiance—of the individual in the face of British tyranny. As president of the Continental Congress during two widely spaced terms—the first from May 24, 1775, to October 30, 1777, and the second from November 23, 1785, to June 5, 1786—Hancock was the presiding officer when members approved the Declaration of Independence. Because of his position, it was his official duty to sign the document first (but not necessarily as dramatically as he did). Hancock figured prominently in another historic event—the battle at Lexington. British troops who fought there on April 10, 1775, had known Hancock and Samuel Adams were in Lexington and had come there to capture these rebel leaders. The two would have been captured if they had not been warned by Paul Revere. As early as 1768 Hancock defied the British by refusing to pay customs charges on the cargo of one of his ships. One of Boston's wealthiest merchants, he was recognized by the citizens as well as the British as a rebel leader and was elected president of the first Massachusetts provincial congress. After he was chosen president of the Continental Congress in 1775, Hancock became known beyond the borders of Massachusetts. Having served as colonel of the Massachusetts Governor's Guards, he hoped to be named commander of the American forces—until John Adams nominated George Washington. In 1778 Hancock was commissioned major general and took part in an unsuccessful campaign in Rhode Island. But it was as a political leader that his real distinction was earned, as the first governor of Massachusetts, as president of Congress, and as president of the Massachusetts constitutional ratification convention. He helped win ratification in Massachusetts, gaining enough popular recognition to make him a contender for the newly created presidency of the United States, but again he saw Washington gain the prize. Like his rival, George Washington, Hancock was a wealthy man who risked much for the cause of independence. Indeed, he was the wealthiest New Englander supporting the patriotic cause, and although he lacked the brilliance of John Adams or Samuel Adams' capacity to inspire, he became one of the foremost leaders of the new nation, perhaps in part because he was willing to commit so much, and at such risk, to the cause of freedom.

HENRY LAURENS (1724-1792)

The only American president ever to be held as a prisoner of war by a foreign power, after he was released Laurens was heralded as "the father of our country" by no less a personage than George Washington. He was of Huguenot extraction, his ancestors having come to America from France after the revocation of the Edict of Nantes made the Reformed faith illegal. Raised and educated for a life of mercantilism at his home in Charleston, he also had the opportunity to spend more than a year in continental travel. It was while in Europe that he began to write revolutionary pamphlets, gaining him renown as a patriot. He served as vice president of South Carolina in 1776. He was then elected to the Continental Congress. He succeeded John Hancock as president of the newly independent but war-beleaguered United States on November 1, 1777 and served until December 9, 1778, at which time he was appointed Ambassador to the Netherlands. Unfortunately for the cause of the young nation, he was captured by an English warship during his cross-Atlantic voyage and was confined to the Tower of London until the end of the war. After the Battle of Yorktown, the American government regained his freedom in a dramatic prisoner exchange— Laurens for Lord Cornwallis. Ever the patriot, Laurens continued to serve his nation as one of the three representatives selected to negotiate terms at the Paris peace conference in 1782.

JOHN JAY (1745-1829)

America's first secretary of state, first chief justice of the Supreme Court, one of its first ambassadors, and author of some of the celebrated Federalist Papers, Jay was a Founding Father who, by a quirk of fate, missed signing the Declaration of Independence—at the time of the vote for independence and the signing, he had temporarily left the Continental

Congress to serve in New York's revolutionary legislature. Nevertheless, he was chosen by his peers to succeed Henry Laurens as president of the United States—serving a term from December 10, 1778, to September 27, 1779. A conservative New York lawyer who was at first against the idea of independence for the colonies, the aristocratic Jay in 1776 became a patriot who was willing to give the next twenty-five years of his life to help establish the new nation. During those years he won the regard of his peers as a dedicated and accomplished statesman and a man of unwavering principle. In the Continental Congress Jay prepared addresses to the people of Canada and Great Britain. In New York he drafted the state constitution and served as chief justice during the war. He was president of the Continental Congress before he undertook the difficult assignment, as ambassador, of trying to gain support and funds from Spain. After helping Franklin, Jefferson, Adams, and Laurens complete peace negotiations in Paris in 1783, Jay returned to become the first secretary of state, then called the "Secretary of Foreign Affairs" under the Articles of Confederation. He negotiated valuable commercial treaties with Russia and Morocco and dealt with the continuing controversy with Britain and Spain over the southern and western boundaries of the United States; he proposed that America and Britain establish a joint commission to arbitrate disputes that remained after the war—a proposal which, though not adopted, influenced the government's use of arbitration and diplomacy in settling later international problems. In this post Jay felt keenly the weakness of the Articles of Confederation and was one of the first to advocate a new governmental compact. He wrote five Federalist Papers supporting the Constitution, and he was a leader in the New York ratification convention. As first chief justice of the Supreme Court, Jay made the historic decision that a state could be sued by a citizen from another state, which led to the Eleventh Amendment to the Constitution. On a special mission to London he concluded the "Jay Treaty," helping avert a renewal of hostilities with Britain but winning little popular favor at home. It is probably for this treaty that this Founding Father is best remembered.

SAMUEL HUNTINGTON (1732-1796)

An industrious youth who mastered his studies of the law without the advantage of a school, a tutor, or a master, borrowing books and snatching opportunities to read and research between odd jobs, he was one of the greatest self-made men among the Founders. He was also one of the greatest legal minds of the age—all the more remarkable for his lack of advantage as a youth. In 1764, in recognition of his obvious abilities and initiative, he was elected to the general assembly of Connecticut. The next year he was chosen to serve on the Executive Council. In 1774 he was appointed associate judge of the Superior Court and as a delegate to the Continental Congress was acknowledged to be a legal scholar of some respect. He served in Congress for five consecutive terms, during the last of which he was elected president, serving in that office from September 28, 1779, until ill health forced him to resign on July 9, 1781. He returned to his home in Connecticut, and as he recuperated, he accepted more counciliar and bench duties. He again took his seat in Congress in 1783, but left it to become chief justice of his state's superior court. He was elected lieutenant governor in 1785 and governor in 1786. According to John Jay, he was "the most precisely trained Christian jurist ever to serve his country."

THOMAS MCKEAN (1734-1817)

During his astonishingly varied fifty-year career in public life he held almost every possible position, from deputy county attorney to president of the United States under the Confederation. Besides signing the Declaration of Independence, he contributed significantly to the development and establishment of constitutional government in both his home state of Delaware and the nation. At the Stamp Act Congress he proposed the voting procedure that Congress adopted: Each colony, regardless of size or population, had one vote—the practice adopted by the Continental Congress and the Congress of the Confederation and the principle of state equality manifest in the composition of the Senate. And as county judge in 1765, he defied the British by ordering his court to work only with documents that did not bear the hated stamps. In June 1776, at the Continental Congress, McKean joined with Caesar Rodney to register Delaware's approval (over the negative vote of the third Delaware delegate, George Read) of the Declaration of Independence, permitting it to be "the unanimous declaration of the thirteen United States." At a special Delaware convention he drafted the constitution for that state. McKean also helped draft—and signed—the Articles of Confederation. It was during his tenure of service as president—from July 10, 1781, to November 4, 1782—that news arrived from General Washington in October 1781 that the British had surrendered following the Battle of Yorktown. As chief justice of the supreme court of Pennsylvania, he contributed to the establishment of the legal system in that state, and, in 1787 he strongly supported the Constitution at the Pennsylvania ratification convention, declaring it "the best the world has yet seen." At sixty-five, after over forty years of public service, McKean resigned from his post as chief justice. A candidate on the Democratic-Republican ticket in 1799, McKean was elected governor of Pennsylvania and followed such a strict policy of appointing only fellow Republicans to office that he became the father of the spoils system in

America. He served three tempestuous terms as governor, completing one of the longest continuous careers of public service of any of the Founding Fathers.

JOHN HANSON (1715-1783)

He was the heir of one of the greatest family traditions in the colonies and became the patriarch of a long line of American patriots. His great grandfather died at Lutzen beside the great King Gustavus Aldophus of Sweden; his grandfather was one of the founders of New Sweden along the Delaware River in Maryland. One of his nephews was the military secretary to George Washington. Another was a signer of the Declaration; one was a signer of the Constitution; and one was governor of Maryland during the Revolution; and still another was a member of the first Congress. Two of his sons were killed in action with the Continental Army, a grandson served as a member of Congress under the new Constitution, and another grandson was a Maryland senator. Thus, even if Hanson had not served as president himself, he would have greatly contributed to the life of the nation through his ancestry and progeny. As a youngster he began a self-guided reading of classics and rather quickly became an acknowledged expert in the jurisprudence of Anselm and the practical philosophy of Seneca—both of whom influenced the political philosophy of the great leaders of the Reformation. It was based upon these legal and theological studies that the young planter (his farm, Mulberry Grove, was just across the Potomac from Mount Vernon) began to espouse the cause of the patriots. In 1775 he was elected to the provincial legislature of Maryland. In 1777 he became a member of Congress, where he distinguished himself as a brilliant administrator. He was elected president in 1781, where he served from November 5, 1781, until November 3, 1782. He was the first president to serve a full term after the full ratification of the Articles of Confederation, and like so many of the southern and New England Founders, he was strongly opposed to the Constitution when it was first discussed. He remained a confirmed anti-Federalist until his untimely death.

ELIAS BOUDINOT (1741-1802)

He did not sign the Declaration, the Articles, or the Constitution. He did not serve in the Continental Army with distinction. He was not renowned for his legal mind or his political skills. He was instead a man who spent his entire career in foreign diplomacy. He earned the respect of his fellow patriots during the dangerous days following the traitorous action of Benedict Arnold. His deft handling of relations with Canada also earned him great praise. After being elected to Congress from his home state of

New Jersey, he served as the new nation's Secretary for Foreign Affairs—managing the influx of aid from France, Spain, and Holland. In 1782 he was elected to the presidency and served in that office from November 4, 1782, until November 2, 1783. Like so many of the other early presidents, he was a classically trained scholar, a practitioner of the Reformed faith, and an anti-Federalist in political matters. He was the father and grandfather of frontiersmen; one of his grandchildren and namesakes eventually became a leader of the Cherokee nation in its bid for independence from the sprawling expansion of the United States.

THOMAS MIFFLIN (1744-1800)

By an ironic sort of providence, Thomas Mifflin served as George Washington's first aide-de-camp at the beginning of the Revolutionary War, and when the war was over, he was the man, as president of the United States, who accepted Washington's resignation of his commission. In the years between Mifflin greatly served the cause of freedom—and apparently his own cause—while serving as the first quartermaster general of the Continental Army. He obtained desperately needed supplies for the new army and was suspected of making excessive profit himself. Although experienced in business and successful in obtaining supplies for the war, Mifflin preferred the front lines, and he distinguished himself in military actions on Long Island and near Philadelphia. Born and reared a Quaker, he was excluded from their meetings for his military activities. He was a controversial figure who lost favor with Washington and was part of the Conway Cabal, a rather notorious plan to replace Washington with General Horatio Gates. Mifflin narrowly missed court-martialing over his handling of funds by resigning his commission in 1778. In spite of these problems (and repeated charges that he was a drunkard) Mifflin continued to be elected to positions of responsibility—as president and governor of Pennsylvania and delegate to the Constitutional Convention, and in the highest office in the land, where he served from November 3, 1783, to November 29, 1784. Most of Mifflin's significant contributions occurred in his earlier years; in the First and Second Continental Congresses he was firm in his stand for independence and for fighting for it, and he helped obtain both men and supplies for Washington's army in the early critical period. In 1784, as president, he signed the treaty with Great Britain that ended the war. Although a delegate to the Constitutional Convention, he did not make a significant contribution beyond signing the document. As governor of Pennsylvania, although he was accused of negligence, he supported improvements of roads and reformed the state penal and judicial systems. Despite the fact that he had gradually become sympathetic to Jefferson's principles regarding state's rights, he directed the Pennsylvania militia to support the federal tax collectors in the Whiskey Rebellion. In spite of charges of corruption, the affable Mifflin remained a popular figure. His magnetic personality and effective speaking ability led him to hold a variety of elective offices for almost thirty years of the critical Revolutionary period.

RICHARD HENRY LEE (1732-1794)

Approved by the Continental Congress on July 2, 1776, Lee's resolution "that these United Colonies are, and of right ought to be, free and independent States," was the first official act of the United Colonies that set them irrevocably on the road to independence. It was not surprising that it came from Lee's pen; as early as 1768 he proposed the idea of committees of correspondence among the colonies, and in 1774 he proposed that the colonies meet in what became the Continental Congress. From the first his eye was on independence. A wealthy Virginia planter whose ancestors had been granted extensive lands by King Charles II, Lee disdained the traditional aristocratic role and view. In the House of Burgesses he flatly denounced the practice of slavery. He saw independent America as "an asylum where the unhappy may find solace, and the persecuted repose." In 1764, when news of the proposed Stamp Act reached Virginia, Lee was a member of the committee of the House of Burgesses that drew up an address to the King—an official protest against such a tax. After the tax was established, Lee organized the citizens of his county into the Westmoreland Association, a group pledged to buy no British goods until the Stamp Act was repealed. At the First Continental Congress, Lee persuaded representatives from all the colonies to adopt his nonimportation idea, leading to the formation of the Continental Association, which was one of the first steps toward union of the colonies. Lee also proposed to the First Continental Congress that a militia be organized and armed—the year before the first shots were fired at Lexington—but this and other proposals of his were considered too radical at the time. Three days after Lee introduced his resolution in June of 1776, he was appointed by Congress to the committee responsible for drafting a declaration of independence, but he was called home when his wife fell ill, and his place was taken by his young protégé, Thomas Jefferson. Thus Lee missed the chance to draft the document, though his influence greatly shaped it and he was able to return in time to sign it. He was elected president, serving from November 30, 1784, to November 22, 1785, when he was succeeded by the second administration of John Hancock. Elected to the Constitutional Convention, Lee refused to attend, but as a member of the Congress of the Confederation, he contributed to another great document, the Northwest Ordinance, which provided for the formation of new states from the

Northwest Territory. When the completed Constitution was sent to the states for ratification, Lee opposed it as antidemocratic and anti-Christian. However, as one of Virginia's first senators, he helped assure passage of the Bill of Rights amendments that he felt corrected many of the document's gravest faults. He was the great uncle of Robert E. Lee and the scion of a great family tradition.

NATHANIEL GORHAM (1738-1796)

Another self-made man, Gorham was one of the many successful Boston merchants who risked all he had for the cause of freedom. He was first elected to the Massachusetts general court in 1771, where his honesty and integrity won him acclaim. He was thus among the first delegates chosen to serve in the Continental Congress. He remained in public service throughout the war and into the Constitutional period, though his greatest contribution was his call for a stronger central government. But even though he was an avid Federalist, he did not believe that the union could—or even should—be maintained peaceably for more than a hundred years. He was convinced that eventually, in order to avoid civil or cultural war, smaller regional interests should pursue an independent course. His support of a new constitution was rooted more in pragmatism than ideology. When John Hancock was unable to complete his second term as president, Gorham was elected to succeed him, serving from June 6, 1786, to February 1, 1787. It was during this time that the Congress actually entertained the idea of asking Prince Henry (the brother of Frederick II of Prussia) and Bonnie Prince Charlie (the leader of the ill-fated Scottish Jacobite Rising and heir of the Stuart royal line) to consider the possibility of establishing a constitutional monarchy in America. It was a plan that had much to recommend it, but eventually the advocates of republicanism held the day. During the final years of his life, Gorham was concerned with several speculative land deals that nearly cost him his entire fortune.

ARTHUR ST. CLAIR (1734-1818)

Born and educated in Edinburgh, Scotland, during the tumultuous days of the final Jacobite Rising and the Tartan Suppression, St. Clair was the only president of the United States born and bred on foreign soil. Though most of his family and friends abandoned their devastated homeland in the years following the Battle of Culloden—after which nearly a third of the land was depopulated through emigration to America—he stayed behind to learn the ways of the hated Hanoverian English in the Royal Navy. His plan was to study the enemy's military might in order to fight another day. During the global conflict of the Seven Years War, generally known as the

French and Indian War, he was stationed in the American theater. Afterward he decided to settle in Pennsylvania, where many of his kin had established themselves. His civic-mindedness quickly became apparent: He helped to organize both the New Jersey and the Pennsylvania militias, led the Continental Army's Canadian expedition, and was elected to Congress; his long years of training in the enemy camp were finally paying off. He was elected president in 1787, and he served from February 2 of that year until January 21 of the next. Following his term of duty in the highest office in the land, he became the first governor of the Northwest Territory and the founder of Cincinnati. Though he briefly supported the idea of creating a constitutional monarchy under the Stuarts' Bonnie Prince Charlie, he was a strident anti-Federalist, believing that the proposed federal constitution would eventually allow for the intrusion of government into virtually every sphere and aspect of life. He even predicted that under the vastly expanded centralized power of the state, the taxing powers of bureaucrats and other unelected officials would eventually confiscate as much as a quarter of the income of the citizens— a notion that seemed laughable at the time but that has proven to be ominously modest in light of our current governmental leviathan. St. Clair lived to see the hated English tyrants who destroyed his homeland defeated. But he despaired that his adopted home might actually create and impose similar tyrannies upon themselves.

CYRUS GRIFFIN (1736-1796)

Like Peyton Randolph, he was trained in London's Inner Temple to be a lawyer, and thus was counted among his nation's legal elite. Like so many other Virginians, he was an anti-Federalist, though he eventually accepted the new Constitution with the promise of the Bill of Rights as a hedge against the establishment of an American monarchy, which remained a danger in the minds of many. The Articles of Confederation afforded such freedoms. He had become convinced that even with the incumbent loss of liberty, some new form of government would be required. A protégé of George Washington, having worked with him on several speculative land deals in the West, he was a reluctant supporter of the Constitutional ratifying process. It was during his term in the office of the presidency—the last before the new national compact went into effect—that ratification was formalized and finalized. He served as the nation's chief executive from January 22, 1788, until George Washington's inauguration on April 30, 1789.

THE FOUNDING FATHERS

The Founding Era was replete with great men. At perhaps no other time in history have so many dynamic, gifted, and courageous leaders been active in public affairs at one time. The lives and careers of these men of valor ought to serve as incentive and inspiration to preserve that which they created.

SAMUEL ADAMS (1722-1803)

A political activist and patriot without peer, Adams was one of the leading architects of the American Revolution. With remarkable singleness of purpose, this cousin of John Adams devoted himself to the cause of independence, largely neglecting his own interests. In articles and speeches he denounced British tyranny, and he led his patriotic followers to such political acts as the Boston Tea Party. The first to question the British right to tax the colonies, he dared to be identified as a rebel leader. It was he, along with John Hancock, that British troops were after when they came to Lexington on April 19, 1775. In 1765 Adams openly encouraged citizens to defy the Stamp Act, and he was the prime mover behind the meeting of all the colonies at the Stamp Act Congress in New York. Adams worked against the British as a member of the Massachusetts legislature in the powerful position of clerk, as well as less openly as founder of the Massachusetts committee of correspondence and a leader of the secret society, Sons of Liberty. This patriotic—and radical—group resorted to violence and demonstrations on several occasions, storming the governor's home and hanging the British tax collector in effigy. On March 5, 1770, a group of colonists threatened British soldiers in Boston, precipitating an incident in which three colonists were killed. Adams and Joseph Warren called it the "Boston Massacre," and news of the "massacre" helped promote anti-British feeling. Adams helped create another incident in December 1773 when the Sons of Liberty, encouraged by Adams, boarded British ships and dumped hundreds of chests of tea overboard to protest the tax on tea. Adams had a genius for daring acts that would strike political flint. He attended the First Continental Congress in 1774, and on April 18, 1775, he was with Hancock in Lexington, about to go to the Second Congress, when Paul Revere arrived with news that British troops were after them. They rode off early the next day before the troops arrived and those first shots were fired. Although he remained active in politics to the end of his life—even serving as the governor of his state—signing the Declaration of Independence was the apex of his career. In his search for freedom and independence Adams was ever impatient, but thanks to his abiding Christian faith, he had the will and the ability to shape events that helped make independence in America a reality in his own time.

CHARLES CARROLL (1737-1832)

One of the largest landholders in America, Charles Carroll was a leader of the Catholic community in Maryland and the only Catholic to sign the Declaration of Independence. Like Washington and Hancock, he risked a great fortune by defying the mother country. After years of study in Europe, Carroll returned to a country indignant over new British taxation, especially the Stamp Act. Although as a Catholic he was unable to hold office, he became a leader of the opposition—partly through newspaper articles he wrote under a pen name. He was a member of the colony's committee of observation, a group directing activities of patriots. He was also a member of both the provincial committee of correspondence and Maryland's unofficial legislature. He actively supported the policy of nonimportation of British goods. In 1776 Congress appointed Carroll, his cousin John, Samuel Chase, and Benjamin Franklin as commissioners to Canada, trying to bring Canada into the struggle on the side of the colonies. However, American troops had already invaded Canada, turning the French Canadians against the American cause, and the mission failed. Carroll returned from Canada in June 1776 in time to take a firm stand for independence in the Maryland legislature, and after helping win the legislature's approval, he was selected as a delegate to the Continental Congress, where he signed the Declaration of Independence. For the next twenty-five years, Carroll played a prominent part in both state and national affairs. In Congress during the war he served with the board of war and other important committees. He was a champion of freedom of religion and contributed to the Maryland constitution. Though he declined to attend the Constitutional Convention, he supported the new national Constitution. As one of Maryland's senators in the first Congress under that new form of government, he was instrumental in bringing Rhode Island, which had not yet ratified the Constitution, into the Union, and he assisted in drafting the amendments to the Constitution known as the Bill of Rights, finally assuring the freedom of worship and other freedoms for which he had risked so much. When Carroll died in 1832 he was reputed to be the wealthiest man in America—and the last surviving signer of the Declaration of Independence.

SAMUEL CHASE (1741-1811)

Like Samuel Adams and Patrick Henry, Chase was a firebrand political activist. His daring speeches against British tyranny stirred fellow Marylanders, as well as members of the Continental Congress, to support the cause of independence. Of powerful build and persuasive manner, Chase won a position of leadership in the Maryland colonial legislature while in his twenties. He vigorously opposed the Stamp Act and helped establish the patriotic committee of correspondence in Maryland. At the Continental Congress he was one of the first to speak out for independence. Early in 1776 he went to Canada, along with Benjamin Franklin, and John and Charles Carroll, as a congressional commissioner. They tried to persuade the French Canadians to join in fighting the British, but the mission was unsuccessful. Chase returned to Philadelphia in time to learn of Richard Lee's resolution on independence, introduced on June 7, but at that time the Maryland delegates were not authorized to vote for independence. Chase left Philadelphia and made a special trip through Maryland to win the people's support, and before the end of June the Maryland Convention voted for independence, authorizing its delegates in Philadelphia to sign the Declaration of Independence. After the war Chase was against the idea of a national government and refused to attend the Constitutional Convention, but by 1790 he was identified with the Federalist party, and President Washington appointed him to the Supreme Court. As an associate justice, Chase became known for his positive, often impressive opinions, some of which provided an enduring base for the new judicial system. But he was on occasion too much the loyal Federalist: He strongly supported the sedition laws passed during the Adams administration, which prohibited political opposition to the government and which Jefferson and his fellow Democratic-Republicans saw as an abridgment of the First Amendment. In 1804, after Chase had uttered some exceedingly intemperate remarks, the House of Representatives initiated impeachment action, but the Senate did not find him guilty. He remained in office, although he was in later years overshadowed by the new chief justice, John Marshall. But he had already made a substantial contribution to the judicial system—and gained the dubious distinction of being the only Founding Father to undergo impeachment proceedings.

GEORGE CLYMER (1739-1813)

The heir of a substantial Philadelphia business and banking fortune, Clymer risked everything to become a leader of the patriots early in the conflict with the King, served in public office for over twenty years, and signed both the Declaration of Independence and the Constitution. A man of unusual intellectual curiosity, he also served as an officer of the Philadelphia Academy of Fine Arts and the Philadelphia Agricultural Society. One of the first members of Pennsylvania's committee of safety, and one of the first to advocate complete independence from Britain, Clymer was called upon by the Continental Congress to serve as the first treasurer for the United Colonies. He undertook the almost impossible assignment of raising money to support the government's operations, chief of which was the new Continental Army. And Clymer devoted not only his great energy but also his own fortune to the cause, exchanging all his money (which was in hard coin) for the shaky continental currency. In late 1776, when Congress fled a threatened Philadelphia, Clymer was one of the committee of three left behind to maintain essential government activities. During this crisis Clymer drove himself almost to a state of exhaustion. Shortly after this ordeal, the British captured Philadelphia and plundered and destroyed his home. In Congress Clymer performed valuable services as a member of committees dealing with financial matters; during the final years of the war, he was again responsible for obtaining funds for the Army. At the Constitutional Convention Clymer, who was not an exceptional speaker, again distinguished himself with his work in committees dealing with his specialty—finance. In 1791, after a term in the first Congress, Clymer served as federal collector of the controversial tax on liquor that led to the Whiskey Rebellion. He concluded his career by negotiating an equitable peace treaty between the United States and the Creek tribe in Georgia. Clymer served the cause from the beginnings of the movement for independence, although he never sought a public office in his life.

JOHN DICKINSON (1732-1808)

Widely known as the "Penman of the Revolution," Dickinson, wrote many of the most influential documents of the period—from the Declaration of Rights in 1765 and the Articles of Confederation in 1776 to the Fabius Letter in 1787 that helped win over Delaware and Pennsylvania, the first States to ratify the Constitution. Having studied law in England, Dickinson was devoted to the English common law system, and his writings before 1776 aimed to correct the misuse of power and preserve the union of the colonies and Britain. His most famous writings were "Letters from a Farmer in Pennsylvania," which condemned the Townshend Acts and were widely read throughout the colonies; "Petition to the King," which was a statement of grievances and an appeal for justice with a pledge of loyalty adopted by Congress, and "Declaration on the Causes and Necessity of Taking up Arms." This last document—which Congress also adopted, defended the colonies' use of arms for "the preservation of our liberties" and stated that the colonists were simply fighting to regain the liberty that was theirs as Englishmen. In the Continental Congress Dickinson first opposed the idea of declaring independence, but once it was done, he supported the cause and prepared a draft of the Articles of Confederation. Although over forty, Dickinson enlisted in the militia and saw action in New Jersey and Pennsylvania. He returned to Congress in 1779 in time to sign the Articles of Confederation. Because Delaware and Pennsylvania were under a single proprietor, a citizen could hold office in either one, and Dickinson served as president first of Delaware and then Pennsylvania. He played the important role of conciliator at the Constitutional Convention; he saw the need for a stable national government, and he joined Roger Sherman of Connecticut in supporting the idea of two legislative bodies, one with proportional and one with equal representation–the Great Compromise that broke the deadlock between the larger and smaller States. After the Constitution was sent to the states, Dickinson published a series of letters that explained and defended the Constitution and that helped win the first ratifications. The Penman had done his work well: Jefferson called him "one of the great worthies of the Revolution."

Benjamin Franklin (1706-1790)

Patriot, inventor, scientist, philosopher, musician, editor, printer, and diplomat, Benjamin Franklin brought the prestige of his unparalleled achievements to the public service that consumed over half of his life. He was a living example of the richness of life that man can achieve with the freedom—and the will—to do so. In many senses he was the first American, and he was a Founding Father of the first rank. His rise from apprentice to man of affairs was paralleled by an ever-widening circle of interests. His curiosity led him from subject to subject: He mastered printing, learned French, invented a stove, discovered electrical principles, organized a postal service, and helped discover the Gulf Stream. Though a free-thinker—an oddity among his overwhelmingly devout Christian peers—he was the close friend and publisher of George Whitefield, the great evangelist. As his country's representative in England in the 1760s, he defended America's position before hostile, arrogant officials; he helped win repeal of the Stamp Act and pleaded for American representation in Parliament. In the 1770s he continued trying to reason with British officials, but they were inflexible, and he returned to America ready to support the cause of independence. In the Continental Congress Franklin headed the committee that organized the American postal system, helped draft the Articles of Confederation, and began negotiations with the French for aid. He also helped draft and signed the Declaration of Independence. Franklin was the colonies' best choice as commissioner to France; well known as a scientist and philosopher, he was warmly welcomed in Paris, and his position as a world figure, coupled with his diplomatic skill, helped him negotiate the 1778 alliance with France that brought America desperately needed military support. Soon after, he began negotiating with the British for peace, but only after the French fleet had joined with Washington to defeat Cornwallis at Yorktown would the British consider granting independence. Franklin signed the peace treaty September 3, 1783. After he returned to America, Franklin had one more vital role to play: At the Constitutional Convention his very presence gave weight and authority to the proceedings, and he used his influence to moderate conflicts. On the final day he appealed to the delegates: "I confess that there are several parts of this Constitution which I do not at present approve, but I am not sure I shall never approve them. For having lived long, I have experienced many instances of being obliged by better information, or fuller consideration, to change opinions even on important subjects, which I once thought right, but found to be otherwise. I cannot help expressing a wish that every member of the Convention who may still have objections to it, would with me, on this occasion, doubt a little of his own infallibility, and to make manifest our unanimity, put his name on this instrument." A few minutes later all but three delegates signed the Constitution.

ELBRIDGE GERRY (1744-1814)

A patriot who signed the Declaration of Independence and the Articles of Confederation but refused to sign the Constitution, Elbridge Gerry worked vigorously for independence from the "prostituted government of Great Britain" yet feared the dangers of "too much democracy." At the Constitutional Convention Gerry refused to sign the Constitution because he could not accept the proposed division of powers or the absence of a bill of rights. Although he championed the people and their rights, he believed that the common man could be too easily swayed by unprincipled politicians for democracy to work. But he was not altogether consistent, for he was also jealous of power and fearful of possible tyranny. Devoted to the patriots' cause in the early 1770s, Gerry was active as a member of the Massachusetts committee of correspondence and the first provincial congress. As one of the members of Congress' committee of safety, he was almost captured by British troops the night before the battles of Lexington and Concord. In the Continental Congress he supported the Articles of

Confederation—with equal representation for all states, large and small. Gerry represented his district in the first session of the Congress, but he refused to run after two terms. However, he was called to further service when, in 1797, President Adams selected him as a commissioner to France. Along with John Marshall and Charles Pinckney, he attempted to improve American relations with the revolutionary French government. French agents—identified as X, Y, and Z—insulted the commissioners by seeking bribes, and Marshall and Pinckney left. Gerry stayed and tried to negotiate with Talleyrand, albeit unsuccessfully. Upon his return, Gerry claimed credit for reducing the tensions between France and America. As governor of Massachusetts, in 1812 Gerry approved an unusual redistricting which favored his Democratic-Republican party; one of the more extreme districts, shaped something like a salamander, was depicted by a cartoonist as a beast labeled "Gerrymander"—a term which has become a part of America's political language. Gerry was elected vice president when Madison was elected to a second term in 1812 and was serving in his official capacity when he died suddenly. Ironically, he was riding to the Capitol to perform the duties of president of the Senate, a constitutional function of the vice president that he had objected to in 1787 and one of the reasons he had refused to sign the U.S. Constitution.

ALEXANDER HAMILTON (1755-1804)

Washington's most valued assistant in war and peace, Hamilton was probably the most brilliant writer, organizer, and political theorist among the Founding Fathers. Time after time from 1776 to 1795 he brought his great powers of intellect to bear on the most critical problems facing the new nation—from obtaining a truly national constitution to establishing a sound national financial system. Born in the British West Indies, he came to America as a teenager. William Livingston of New Jersey, who later joined Hamilton in signing the Constitution, gave the talented young man a home and sent him to college. By 1775 Hamilton had written two pamphlets defending the American cause that displayed an exceptional grasp of the principles of government. During the war Hamilton distinguished himself in battle and served as Washington's aide. He organized Washington's headquarters and wrote many of Washington's statements and a complete set of military regulations. An advocate of a strong central government, Hamilton led the delegates at the inconclusive Annapolis Convention to agree to meet in Philadelphia the next year "to take into consideration the situation of the United States . . . to render the Constitution of the Federal Government adequate to the exigencies of the Union." His carefully worded proposal permitted more than it seemed to say; he opened the way for the Constitutional Convention. His influence was not so great at the Convention as after it, when he wrote fifty of the eighty-five Federalist Papers that won the necessary public support. As the first secretary of the treasury, Hamilton devised a comprehensive financial system that proved almost immediately successful: He proposed that the federal government assume the states' war debts, and to settle these and foreign debts, that there be an excise tax, a national bank, and a protective tariff that would also encourage American industry. The businessmen favored by these measures gradually grew into a political party under Hamilton. As the first leader of the Federalist party, Hamilton was, with Jefferson—who founded the Democratic-Republican party—a founder of the two-party system. Hamilton, who had little faith in the people, stood for an industrial society, a strong national government, and an aristocracy of power, while Jefferson advocated an agricultural society, strong state government, and political democracy. Jefferson was more concerned with individual rights and freedom and Hamilton with governmental systems and procedures. Rivalry between the factions came to a head when Hamilton was killed in a duel by his New York rival, Aaron Burr. The Constitution and the Federalist Papers, the national financial system and the American two-party system—in a very real sense these are the legacy of the brilliant man who came to America a penniless youth.

Benjamin Harrison (1726-1791)

A wealthy Virginia planter and political leader, Harrison risked his vast holdings along the James River by embracing the cause of independence from the time of the Stamp Act through the Revolution. He suffered severe losses during the war when British troops plundered his property. While serving in the Virginia legislature, Harrison helped draft an official protest against the Stamp Act, and his activities as a member of the committee of correspondence and of the first provincial congress led to his selection as a delegate to the Continental Congress. There he served on three important committees dealing with foreign affairs, the army, and the navy—the working committees that formed the nucleus of what later became major departments of the federal government. Harrison also served in Congress as chairman of the committee of the whole, and on July 2, 1776, he presided over the discussions that led to the vote in favor of Richard Lee's resolution for independence. Harrison's signature on the Declaration of Independence is next to that of his fellow Virginian, Thomas Jefferson. In the Congress Harrison also presided over the debates that led to the adoption of the Articles of Confederation. During the war Harrison served as speaker of the Virginia legislature and as governor, the position he held when the British surrendered at Yorktown. During his tenure in that latter office, Virginia ceded to the federal government her claim to the lands north and west of the Ohio River, an action in which Jefferson played a major role, and one that helped strengthen the new Union. As a member of the Virginia convention that met to consider ratifying the Constitution, Harrison was chairman of the committee on elections, but he did not participate in many debates. He did, however, join Patrick Henry in refusing to support the Constitution without a bill of rights. Of all the Founding Fathers, Harrison is the only one who has the distinction of having two direct descendants—a son and a great-grandson—serve as president of the United States: William Henry Harrison, the ninth president under the current constitution and Benjamin Harrison, the twenty-third under the current constitution.

Patrick Henry (1736-1799)

The most famous orator of the Revolution, Henry delivered dramatic speeches which kindled the spark of liberty in colonial Virginians and was, according to Thomas Jefferson, "far above all in maintaining the spirit of the Revolution." In 1765, before the House of Burgesses, Henry spoke out boldly against the Stamp Act, firing the colony's opposition, and in 1775, just weeks before Lexington and Concord, he closed a stirring appeal to arm the militia with the immortal phrase, "Give me liberty, or give me death!" A failure as a farmer and storekeeper, Henry studied law and quickly won a reputation as a lawyer. In 1763, in the "Parson's Cause" case, he gained fame throughout Virginia by winning a point of law against the King's nullification of a Virginia law. In the House of Burgesses in 1765 he responded to news of the Stamp Act by offering five daring resolutions that declared the colonists' rights, including the exclusive right to tax themselves, and he sought support with a fiery speech that evoked accusations of treason. But Henry's powerful words helped stiffen resistance to the Stamp Act throughout the colonies and added to his reputation. In Virginia he had more real power than the governor. At the First Continental Congress, Henry strongly supported the Continental Association, a union of colonies with the purpose of boycotting British imports. It was at Virginia's revolutionary convention at Richmond that Henry, after proposing immediate arming of the militia, delivered the most famous speech of the Revolution, concluding, "Gentlemen may cry peace, peace—but there is no peace. The war is actually begun. Is life so dear, or peace so sweet, as to be purchased at the price of chains and slavery? Forbid it, Almighty God! I know not what course others may take, but as for me, give me liberty, or give me death!" The convention promptly approved his proposal, crying out, "To arms! To arms!" In the Continental Congress in 1775 Henry favored the idea of a Continental Army. No soldier himself, he resigned a commission after a short time. As a member of the Virginia patriotic convention, he helped draft the state's constitution and bill of rights. He became Virginia's first governor on July 5, 1776, and held the position for the legal limit of three years. Although a leader of the Revolution, Henry was first and foremost a Virginian; when the Constitution came to Virginia for ratification, he fought it, believing it placed too much power in the federal government and deprived the states and the people of essential rights. His fight against the Constitution brought that issue to public notice throughout the colonies, contributing to the early adoption of the Bill of Rights amendments.

WILLIAM JOHNSON (1727-1819)

The only Founding Father who in 1776 was not in favor of independence, Johnson grew into a strong supporter of the new nation; he helped draft the Constitution, signed it, and stoutly defended it at the Connecticut ratification convention. Although he attended the Stamp Act Congress in 1765 and served as a special agent for Connecticut in England, Johnson was firmly convinced during these years that the colonies and Great Britain would settle their differences. His stay in London, where he associated with Dr. Samuel Johnson, the great critic and lexicographer, and other notables, undoubtedly strengthened his ties with England. However, in London he worked closely with Benjamin Franklin, then agent for Pennsylvania and other colonies, in representing colonial interests. And he supported the American policy of nonimportation of British goods as a protest against the Townshend Acts. After returning, Johnson was elected to serve in the first Continental Congress, but since he was against the idea of independence, he declined the position. Still devoted to the idea of a peaceful settlement, in 1775 he visited the British commander, General Thomas Gage, in Boston—sent by the Connecticut legislature. His mission was unsuccessful, and he was for a time held by patriots there. He resigned from the Connecticut legislature, and from 1777 to 1779 his refusal to support independence cost him his law practice, which the State permitted him to resume after he swore allegiance to Connecticut. Despite his tardy adoption of the cause of independence, Johnson was an influential member of the Congress of Confederation. At the Constitutional Convention Johnson, a soft-spoken but effective speaker, helped defend and explain the "Connecticut Compromise," the proposal for representing the states in the Senate and the people in the House of Representatives that was finally adopted to settle the dispute between the larger and smaller States. The scholarly Johnson, who was one of the colonies' leading classicists and who was then serving as president of Columbia College, was chairman of the committee on style that produced the final version of the Constitution—though Gouverneur Morris wrote most of it. Johnson eloquently defended the Constitution at the Connecticut ratification convention, and after ratification, his state selected him to serve as one of the men to sit in the newly formed Senate.

RUFUS KING (1755-1827)

For over forty years King served his country as a state legislator, member of Congress, delegate to the Constitutional Convention, senator, minister to Great Britain, and candidate for vice president and president. He helped draft both the Northwest Ordinance and the Constitution, which he signed and later supported at the Massachusetts ratification convention. A student during most of the war, King began his public service as a member of the Massachusetts legislature, where he demonstrated his interest in the national cause by championing a bill that provided for regular financial support to the Congress of the Confederation. Later, while serving in Congress, he joined with Jefferson in contributing an antislavery provision to the Northwest Ordinance, the document that prescribed the conditions for the formation of new states from the Northwest Territory. At the Constitutional Convention, where he was recognized as one of the most eloquent speakers, King maintained his position against slavery and supported the idea of a national government with clear authority beyond that of the states. As a member of the first Senate, the Federalist King supported the policies and programs of Washington's administration. He backed Hamilton's financial plans and served as a director of the Bank of the United States, which he helped establish. In 1796 he resigned from the Senate to become minister to Great Britain, a position which taxed his considerable diplomatic ability, helping to keep America neutral while France and Britain were at war. In the elections of 1804 and 1808, King was a vice-presidential candidate, running both times on the unsuccessful Federalist ticket with Charles Cotesworth Pinckney of South Carolina. In 1816 King was himself the Federalist candidate for president, losing to James Monroe. In 1820 King opposed the Missouri Compromise—with the admission of Missouri as a slave state—as a failure to deal squarely with the problem of slavery. Forcefully but unsuccessfully he advocated the abolition of slavery. Handsome and sociable, King achieved success as a legislator and diplomat, and he won high praise as a speaker from one of America's most celebrated speakers. Of King, Daniel Webster wrote: "You never heard such a speaker. In strength, and dignity, and fire; in ease, in natural effect, and gesture as well as in matter, he is unequaled."

JOHN MARSHALL (1755-1835)

Unique among the Founding Fathers, Marshall was a young officer in the Continental Army who played only a minor role in the Revolution. In addition, he did not contribute to or sign either the Declaration of Independence or the Constitution. But as chief justice of the Supreme Court, he did more than any other man to institutionalize the new national government by establishing the authority of the Court as co-equal with the legislative and executive branches and by clarifying the fundamental relationship between the states and the national government. Contributions of such magnitude place John Marshall among the first rank of the nation's founders. Although Marshall was only a junior officer in the Revolution— he fought at Brandywine, Germantown, and Monmouth, and endured Valley Forge—his experience in the war led him to see the need for a strong national government. He believed that a stronger, better-organized government might have more effectively managed the limited resources available to the colonies to wage war. In addition, his military service provided the kind of experience that permitted him to think in national terms. Raised in the near wilderness of the frontier, Marshall was thrust into the world of the Continental Army as a teenager. Later he acknowledged that he became an American before he had had a chance to become a Virginian. In the 1790s Marshall was well established as a leader of the Federalists in Virginia. He declined President Washington's offer of the position of attorney general, he publicly defended the Jay Treaty, and in 1797 he was appointed by President Adams as a commissioner to France—for what became known as the XYZ Affair. When Marshall was appointed chief justice, the Supreme Court stood far below the executive and legislative branches in power and prestige. By sheer force of intellect he produced decisions that won wide approval from constitutional lawyers, associates on the Court, and eventually the general American citizens. He was so successful, so inevitably right in many of his views, that he made the Court the recognized interpreter of the Constitution. From 1801 to 1835 he delivered the opinion in more than five hundred cases, over twenty-five of which were fundamental constitutional questions. Marshall's influence on our system was so great that the Constitution as we know it is based in large measure on Marshall's interpretation of it. A century and a half later, Marshall is still considered the foremost of constitutional lawyers. According to a contemporary, Judge Jeremiah Mason, without Marshall's monumental efforts the government of the new nation "would have fallen to pieces."

GEORGE MASON (1725-1792)

Thomas Jefferson called him, "The wisest man of his generation." Although he signed neither the Declaration of Independence nor the Constitution, Mason was the source of some of the most revolutionary ideas in both of those documents. The drafters of both drew ideas from documents that were largely his—the Virginia declaration of rights and the Virginia constitution. A southern aristocrat with a five-thousand-acre plantation that he managed himself, Mason was a neighbor and friend of Washington. As a member of the House of Burgesses in 1769, Mason prepared resolutions, which Washington presented and the legislature adopted, against the importing of British goods . In 1774 Mason wrote the Fairfax Resolves, advocating that all of the colonies meet in congress and that Virginia cease all relations with Britain. He was also primarily responsible for Virginia's relinquishing its claim to the lands beyond the Ohio River, and he influenced Jefferson in his drafting of the Northwest Ordinance with its prohibition of slavery and its provision for the formation of new states. This Virginia planter played an unusual role at the Constitutional Convention, for he hated slavery, which he called "diabolical in itself and disgraceful to mankind," and he urged delegates at the Convention to give the new government the power to prevent the expansion of slavery. When the Constitution was completed, he refused to sign, partly because he felt the Constitution failed to deal strongly enough with the institution of slavery (permitting the importing of slaves until 1808) and partly because it gave the Senate and president too much power and provided no protective bill of rights. He continued his opposition at the Virginia ratification convention, joining Patrick Henry, Benjamin Harrison, Richard Henry Lee, and others who feared too powerful a central government. But Mason lived to see his most cherished ideas of the rights of the individual incorporated into the Constitution as the Bill of Rights amendments in December 1791. A rationalist who had little faith in the workings of governmental bodies, Mason fought passionately for the freedom of the individual—citizen or slave—and he was largely responsible for ensuring that protection of the rights of the individual would be an essential part of the American system.

GOUVERNEUR MORRIS (1752-1816)

His words are among the most recognizable of any of the Founding Fathers: "We, the people of the United States, in order to form a more perfect union, establish justice, insure domestic tranquility." Morris, who was primarily responsible for the final draft of the Constitution, was also an eloquent, though sometimes windy, speaker, and members of the New

York legislature, the Constitutional Convention, and the Senate were often swayed by his masterful blend of logic, wit, and imagination. Although he had strong aristocratic tendencies and as late as 1774 wrote, "It is in the interest of all men to seek for reunion with the parent state," in 1776 Morris spoke in the New York legislature on behalf of the colonies and against the King. He early recognized the need for a united, strong national congress. Of Morris, historian David Muzzey wrote, "he was a nationalist before the birth of the nation."

In the Continental Congress Morris was chairman of several committees, and his gifted pen produced such important documents as instructions to Franklin as the minister to France and detailed instructions to the peace commissioners, which contained provisions that ultimately appeared in the final treaty. As a member of Congress, he supported and signed the Articles of Confederation, and at the Constitutional Convention he participated in more debates than any other delegate. He argued that the president and the Senate should be elected for life, and that the Senate should represent the rich and propertied, which would counterbalance the democratic character of the House of Representatives. This was of course rejected, but his proposal for a council of state led to the idea of the president's Cabinet, and he proposed that the president be elected, not by Congress, but by the people. When the Constitution was completed, Morris was given the task of editing and revising it, and he then wrote the famous words of the Preamble. Once the Constitution was formally accepted, Morris proved one of its most devoted supporters. On September 17, the day the delegates signed it, Morris made an impassioned speech answering Edmund Randolph, who refused to sign. As minister to France in the 1790s, Morris found himself in the wrong country at the wrong time, for although he was recognized by the French revolutionists as one of the leaders of the American Revolution, he was nonetheless a Federalist with clear aristocratic sympathies. In Paris he became involved in attempts to help French nobles escape—including the Marquis de Lafayette and the King—and the revolutionists demanded his removal. After he returned he served in the Senate and later as chairman of the group that developed the plan for the Erie Canal, the waterway that opened the path for westward expansion.

Robert Morris (1734-1806)

A Philadelphia merchant of great wealth who became the "financier of the Revolution," Morris frequently risked his fortune on behalf of the Continental Army and in the end lost everything. With Roger Sherman, Morris shares the distinction of having signed all three of the principal founding documents—the Declaration of Independence, the Articles of Confederation, and the Constitution. A conservative among the patriots, Morris did little besides sign a protest against the Stamp Act before he was elected to Congress in 1775, and he did not originally support the idea of independence, believing that the time was not ripe. He did, however, sign the Declaration—after he had abstained from the vote. And in 1778 he signed the Articles of Confederation. In 1776, as chairman of the executive committee of Congress, Morris was left in charge of the government when Congress fled Philadelphia, then threatened by the British. Later that year Washington requested funds for an offensive, and Morris, pledging his personal credit, obtained the money that enabled Washington to defeat the Hessians at Trenton in December. For the remainder of the war, Morris was either officially or unofficially the chief civilian in charge of finance and supply. In May 1781 Congress appointed him to the new position of superintendent of finance, and that summer he worked closely with Washington in planning the support for the major offensive against Cornwallis at Yorktown. Again Morris backed the purchase of ammunition and supplies with his personal pledge. After the war Morris continued as the principal finance officer for Congress, caught between the obligations of the Confederation and the states' continued refusal to support it. He all but exhausted his own credit and repeatedly planned to resign, but stayed on. He established the first national bank, but Pennsylvania challenged its charter. By 1784, when he finally resigned, the United States had practically no credit abroad, and he himself was nearly bankrupt. As a result, he urged the establishment of a stronger national government. At the Annapolis convention he supported the idea of the convention in Philadelphia. Host to George Washington during the Constitutional Convention, Morris nominated Washington to preside and signed the completed document in September. Morris declined Washington's offer of the position of secretary of the treasury in the new government but was elected one of Pennsylvania's first senators. After he returned to private life his debts finally caught up to him. From 1798 to 1801 he was incarcerated in Philadelphia's debtor's prison. He came out a broken and forgotten man.

CHARLES PINCKNEY (1757-1824)

The "Pinckney Plan" was one of the three plans offered to the Constitutional Convention in Philadelphia. No record of it exists, but Pinckney is generally given credit for many provisions—possibly as many as thirty—of the finished Constitution. In an extremely active career, Pinckney also served four terms as governor of South Carolina, congressman, senator, and minister to Spain. Educated in England, Pinckney returned to assist and then replace his father in South Carolina's patriotic movement. Before he was twenty he had served on the state's executive council and helped draft its first constitution. In the war he served with the militia, was captured, and spent a year in a British prison. Pinckney was elected to the Congress of the Confederation in 1784 and gradually became convinced of the weakness of the government under the Articles of Confederation. As chairman of a congressional committee considering measures to strengthen the Articles of Confederation, Pinckney gained experience that prepared him for his role at the Constitutional Convention. In 1786, in an address to Congress, he urged that a general convention be called to revise the Articles of Confederation. When Pinckney arrived at the Constitutional Convention in Philadelphia in May 1787, he had already prepared his "Plan." Unfortunately, he presented it to the Convention immediately after Edmund Randolph completed a three-hour description of his own plan, and Pinckney's was never debated point by point but simply referred with other plans to the committee on detail. And that committee did not identify in its comprehensive report the source of each recommended element of the Constitution. Though the exact extent of Pinckney's contribution to the Constitution remains unknown, Pinckney in later life made such extravagant claims that he became known as "Constitution Charlie." Pinckney also prepared a large part of South Carolina's new constitution, adopted in 1790 and modeled after the national Constitution. For more than thirty years after the Constitution was ratified, Pinckney served in public office. In the 1790s he left the Federalist party to support Jefferson. In 1795 he denounced the Jay Treaty, and in the 1800 election, he helped Jefferson carry South Carolina even though his cousin, Charles Cotesworth Pinckney, was the vice-presidential candidate on the Federalist ticket. President Jefferson's appointment of Pinckney as minister to Spain looked very much like a reward, but Pinckney had little success in dealing with Spain. After his return he continued to be elected to public office, completing his career in the Congress, where one of his final acts was to oppose the Missouri Compromise.

CHARLES COTESWORTH PINCKNEY (1746-1825)

"If I had a vein that did not beat with the love of my country, I myself would open it." Such were the sentiments of this southern patriot who, though educated in England, was one of the principal leaders of the new nation. Charles Cotesworth Pinckney was twice the unsuccessful

Federalists' candidate for president—in 1804 against Jefferson and 1808 against Madison—but he is remembered primarily as a courageous Army officer, a signer of the Constitution, and as the commissioner to France who in 1798 refused a veiled request for bribes with, "Millions for defense but not one cent for tribute." After studying law under William Blackstone at Oxford, Pinckney attended the Royal Military Academy in France, gaining training that helped him, after he returned to America, to win a commission as a captain in the Continental Army in 1775. He fought in several battles and was captured when the British took Charleston in 1780. By the end of the war he was a brigadier general. Even before the war Pinckney was active in the patriotic movement. In 1775 he was a member of a group responsible for the local defense, and in February 1776 he was chairman of a committee that drafted a plan for the temporary government of South Carolina. At the Constitutional Convention Pinckney stoutly defended southern interests and state's rights; he revealed little faith in elections by the people, but he accepted the decisions of the convention, signed the Constitution, and supported it at the South Carolina ratification convention. One of the most successful lawyers in South Carolina, Pinckney was offered a seat on the Supreme Court by Washington, but he declined, as he did later offers for the positions of secretary of war and secretary of state. In 1796 he accepted the position of minister to France, but after he arrived in Paris, the French Directory chose not to accept him, and he went to Holland instead. In 1797 President Adams appointed Pinckney, John Marshall, and Elbridge Gerry as commissioners to France in an attempt to settle differences, but the three were insulted by the French officials known as X, Y, and Z, and Pinckney made his famous reply and returned home something of a hero. He was soon appointed major general in the newly formed Army, hastily organized by Washington because of the rupture with France, but by 1800 tensions were reduced. Although he was twice unsuccessful in seeking the presidency, Pinckney was honored by his fellow officers of the Revolution and served from 1805 until his death as president of their association, the Society of the Cincinnati.

EDMUND RANDOLPH (1753-1813)

On May 29, 1787, Randolph introduced the Virginia Plan to the Constitutional Convention—the first time the idea of a new national form of government was formally presented to the delegates at Philadelphia. Although Madison contributed much to the plan, it was this handsome, thirty-three-year-old governor of Virginia, the spokesman for his state, who began the Convention's serious deliberations by outlining the fifteen resolves calling for national executive, judiciary and legislative branches. It was a dramatic moment as the delegates, officially gathered "for the sole and express purpose of revising the Articles of Confederation," were confronted with a radical proposal to create a completely different governmental system. That they heard Randolph out for over three hours and even considered the plan he offered testifies to Randolph's success. But he was not pleased with some of the additions and revisions to the Virginia Plan that delegates later introduced, and he several times shifted his position for and against a new constitution; in September he refused to sign the final document. However, at the Virginia ratification convention he shocked anti-Federalists like Patrick Henry by reversing his position and supporting the Constitution. Randolph explained his new position: by this time eight states had already ratified the Constitution, only one more was needed, and other states had already urged that bill of rights amendments should be enacted soon after ratification, thus satisfying his objection to the original Constitution. In a telling speech Patrick Henry slyly suggested that perhaps there were other reasons. He never went as far as mentioning a promised post in the new government, but the hint was enough, and the two men came close to fighting a duel. After Washington was elected president, he named Randolph the first attorney general, but Randolph denied this was in any way related to his supporting the Constitution. As attorney general he established the office and the beginnings of the Justice Department, and after Jefferson resigned as secretary of state, Randolph assumed that position also. In 1795 he was accused of seeking bribes from the French ambassador, and though he proved himself innocent, he resigned and never held another public office.

ROGER SHERMAN (1721-1793)

A Yankee cobbler who taught himself law and became a judge and a legislator, Roger Sherman helped draft four of the major American founding documents—the Declaration of Independence, the Articles of Confederation, the Constitution, and the Bill of Rights. Sherman had almost twenty years of experience as a colonial legislator behind him when he came to the First Continental Congress in 1774, and he quickly won the respect of his fellow delegates for his wisdom, industry, and sound judgment; John Adams called him "one of the soundest and strongest pillars of the Revolution." In Congress Sherman was one of the first to deny Parliament's authority to make laws for America, and he strongly supported the boycott of British goods. In the following years he served with Jefferson and Franklin on the committees that drafted the Declaration of Independence and the Articles of Confederation. He also served on the maritime committee, the board of treasury and the board of war—all of first importance to the Revolution. A Puritan of simple habits who performed all tasks with thoroughness and accuracy, Sherman gained more legislative experience in his years in Congress than any other member; by the time he left he was perhaps the most powerful—and most overworked—of congressmen. Sherman's greatest contribution, and the best known, was the "Connecticut Compromise" he proposed at the Constitutional Convention: by proposing that Congress have two branches, one with proportional and one with equal representation, he satisfied both the smaller and larger states, providing a solution to one of the most stubborn problems of the Convention. In Connecticut he defended the Constitution, writing articles in the _New Haven Gazette,_ and helped win ratification in January 1788. Connecticut was the fifth state to ratify. Sherman was the oldest man elected to the new national House of Representatives. In the first Congress he served on the committee that prepared and reviewed the Bill of Rights amendments. By coincidence, the year that the Bill of Rights became part of the Constitution, Sherman was elected senator, so the man who conceived the "Connecticut Compromise" had the opportunity to represent that State in both of the legislative branches he helped to create.

JAMES WILSON (1742-1808)

"The best form of government which has ever been offered to the world," James Wilson called the Constitution, which he helped draft and later signed. He also signed the Declaration of Independence and served as associate justice of the first Supreme Court. Although born and educated in Scotland, Wilson became a leader of the patriots after fleeing the English oppression of his homeland. He studied law under John Dickinson in Philadelphia, and the two served in the Continental Congress together. In 1774, before he was elected to Congress, Wilson wrote a carefully reasoned pamphlet, "Considerations on the Legislative Authority of the British Parliament," which boldly concluded that Parliament had no authority over the colonies. In Congress he was one of three Pennsylvanian members to vote for independence. In a bizarre incident in 1779 Wilson's home was attacked by a faction of patriots who felt Wilson had betrayed the cause by defending in court merchants charged with treason. However, after the war he continued to represent Pennsylvania in Congress and at the Constitutional Convention. At the Constitutional Convention he had a dual role—as a delegate and as spokesman for the elderly and infirm Benjamin Franklin. As a lawyer and political theorist, Wilson was deeply committed to the principle that sovereignty resides with the people, and he advocated popular elections for both the president and Congress. A member of the committee on detail, he wrote a draft of the Constitution that provided the basis for the final document, and throughout the convention he delivered the persuasive words of Franklin that moved the delegates to overlook minor differences and finally approve the Constitution. Later in 1787, at the Pennsylvania ratification convention, Wilson delivered a persuasive speech of his own, winning the votes necessary for ratification. Two years later his state called on him to draft a new state constitution. During the first years under the new Constitution, Wilson served on the Supreme Court. In addition, as a lecturer in law at the College of Philadelphia, he undertook to translate the principle of the sovereignty of the people into the realm of law, providing legal justification for the Revolution and the beginnings of a uniquely American system of jurisprudence.

PRESIDENTIAL FATHERS

Once the new constitution was ratified, the office of the presidency took on a whole new importance. The next four men to hold the office were therefore vitally important to the life and stability of the nation. Their stories, though familiar, remain among the most eloquent testimonies to the substantiveness of the great American experiment in liberty.

GEORGE WASHINGTON (1732-1799)

To General Washington fell the unprecedented task of organizing a national administration that was somehow to govern the thirteen separate states and yet preserve the freedoms for which the independent men of these states had so recently fought. It was his extraordinary task to make the radical idea of a government of free men, by free men, actually work with nothing but the noble words of the freshly written Constitution to guide him. There were no existing buildings or departments, no procedures, precedents or traditions; there was no Capitol. There was simply the Constitution and the man and the mighty task. Like other colonial landholders, Washington was a new kind of man in history—part cultivated gentleman, part rugged pioneer, a man in whom the ideas of Western civilization were combined with the great physical strength and fierce spirit of independence of the frontiersman. Among such men Washington was outstanding. His performance as a surveyor and a soldier on the western frontier earned him, at twenty-three, the command of Virginia's troops, and he served in the House of Burgesses for years before the Continental Congress chose him to lead the Continental Army. As its commander he held the struggling patriots together during the long war years; with victory, he quietly retired from the field. The presidential electors from the nearly sovereign states, cautious in selecting the man who would hold power over all the states, had little to fear from one who had so willingly relinquished control of a victorious army. Already one of the country's leading citizens, Washington carried out his duties as president with simple dignity. Although he tried to remain free of parties, he was closer to the Federalist Hamilton, his secretary of the treasury, than to the Democrat Jefferson, his secretary of state. He firmly declined a third term and spent his last years peacefully at his beautiful plantation, Mount Vernon, where his tomb now stands. Of all memorials, the most dramatic is the graceful shaft of the monument in the District of Columbia that symbolizes the aspirations of America as they were so nobly embodied in this "first citizen."

JOHN ADAMS (1735-1826)

It was natural that Washington's vice president, Adams, should succeed Washington, for in his own contentious but courageous way he had contributed much to the new nation. Unlike Washington, Adams was not a great leader. He had neither a commanding nor a magnetic personality; he was a lawyer and an intellectual who made his greatest contributions before he became president. A man of bristling integrity, he could devote himself to a cause with a fierce intensity: he condemned the Stamp Act of 1765, was one of the first to support the idea of independence, and at the Continental Congress when the colonies wavered before the mighty decision, he vigorously fought for acceptance of the Declaration of Independence. He further distinguished himself by representing the infant country with dignity and success in the leading courts of Europe. By 1789 Adams was a respected but not popular figure. In finishing second to Washington he barely received enough votes to secure the vice presidency, and for eight years he was continually in the shadow of the commanding figure of Washington. Unfortunately, his own term was little better. His struggle with Alexander Hamilton and his Cabinet members created factional strife in both the Federalist party and the government. Through the bitter disputes Adams remained essentially a Federalist, maintaining the strong central government established by Washington and Hamilton. When the Federalists passed the oppressive Alien and Sedition Laws in 1789, they assumed such sweeping powers over all critics of government that they challenged the essential freedoms of the individual; the party, already too closely allied with the propertied colonial aristocracy, carried the idea of a strong central government too far. Both Adams and the party lost favor, and in the 1800 election Adams was defeated by Jefferson and the new Republican party. Interestingly, Jefferson and Adams—once fierce rivals—became close friends in their elder years. They even died on the same day, within hours of one another, on July 4, 1826.

THOMAS JEFFERSON (1743-1826)

Called the "Bloodless Revolution of 1800," Jefferson's election marked a profound but peaceful change in the administration of the young nation. The revolutionist who boldly wrote Enlightenment ethics into the Declaration of Independence brought to the presidency a philosophy of government firmly rooted in those same beliefs—a philosophy that concerned itself above all with the rights and liberties of the individual. It was Jefferson's democratic views, with his enduring faith in the individual, that more than anything else turned the country away from the class rule of the Federalists. Few men have been better equipped to become president; a graduate of William and Mary College and an able lawyer, Jefferson helped shape the destiny of the struggling nation from the beginning. He served in the Virginia house of burgesses, in the Continental Congress— writing the final draft of the Declaration and serving as a minister in the French court—as governor of Virginia, as secretary of state under Washington, and vice president under Adams. But as president Jefferson proved that philosophic ability and experience in office were no replacements for political leadership. He was a remarkable inventor, scientist, writer, artist, planter, architect, musician, and educator, but he was a poor politician and administrator. He was able, however, to bring a profound sense of democracy to the nation's highest office, an accomplishment that ranks with the celebrated purchase of the Louisiana Territory as an outstanding achievement of his administration. A complex, brilliant man, Jefferson was one of the most accomplished of our presidents. He was talented as are few men in any age—the living example of his own abiding belief in the capacity of the individual to learn and to grow under freedom.

JAMES MADISON (1751-1836)

A devoted disciple of Jefferson, Madison became the active leader of the Democratic-Republican party when he was elected president. And like his mentor, he was never able to provide the kind of administrative leadership necessary to guide the nation. Like John Adams, Madison performed his greatest service to the nation before he was elected president. Increasingly aware of the weaknesses of the confederation that loosely bound the states after the Revolution, he helped frame the Constitution in the Convention of 1787 and eloquently defended it in the Virginia ratifying convention and in the famed Federalist Papers. After the new government was formed, it was Madison who introduced the Bill of Rights to Congress as the first amendments to the Constitution. The smallest man ever to become president, the soft-spoken, retiring Madison was more a scholar than an executive. He developed the habit of serious study at the College of New Jersey—under the tutelage of John Witherspoon—and became a devoted student of history and law. Besides the Constitution and the Federalist Papers, other documents that helped shape the new nation can be traced to his pen: the petition for religious freedom in Virginia, the defense of American navigation rights on the Mississippi, and the Virginia Resolution—a ringing denouncement of the oppressive Alien and Sedition Laws. Foreign problems dominated Madison's years as president. Conflict with Britain over naval rights finally led to a war that brought little credit to either nation and made Madison the most unpopular president the country had thus far known. Federalists demanded that he resign, but he weathered the criticism; with peace he regained a measure of popularity. But nothing he accomplished as president, or as member of Congress or secretary of state, won him the high place he had already gained as one of the founders of the nation—a place of enduring fame as the Father of the Constitution.

PART III

MANIFEST DESTINY

We have staked the whole future of American civilization, not upon the power of government, far from it. We have staked the future upon the capacity of each and all of us to govern ourselves, to sustain ourselves, according to the Ten Commandments of God.

JAMES MADISON

FAREWELL PEACE

By Joseph Hopkinson

The War of 1812 was perceived by many Americans as a kind of second war of independence from Britain, though in fact it may have been American territorial ambitions along the Gulf Coast and in Canada that actually sparked the hostilities. Particularly in New England, opposition to the war was strong—even to the point of threatening secession. Nevertheless, the people rallied for the most part to the patriotic cause. This verse exemplifies the resigned determination that accompanied the conflict.

Farewell, Peace! Another crisis
    Calls us to " the last appeal,"
Made when monarchs and their vices
    Leave no argument but steel.
When injustice and oppression
    Dare avow the tyrant's plea.
Who would recommend submission?
    Virtue bids us to be free.

History spreads her page before us,
    Time unrolls his ample scroll;
Truth unfolds them, to assure us,
    States, united, ne'er can fall.
See, in annals Greek and Roman,
    What immortal deeds we find;
When those gallant sons of woman
    In their country's cause combined.

Sons of Freedom! Brave descendants
    From a race of heroes tried,
To preserve our independence
    Let all Europe be defied.
Let not all the world, united,
    Rob us of one sacred right:
Every patriot heart's delighted
    In his country's cause to fight.

Come then, War! With hearts elated
    To thy standard we will fly;
Every bosom animated
    Either to live free or die.
May the wretch that shrinks from duty,
    Or deserts the glorious strife,
Never know the smile of beauty,
    Nor the blessing of a wife.

FIRST FRUITS IN 1812

By Wallace Rice

To a large degree the War of 1812 was a naval war. Though outgunned and outmanned, America's small fleet of converted merchant vessels and their commanders made a strong showing for themselves and initiated a great naval tradition. This popular poem vividly recaptures the import of the conflict.

W hat is that a-billowing there
Like a thunderhead in air?
    Why should such a sight be whitening the seas;
That's a Yankee man-o'-war,
And three things she's seeking for:
    For a prize, and for a battle, and a breeze.

When the war blew o'er the sea
Out went Hull and out went we
    In the Constitution, looking for the foe;
But five British ships came down—
And we got to Boston-town
    By a mighty narrow margin, you must know!

Captain Hull can't fight their fleet,
But he fairly aches to meet
    Quite the prettiest British ship of all there were;
So he stands again to sea
In the hope that on his lee
    He'll catch Dacres and his pretty Guerriere.

'Tis an August afternoon
Not a day too late or soon,
    When we raise a ship whose lettered mainsail reads:
All who meet me have a care,
I am England's Guerriere;
    So Hull gaily clears for action as he speeds.

Cheery bells had chanted five
On the happiest day alive
    When we Yankees dance to quarters at his call;
While the British bang away
With their broadsides' screech and bray;
    But the Constitution never fires a ball.

We send up three times to ask
If we sha'n't begin our task?
    Captain Hull sends back each time the answer No;
Till to half a pistol-shot
The two frigates he had brought,
    Then he whispers, Lay along! And we let go.

Twice our broadside lights and lifts,
And the Briton, crippled, drifts
    With her mizzen dangling hopeless at her poop:
Laughs a Yankee, She's a brig!
Says our Captain, "That's too big;
    Try another, so we'll have her for a sloop!"

We huzzah, and fire again,
Lay aboard of her like men,
    And, like men, they beat us off, and try in turn;
But we drive bold Dacres back
With our muskets' snap and crack
    All the while our crashing broadsides boom and burn.

'Tis but half an hour, bare,
When that pretty Guerriere
    Not a stick calls hers aloft or hers alow,
Save the mizzen's shattered mast,
Where her "meteor flag" is nailed fast
    Till, a fallen star, we quench its ruddy glow.

Dacres, injured, o'er our side
Slowly bears his sword of pride,
  Holds it out, as Hull stands there in his renown:
No, no! Says th' American,
Never, from so brave a man:
  But I see you're wounded, let me help you down.

All that night we work in vain
Keeping her upon the main,
  But we've hulled her far too often, and at last
In a blaze of fire there
Dies the pretty Guerriere;
  While away we cheerly sail upon the blast.

Oh, the breeze that blows so free!
Oh, the prize beneath the sea!
  Oh, the battle! Was there ever better won?
Still the happy Yankee cheers
Are a-ringing in our ears
  From old Boston, glorying in what we've done.

What is that a-billowing there
Like a thunderhead in air?
  Why should such a sight be whitening the seas?
That's Old Ir'nsides, trim and taut,
And she's found the things she sought:
  Found a prize, a bully battle, and a breeze!

THE STAR SPANGLED BANNER

By Francis Scott Key

During the night of September 13, 1814, as a Washington attorney was sent to the British command to secure the release of a prisoner, the fleet began to bombard the placements of American fortifications in Baltimore at Fort McHenry. Though the battle raged through the night, the defenses stood firm. The sight of the flag still flying over the fort the next morning inspired the young lawyer to pen these words. Set to a popular English song, Anacreon in Heaven, *it was officially declared to be the national anthem more than a hundred years later, just before the First World War.*

O! say, can you see, by the dawn's early light,
What so proudly we hailed at the twilight's last gleaming:
Whose broad stripes and bright stars, through the perilous fight,
O'er the ramparts we watched were so gallantly streaming,
And the rocket's red glare, the bombs bursting in air,
Gave proof through the night that our flag was still there:

    O! say, does the star-spangled banner still wave
    O'er the land of the free and the home of the brave?

On the shore, dimly seen through the mist of the deep,
Where the foe's haughty host in dread silence reposes,
What is that which the breeze, o'er the towering steep,
As it fitfully blows, half conceals, half discloses?
Now it catches the gleam of the morning's first beam—
In full glory reflected, now shines on the stream.

    'Tis the star-spangled banner, O! long may it wave
    O'er the land of the free and the home of the brave.

And where is the band who so vauntingly swore
That the havoc of war and the battle's confusion
A home and a country would leave us no more?
Their blood has washed out their foul footsteps' pollution.
No refuge could save the hireling and slave
From the terror of flight or the gloom of the grave!

    And the star-spangled banner in triumph doth wave
    O'er the land of the free and the home of the brave.

O! thus be it ever when freemen shall stand
Between their loved homes and the foe's desolation;
Bless'd with victory and peace, may our heaven-rescued land
Praise the Power that hath made and preserved us a nation.
Then conquer we must, for our cause it is just—
And this be our motto—"In God is our trust!"

    And the star-spangled banner in triumph shall wave
    O'er the land of the free and the home of the brave.

THE MISSOURI COMPROMISE

By Henry Clay

The question of the admission of Maine and Missouri as states in 1818 provoked the first major clash over slavery in American national politics. Henry Clay, a perennial contender for the presidency, and Jesse Thomas of Illinois hammered out a compromise they hoped would preserve the Union in perpetuity. In the end it only delayed the inevitable. The bill was passed on March 6, 1820.

An act to authorize the people of the Missouri Territory to form a constitution and state government, and for the admission of such state into the Union on an equal footing with the original states, and to prohibit slavery in certain territories.

Be it enacted, That the inhabitants of that portion of the Missouri Territory included within the boundaries hereinafter designated, be, and they are hereby authorized to form for themselves a constitution and state government, and to assume such name as they shall deem proper; and the said state, when formed, shall be admitted into the Union, upon an equal footing with the original states, in all respects whatsoever.

That the said state shall consist of all the territory included within the following boundaries, to wit: Beginning in the middle of the Mississippi River, on the parallel of thirty-six degrees of north latitude; thence west, along that parallel of latitude, to the St. Francois River; thence up, and following the course of that river, in the middle of the main channel thereof, to the parallel of latitude of thirty-six degrees and thirty minutes; thence west, along the same, to a point where the said parallel is intersected by a meridian line passing through the middle of the mouth of the Kansas River, where the same empties into the Missouri River, thence, from the point aforesaid north, along the said meridian line, to the intersection of the parallel of latitude which passes through the rapids of the river Des Moines, making the said line to correspond with the Indian boundary line; thence east, from the point of intersection last aforesaid, along the said parallel of latitude, to the middle of the channel of the main fork of the said river Des Moines; thence down and along the middle of the main channel of the said river Des Moines, to the mouth of the same, where it empties into the Mississippi River; thence, due east, to the middle of the main channel of the Mississippi River; thence down, and following the course of the Mississippi River, in the middle of the main channel thereof, to the place of beginning....

That all free white male citizens of the United States, who shall have arrived at the age of twenty-one years, and have resided in said territory three months previous to the day of election, and all other persons qualified to vote for representatives to the general assembly of the said territory, shall be qualified to be elected, and they are hereby qualified and authorized to vote, and choose representatives to form a convention.

That in all that territory ceded by France to the United States, under the name of Louisiana, which lies north of thirty-six degrees and thirty minutes north latitude, not included within the limits of the state contemplated by this act, slavery and involuntary servitude, otherwise than in the punishment of crimes whereof the parties shall have been duly convicted, shall be, and is hereby, forever prohibited: Provided always, that any person escaping into the same, from whom labor or service is lawfully claimed, in any state or territory of the United States, such fugitive may be lawfully reclaimed and conveyed to the person claiming his or her labor or service as aforesaid.

THE MONROE DOCTRINE

By James Monroe

The Monroe Doctrine, excerpted from the president's message to Congress on December 2, 1823, was actually formulated by Secretary of State John Quincy Adams. Its design was to head off the colonial intentions of both the Russians, who claimed the coastal lands south of the Bering Straits to an undetermined line in the American northwest, and the Spanish, who were determined to put down a rash of rebellions in their American colonies. Though rarely enforced until the administration of Theodore Roosevelt, the statement was recognized quickly as the clearest enunciation of American foreign policy—and has remained so to this day.

At the proposal of the Russian imperial government, made through the minister of the Emperor residing here, full power and instructions have been transmitted to the Minister of the United States at St. Petersburg, to arrange, by amicable negotiation, the respective rights and interests of the two nations on the northwest coast of this continent. A similar proposal has been made by his Imperial Majesty to the government of Great Britain, which has likewise been acceded to.

The government of the United States has been desirous, by this friendly proceeding, of manifesting the great value which they have invariably attached to the friendship of the emperor, and their solicitude to cultivate the best understanding with his government. In the discussions to which this interest has given rise, and in the arrangements by which they may terminate, the occasion has been judged proper for asserting, as a principle in which the rights and interests of the United States are involved, that the American continents, by the free and independent condition which they have assumed and maintain, are henceforth not to be considered as subjects for future colonization by any European powers.

It was stated at the commencement of the last session, that a great effort was then making in Spain and Portugal, to improve the condition of the people of those countries; and that it appeared to be conducted with extraordinary moderation. It need scarcely be remarked, that the result has been, so far, very different from what was then anticipated. Of events in that quarter of the globe, with which we have so much intercourse, and from which we derive our origin, we have always been anxious and interested spectators. The citizens of the United States cherish sentiments the most friendly, in favor of the liberty and happiness of their fellow men on that side of the Atlantic. In the wars of the European powers, in matters relating to themselves, we have never taken any part, nor does it comport with our policy so to do. It is only when our rights are invaded, or seriously menaced, that we resent injuries, or make preparation for our defense. With the movements in this hemisphere, we are, of necessity, more immediately connected, and by causes which must be obvious to all enlightened and impartial observers. The political system of the allied powers is essentially different, in this respect, from that of America. This difference proceeds from that which exists in their respective governments. And to the defence of our own, which has been achieved by the loss of so much blood and treasure, and matured by the wisdom of their most enlightened citizens, and under which we have enjoyed unexampled felicity, this whole nation is devoted. We owe it, therefore, to candor, and to the amicable relations existing between the United States and those powers, to declare, that we should consider any attempt on their part to extend their system to any portion of this hemisphere, as dangerous to our peace and safety. With the existing colonies or dependencies of any European power, we have not interfered, and shall not interfere. But, with the governments who have declared their independence and maintained it, and whose independence we have, on great consideration, and on just principles, acknowledged, we could not view any interposition for the purpose of oppressing them, or controlling, in any other manner, their destiny, by any European power, in any other light than as the manifestation of an unfriendly disposition towards the United States. In the war between these new governments and Spain, we declared our neutrality at the time of their recognition, and to this we have adhered, and shall continue to adhere, provided no change shall occur, which, in the judgment of the competent authorities of this government, shall make a corresponding change, on the part of the United States, indispensable to their security.

The late events in Spain and Portugal, shew that Europe is still unsettled. Of this important fact, no stronger proof can be adduced than that the allied powers should have thought it proper, on any principle satisfactory to themselves, to have interposed, by force, in the internal concerns of Spain. To what extent such interposition may be carried, on the same principle, is a question, in which all independent powers, whose governments differ from theirs, are interested; even those most remote, and surely none more so than the United States. Our policy, in regard to Europe, which was adopted at an early stage of the wars which have so long agitated that quarter of the globe, nevertheless remains the same, which is, not to interfere in the internal concerns of any of its powers; to consider the government de facto as the legitimate government for us; to cultivate friendly relations with it, and to preserve those relations by a frank, firm, and manly policy, meeting, in all instances, the just claims of every power; submitting to injuries from none. But, in regard to those continents, circumstances are eminently and conspicuously different.

It is impossible that the allied powers should extend their political system to any portion of either continent, without endangering our peace and happiness; nor can any one believe that our Southern Brethren, if left to themselves, would adopt it of their own accord. It is equally impossible, therefore, that we should behold such interposition, in any form, with indifference. If we look to the comparative strength and resources of Spain and those new governments, and their distance from each other, it must be obvious that she can never subdue them. It is still the true policy of the United States, to leave the parties to themselves, in the hope that other powers will pursue the same course.

NATIONAL BANK VETO

By Andrew Jackson

Presented with a Bank Renewal Bill from Congress in 1832, the president declined to sign based upon his concerns regarding a new and narrow concentration of wealth and power in America—thus denying the central bank its monopolistic charter. Such a monopoly, he believed, only exacerbated the tendency toward tyranny to which all nations eventually drift. Eventually the principle of his argument became one of the cornerstones of American conservatism, so despite the fact that its economics no longer enliven the national debate, its politics do.

The bill "to modify and continue" the act entitled "An act to incorporate the subscribers to the Bank of the United States" was presented to me on the 4th July instant. Having considered it with that solemn regard to the principles of the Constitution which the day was calculated to inspire, and come to the conclusion that it ought not to become a law, I herewith return it to the Senate, in which it originated, with my objections.

A bank of the United States is in many respects convenient for the Government and useful to the people. Entertaining this opinion, and deeply impressed with the belief that some of the powers and privileges possessed by the existing bank are unauthorized by the Constitution, subversive of the rights of the States, and dangerous to the liberties of the people, I felt it my duty at an early period of my Administration to call the attention of Congress to the practicability of organizing an institution combining all its advantages and obviating these objections. I sincerely regret that in the act before me I can perceive none of those modifications of the bank charter which are necessary, in my opinion, to make it compatible with justice, with sound policy, or with the Constitution of our country.

The present corporate body, denominated the president, directors, and company of the Bank of the United States, will have existed at the time this act is intended to take effect, twenty years. It enjoys an exclusive privilege of banking under the authority of the General Government, a monopoly of its favor and support, and, as a necessary consequence, almost monopoly of the foreign and domestic exchange. The powers, privileges, and favors bestowed upon it in the original charter, by increasing the value of the stock far above its par value, operated as a gratuity of many millions to the stockholders.

An apology may be found for the failure to guard against this result in the consideration that the effect of the original act of incorporation could not be certainly foreseen at the time of its passage. The act before me proposes another gratuity to the holders of the same stock, and in many cases to the same men, of at least seven millions more. This donation finds no apology in any uncertainty as to the effect of the act. On all hands it is conceded that its passage will increase at least 20 or 30 per cent more the market price of the stock, subject to the payment of the annuity of $200,000 per year secured by the act, thus adding in a moment one fourth to its par value. It is not our own citizens only who are to receive the bounty of our Government. More than eight millions of the stock of this bank are held by foreigners. By this act the American Republic proposes virtually to make them a present of some millions of dollars. For these gratuities to foreigners, and to some of our own opulent citizens the act secures no equivalent whatever. They are the certain gains of the present stockholders under the operation of this act, after making full allowance for the payment of the bonus.

Every monopoly and all exclusive privileges are granted at the expense of the public, which ought to receive a fair equivalent. The many millions which this act proposes to bestow on the stockholders of the existing bank must come directly or indirectly out of the earnings of the American people. It is due to them, therefore, if their Government sell monopolies and exclusive privileges, that they should at least exact for them as much as they are worth in open market. The value of the monopoly in this case may be correctly ascertained. The twenty-eight millions of stock would probably be at an advance of 50 per cent, and command in market at least $42,000,000, subject to the payment of the present bonus. The present value of the monopoly, therefore, is $17,000,000, and this the act proposes to sell for three millions, payable in fifteen annual installments of $200,000 each.

It is not conceivable how the present stockholders can have any claim to the special favor of the Government. The present corporation has enjoyed its monopoly during the period stipulated in the original contract. If we must have such a corporation, why should not the Government sell out the whole stock and thus secure to the people the full market value of the privileges granted? Why should not Congress create and sell twenty-eight millions of stock, incorporating the purchases with all the powers and privileges secured in this act and putting the premium upon the sales into the Treasury?

But this act does not permit competition in the purchase of this monopoly. It seems to be predicated on the erroneous idea that the present stockholders have a prescriptive right not only to the favor but to the bounty of Government. It appears that more than a fourth part of the stock is held by foreigners and the residue is held by a few hundred of our own citizens, chiefly of the richest class. For their benefit does this act exclude the whole American people from competition in the purchase of this monopoly and dispose of it for many millions less than its worth. This seems the less excusable because some of our citizens not now stockholders petitioned that the door of competition might be opened, and offered to take a charter on terms much more favorable to the Government and country.

But this proposition, although made by men whose aggregate wealth is believed to be equal to all the private stock in the existing bank, has been set aside, and the bounty of our Government is proposed to be again bestowed on the few who have been fortunate enough to secure the stock and at this moment wield the power of the existing institution. I can not perceive the justice or policy of this course. If our Government must sell monopolies, it would seem to be its duty to take nothing less than their full value, and if gratuities must be made once in fifteen or twenty years let them not be bestowed on the subjects of a foreign government nor upon a designated and favored class of men in our own country. It is but justice and good policy as far as the nature of the case will admit, to confine our favors to our own fellow-citizens, and let each in his turn enjoy an opportunity to profit by our bounty. In the bearings of the act before me upon these points I find ample reasons why it should not become a law.

It has been urged as an argument in favor of rechartering the present bank that the calling in its loans will produce great embarrassment and distress. The time allowed to close its concerns is ample, and if it has been well managed, its pressure will be light, and heavy only in case its management has been bad. If, therefore, it shall produce distress, the fault will be its own, and it would furnish a reason against renewing a power which has been so obviously abused. But will there ever be a time when this reason will be less powerful? To acknowledge its force is to admit that the bank ought to be perpetual and as a consequence the present stockholder and those inheriting their rights as successors be established a privileged order, clothed both with great political power and enjoying immense pecuniary advantages from their connection with the Government.

The modifications of the existing charter proposed by this act are not such, in my view, as make it consistent with the rights of the States or the liberties of the people. The qualification of the right of the bank to hold real estate, the limitation of its power to establish branches, and the power reserved to Congress to forbid the circulation of small notes are restrictions comparatively of little value or importance. All the objectionable principles of the existing corporation, and most of its odious features, are retained without alleviation.

In another of its bearings this provision is fraught with danger. Of the twenty-five directors of this bank five are chosen by the Government and twenty by the citizen stockholders. From all voice in these elections the foreign stockholders are excluded by the charter. In proportion, therefore, as the stock is transferred to foreign holders the extent of suffrage in the choice of directors is curtailed. Already is almost a third of the stock in foreign hands and not represented in elections. It is constantly passing out of the country, and this act will accelerate its departure. The entire control of the institution would necessarily fall into the hands of a few citizen stockholders, and the ease with which the object would be accomplished would be a temptation to designing men to secure that control in their own hands by monopolizing the remaining stock. There is danger that a president and directors would then be able to elect themselves from year to year, and without responsibility or control manage the whole concerns of the bank during the existence of its charter. It is easy to conceive that great evils to our country and its institutions might flow from such a concentration of power in the hands of a few men irresponsible to the people.

Is there no danger to our liberty and independence in a bank that in its nature has so little to bind it to our country? The president of the bank has told us that most of the State banks exist by its forbearance. Should its influence become concentered, as it may under the operation of such an act as this, in the hands of a self-elected directory whose interests are identified with those of the foreign stockholder, will there not be cause to tremble for the purity of our elections in peace and for the independence of our country in war? Their power would be great whenever they might choose to exert it; but if this monopoly were regularly renewed every fifteen or twenty years on terms proposed by themselves, they might seldom in peace put forth their strength to influence elections or control the affairs of the nation. But if any private citizen or public functionary should interpose to curtail its powers or prevent a renewal of its privileges, it can not be doubted that he would be made to feel its influence.

Should the stock of the bank principally pass into the hands of the subjects of a foreign country, and we should unfortunately become involved in a war with that country, what would be our condition? Of the course which would be pursued by a bank almost wholly owned by the subjects of a foreign power, and managed by those whose interests, if not affections, would run in the same direction there can be no doubt. All its operations within would be in aid of the hostile fleets and armies without. Controlling our currency, receiving our public moneys, and holding thousands of our citizens in dependence, it would be more formidable and dangerous than the naval and military power of the enemy.

If we must have a bank with private stockholders, every consideration of sound policy and every impulse of American feeling admonishes that it should be purely American. Its stockholders should be composed exclusively of our own citizens, who at least ought to be friendly to our Government and willing to support it in times of difficulty and danger. So abundant is domestic capital that competition in subscribing for the stock of local banks has recently led almost to riots. To a bank exclusively of American stockholders, possessing the powers and privileges granted by this act, subscriptions for $200,000,000 could readily be obtained. Instead of sending abroad the stock of the bank in which the Government must deposit its funds and on which it must rely to sustain its credit in times of emergency, it would rather seem to be expedient to prohibit its sale to aliens under penalty of absolute forfeiture.

It is maintained by the advocates of the bank that its constitutionality in all its features ought to be considered as settled by precedent and by the decision of the Supreme Court. To this conclusion I can not assent. Mere precedent is a dangerous source of authority, and should not be regarded as deciding questions of power except where the acquiescence of the people and the States can be considered as well settled. So far from this being the case on this subject, an argument against the bank might be based on precedent. One Congress, in 1791, decided in favor of a bank; another, in 1811, decided against it. One Congress, in 1815, decided against a bank; another, in 1816, decided in its favor. Prior to the present Congress, therefore, the precedents drawn from that source were equal. If we resort to the States, the expressions of legislative, judicial, and executive opinion against the bank have been probably to those in its favor as 4 to 1. There is nothing in precedent, therefore, which, if its authority were admitted, ought to weigh in favor of the act before me.

If the opinion of the Supreme Court covered the whole ground of this act, it ought not to control the coordinate authorities of this Government. The Congress, the Executive, and the Court must each for itself be guided by its own opinion of the Constitution. Each public officer who takes an oath to support the Constitution swears that he will support it as he understands it, and not as it is understood by others. It is as much the duty of the House of Representatives, of the Senate, and of the President to decide upon the constitutionality of any bill or resolution which may be presented to them for passage or approval as it is of the supreme judges when it may be brought before them for judicial decision. The opinion of the judges has no more authority over Congress than one opinion of Congress has over the judges, and on that point the President is independent of both. The authority of the Supreme Court must not, therefore, be permitted to control the Congress or the Executive when acting in their legislative capacities, but to have only such influence as the force of their reasoning may deserve.

The bank is professedly established as an agent of the executive branch of the Government, and its constitutionality is maintained on that ground. Neither upon the propriety of present action nor upon the provisions of this act was the Executive consulted. It has had no opportunity to say that it neither needs nor wants an agent clothed with such powers and favored by such exemptions. There is nothing in its legitimate functions which makes it necessary or proper. Whatever interest or influence, whether public or private, has given birth to this act, it can not be found either in the wishes or necessities of the executive department, by which present action is deemed premature, and the powers conferred upon its agent not only unnecessary, but dangerous to the Government and country.

It is to be regretted that the rich and powerful too often bend the acts of government to their selfish purposes. Distinctions in society will always exist under every just government. Equality of talents, of education, or of wealth can not be produced by human institutions. In the full enjoyment of those gifts of Heaven and the fruits of superior industry, economy, and virtue, every man is equally entitled to protection by law; but when the laws undertake to add to these natural and just advantages artificial distinctions, to grant titles, gratuities, and exclusive privileges, to make the rich richer and the potent more powerful, the humble members of society—the farmers, mechanics, and laborers—who have neither the time nor the means of securing like favors to themselves, have a right to complain of the injustice of their Government. There are no necessary evils in government. Its evils exist only in its abuses. If it would confine itself to equal protection, and, as Heaven does its rains, shower its favors alike on the high and the low, the rich and the poor, it would be an unqualified blessing. In the act before me there seems to be a wide and unnecessary departure from these just principles.

Nor is our Government to be maintained or our Union preserved by invasions of the rights and powers of the several States. In thus attempting to make our General Government strong we make it weak. Its true strength consists in leaving individuals and States as much as possible to themselves—in making itself felt, not in its power, but in its beneficence; not in its control, but in its protection; not in binding the States more closely to the center, but leaving each more unobstructed in its proper orbit.

Experience should teach us wisdom. Most of the difficulties our Government now encounters and most of the dangers which impend over our Union have sprung from an abandonment of the legitimate objects of Government by our national legislation, and the adoption of such principles as are embodied in this act. Many of our rich men have not been content with equal protection and equal benefits, but have besought us to make them richer by act of Congress. By attempting to gratify their desires we have in the results of our legislation arrayed section against section, interest against interest, and man against man, in a fearful commotion which threatens to shake the foundations of our Union. It is time to pause in our career to review our principles, and if possible revive that devoted patriotism and spirit of compromise which distinguished the saga of the Revolution and the fathers of our Union. If we can not at once, in justice to interests vested under improvident legislation, make our Government what it ought to be, we can at least take a stand against all new grants of monopolies and exclusive privileges, against any prostitution of our Government to the advancement of the few at the expense of the many, and in favor of compromise and gradual reform in our code of laws and system of political economy.

THE DEFENSE OF THE ALAMO

By Joaquin Miller

In February 1836, while garrisoned in a little Franciscan mission church at San Antonio de Valero, a beleaguered group of 183 Texan freedom fighters and American volunteers were attacked by the full force of the Mexican national army. Despite all odds, the small force was able to hold off the swarming assaults of the well-equipped Mexicans until March 6. Defying the demands of the Mexican dictator Santa Anna to surrender, they fought to the last man—in the end resorting to hand-to-hand combat. The news of their courageous defense inspired and reinvigorated the Texan bid for independence. "Remember the Alamo" became their battle cry.

Santa Ana came storming, as a storm might come;
There was rumble of cannon; there was rattle of blade;
There was cavalry, infantry, bugle, and drum,
Full seven thousand in pomp and parade.
The chivalry, flower of Mexico;
And a gaunt two hundred in the Alamo!

And thirty lay sick, and some were shot through;
For the siege had been bitter, and bloody, and long.
"Surrender, or die!— Men, what will you do?"
And Travis, great Travis, drew sword, quick and strong;

Drew a line at his feet.... "Will you come? Will you go?
I die with my wounded, in the Alamo."

Then Bowie gasped, "Lead me over that line!"
Then Crockett, one hand to the sick, one hand to his gun,
Crossed with him; then never a word or a sign
Till all, sick or well, all, all save but one,
One man. Then a woman stepped, praying, and slow
Across; to die at her post in the Alamo.

Then that one coward fled, in the night, in that night
When all men silently prayed and thought
Of home; of tomorrow; of God and the right,
Till dawn; and with dawn came Travis's cannon-shot,
In answer to insolent Mexico,
From the old bell-tower of the Alamo.

Then came Santa Ana; a crescent of flame!
Then the red escalade; then the fight hand to hand;
Such an unequal fight as never had name
Since the Persian hordes butchered that doomed Spartan band.
All day—all day and all night; and the morning? so slow,
Through the battle smoke mantling the Alamo.

Now silence! Such silence! Two thousand lay dead
In a crescent outside! And within? Not a breath
Save the gasp of a woman, with gory gashed head,
All alone, all alone there, waiting for death;
And she but a nurse. Yet when shall we know
Another like this of the Alamo?

Shout, "Victory, victory, victory ho!"
I say 'tis not always to the hosts that win!
I say that the victory, high or low,
Is given the hero who grapples with sin,
Or legion or single; just asking to know
When duty fronts death in his Alamo.

LIBERTY FOR ALL

By William Lloyd Garrison

A poorly educated, failed journalist and publisher, William Lloyd Garrison found his cause and calling in the abolitionist movement. In 1831 he began publishing a rather radical antislavery paper, The Liberator. Though it never attracted a circulation of more than three thousand, it became the driving force toward the abolition of the institution of chattel servitude. This poem, which attracted a wide popular following, became a clarion call throughout New England for the freedom of African slaves.

They tell me, Liberty! that in thy name
I may not plead for all the human race;
That some are born to bondage and disgrace,
Some to a heritage of woe and shame,
And some to power supreme, and glorious fame:
With my whole soul I spurn the doctrine base,
And, as an equal brotherhood, embrace
All people, and for all fair freedom claim!
Know this, O man! whate'er thy earthly fate,
God never made a tyrant nor a slave:
Woe, then, to those who dare to desecrate
His glorious image!—for to all He gave
Eternal rights, which none may violate;
And, by a mighty hand, the oppressed He yet shall save!

THE SLAVERY QUESTION

By John C. Calhoun

Slavery was but one of many issues that divided North and South—but it was, of course, the issue that carried the most moral and emotional weight. All other issues, however vital economically, politically, and historically, tend to pale in comparison. Feeling the inordinate weight of that single question, the greatest of the South's spokesmen made his final speech in the Senate on March 4, 1850, in response to the Great Compromise devised—once again—by Henry Clay. It was as brilliant and articulate as it was somber and uncompromising. In the end, it only emphasized the divide that existed in the nation. Within weeks the old warrior who had served the Union so faithfully since the twilight of the Founding Era was dead—and so were his hopes for some kind of a negotiated peace.

I have, Senators, believed from the first that the agitation of the subject of slavery would, if not prevented by some timely and effective measure, end in disunion. Entertaining this opinion, I have, on all proper occasions, endeavored call the attention of both the two great parties which divide the country to adopt some measure to prevent so great a disaster, but without success. The agitation has been permitted to proceed, with almost no attempt to resist it, until it has reached a point when it can no longer be disguised or denied that the Union is in danger. You have thus had forced upon you the greatest and the gravest question that can ever come under your consideration: How can the Union be preserved?

To give a satisfactory answer to this mighty question, it is indispensable to have an accurate and thorough knowledge of the nature and the character of the cause by which the Union is endangered. Without such knowledge it is impossible to pronounce, with any certainty, by what measure it can be saved; just as it would be impossible for a physician to pronounce, in the case of some dangerous disease, with any certainty, by what remedy the patient could be saved, without similar knowledge of the nature and character of the cause which produced it. The first question, then, presented for consideration, in the investigation I propose to make, in order to obtain such knowledge, is, What is it that has endangered the Union?

To this question there can be but one answer: that the immediate cause is the almost universal discontent which pervades all the States composing the Southern section of the Union. This widely extended discontent is not of recent origin. It commenced with the agitation of the slavery question, and has been increasing ever since. The next question, going one step further back, is—What has caused this widely diffused and almost universal discontent?

It is a great mistake to suppose, as is by some, that it originated with demagogues, who excited the discontent with the intention of aiding their personal advancement, or with the disappointed ambition of certain politicians, who resorted to it as the means of retrieving their fortunes. On the contrary, all the great political influences of the section were arrayed against excitement, and exerted to the utmost to keep the people quiet. The great mass of the people of the South were divided, as in the other section, into Whigs and Democrats. The leaders and the presses of both parties in the South were very solicitous to prevent excitement and to preserve quiet; because it was seen that the effects of the former would necessarily tend to weaken, if not destroy, the political ties which united them with their respective parties in the other section. Those who know the strength of party ties will readily appreciate the immense force which this cause exerted against agitation, and in favor of preserving quiet. But, great as it was, it was not sufficient to prevent the widespread discontent which now pervades the section. No; some cause, far deeper and more powerful than the one supposed, must exist, to account for discontent so wide and deep. The question then recurs, What is the cause of this discontent? It will be found in the belief of the people of the Southern States, as prevalent as the discontent itself, that they cannot remain, as things now are, consistently with honor and safety, in the Union. The next question to be considered is, What has caused this belief?

One of the causes is, undoubtedly, to be traced to the long continued agitation of the slave question on the part of the North, and the many aggressions which they have made on the rights of the South during the time.

There is another lying back of it, with which this is intimately connected, that may be regarded as the great and primary cause. This is to be found in the fact that the equilibrium between the two sections, in the Government as it stood when the constitution was ratified and the Government put in action, has been destroyed. At that time there was nearly a perfect equilibrium between the two, which afforded ample means to each to protect itself against the aggression of the other; but, as it now stands, one section has the exclusive power of controlling the Government, which leaves the other without any adequate means of protecting itself against its encroachrnent and oppression. To place this subject distinctly before you, I have, Senators, prepared a brief statistical statement, showing the relative weight of the two sections in the Government under the first census of 1790 and the last census of 1840.

According to the former, the population of the United States, including Vermont, Kentucky, and Tennessee, which then were in their incipient condition of becoming States, but were not actually admitted, amounted to 3,929,827. Of this number the Northern States had 1,997,899, and the Southern 1,952,072, making a difference of only 45,827 in favor of the former States. The number of States, including Vermont, Kentucky, and Tennessee, were sixteen; of which eight, including Vermont, belonged to the Northern section, and eight, including Kentucky and Tennessee, to the Southern—making an equal division of the States between the two sections under the first census. There was a small preponderance in the House of Representatives, and in the Electoral College, in favor of the Northern, owing to the fact that, according to the provisions of the constitution, in estimating federal numbers five slaves count but three; but it was too small to affect sensibly the perfect equilibrium which, with that exception, existed at the time. Such was the equality of the two sections when the States composing them agreed to enter into a Federal Union. Since then the equilibrium between them has been greatly disturbed.

According to the last census the aggregate population of the United States amounted to 17,063,357, of which the Northern section contained 9,728,920, and the Southern 7,334,437, making a difference, in round numbers, of 2,400,000. The number of States has increased from sixteen to twenty-six, making an addition of ten States. In the meantime the position of Delaware had become doubtful as to which section she properly belonged. Considering her as neutral, the Northern States will have thirteen and the Southern States twelve, making a difference in the Senate of two Senators in favor of the former. According to the apportionment under the census of 1840, there were two hundred and twenty-three members of the House of Representatives, of which the Northern States had one hundred and thirty-five, and the Southern States (considering Delaware as neutral) eighty-seven, making a difference in favor of the former in the House of Representatives of forty-eight. The difference in the Senate of two members, aided to this, gives to the North in the electoral college, a majority of fifty. Since the census of 1840, four States hare been added to the Union—Iowa, Wisconsin, Florida, and Texas. They leave the difference in the Senate as it stood when the census was taken; but add two to the side of the North in the House, making the present majority in the House in its favor fifty, and in the electoral college fifty-two.

The result of the whole is to give the Northern section a predominance in every department of the Government, and thereby concentrate in the two elements which constitute the Federal Government—majority of States, and a majority of their population, estimated in federal numbers. Whatever section concentrates the two in itself possesses the control of the entire Government.

But we are just at the close of the sixth decade, and the commencement of the seventh. The census is to be taken this year, which must add greatly to the decided preponderance of the North in the House of Representatives and in the electoral college. The prospect is, also, that a great increase will be added to its present preponderance in the Senate, during the period of the decade, by the addition of new States. Two territories, Oregon and Minnesota, are already in progress, and strenuous efforts are making to bring in three additional States from the territory recently conquered from Mexico; which, if successful, will add three other States in a short time to the Northern section, making five States; and increasing the present number of its States from fifteen to twenty, and of its Senators from thirty to forty. On the contrary, there is not a single territory in progress in the Southern section, and no certainty that any additional State will be added to it during the decade. The prospect then is that the two sections in the Senate, should the efforts now made to exclude the South from the newly acquired territories succeed, will stand, before the end of the decade, twenty Northern States to fourteen Southern (considering Delaware as neutral), and forty Northern Senators to twenty-eight Southern. This great increase of Senators, added to the great increase of members of the House of Representatives and the electoral college on the part of the North, which must take place under the next decade, will effectually and irretrievably destroy the equilibrium which existed when the Government commenced.

Had this destruction been the operation of time, without the interference of government, the South would have had no reason to complain; but such was not the fact. It was caused by the legislation of this Government, which was appointed as the common agent of all, and charged with the protection of the interests and security of all. The legislation which has been effected may be classed under three heads. The first, is that series of acts by which the South has been excluded from the common territory belong-ing to all the States as members of the Federal Union—which have had the effect of extending vastly the portion allotted to the Northern section and restricting within narrow limits the portion left the South. The next consists in adopting a system of revenue and disbursements, by which an undue proportion of the burden of taxation has been imposed upon the South, and an undue proportion of proceeds appropriated to the North; and the last is a system of political measures, by which the original character of the Government has been radically changed. I propose to bestow upon each of these, in the order they stand, a few remarks, with the view of showing that it is owing to the action of this Government, that the equilibrium between the two sections has been destroyed, and the whole powers of the system centered in a sectional majority.

The result of the whole of these causes combined is, that the North has acquired a decided ascendancy over every department of this Government, and through it a control over all the powers of the system. A single section governed by the will of the numerical majority, has now, in fact, the control of the Government and the entire powers of the system.

As, then, the North has the absolute control over the Government, it is manifest, that on all questions between it and the South, where there is a diversity of interests, the interest of the latter will be sacrificed to the former, however oppressive the effects may be; as the South possesses no means by which it can resist, through the action of the Government. But if there was no question of vital importance to the South, in reference to which there was a diversity of views between the two sections, this state of things might be endured, without the hazard of destruction to the South. But such is not the fact. There is a question of vital importance to the Southern section, in reference to which the views and feelings of the two sections are as opposite and hostile as they can possibly be.

I refer to the relation between the two races in the Southern section, which constitutes a vital portion of her social organization. Every portion of the North entertains views and feelings more or less hostile to it. Those most opposed and hostile, regard it as a sin, and consider themselves under the most sacred obligation to use every effort to destroy it. Indeed, to the extent that they conceive that they have power, they regard themselves as implicated in the sin, and responsible for not suppressing it by the use of all and every means. Those less opposed and hostile, regard it as a crime— an offense against humanity, as they call it; and although not so fanatical, feel themselves bound to use all efforts to effect the same object; while those who are least opposed and hostile, regard it as a blot and a stain on the character of what they call the Nation, and feel themselves accordingly bound to give it no countenance or support. On the contrary, the Southern section regards the relation as one which cannot be destroyed without subjecting the two races to the greatest calamity; and the section to poverty, desolation, and wretchedness; and accordingly they feel bound, by every consideration of interest and safety, to defend it.

This hostile feeling on the part of the North towards the social organization of the South long lay dormant, but it only required some cause to act on those who felt most intensely that they were responsible for its continuance, to call it into action. The increasing power of this Government, and of the control of the Northern section over all its departments, furnished the cause. It was this which made an impression on the minds of many, that there was little or no restraint to prevent the

Government from doing whatever it might choose to do. This was sufficient of itself to put the most fanatical portion of the North in action, for the purpose of destroying the existing relation between the two races in the South.

The first organized movement towards it commenced in 1835. Then, for the first time, societies were organized, presses established, lecturers sent forth to excite the people of the North and incendiary publications scattered over the whole South through the mail. The South was thoroughly aroused. Meetings were held and resolutions adopted, calling upon the North to apply a remedy to arrest the threatened evil, and pledging themselves to adopt measures for their own protection, if it was not arrested.

As for myself, I believed at that early period that agitation would follow, and that it would in the end, if not arrested, destroy the Union. I then so expressed myself in debate, but in vain. Had my voice been heeded, the agitation which followed would have been prevented, and the fanatical zeal which has brought us to our present perilous condition, would have become extinguished, from the want of fuel to feed the flame. That was the time for the North to have shown her devotion to the Union: but, unfortunately, both of the great parties of that section were so intent on obtaining or retaining party ascendancy, that all other considerations were overlooked or forgotten.

What has since followed are but natural consequences. With the success of their first movement, this small fanatical party began to acquire strength; and with that, to become an object of courtship to both the great parties. The necessary consequence was, a further increase of power, and a gradual tainting of the opinions of both of the other parties with their doctrines, until the infection has extended over both; and the great mass of the population of the North, who, whatever may be their opinion of the original abolition party, which still preserves its distinctive organization, hardly ever fail, when it comes to acting, to cooperate in carrying out their measures.

Such is a brief history of the agitation, as far as it has yet advanced. Now I ask, Senators, what is there to prevent its further progress, until it fulfills the ultimate end proposed, unless some decisive measure should be adopted to prevent it? Has any one of the causes, which has added to its increase from its original small and contemptible beginning until it has attained its present magnitude, diminished in force? Is the original cause of the movement—that slavery is a sin, and ought to be suppressed—weaker now than at the commencement? Or is the abolition party less numerous or influential, or have they less influence with, or control over the two great parties of the North in elections? Or has the South greater means of influencing or controlling the movements of this Government now, than it had when the agitation commenced? To all these questions but one answer can be given: No, no, no. The very reverse is true. Instead of being weaker, all the elements in favor of agitation are stronger now than they were in 1835, when it first commenced, while all the elements of influence on the part of the South are weaker. Unless something decisive is done, I again ask what is to stop this agitation, before the great and final object at which it aims—the abolition of slavery in the States—is consummated? Is it, then, not certain, that if something is not done to arrest it, the South will be forced to choose between abolition and secession? Indeed, as events are now moving, it will not require the South to secede, in order to dissolve the Union. Agitation will of itself effect it, of which its past history furnishes abundant proof—as I shall next proceed to show.

It is a great mistake to suppose that disunion can be effected by a single blow. The cords which bound these States together in one common Union, are far too numerous and powerful for that. Disunion must be the work of time. It is only through a long process, and successively, that the cords can be snapped, until the whole fabric falls asunder. Already the agitation of the slavery question has snapped some of the most important, and has greatly weakened all the others, as I shall proceed to show.

The cords that bind the States together are not only many, but various in character. Some are spiritual or ecclesiastical; some political; others social. Some appertain to the benefit conferred by the Union, and others to the feeling of duty and obligation.

The strongest of those of a spiritual and ecclesiastical nature, consisted in the unity of the great religious denominations, all of which originally embraced the whole Union. All these denominations, with the exception, perhaps, of the Catholics, were organized very much upon the principle of our political institutions. Beginning with smaller meetings, corresponding with the political divisions of the country, their organization terminated in one great central assemblage, corresponding very much with the character of Congress. At these meetings the principal clergymen and lay members of the respective denominations, from all parts of the Union, met to transact business relating to their common concerns. It was not confined to what appertained to the doctrines and discipline of the respective denominations, but extended to plans for disseminating the Bible, establishing missions, distributing tracts, and of establishing presses for the publications of tracts, newspapers, and periodicals, with a view of diffusing religious information, and for the support of their respective doctrines and creeds. All this combined contributed greatly to strengthen the bonds of the Union. The ties which held each denomination together formed a strong cord to hold the whole Union together; but, powerful as they were, they have not been able to resist the explosive effect of slavery agitation.

The strongest cord, of a political character, consists of the many and powerful ties that have held together the two great parties which have, with some modifications, existed from the beginning of the Government. They both extended to every portion of the Union, and strongly contributed to hold all its parts together. But this powerful cord has fared no better than the spiritual. It resisted, for a long time, the explosive tendency of the agitation, but has finally snapped under its force—if not entirely, in a great measure. Nor is there one of the remaining cords which has not been greatly weakened. To this extent the Union has already been destroyed by agitation, in the only way it can be, sundering and weakening the cords which bind it together.

If the agitation goes on, the same force, acting with increased intensity, as has been shown, will finally snap every cord, when nothing will be left to hold the States together except force. But surely, that can, with no propriety of language, be called a Union, when the only means by which the weaker is held connected with the stronger portion is force. It may, indeed, keep them connected; but the connection will partake much more of the character of subjugation, on the part of the weaker to the stronger, than the union of free, independent, and sovereign States, in one confederation as they stood in the early stages of the Government, and which only is worthy of the sacred name of Union.

Having now, Senators, explained what it is that endangers Union, and traced it to its cause, and explained its nature and character, the question again recurs, How can the Union be saved? To this I answer: There is but one way by which it can be, and that is, by adopting such measures as will satisfy the States belonging to the Southern section, that they can remain in the Union consistently with their honor and their safety. There is, again, only one way by which this can be effected, and that is by removing the causes by which this belief has been produced. Do this, and discontent will cease, harmony and kind feelings between the sections be restored, and every apprehension of danger to the Union removed. The question then, is, How can this be done? But, before I undertake to answer this question, I propose to show by what the Union cannot be saved.

It cannot, then, be saved by eulogies on the Union, however splendid or numerous. The cry of "Union, Union, the glorious Union!" can no more prevent disunion than the cry of "Health, health, glorious health!" on the part of the physician, can save a patient lying dangerously ill. So long as the Union, instead of being regarded as a protector, is regarded in the opposite character, by not much less than a majority of the States, it will be in vain to attempt to conciliate them by pronouncing eulogies on it.

Besides, this cry of Union comes commonly from those whom we cannot believe to be sincere. It usually comes from our assailants. But we cannot believe them to be sincere; for, if they loved the Union, they would necessarily be devoted to the Constitution. It made the Union, and to destroy the Constitution would be to destroy the Union. But the only reliable and certain evidence of devotion to the Constitution is, to abstain, on the one hand, from violating it, and to repel, on the other, all attempts to violate it. It is only by faithfully performing these high duties that the Constitution can be preserved, and with it the Union.

But how stands the profession of devotion to the Union by our assailants, when brought to this test? Have they abstained from violating the Constitution? Let the many acts passed by the Northern States to set aside and annul the clause of the Constitution providing for the delivery up of fugitive slaves answer. I cite this, not that it is the only instance (for there are many others), but because the violation in this particular is too notorious and palpable to be denied. Again, have they stood forth faithfully to repel violations of the Constitution? Let their course in reference to the agitation of the slavery question, which was commenced and has been carried on for fifteen years, avowedly for the purpose of abolishing slavery in the States—an object all acknowledged to be unconstitutional—answer. Let them show a single instance, during this long period, in which they have denounced the agitators or their attempts to effect what is admitted to be unconstitutional, or a single measure which they have brought forward for that purpose. How can we, with all these facts before us, believe that they are sincere in their profession of devotion to the Union, or avoid believing their profession is but intended to increase the vigor of their assaults and to weaken the force of our resistance?

Nor can we regard the profession of devotion to the Union, on the part of those who are not our assailants, as sincere, when they pronounce eulogies upon the Union, evidently with the intent of charging us with disunion, without uttering one word of denunciation against our assailants. If friends of the Union, their course should be to unite with us in repelling these assaults, and denouncing the authors as enemies of the Union. Why they avoid this, and pursue the course they do, it is for them to explain.

Nor can the Union be saved by invoking the name of the illustrious Southerner whose mortal remains repose on the western bank of the Potomac. He was one of us—a slaveholder and a planter. We have studied his history, and find nothing in it to justify submission to wrong. On the contrary, his great fame rests on the solid foundation, that, while he was careful to avoid doing wrong to others, he was prompt and decided in repelling wrong. I trust that, in this respect, we profited by his example.

Nor can we find any thing in his history to deter us from seceding from the Union, should it fail to fulfill the objects for which it was instituted, by being permanently and hopelessly converted into the means of oppressing instead of protecting us. On the contrary, we find much in his example to encourage us, should we be forced to the extremity of deciding between submission and disunion.

Having now shown what cannot save the Union, I return to the question with which I commenced. How can the Union be saved? There is but one way by which it can with any certainty; and that is, by a full and final settlement, on the principle of justice, of all the questions at issue between the two sections. The South asks for justice, simple justice, and less she ought not to take. She has no compromise to offer, but the Constitution; and no concession or surrender to make. She has already surrendered so much that she has little left to surrender. Such a settlement would go to the root of the evil, and remove all cause of discontent, by satisfying the South, that she could remain honorably and safely in the Union, and thereby restore the harmony and fraternal feeling between the sections, which existed anterior to the Missouri agitation. Nothing else can, with any certainty, finally and for ever settle the questions at issue, terminate agitation, and save the Union.

But can this be done? Yes, easily; not by the weaker party, for it can of itself do nothing, not even protect itself, but by the stronger. The North has only to will it to accomplish it, to do justice by conceding to the South an equal right in the acquired territory, and to do her duty by causing the stipulations relative to fugitive slaves to be faithfully fulfilled, to cease the agitation of the slave question, and to provide for the insertion of a provision in the Constitution, by an amendment, which will restore to the South, in substance, the power she possessed of protecting herself, before the equilibrium between the sections was destroyed by the action of this Government. There will be no difficulty in devising such a provision, one that will protect the South, and which, at the same time, will improve and strengthen the Government, instead of impairing and weakening it.

But will the North agree to this? It is for her to answer the question. But, I will say, she cannot refuse, if she has half the love of the Union which she professes to have, or without justly exposing herself to the charge that her love of power and aggrandizement is far greater than her love of the Union. At all events, the responsibility of saving the Union rests on the North, and not on the South. The South cannot save it by any act of hers, and the North may save it without any sacrifice whatever, unless to do justice, and to perform her duties under the Constitution, should be regarded by her as a sacrifice.

It is time, Senators, that there should be an open and manly avowal on all sides, as to what is intended to be done. If the question is not now settled, it is uncertain whether it ever can hereafter be; and we, the representatives of the States of this Union, regarded as governments, should come to a distinct understanding as to our respective views, in order to ascertain whether the great questions at issue can be settled or not. If you, who represent the stronger portion, cannot agree to settle them on the broad principle of justice and duty, say so; and let the States we both represent agree to separate and part in peace. If you are unwilling we should part in peace, tell us so; and we shall know what to do, when you reduce the question to submission or resistance. If you remain silent, you will compel us to infer by your acts what you intend. In that case, California will become the test question. If you admit her under all the difficulties that oppose her admission, you compel us to infer that you intend to exclude us from the whole of the acquired territories, with the intention of destroying, irretrievably, the equilibrium between the two sections. We would be blind not to perceive in that case, that your real objects are power and aggrandizement, and infatuated not to act accordingly.

I have now, Senators, done my duty in expressing my opinions fully, freely, and candidly, on this solemn occasion. In doing so, I have been governed by the motives which have governed me in all the stages of the agitation of the slavery question since its commencement. I have exerted myself, during the whole period, to arrest it, with the intention of saving the Union, if it could be done, and if it could not, save the section where it has pleased Providence to cast my lot, and which I sincerely believe has justice and the Constitution on its side. Having faithfully done my duty to the best of my ability, both to the Union and my section, throughout this agitation, I shall have the consolation, let what will come, that I am free from all responsibility.

DRED SCOTT V. SANFORD

By Roger B. Taney

*Deciding the case of a fugitive slave in 1857, the Supreme Court argued in very
careful terms that the common law and constitutional definitions of citizenship
and personhood excluded fugitive slaves and their families. Written by the chief
justice, the decision outraged abolitionists and their more moderate antislavery
allies. It eventually became the legal wedge driven between North and South.*

There are two leading questions presented by the record. First, had
the Circuit Court of the United States jurisdiction to hear and
determine the case between these parties? And, Second, if it had
jurisdiction, is the judgment it has given erroneous or not?

The plaintiff in error was, with his wife and children, held as slaves by
the defendant, in the State of Missouri, and he brought this action in the
Circuit Court of the United States for that district, to assert the title of
himself and his family to freedom.

The declaration is that he and the defendant are citizens of different
States; that is, that he is a citizen of Missouri, and the defendant a citizen
of New York.

The defendant pleaded in abatement to the jurisdiction of the court, that
the plaintiff was not a citizen of the State of Missouri as alleged in his
declaration, being a Negro of African descent whose ancestors were of
pure African blood, and who were brought into this country and sold as
slaves.

Before we speak of the pleas in bar, it will be proper to dispose of the
questions which have arisen on the plea in abatement.

That plea denies the right of the plaintiff to sue in a court of the United
States, for the reasons therein stated.

If the question raised by it is legally before us, and the court should be
of opinion that the facts stated in it disqualify the plaintiff from becoming
a citizen, in the sense in which that word is used in the Constitution of the
United States, then the judgment of the Circuit Court is erroneous, and
must be reversed.

The question to be decided is, whether the plaintiff is not entitled to sue
as a citizen in a court of the United States.

The question is simply this: Can a Negro, whose ancestors were
imported into this country, and sold as slaves, become a member of the
political community formed and brought into existence by the Constitution

of the United States, and as such become entitled to all the rights, and privileges, and immunities, guaranteed by that instrument to the citizen? One of which rights is the privilege of suing in a court of the United States in the cases specified in the Constitution.

It will be observed, that the plea applies to that class of persons only whose ancestors were Negroes of the African race, and imported into this country, and sold and held as slaves. The only matter in issue before the court, therefore, is whether the descendants of such slaves, when they shall be emancipated, or who are born of parents who had become free before their birth, are citizens of a State, in the sense in which the word citizen is used in the Constitution of the United States.

The words "people of the United States" and "citizens" are synonymous terms, and mean the same thing. They both describe the political body who, according to our republican institutions, form the sovereignty, and who hold the power and conduct the government through their representatives. They are what we familiarly call the "sovereign people," and every citizen is one of this people, and a constituent member of this sovereignty. The question before us is, whether the class of persons described in the plea in abatement compose a portion of this people, and are constituent members of this sovereignty? We think they are not, and that they are not included, and were not intended to be included, under the word "citizens" in the Constitution, and can, therefore, claim none of the rights and privileges which that instrument provides for and secures to citizens of the United States. On the contrary, they were at that time considered as a subordinate and inferior class of being, who had been subjugated by the dominant race, and whether emancipated or not, yet remained subject to their authority, and had no rights or privileges but such as those who held the power and the government might choose to grant them.

In discussing this question, we must not confound the rights of citizenship which a State may confer within its own limits, and the rights of citizenship as a member of the Union. It does not by any means follow, because he has all the rights and privileges of a citizen of a State, that he must be a citizen of the United States. He may have all of the rights and privileges of the citizen of a State, and yet not be entitled to the rights and privileges of a citizen in any other State. For, previous to the adoption of the Constitution of the United States, every State had the undoubted right to confer on whomsoever it pleased the character of a citizen, and to endow him with all its rights. But this character, of course, was confined to the boundaries of the State, and gave him no rights or privileges in other States beyond those secured to him by the laws of nations and the community of States. Nor have the several States surrendered the power of conferring these rights and privileges by adopting the Constitution of the United

States. Each State may still confer them upon an alien, or any one it thinks proper, or upon any class or description of persons; yet he would not be a citizen in the sense in which that word is used in the Constitution of the United States, nor entitled to sue as such in one of its courts, nor to the privileges and immunities of a citizen in the other States. The rights which he would acquire would be restricted to the State which gave them.

It is very clear, therefore, that no State can, by any act or law of its own, passed since the adoption of the Constitution, introduce a new member into the political community created by the Constitution of the United States. It cannot make him a member of this community by making him a member of its own. And for the same reason it cannot introduce any person, or description of persons, who were not intended to be embraced in this new political family, which the Constitution brought into existence, but were intended to be excluded from it.

The question then arises, whether the provisions of the Constitution, in relation to the personal rights and privileges to which the citizen of a State should be entitled, embraced the Negro African race, at that time in this country, or who might afterwards be imported, who had then or should afterwards be made free in any State, and to put it in the power of a single State to make him a citizen of the United States, and endue him with the full rights of citizenship in every other State without their consent. Does the Constitution of the United States act upon him whenever he shall be made free under the laws of a State, and raised there to the rank of a citizen, and immediately clothe him with all the privileges of a citizen in every other State, and in its own courts?

The court think the affirmative of these propositions cannot be maintained. And if it cannot, the plaintiff in error could not be a citizen of the State of Missouri, within the meaning of the Constitution of the United States, and, consequently, was not entitled to sue in its courts.

It is true, every person, and every class and description of persons, who were at the time of the adoption of the Constitution recognized as citizens in the several States, became also citizens of this new political body; but none other; it was formed by them, and for them and their posterity, but for no one else. And the personal rights and privileges guaranteed to citizens of this new sovereignty were intended to embrace those only who were then members of the several state communities, or who should afterwards, by birthright or otherwise, become members, according to the provisions of the Constitution and the principles on which it was founded.

It becomes necessary, therefore, to determine who were citizens of the several States when the Constitution was adopted. And in order to do this, we must recur to the governments and institutions of the thirteen Colonies, when they separated from Great Britain and formed new sovereignties. We must inquire who, at that time, were recognized as the people or citizens of a State.

In the opinion of the court, the legislation and histories of the times, and the language wed in the Declaration of Independence, show, that neither the class of persons who had been imported as slaves, nor their descendants, whether they had become free or not, were then acknowledged as a part of the people, nor intended to be included in the general words used in that memorable instrument.

It is difficult at this day to realize the state of public opinion in relation to that unfortunate race, which prevailed in the civilized and enlightened portions of the world at the time of the Declaration of Independence, and when the Constitution of the United States was framed and adopted.

They had for more than a century before been regarded as beings of an inferior order and altogether unfit to associate with the white race, either in social or political relations; and so far inferior that they had no rights which the white man was bound to respect; and that the Negro might justly and lawfully be reduced to slavery for his benefit. He was bought and sold and treated as an ordinary article of merchandise and traffic whenever a profit could be made by it. This opinion was at that time fixed and universal in the civilized portion of the white race. It was regarded as an axiom in morals as well as in politics, which no one thought of disputing, or supposed to be open to dispute; and men in every grade and position in society daily and habitually acted upon it in their private pursuits, as well as in matters of public concern, without doubting for a moment the correctness of this opinion.

A Negro of the African race was regarded as an article of property and held and bought and sold as such in every one of the thirteen Colonies which united in the Declaration of Independence and afterward formed the Constitution of the United States. The slaves were more or less numerous in the different Colonies, as slave labor was found more or less profitable. But no one seems to have doubted the correctness of the prevailing opinion of the time.

The legislation of the different Colonies furnished positive and indisputable proof of this fact.

The language of the Declaration of Independence is equally conclusive:

It begins by declaring that "When, in the course of human events, it becomes necessary for one people to dissolve the political bands which have connected them with another, and to assume, among the powers of the earth the separate and equal station to which the laws of nature and nature's God entitle them, a decent respect for the opinions of mankind requires that they should declare the causes which impel them to the separation."

It then proceeds to say: "We hold these truths to be self-evident: that all men are created equal; that they are endowed by their Creator with certain inalienable rights; that among these are life, liberty, and the pursuit of happiness; that to secure these rights, governments are instituted, deriving their just powers from the consent of the governed."

The general words above quoted would seem to embrace the whole human family, and if they were used in a similar instrument at this day would be so understood. But it is too clear for dispute that the enslaved African race were not intended to be included and formed no part of the people who framed and adopted this declaration; for if the language, as understood in that day would embrace them, the conduct of the distinguished men who framed the Declaration of Independence would have been utterly and flagrantly inconsistent with the principles they asserted; and instead of the sympathy of mankind, to which they so confidently appealed, they would have deserved and received universal rebuke and reprobation.

Yet the men who framed this declaration were great men—high in literary acquirements—high in their sense of honor, and incapable of asserting principles inconsistent with those on which they were acting. They perfectly understood the meaning of the language they used and how it would be understood by others; and they knew that it would not in any part of the civilized world be supposed to embrace the Negro race, which, by common consent, had been excluded from civilized governments and the family of nations and doomed to slavery. They spoke and acted according to the then established doctrine and principles and in the ordinary language of the day, and no one misunderstood them. The unhappy black race were separated from the white by indelible marks, and laws long before established, and were never thought of or spoken of except as property and when the claims of the owner or the profit of the trader were supposed to need protection.

This state of public opinion had undergone no change when the Constitution was adopted, as is equally evident from its provisions and language.

The brief preamble sets forth by whom it was formed, for what purposes, and for whose benefit and protection. It declares that it is formed by the people of the United States; that is to say, by those who were members of the different political communities in the several states; and its great object is declared to be to secure the blessing of liberty to themselves and their posterity. It speaks in general terms of the people of the United States, and of citizens of the several states, when it is providing for the exercise of the powers granted or the privileges secured to the citizen. It does not define what description of persons are intended to be included under these terms, or who shall be regarded as a citizen and one of the people. It uses them as terms so well understood that no further description or definition was necessary.

But there are two clauses in the Constitution which point directly and specifically to the Negro race as a separate class of persons, and show clearly that they were not regarded as a portion of the people or citizens of the Government then formed.

One of these clauses reserves to each of the thirteen States the right to import slaves until the year 1808, if it thinks it proper. And the importation which it thus sanctions was unquestionably of persons of the race of which we are speaking, as the traffic in slaves in the United States had always been confined to them. And by the other provision the States pledge themselves to each other to maintain the right of property of the master, by delivering up to him any slave who may have escaped from his service, and be found within their respective territories. And these two provisions show, conclusively, that neither the description of persons therein referred to, nor their descendants, were embraced in any of the other provisions of the Constitution; for certainly these two clauses were not intended to confer on them or their posterity the blessings of liberty, or any of the personal rights so carefully provided for the citizen.

Indeed, when we look to the condition of this race in the several States at the time, it is impossible to believe that these rights and privileges were intended to be extended to them.

The legislation of the States therefore shows, in a manner not to be mistaken, the inferior and subject condition of that race at the time the Constitution was adopted, and long afterwards, throughout the thirteen States by which that instrument was framed, and it is hardly consistent with the respect due to these States, to suppose that they regarded at that time, as fellow-citizens and members of the sovereignty, a class of beings whom they had thus stigmatized. More especially, it cannot be believed that the large slave-holding States regarded them as included in the word "citizens," or would have consented to a constitution which might compel them to receive them in that character from another State. For if they were so received, and entitled to the privileges and immunities of citizens, it would exempt them from the operation of the special laws and from the police regulations which they considered to be necessary for their own safety. And all of this would be done in the face of the subject race of the same color, both free and slaves, inevitably producing discontent and insubordination among them, and endangering the peace and safety of the State.

Upon a full and careful consideration of the subject, the court is of the opinion that, upon the facts stated in the plea in abatement, Dred Scott was not a citizen of Missouri within the meaning of the Constitution of the

United States, and not entitled as such to sue in its courts; and, consequently, that the Circuit Court had no jurisdiction of the case, and that the judgment on the plea in abatement is erroneous.

We proceed, therefore, to inquire whether the facts relied on by the plaintiff entitled him to his freedom.

In considering this part of the controversy, two questions arise: Was he, together with his family, free in Missouri by reason of the stay in the territory of the United States hereinbefore mentioned? If they were not, is Scott himself free by reason of his removal to Rock Island, in the State of Illinois, as stated in the above admissions?

We proceed to examine the first question.

The Act of Congress, upon which the plaintiff relies, declares that slavery and involuntary servitude, except as a punishment for crime, shall be forever prohibited in all that part of the territory ceded by France, under the name of Louisiana, which lies north of thirty-six degrees thirty minutes north latitude, and not included within the limits of Missouri. And the difficulty which meets us at the threshold of this part of the inquiry is, whether Congress was authorized to pass this law under any of the powers granted to it by the Constitution; for if the authority is not given by that instrument, it is the duty of this court to declare it void and inoperative, and incapable of conferring freedom upon any one who is held as a slave under the laws of any one of the States.

The counsel for the plaintiff has laid much stress upon that article in the Constitution which confers on Congress the power "to dispose of and make all needful rules and regulations respecting the territory or other property belonging to the United States," but, in the judgment of the court, that provision has no bearing on the present controversy, and the power there given, whatever it may be, is confined, and was intended to be confined, to the territory which at that time belonged to, or was claimed by, the United States, and was within their boundaries as settled by the treaty with Great Britain, and can have no influence upon a territory afterwards acquired from a foreign Government. It was a special provision for a known and particular territory, and to meet a present emergency, and nothing more.

If this clause is construed to extend to territory acquired by the present Government from a foreign nation, outside of the limits of any charter from the British Government to a colony, it would be difficult to say, why it was deemed necessary to give the Government the power to sell any vacant lands belonging to the sovereignty which might be found within it; and if this was necessary, why the grant of this power should precede the power to legislate over it and establish a Government there; and still more difficult to say, why it was deemed necessary so specially and particularly to grant the power to make needful rules and regulations in relation to any personal or movable property it might acquire there. For the words, other property necessarily, by every known rule of interpretation, must mean property of a different description from territory or land. And the difficulty would perhaps be insurmountable in endeavoring to account for the last member of the sentence, which provides that "nothing in this Constitution shall be so construed as to prejudice any claims of the United States or any particular State," or to say how any particular State could have claims in or to a territory ceded by a foreign Government, or to account for associating this provision with the preceding provisions of the clause, with which it would appear to have no connection.

But the power of Congress over the person or property of a citizen can never be a mere discretionary power under our Constitution and form of Government. The powers of the Government and the rights and privileges of the citizen are regulated and plainly defined by the Constitution itself. And when the Territory becomes a part of the United States, the Federal Government enters into possession in the character impressed upon it by those who created it. It enters upon it with its powers over the citizen strictly defined, and limited by the Constitution, from which it derives its own existence, and by virtue of which alone it continues to exist and act as a government and sovereignty. It has no power of any kind beyond it; and it cannot, when it enters a Territory of the United States, put off its character, and assume discretionary or despotic powers which the Constitution has denied to it. It cannot create for itself a new character separated from the citizens of the United States, and the duties it owes them under the provisions of the Constitution. The Territory being a part of the United States, the Government and the citizen both enter it under the authority of the Constitution, with their respective rights defined and marked out; and the Federal Government can exercise no power over his person or property, beyond what that instrument confers, nor lawfully deny any right which it has reserved.

The rights of private property have been guarded with equal care. Thus the rights of property are united with the rights of person, and placed on the same ground by the fifth amendment to the Constitution. An Act of Congress which deprives a person of the United States of his liberty or property merely because he came himself or brought his property into a particular Territory of the United States, and who had committed no offense against the laws, could hardly be dignified with the name of due process of law.

And this prohibition is not confined to the States, but the words are general, and extend to the whole territory over which the Constitution gives it power to legislate, including those portions of it remaining under territorial government, as well as that covered by States. It is a total absence of power everywhere within the dominion of the United States, and places the citizens of a territory, so far as these rights are concerned, on the same footing with citizens of the States, and guards them as firmly and plainly against any inroads which the general government might attempt, under the plea of implied or incidental powers. And if Congress itself cannot do this—if it is beyond the powers conferred on the Federal Government—it will be admitted, we presume, that it could not authorize a territorial government to exercise them. It could confer no power on any local government, established by its authority, to violate the provisions of the Constitution.

It seems, however, to be supposed, that there is a difference between property in a slave and other property, and that different rules may be applied to it in expounding the Constitution of the United States.

But if the Constitution recognizes the right of property of the master in a slave, and makes no distinction between that description of property and other property owned by a citizen, no tribunal, acting under the authority of the United States, whether it be legislative, executive, or judicial, has a right to draw such a distinction, or deny to it the benefit of the provisions and guarantees which have been provided for the protection of private property against the encroachments of the Government.

Now the right of property in a slave is distinctly and expressly affirmed in the Constitution. The right to traffic in it, like an ordinary article of merchandise and property, was guaranteed to the citizens of the United States, in every State that might desire it, for twenty years. And the Government in express terms is pledged to protect it in all future time, if the slave escapes from his owner. And no word can be found in the Constitution which gives Congress a greater power over slave property, or which entitles property of that kind to less protection than property of any other description. The only power conferred is the power coupled with the duty of guarding and protecting the owner in his rights.

Upon these considerations, it is the opinion of the court that the Act of Congress which prohibited a citizen from holding and owning property of this kind in the territory of the United States north of the line therein mentioned, is not warranted by the Constitution, and is therefore void; and that neither Dred Scott himself, nor any of his family, were made free by being carried into this territory; even if they had been carried there by the owner, with the intention of becoming a permanent resident.

Upon the whole, therefore, it is the judgment of this court, that it appears by the record before us that the plaintiff in error is not a citizen of Missouri, in the sense in which that word is used in the Constitution; and that the Circuit Court of the United States, for that reason, had no jurisdiction in the case, and could give no judgment in it.

Its judgment for the defendant must, consequently, be reversed, and a mandate issued directing the suit to be dismissed for want of jurisdiction.

A HOUSE DIVIDED

By Abraham Lincoln

At the Illinois state Republican convention on June 7, 1858, a somewhat obscure Springfield attorney and failed politician made a startling speech that ultimately electrified the nation. Decrying the halfhearted attempts at compromise over the slavery issue—and particularly the infamous Dred Scott case—he made an incendiary case for enforced unity on the issue. It was this speech more than anything else that ultimately provoked the secession of the southern states two years later.

Mr. President and Gentlemen of the Convention: If we could first know where we are, and whither we are tending, we could better judge what to do, and how to do it. We are now far into the fifth year since a policy was initiated with the avowed object and confident promise of putting an end to slavery agitation. Under the operation of that policy, that agitation has not only not ceased but has constantly augmented. In my opinion, it will not case until a crisis shall have been reached and passed.

"A house divided against itself cannot stand." I believe this government cannot endure permanently half slave and half free. I do not expect the Union to be dissolved; I do not expect the house to fall; but I do expect it will cease to be divided. It will become all one thing, or all the other. Either the opponents of slavery will arrest the further spread of it, and place it where the public mind shall rest in the belief that it is in the course of ultimate extinction, or its advocates will push it forward till it shall become alike lawful in all the states, old as well as new, North as well as South.

Have we no tendency to the latter condition?

Let anyone who doubts carefully contemplate that now almost complete legal combination—piece of machinery, so to speak—compounded of the Nebraska doctrine and the Dred Scott decision. Let him consider not only what work the machinery is adapted to do, and how well adapted, but also let him study the history of its construction, and trace, if he can, or rather fail, if he can, to trace the evidences of design, and concert of action, among its chief architects, from the beginning.

The new year of 1854 found slavery excluded from more than half the states by state constitutions, and from most of the national territory by congressional prohibition. Four days later commenced the struggle which ended in repealing that congressional prohibition. This opened all the national territory to slavery and was the first point gained....

While the Nebraska Bill was passing through Congress, a law case, involving the question of a Negro's freedom, by reason of his owner having voluntarily taken him first into a free state, and then into a territory covered by the congressional prohibition, and held him as a slave for a long time in each, was passing through the United States Circuit Court for the District of Missouri; and both Nebraska Bill and lawsuit were brought to a decision in the same month of May 1854. The Negro's name was Dred Scott, which name now designates the decision finally made in the case. Before the then next presidential election, the law case came to, and was argued in, the Supreme Court of the United States; but the decision of it was deferred until after the election.

The election came. Mr. Buchanan was elected, and the endorsement, such as it was, secured. That was the second point gained.

The reputed author of the Nebraska Bill finds an early occasion to make a speech at this capital endorsing the Dred Scott decision, and vehemently denouncing all opposition to it. The new president, too, seizes the early occasion of the Silliman letter to endorse and strongly construe that decision, and to express his astonishment that any different view had ever been entertained!

The several points of the Dred Scott decision, in connection with Senator Douglas's "care not" policy, constitute the piece of machinery, in its present state of advancement. This was the third point gained. The working points of that machinery are:

Firstly, That no Negro slave, imported as such from Africa, and no descendant of such slave, can ever be a citizen of any state, in the sense of that term as used in the Constitution of the United States. This point is made in order to deprive the Negro, in every possible event, of the benefit of that provision of the United States Constitution which declares that "the citizens of each state shall be entitled to all privileges and immunities of citizens in the several states."

Secondly, That, "subject to the Constitution of the United States," neither Congress nor a territorial legislature can exclude slavery from any United States territory. This point is made in order that individual men may fill up the territories with slaves, without danger of losing them as property, and thus to enhance the chances of permanency to the institution through all the future.

Thirdly, That whether the holding a Negro in actual slavery in a free state makes him free, as against the holder, the United States courts will not decide, but will leave to be decided by the courts of any slave state the Negro may be forced into by the master. This point is made, not to be pressed immediately; but, if acquiesced in for a while, and apparently endorsed by the people at an election, then to sustain the logical conclusion that what Dred Scott's master might lawfully do with Dred Scott in the free state of Illinois, every other master may lawfully do with any other one, or one thousand slaves, in Illinois, or in any other free state.

It will throw additional light on the latter, to go back and run the mind over the string of historical facts already stated. Several things will now appear less dark and mysterious than they did when they were transpiring. The people were to be left "perfectly free," "subject only to the Constitution." What the Constitution had to do with it outsiders could not then see. Plainly enough now, it was an exactly fitted niche for the Dred Scott decision afterward to come in and declare that perfect freedom of the people to be just no freedom at all. Why was the amendment expressly declaring the right of the people to exclude slavery voted down? Plainly enough now, the adoption of it would have spoiled the niche for the Dred Scott decision. Why was the court decision held up? Why even a senator's individual opinion withheld till after the presidential election? Plainly enough now, the speaking out then would have damaged the "perfectly free" argument upon which the election was to be carried. Why the outgoing president's felicitation on the endorsement? Why the delay of a re-argument? Why the incoming president's advance exhortation in favor of the decision?

We cannot absolutely know that all these exact adaptations are the result of preconcert. But when we see a lot of framed timbers, different portions of which we know have been gotten out at different times and places and by different workmen—Stephen, Franklin, Roger, and James, for instance—and when we see these timbers joined together, and see they exactly make the frame of a house or a mill, all the tenons and mortices exactly fitting, and all the lengths and proportions of the different pieces exactly adapted to their respective places, and not a piece too many or too few, not omitting even scaffolding—or, if a single piece be lacking, we see the place in the frame exactly fitted and prepared to yet bring such piece in—in such a case we find it impossible not to believe that Stephen and Franklin and Roger and James all understood one another from the beginning, and all worked upon a common plan or draft drawn up before the first blow was struck.

While the opinion of the court, by Chief Justice Taney, in the Dred Scott case, and the separate opinions of all the concurring judges, expressly declare that the Constitution of the United States neither permits Congress nor a territorial legislature to exclude slavery from any United States territory, they all omit to declare whether or not the same Constitution permits a state, or the people of a state, to exclude it. We may, ere long, see another Supreme Court decision declaring that the Constitution of the United States does not permit a state to exclude slavery from its limits. And this may especially be expected if the doctrine of "care not whether slavery be voted down or voted up" shall gain upon the public mind sufficiently to give promise that such a decision can be maintained when made.

Such a decision is all that slavery now lacks of being alike lawful in all the states. Welcome, or unwelcome, such decision is probably coming, and will soon be upon us, unless the power of the present political dynasty shall be met and overthrown. We shall lie down pleasantly dreaming that the people of Missouri are on the verge of making their state free, and we shall awake to the reality instead that the Supreme Court has made Illinois a slave state. To meet and overthrow the power of that dynasty is the work now before all those who would prevent that consummation. That is what we have to do. How can we best do it?

There are those who denounce us openly to their own friends, and yet whisper us softly that Senator Douglas is the aptest instrument there is with which to effect that object. They do not tell us, nor has he told us, that he wishes any such object to be effected. They wish us to infer all from the facts that he now has a little quarrel with the present head of the dynasty; and that he has regularly voted with us on a single point upon which he and we have never differed. They remind us that he is a very great man, and that the largest of us are very small ones. Let this be granted. But "a living dog is better than a dead lion." Judge Douglas, if not a dead lion for this work, is at least a caged and toothless one.

Our cause, then, must be entrusted to, and conducted by, its own undoubted friends—those whose hands are free, whose hearts are in the work, who do care for the result. Two years ago the Republicans of the nation mustered over thirteen hundred thousand strong. We did this under the single impulse of resistance to a common danger, with every external circumstance against us. Of strange, discordant, and even hostile elements, we gathered from the four winds, and formed and fought the battle through, under the constant hot fire of a disciplined, proud, and pampered enemy. Did we brave all then to falter now? Now, when that same enemy is wavering, dissevered, and belligerent? The result is not doubtful. We shall not fail—if we stand firm, we shall not fail. Wise counsels may accelerate or mistakes delay it, but, sooner or later, the victory is sure to come.

INAUGURAL ADDRESS

By Jefferson Davis

Upon news of the election of Abraham Lincoln, South Carolina, claiming strong constitutional warrant, seceded from the Union on December 20, 1860. Six other states followed—Mississippi, Florida, Alabama, Georgia, Louisiana, and Texas. Together they formed the Confederate States of America in February 1861. Kentucky, Arkansas, Virginia, North Carolina, and Tennessee were to follow—while Maryland and Missouri were prevented from formal secession only by Federal action. The Constitutional Convention in Montgomery, Alabama, chose Jefferson Davis as the Confederacy's first president, and he took the oath of office on February 18. The cumulative haste of these events undermined the efforts of the Confederacy to create a fully functioning government prior to Lincoln's inauguration. The Confederate Congress soon adopted a permanent constitution, which allowed for presidential election by popular vote. On February 22, 1862, Davis took a second oath of office at Richmond, Virginia, and gave this inaugural address.

Fellow Citizens: On this the birthday of the man most identified with the establishment of American independence, and beneath the monument erected to commemorate his heroic virtues and those of his compatriots, we have assembled to usher into existence the permanent government of the Confederate States. Through this instrumentality, under the favor of Divine Providence, we hope to perpetuate the principles of our Revolutionary fathers. The day, the memory, and the purpose seem fitly associated.

It is with mingled feelings of humility and pride that I appear to take, in the presence of the people and before high heaven, the oath prescribed as a qualification for the exalted station to which the unanimous voice of the people has called me. Deeply sensible of all that is implied by this manifestation of the people's confidence, I am yet more profoundly impressed by the vast responsibility of the office and humbly feel my own unworthiness.

When a long course of class legislation, directed not to the general welfare but to the aggrandizement of the Northern section of the Union, culminated in a warfare on the domestic institutions of the Southern states—when the dogmas of a sectional party, substituted for the provisions of the constitutional compact, threatened to destroy the sovereign rights of the states—six of those states, withdrawing from the Union, confederated together to exercise the right and perform the duty of instituting a government which would better secure the liberties for the preservation of which that Union was established.

Whatever of hope some may have entertained that a returning sense of justice would remove the danger with which our rights were threatened, and render it possible to preserve the Union of the Constitution, must have been dispelled by the malignity and barbarity of the Northern states in the prosecution of the existing war. The confidence of the most hopeful among us must have been destroyed by the disregard they have recently exhibited for all the time-honored bulwarks of civil and religious liberty.

Bastilles filled with prisoners, arrested without civil process or indictment duly found; the writ of habeas corpus suspended by executive mandate; a state legislature controlled by the imprisonment of members whose avowed principles suggested to the federal executive that there might be another added to the list of seceded states; elections held under threats of a military power; civil officers, peaceful citizens, and gentlewomen incarcerated for opinion's sake—proclaimed the incapacity of our late associates to administer a government as free, liberal, and humane as that established for our common use.

For proof of the sincerity of our purpose to maintain our ancient institutions, we may point to the Constitution of the Confederacy and the laws enacted under it, as well as to the fact that through all the necessities of an unequal struggle there has been no act on our part to impair personal liberty or the freedom of speech, of thought, or of the press. The courts have been open, the judicial functions fully executed, and every right of the peaceful citizen maintained as securely as if a war of invasion had not disturbed the land.

The people of the states now confederated became convinced the government of the United States had fallen into the hands of a sectional majority, who would pervert that most sacred of all trusts to the destruction of the rights which it was pledged to protect. They believed that to remain longer in the Union would subject them to a continuance of a disparaging discrimination, submission to which would be inconsistent with their welfare and intolerable to a proud people. They therefore determined to sever its bonds and establish a new confederacy for themselves.

The first year in our history has been the most eventful in the annals of this continent. A new government has been established, and its machinery put in operation over an area exceeding seven hundred thousand square miles. The great principles upon which we have been willing to hazard everything that is dear to man have made conquests for us which could never have been achieved by the sword. Our Confederacy has grown from six to thirteen states; and Maryland, already united to us by hallowed memories and material interests, will, I believe, when able to speak with unstifled voice, connect her destiny with the South.

Our people have rallied with unexampled unanimity to the support of the great principles of constitutional government, with firm resolve to perpetuate by arms the right which they could not peacefully secure. A million of men, it is estimated, are now standing in hostile array and waging war along a frontier of thousands of miles. Battles have been fought, sieges have been conducted, and although the contest is not ended, and the tide for the moment is against us, the final result in our favor is not doubtful.

This great strife has awakened in the people the highest emotions and qualities of the human soul. It is cultivating feelings of patriotism, virtue, and courage. Instances of self-sacrifice and of generous devotion to the noble cause for which we are contending are rife throughout the land. Never has a people evinced a more determined spirit than that now animating men, women, and children in every part of our country. Upon the first call, the men fly to arms; and wives and mothers send their husbands and sons to battle without a murmur of regret.

It is a satisfaction that we have maintained the war by our unaided exertions. We have neither asked nor received assistance from any quarter. Yet the interest involved is not wholly our own. The world at large is concerned in opening our markets to its commerce. When the independence of the Confederate States is recognized by the nations of the earth, and we are free to follow our interests and inclinations by cultivating foreign trade, the Southern states will offer to manufacturing nations the most favorable markets which ever invited their commerce. Cotton, sugar, rice, tobacco, provisions, timber, and naval stores will furnish attractive exchanges.

The tyranny of an unbridled majority, the most odious and least responsible form of despotism, has denied us both the rights and the remedy. Therefore we are in arms to renew such sacrifices as our fathers made to the holy cause of constitutional liberty. At the darkest hour of our struggle the provisional gives place to the permanent government. After a series of successes and victories, which covered our arms with glory, we have recently met with serious disasters. But in the heart of a people resolved to be free, these disasters tend but to stimulate to increased resistance.

To show ourselves worthy of the inheritance bequeathed to us by the patriots of the Revolution, we must emulate that heroic devotion which made reverse to them but the crucible in which their patriotism was refined.

With confidence in the wisdom and virtue of those who will share with me the responsibility and aid me in the conduct of public affairs; securely relying on the patriotism and courage of the people, of which the present war has furnished so many examples, I deeply feel the weight of the responsibilities I now, with unaffected diffidence, am about to assume; and fully realizing the inequality of human power to guide and to sustain, my hope is reverently fixed on Him whose favor is ever vouchsafed to the cause which is just. With humble gratitude and adoration, acknowledging the Providence which has so visibly protected the Confederacy during its brief but eventful career, to Thee, O God! I trustingly commit myself, and prayerfully invoke Thy blessing on my country and its cause.

CONSTITUTION OF THE CONFEDERATE STATES

The form of government the southern states adopted for their confederacy was a deliberate imitation of the original American Constitution; the Confederates believed they were the philosophical heirs of the Founders and the Northern states had departed from that decentralized vision. Drafted on March 11, 1861, the confederation also drew from the old Articles of Confederation in protecting the autonomy and rights of the individual states. Though its cause was lost, the essence of its flexible form has served as a model for a number of conservative republican experiments in the years since.

We, the people of the Confederate States, each state acting in its sovereign and independent character, in order to form a permanent federal government, establish justice, insure domestic tranquillity, and secure the blessings of liberty to ourselves and our posterity—invoking the favor and guidance of Almighty God—do ordain and establish this Constitution for the Confederate States of America.

ARTICLE I

Section 1: All legislative powers herein delegated shall be vested in a Congress of the Confederate States, which shall consist of a Senate and House of Representatives.

Section 2: The House of Representatives shall be composed of members chosen every second year by the people of the several States: and the electors in each State shall be citizens of the Confederate States, and have the qualifications requisite for electors of the most numerous branch of the State Legislature, but no person of foreign birth, not a citizen of the

Confederate States, shall be allowed to vote for any officer, civil or political, State or Federal.

No person shall be a Representative who shall not have attained the age of twenty five years, and be a citizen of the Confederate States, and who shall not, when elected, be an inhabitant of that State in which he shall be chosen.

Representatives and direct taxes shall be apportioned among the several States, which may be included within this Confederacy, according to their respective numbers, which shall be determined by adding to the whole number of free persons, including those bound to service for a term of years and excluding Indians not taxed, three fifths of all slaves. The actual enumeration shall be made within three years after the first meeting of the Congress of the Confederate States, and within every subsequent term of ten years, in such manner as they shall by law direct. The number of Representatives shall not exceed one for every fifty thousand, but each State shall have at least one Representative; and until such enumeration shall be made, the State of South Carolina shall be entitled to choose six, the State of Georgia ten, the State of Alabama nine; the State of Florida two; the State of Mississippi seven; the State of Louisiana six; and the State of Texas six.

When vacancies happen in the representation from any State the executive authority thereof shall issue writs of election to fill such vacancies

The House of Representatives shall choose their Speaker and other officers, and shall have the sole power of impeachment; except that any judicial or other Federal officer, resident and acting solely within the limits of any State, may be impeached by a vote of two thirds of both branches of the Legislature thereof.

Section 3: The Senate of the Confederate States shall be composed of two Senators from each State, chosen for six years by the Legislature thereof, at the regular session next immediately preceding the commencement of the term of service; and each Senator shall have one vote.

Immediately after they shall be assembled, in consequence of the first election they shall be divided as casually as may be into three classes. The seats of the Senators of the first class shall be vacated at the expiration of the second year; of the second class at the expiration of the fourth year; and of the third class at the expiration of the sixth year, so that one third may be chosen every second year; and if vacancies happen by resignation, or otherwise, during the recess of the Legislature of any State, the executive thereof may make temporary appointments until the next meeting of the Legislature, which shall then fill such vacancies.

No Person shall be a Senator who shall not have attained the age of thirty years, and be a citizen of the Confederate States; and who shall not, when elected, be an inhabitant of the State for which he shall be chosen.

The Vice President of the Confederate States shall be president of the Senate, but shall have no vote unless they be equally divided.

The Senate shall choose their other officers; and also a president pro-tempore in the absence of the Vice President or when he shall exercise the office of President of the Confederate States.

The Senate shall have the sole power to try all impeachments. When sitting for that purpose, they shall be on oath or affirmation. When the President of the Confederate States is tried, the Chief Justice shall preside; and no person shall be convicted without the concurrence of two thirds of the members present.

Judgment in cases of impeachment shall not extend further than to removal from office, and disqualification to hold and enjoy any office of honor, trust or profit under the Confederate States, but the party convicted shall, nevertheless, be liable and subject to indictment, trial, judgment, and punishment according to law.

Section 4: The times, places, and manner of holding elections for Senators and Representatives shall be prescribed in each State by the Legislatures thereof, subject to the provisions of this Constitution; but the Congress may, at any time, by law, make or alter such regulations, except as to the times and places of choosing Senators.

The Congress shall assemble at least once in every year; and such meeting shall be on the first Monday in December, unless they shall, by law, appoint a different day.

Section 5: Each House shall be the judge of the elections, returns, and qualifications of its members, and a majority of each shall constitute a quorum to do business; but a smaller number may adjourn from day to day, and may be authorized to compel the attendance of absent members, in such manner and under such penalties as each House may provide.

Each House may determine the rules of its proceedings, punish its members for disorderly behavior, and, with the concurrence of two thirds of the whole number, expel a member.

Each House shall keep a journal of its proceedings, and from time to time publish the same, excepting such parts as may in their judgment require secrecy; and the yeas and nays of the members of either House, on any question, shall, at the desire of one fifth of those present, be entered on the journal.

Neither House, during the session of Congress, shall, without the consent of the other, adjourn for more than three days, nor to any other place than that in which the two Houses shall be sitting.

Section 6: The Senators and Representatives shall receive a

compensation for their services, to be ascertained by law, and paid out of the Treasury of the Confederate States. They shall, in all cases, except treason, felony, and breach of the peace, be privileged from arrest during their attendance at the session of their respective Houses, and in going to or returning from the same, and from any speech or debate in either House, they shall not be questioned in any other place.

No Senator or Representative shall, during the time for which he was elected, be appointed to any civil office under the authority of the Confederate States, which shall have been created, or the emoluments whereof shall have been increased during such time, and no person holding any office under the Confederate States shall be a member of either House during his continuance in office. But Congress may, by law, grant to the principal officer in each of the Executive Departments a seat upon the floor of either House, with the privilege of discussing any measures appertaining to his department.

Section 7: All bills for raising revenue shall originate in the House of Representatives; but the Senate may propose or concur with amendments, as on other bills.

Every bill which shall have passed both Houses, shall, before it becomes a law, be presented to the President of the Confederate States; if he approve, he shall sign it; but if not, he shall return it, with his objections, to that House in which it shall have originated, who shall enter the objections at large on their journal, and proceed to reconsider it. If, after such reconsideration, two-thirds of that House shall agree to pass the bill, it shall be sent, together with the objections, to the other House, by which it shall likewise be reconsidered, and if approved by two thirds of that House, it shall become a law. But in all such cases, the votes of both Houses shall be determined by yeas and nays, and the names of the persons voting for and against the bill shall be entered on the journal of each House respectively. If any bill shall not be returned by the President within ten days (Sundays excepted) after it shall have been presented to him, the same shall be a law, in like manner as if he had signed it, unless the Congress, by their adjournment, prevent its return; in which case it shall not be a law. The President may approve any appropriation and disapprove any other appropriation in the same bill. In such case he shall, in signing the bill, designate the appropriations disapproved; and shall return a copy of such appropriations, with his objections, to the House in which the bill shall have originated; and the same proceedings shall then be had as in the case of other bills disapproved by the President.

Every order, resolution, or vote, to which the concurrence of both Houses may be necessary (except on a question of adjournment) shall be presented to the President of the Confederate States; and before the same shall take effect shall be approved by him: or, being disapproved by him, shall be re-passed by two thirds of both Houses, according to the rules and limitations prescribed in case of a bill.

Section 8: The Congress shall have power—

To lay and collect taxes, duties, imposts, and excises for revenue, necessary to pay the debts, provide for the common defense, and carry on the Government of the Confederate States: but no bounties shall be granted from the Treasury; nor shall any duties or taxes on importations from foreign nations be laid to promote or foster any branch of industry; and all duties, imposts, and excises shall be uniform throughout the Confederate States.

To borrow money on the credit of the Confederate States.

To regulate commerce with foreign nations, and among the several States, and with the Indian tribes, but neither this, nor any other clause contained in the Constitution, shall ever be construed to delegate the power to Congress to appropriate money for any internal improvement intended to facilitate commerce; except for the purpose of furnishing lights, beacons, and buoys, and other aids to navigation upon the coasts, and the improvement of harbors and the removing of obstructions in river navigation, in all which cases such duties shall be laid on the navigation facilitated thereby as may be necessary to pay the costs and expenses thereof.

To establish uniform laws of naturalization, and uniform laws on the subject of bankruptcies, throughout the Confederate States, but no law of Congress shall discharge any debt contracted before the passage of the same.

To coin money, regulate the value thereof, and of foreign coin, and fix the standard of weights and measures.

To provide for the punishment of counterfeiting the securities and current coin of the Confederate States.

To establish post offices and post routes; but the expenses of the Post Office Department, after the first day of March in the year of our Lord eighteen hundred and sixty three, shall be paid out of its own revenues.

To promote the progress of science and useful arts, by securing for limited times to authors and inventors the exclusive right to their respective writings and discoveries.

To constitute tribunals inferior to the Supreme Court.

To define and punish piracies and felonies committed on the high seas, and offenses against the law of nations.

To declare war, grant letters of marque and reprisal, and make rules concerning captures on land and water.

To raise and support armies; but no appropriations of money to that use shall be for a longer term than two years.

To provide and maintain a navy.

To make rules for the government and regulation of the land and naval forces.

To provide for calling forth the militia to execute the laws of the Confederate States, suppress insurrections, and repel invasions.

To provide for organizing, arming, and disciplining the militia, and for governing such part of them as may be employed in the service of the Confederate States; reserving to the States, respectively, the appointment of officers, and the authority of training the militia according to the discipline prescribed by Congress.

To exercise exclusive legislation, in all cases whatsoever, over such district (not exceeding ten miles square) as may, by cession of one or more States and the acceptance of Congress, become the seat of the Government of the Confederate States; and to exercise like authority over all places purchased by the consent of the Legislature of the State in which the same shall be, for the erection of forts, magazines, arsenals, dockyards, and other needful buildings.

To make all laws which shall be necessary and proper for carrying into execution the foregoing powers, and all other powers vested by this Constitution in the Government of the Confederate States, or in any department or officer hereof.

Section 9: The importation of negroes of the African race from any foreign country other than the slaveholding States or Territories of the United States of America, is hereby forbidden: and Congress is required to pass such laws as shall effectually prevent the same.

Congress shall also have power to prohibit the introduction of slaves from any State not a member of, or Territory not belonging to, this Confederacy.

The privilege of the writ of habeas corpus shall not be suspended, unless when in cases of rebellion or invasion the public safety may require it.

No bill of attainder, ex post facto law, or law denying or impairing the right of property in negro slaves shall be passed.

No capitation or other direct tax shall be laid, unless in proportion to the census or enumeration herein before directed to be taken.

No tax or duty shall be laid on articles exported from any State, except by a vote of two thirds of both Houses.

No preference shall be given by any regulation of commerce or revenue to the ports of one State over those of another.

No money shall be drawn from the Treasury, but in consequence of appropriations made by law; and a regular statement and account of the receipts and expenditures of all public money shall be published from time to time.

Congress shall appropriate no money from the Treasury except by a vote of two thirds of both Houses, taken by yeas and nays, unless it be asked and estimated for by some one of the heads of departments and submitted to Congress by the President: or for the purpose of paying its own expenses and contingencies: or for the payment of claims against the Confederate States the justice of which shall have been judicially declared by a tribunal for the investigation of claims against the Government, which it is hereby made the duty of Congress to establish.

All bills appropriating money shall specify in Federal currency the exact amount of each appropriation and the purposes for which it is made: and Congress shall grant no extra compensation to any public contractor, officer, agent, or servant, after such contract shall have been made or such service rendered.

No title of nobility shall be granted by the Confederate States: and no person holding any office of profit or trust under them shall, without the consent of Congress, accept any present, emolument, office, or title of any kind whatever, from any king, prince, or foreign state.

Congress shall make no law respecting an establishment of religion, or prohibiting the free exercise thereof; or abridging the freedom of speech, or of the press; or the right of the people peaceably to assemble and petition the Government for a redress of grievances.

A well-regulated militia being necessary to the security of a free State, the right of the people to keep and bear arms shall not be infringed.

No soldier shall, in time of peace, be quartered in any house without the consent of the owner; nor in time of war, but in a manner to be prescribed by law.

The right of the people to be secure in their persons, houses, papers, and effects, against unreasonable searches and seizures, shall not be violated, and no warrants shall issue but upon probable cause, supported by oath or affirmation, and particularly describing the place to be searched and the persons or things to be seized.

No person shall be held to answer for a capital or otherwise infamous crime, unless on a presentment or indictment of a grand jury, except in cases arising in the land or naval forces, or in the militia, when in actual service in time of war or public danger; nor shall any person be subject for the same offense to be twice put in jeopardy of life or limb; nor be compelled, in any criminal case, to be a witness against himself; nor be deprived of life, liberty, or property without due process of law; nor shall private property be taken for public use, without just compensation.

In all criminal prosecutions the accused shall enjoy the right to a speedy and public trial, by an impartial jury of the State and district wherein the crime shall have been committed, which district shall have been previously ascertained by law, and to be informed of the nature and cause of the accusation; to be confronted with the witnesses against him: to have compulsory process for obtaining witnesses in his favor; and to have the assistance of counsel for his defense.

In suits at common law, where the value in controversy shall exceed twenty dollars, the right of trial by jury shall be preserved; and no fact so tried by a jury shall be otherwise reexamined in any court of the Confederacy, than according to the rules of common law.

Excessive bail shall not be required, nor excessive fines imposed, nor cruel and unusual punishments inflicted.

Every law, or resolution having the force of law shall relate to but one subject, and that shall be expressed in the title.

Section 10: No State shall enter into any treaty, alliance, or confederation, grant letters of marque and reprisal: coin money; make anything but gold and silver coin a tender in payment of debts: pass any bill of attainder, or ex post facto law, or law impairing the obligation of contracts; or grant any title of nobility.

No State shall, without the consent of Congress, lay any imposts or duties on imports or exports, except what may be absolutely necessary for executing its inspection laws: and the net produce of all duties and imposts, laid by any State on imports or exports, shall be for the use of the Treasury of the Confederate States; and all such laws shall be subject to the revision and control of Congress.

No State shall, without the consent of Congress, lay any duty on tonnage, except on seagoing vessels, for the improvement of its rivers and harbors navigated by the said vessels; but such duties shall not conflict with any treaties of the Confederate States with foreign nations; and any surplus revenue thus derived shall, after making such improvement, be paid into the common treasury. Nor shall any State keep troops or ships of war in time of peace, enter into any agreement or compact with another State, or with a foreign power, or engage in war unless actually invaded, or in such imminent danger as will not admit of delay. But when any river divides or flows through two or more States they may enter into compacts with each other to improve the navigation thereof.

ARTICLE II

Section 1: The executive power shall be vested in a President of the Confederate States of America. He and the Vice President shall hold their offices for the term of six years; but the President shall not be re-eligible. The President and Vice President shall be elected as follows:

Each State shall appoint, in such manner as the Legislature thereof may direct, a number of electors equal to the whole number of Senators and Representatives to which the State may be entitled in the Congress, but no Senator or Representative or person holding an office of trust or profit under the Confederate States shall be appointed an elector.

The electors shall meet in their respective States and vote by ballot for President or Vice President, one of whom at least, shall not be an inhabitant of the same State with themselves; they shall name in their ballots the person voted for as President, and in distinct ballots the person voted for as Vice President, and they shall make distinct lists of all persons voted for as President, and of all persons voted for as Vice President, and of the number of votes for each, which lists they shall sign and certify, and transmit, sealed, to the seat of the Government of the Confederate States, directed to the President of the Senate; the President of the Senate shall in the presence of the Senate and House of Representatives open all the certificates, and the votes shall then be counted. The person having the greatest number of votes for President shall be the President, if such number be a majority of the whole number of electors appointed, and if no person have such majority, then from the persons having the highest numbers, not exceeding three, on the list of those voted for as president, the House of Representatives shall choose immediately, by ballot, the President. But in choosing the President the votes shall be taken by States—the representation from each State having one vote; a quorum for this purpose shall consist of a member or members from two thirds of the States, and a majority of all the States shall be necessary to a choice. And if the House of Representatives shall not choose a President, whenever the right of choice shall devolve upon them, before the 4th day of March next following, then the Vice President shall act as President, as in case of the death, or other constitutional disability of the President.

The person having the greatest number of votes as Vice President shall be the Vice President, if such number be a majority of the whole number of electors appointed; and if no person have a majority, then, from the two highest numbers on the list, the Senate shall choose a Vice President; a quorum for the purpose shall consist of two thirds of the whole number of Senators, and a majority of the whole number shall be necessary to a choice.

But no person constitutionally ineligible to the office of President shall be eligible to that of Vice President of the Confederate States.

The Congress may determine the time of choosing the electors, and the day on which they shall give their votes, which day shall be the same throughout the Confederate States.

No person except a natural born citizen of the Confederate States. or a citizen thereof at the time of the adoption of this Constitution, or a citizen thereof born in the United States prior to the 20th of December, 1860, shall be eligible to the office of President; neither shall any person be eligible to that office who shall not have attained the age of thirty five years, and been fourteen years a resident within the limits of the Confederate States, as they may exist at the time of his election.

In case of the removal of the President from office or of his death, resignation, or inability to discharge the powers and duties of said office, the same shall devolve on the Vice President, and the Congress may by law provide for the case of removal, death, resignation, or inability, both of the President and Vice President, declaring what officer shall then act as President; and such officer shall act accordingly until the disability be removed or a President shall be elected.

The President shall, at stated times, receive for his services a compensation, which shall neither be increased nor diminished during the period for which he shall have been elected; and he shall not receive within that period any other emolument from the Confederate States, or any of them.

Before he enters on the execution of his office he shall take the following oath or affirmation: "I do solemnly swear (or affirm) that I will faithfully execute the office of President of the Confederate States, and will, to the best of my ability, preserve, protect, and defend the Constitution thereof."

Section 2: The President shall be Commander in Chief of the Army and Navy of the Confederate States, and of the militia of the Several States, when called into the actual service of the Confederate States; he may require the opinion, in writing, of the principal officer in each of the Executive Departments, upon any subject relating to the duties of their respective offices; and he shall have power to grant reprieves and pardons for offenses against the Confederate States, except in cases of impeachment.

He shall have power, by and with the advice and consent of the Senate, to make treaties, provided two thirds of the Senators present concur; and he shall nominate, and by and with the advice and consent of the Senate shall appoint ambassadors, other public ministers and consuls, judges of the Supreme Court, and all other officers of the Confederate States whose appointments are not herein otherwise provided for, and which shall be established by law; but the Congress may, by law, vest the appointment of such inferior officers, as they think proper, in the President alone, in the courts of law, or in the heads of departments.

The principal officer in each of the Executive Departments, and all persons connected with the diplomatic service may be removed from office at the pleasure of the President. All other civil officers of the Executive Departments may be removed at any time by the President, or other appointing power, when their services are unnecessary, or for dishonesty, incapacity, inefficiency, misconduct, or neglect of duty; and when so removed, the removal shall be reported to the Senate, together with the reasons therefor.

The President shall have power to fill all vacancies that may happen during the recess of the Senate, by granting commissions which shall expire at the end of their next session, but no person rejected by the Senate shall be reappointed to the same office during their ensuing recess.

Section 3: The President shall, from time to time, give the Congress information of the state of the Confederacy, and recommend to their consideration such measures as he shall judge necessary and expedient; he may, on extraordinary occasions, convene both Houses, or either of them, and in case of disagreement between them, with respect to the time of adjournment, he may adjourn them to such time as he shall think proper; he shall receive ambassadors and other public ministers; he shall take care that the laws be faithfully executed, and shall commission all the officers of the Confederate States.

Section 4: President, Vice President, and all civil officers of the Confederate States, shall be removed from office on impeachment for and conviction of treason, bribery, or other high crimes and misdemeanors.

ARTICLE III

Section 1: The judicial power of the Confederate States shall be vested in one Supreme Court, and in such inferior courts as the Congress may, from time to time, ordain and establish. The judges, both of the Supreme and inferior courts, shall hold their offices during good behavior, and shall, at stated times, receive for their services a compensation which shall not be diminished during their continuance in office.

Section 2: The judicial power shall extend to all cases arising under this Constitution, the laws of the Confederate States, and treaties made, or which shall be made, under their authority; to all cases affecting ambassadors, other public ministers and consuls; to all cases of admiralty and maritime jurisdiction; to controversies to which the Confederate States shall be a party; to controversies between two or more States; between a State and citizens of another State, where the State is plaintiff; between citizens claiming lands under grants of different States; and between a State or the citizens thereof, and foreign states, citizens, or subjects; but no State shall be sued by a citizen or subject of any foreign state.

In all cases affecting ambassadors, other public ministers and consuls, and those in which a State shall be a party, the Supreme Court shall have original jurisdiction. In all the other cases before mentioned, the Supreme Court shall have appellate jurisdiction both as to law and fact, with such exceptions and under such regulations as the Congress shall make.

The trial of all crimes, except in cases of impeachment, shall be by jury, and such trial shall be held in the State where the said crimes shall have been committed, but when not committed within any State, the trial shall be at such place or places as the Congress may by law have directed.

Section 3: Treason against the Confederate States shall consist only in levying war against them, or in adhering to their enemies, giving them aid and comfort. No person shall be convicted of treason unless on the testimony of two witnesses to the same overt act, or on confession in open court.

The Congress shall have power to declare the punishment of treason; but no attainder of treason shall work corruption of blood, or forfeiture, except during the life of the person attained.

ARTICLE IV

Section 1: Full faith and credit shall be given in each State to the public acts, records, and judicial proceedings of every other State; and the Congress may, by general laws, prescribe the manner in which such acts, records, and proceedings shall be proved, and the effect thereof.

Section 2: The citizens of each State shall be entitled to all the privileges and immunities of citizens in the several States; and shall have the right of transit and sojourn in any State of this Confederacy, with their slaves and other property; and the right of property in said slaves shall not be thereby impaired.

A person charged in any State with treason, felony, or other crime against the laws of such State, who shall flee from justice, and be found in another State, shall, on demand of the executive authority of the State from which he fled, be delivered up, to be removed to the State having jurisdiction of the crime.

No slave or other person held to service or labor in any State or Territory of the Confederate States, under the laws thereof, escaping or lawfully carried into another, shall in consequence of any law or regulation therein, be discharged from such service or labor, but shall be delivered up on claim of the party to whom such slave belongs, or to whom such service or labor may be due.

Section 3: Other States may be admitted into this Confederacy by a vote of two thirds of the whole House of representatives and two thirds of the Senate, the Senate voting by States; but no new State shall be formed or erected within the jurisdiction of any other State, nor any State shall be formed by the junction of two or more States, or parts of States, without the consent of the Legislatures of the States concerned, as well as of the Congress.

The Congress shall have the power to dispose of and make all needful rules and regulations concerning the property of the Confederate States, including the lands thereof.

The Confederate States may acquire new territory and Congress shall have power to legislate and provide governments for the inhabitants of all territory belonging to the Confederate States, lying without the limits of the several States; and may permit them, at such times, and in such manner as it may by law provide, to form States to be admitted into the Confederacy. In all such territory the institution of negro slavery as it now exists in the Confederate States, shall be recognized and protected by Congress and by the Territorial government; and the inhabitants of the several Confederate States and Territories shall have the right to take to such Territory any slaves lawfully held by them in any of the States or Territories of the Confederate States.

The Confederate States shall guarantee to every State that now is, or hereafter may become, a member of this Confederacy, a republican form of government; and shall protect each of them against invasion; and on application of the Legislature (or of the Executive when the Legislature is not in session) against domestic violence.

ARTICLE V

Section 1: Upon the demand of any three States, legally assembled in their several conventions, the Congress shall summon a convention of all the States, to take into consideration such amendments to the Constitution as the said States shall concur in suggesting at the time when the said demand is made; and should any of the proposed amendments to the Constitution be agreed on by the said convention—voting by States—and the same be ratified by the Legislatures of two thirds of the several States, or by conventions in two thirds thereof—as the one or the other mode of ratification may be proposed by the general convention—they shall thenceforward form a part of this Constitution. But no State shall, without its consent, be deprived of its equal representation in the Senate.

ARTICLE VI

Section 1: The Government established by this Constitution is the successor of the Provisional Government of the Confederate States of America, and all the laws passed by the latter shall continue in force until the same shall be repealed or modified and all the officers appointed by the same shall remain in office until their successors are appointed and qualified, or the offices abolished.

Section 2: All debts contracted and engagements entered into before the adoption of this Constitution shall be as valid against the Confederate States under this Constitution, as under the Provisional Government.

Section 3: This Constitution, and the laws of the Confederate States made in pursuance thereof, and all treaties made, or which shall be made, under the authority of the Confederate States, shall be the supreme law of the land; and the judges in every State shall be bound thereby, anything in the constitution or laws of any State to the contrary notwithstanding.

Section 4: The Senators and Representatives before mentioned, and the members of the several State Legislatures, and all executive and judicial officers, both of the Confederate States and of the several States, shall be bound by oath or affirmation to support this Constitution; but no religious test shall ever be required as a qualification to any office or public trust under the Confederate States.

Section 5: The enumeration, in the Constitution, of certain rights shall not be construed to deny or disparage others retained by the people of the Several States.

Section 6: The powers not relegated to the Confederate States by the Constitution, nor prohibited by it to the States, are reserved to the States, respectively, or to the people thereof.

ARTICLE VII

Section 1: The ratification of the conventions of five States shall be sufficient for the establishment of this Constitution between the States so ratifying the same.

Section 2: When five States shall have ratified this Constitution, in the manner before specified, the Congress under the Provisional Constitution, shall prescribe the time for holding the election of President and Vice President, and for the meeting of the Electoral College; and for counting the votes, and inaugurating the President. They shall, also, prescribe the time for holding the first election of members of Congress under this Constitution, and the time for assembling the same. Until the assembling of such Congress, the Congress under the Provisional Constitution shall continue to exercise the legislative powers granted them, not extending beyond the time limited by the Constitution of the Provisional Government.

Adopted unanimously by the Congress of the Confederate States of South Carolina, Georgia, Florida, Alabama, Mississippi, Louisiana, and Texas, sitting in convention at the capital, in the city of Montgomery, Ala., on the eleventh day of March, in the year eighteen hundred and sixty one.

THE BATTLE HYMN OF THE REPUBLIC

By Julia Ward Howe

First published in the February 1862 issue of the Atlantic Monthly, *this famous Unitarian hymn quickly became a popular anthem for the most radical forces in northern politics during the War between the States. Though utilizing Christian imagery, its purpose is to exalt a messianic state and the coercive force of military adventurism. Written by an avid antagonist to traditional faith and politics, it was a reflection of her enmity toward the American system. Nevertheless, following the war it was slowly absorbed into the canon of acceptable patriotic musicology.*

Mine eyes have seen the glory of the coming of the Lord;
He is trampling out the vintage where the grapes of wrath are stored;
He hath loosed the fateful lightning of His terrible swift sword:
His truth is marching on.

I have seen Him in the watch-fires of a hundred circling camps;
They have builded Him an altar in the evening dews and damps;
I can read His righteous sentence by the dim and flaring lamps:
His day is marching on.

I have read a fiery gospel writ in burnished rows of steel:
"As ye deal with my contemners, so with you my grace shall deal;
Let the Hero, born of woman, crush the serpent with his heel,
Since God is marching on."

He has sounded forth the trumpet that shall never call retreat;
He is sifting out the hearts of men before His judgment seat:
Oh, be swift, my soul, to answer Him! be jubilant, my feet!
Our God is marching on.

In the beauty of the lilies Christ was born across the sea,
With a glory in his bosom that transfigures you and me:
As he died to make men holy, let us die to make men free,
While God is marching on.

THE VOLUNTEER

By _Elbridge Jefferson Cutler_

The War between the States was brutal and devastating. It was among the first of the modern conflicts in which professional armies did not bear the brunt of the suffering. The soldiers were for the most part conscripts or volunteers—more often than not barely out of adolescence. This poignant poem conveys the weight of misery such a war naturally entails.

"At dawn," he said, "I bid them all farewell,
    To go where bugles call and rifles gleam."
And with the restless thought asleep he fell,
    And glided into dream.

A great hot plain from sea to mountain spread,
    Through it a level river slowly drawn:
He moved with a vast crowd, and at its head
    Streamed banners like the dawn.

There came a blinding flash, a deafening roar,
    And dissonant cries of triumph and dismay;
Blood trickled down the river's reedy shore,
    And with the dead he lay.

The morn broke in upon his solemn dream,
    And still, with steady pulse and deepening eye,
"Where bugles call," he said, "and rifles gleam,
    I follow, though I die!"

STONEWALL JACKSON'S WAY

By John Williamson Palmer

Virginia-bred and West Point trained, Thomas Jackson turned out to be the South's most versatile—and unbeatable—military commander. Nicknamed "Stonewall," his quirky habits, sincere piety, and brilliant battlefield maneuvers made him a legend on both sides of the battlefield. This verse was set to music and became a favorite marching tune among the southern troops.

Come, stack arms, men! Pile on the rails,
Stir up the camp-fire bright;
No growling if the canteen fails,
We'll make a roaring night.
Here Shenandoah brawls along,
There burly Blue Ridge echoes strong,
To swell the Brigade's rousing song
Of "Stonewall Jackson's way."

We see him now—the queer slouched hat
Cocked o'er his eye askew;
The shrewd, dry smile, the speech so pat,
So calm, so blunt, so true.
The "Blue-light Elder" knows 'em well;
Says he, "That's Banks—he's fond of shell;
Lord save his soul! We'll give him—" well!
That's "Stonewall Jackson's way."

Silence! Ground arms! Kneel all! Caps off!
Old Massa's goin' to pray.
Strangle the fool that dares to scoff!
Attention! It's his way.
Appealing from his native sod
In forma pauperis to God:
"Lay bare Thine arm; stretch forth Thy rod!
Amen! "That's "Stonewall's way."

He's in the saddle now. Fall in!
Steady! The whole brigade!

Hill's at the ford, cut off; we'll win
His way out, ball and blade!
What matter if our shoes are worn?
What matter if our feet are torn?
"Quick step! We're with him before morn!"
That's "Stonewall Jackson's way."

The sun's bright lances rout the mists
Of morning, and, by George!
Here's Longstreet, struggling in the lists,
Hemmed in an ugly gorge.
Pope and his Dutchmen, whipped before;
"Bay'nets and grape!" Hear Stonewall roar;
"Charge, Stuart! Pay off Ashby's score!"
In "Stonewall Jackson's way."

Ah, Maiden! wait and watch and yearn
For news of Stonewall's band.
Ah, Widow! Read, with eyes that burn,
That ring upon thy hand.
Ah, Wife! sew on, pray on, hope on;
Thy life shall not be all forlorn;
The foe had better ne'er been born
That gets in "Stonewall's way."

STONEWALL'S DYING WORDS

By Sidney Lanier

_At the Battle of Chancellorsville in 1863, Jackson was accidentally struck by the
fire of his own men and mortally wounded. It was one of the severest blows to the
cause of the South. Robert E. Lee lamented that he had, in fact, lost his "own
right arm."_

T he stars of Night contain the glittering Day
And rain his glory down with sweeter grace
Upon the dark World's grand, enchanted face
All loth to turn away.

And so the Day, about to yield his breath,
Utters the stars unto the listening Night,
To stand for burning fare-thee-wells of light
Said on the verge of death.

O hero-life that lit us like the sun!
O hero-words that glittered like the stars
And stood and shone above the gloomy wars
When the hero-life was done!

The phantoms of a battle came to dwell
In the fitful vision of his dying eyes
Yet even in battle-dreams, he sends supplies
To those he loved so well.

His army stands in battle-line arrayed:
His couriers fly: all's done: now God decide!
And not till then saw he the Other Side
Or would accept the shade.

Thou land whose sun is gone, thy stars remain!
Still shine the words that miniature his deeds.
O thrice-beloved, where'er thy great heart bleeds,
Solace hast thou for pain!

DREAMING IN THE TRENCHES

By William Gordon McCabe

*In the trenches thoughts inevitably turned toward home. Reading the
correspondence of soldiers wearing both the blue and the gray is a heartrending
experience. This poem was actually drawn from that correspondence, and it well
conveys the timeless tragedy of war.*

I picture her there in the quaint old room,
    Where the fading fire-light starts and falls
Alone in the twilight's tender gloom
    With the shadows that dance on the dim-lit walls.

Alone, while those faces look silently down
    From their antique frames in a grim repose
Slight scholarly Ralph in his Oxford gown,
    And stanch Sir Alan, who died for Montrose.

There are gallants gay in crimson and gold,
    There are smiling beauties with powdered hair,
But she sits there, fairer a thousand-fold,
    Leaning dreamily back in her low arm-chair.

And the roseate shadows of fading light
    Softly clear steal over the sweet young face,
Where a woman's tenderness blends tonight
    With the guileless pride of a knightly race.

Her hands lie clasped in a listless wave
    On the old Romance—which she holds on her knee
Of Tristram, the bravest of knights in the fray,
    And Iseult, who waits by the sounding sea.

And her proud, dark eyes wear a softened look
    As she watches the dying embers fall:
Perhaps she dreams of the knight in the book,
    Perhaps of the pictures that smile on the wall.

What fancies I wonder are thronging her brain,
    For her cheeks flush warm with a crimson glow
Perhaps—Ah! me, how foolish and vain!
    But I'd give my life to believe it so!

Well, whether I ever march home again
    To offer my love and a stainless name,
Or whether I die at the head of my men,
    I'll be true to the end all the same.

CHRISTMAS NIGHT OF '62

By William Gordon McCabe

Almost any soldier will tell you that the most difficult time to be away from home is during the holidays. Again drawn from actual personal correspondence of soldiers in the field, this poem is a poignant reminder of the hellish agonies of wartime.

The wintry blast goes wailing by,
The snow is falling overhead;
I hear the lonely sentry's tread,
And distant watch-fires light the sky.

Dim forms go flitting through the gloom;
The soldiers cluster round the blaze
To talk of other Christmas days,
And softly speak of home and home.

My sabre swinging overhead
Gleams in the watch-fire's fitful glow,
While fiercely drives the blinding snow,
And memory leads me to the dead.

My thoughts go wandering to and fro,
Vibrating 'twixt the Now and Then;
I see the low-browed home again,
The old hall wreathed with mistletoe.

And sweetly from the far-off years
Comes borne the laughter faint and low,
The voices of the Long Ago!
My eyes are wet with tender tears.

I feel again the mother-kiss,
I see again the glad surprise
That lightened up the tranquil eyes
And brimmed them o'er with tears of bliss,

As, rushing from the old hall-door,
She fondly clasped her wayward boy
Her face all radiant with the joy
She felt to see him home once more.

My sabre swinging on the bough
Gleams in the watch-fire's fitful glow,
While fiercely drives the blinding snow
Aslant upon my saddened brow.

Those cherished faces all are gone!
Asleep within the quiet graves
Where lies the snow in drifting waves.
And I am sitting here alone.

There's not a comrade here tonight
But knows that loved ones far away
On bended knees this night will pray:
"God bring our darling from the fight."

But there are none to wish me back,
For me no yearning prayers arise.
The lips are mute and closed the eyes
My home is in the bivouac.

JOHN BURNS OF GETTYSBURG

By Bret Harte

The decisive Battle of Gettysburg quickly became fertile ground for legend and lore. This tale, told by one of America's best and most humorous writers, captures the sense of irony that surrounded the war for many of the combatants.

Have you heard the story that gossips tell
Of Burns of Gettysburg? No? Ah, well:
Brief is the glory that hero earns,
Briefer the story of poor John Burns:

He was the fellow who won renown,
The only man who didn't back down
When the rebels rode through his native town;
But held his own in the fight next day,
When all his townsfolk ran away.
That was in July, sixty-three
The very day that General Lee,
Flower of Southern chivalry,
Baffled and beaten, backward reeled
From a stubborn Meade and a barren field.

I might tell how, but the day before,
John Burns stood at his cottage door,
Looking down the village street,
Where, in the shade of his peaceful vine,
He heard the low of his gathered kine,
And felt their breath with incense sweet;
Or I might say, when the sunset burned
The old farm gable, he thought it turned
The milk that fell like a babbling flood
Into the milk-pail, red as blood!
Or how he fancied the hum of bees
Were bullets buzzing among the trees.
But all such fanciful thoughts as these
Were strange to a practical man like Burns,
Who minded only his own concerns,
Troubled no more by fancies fine
Than one of his calm-eyed, long-tailed kine,
Quite old-fashioned and matter-of-fact,
Slow to argue, but quick to act.
That was the reason, as some folks say,
He fought so well on that terrible day.
And it was terrible. On the right
Raged for hours the heady fight,
Thundered the battery's double bass,
Difficult music for men to face;
While on the left—where now the graves
Undulate like the living waves
That all that day unceasing swept
Up to the pits the rebels kept,
Round-shot ploughed the upland glades,
Sown with bullets, reaped with blades;

Shattered fences here and there
Tossed their splinters in the air;
The very trees were stripped and bare;
The barns that once held yellow grain
Were heaped with harvests of the slain;
The cattle bellowed on the plain,
The turkeys screamed with might and main,
The brooding barn-fowl left their rest
With strange shells bursting in each nest.

Just where the tide of battle turns,
Erect and lonely, stood old John Burns.
How do you think the man was dressed?
He wore an ancient long buff vest,
Yellow as saffron—but his best;
And, buttoned over his manly breast,
Was a bright blue coat, with a rolling collar,
And large gilt buttons—size of a dollar,
With tails that the country-folk called "swaller."
He wore a broad-brimmed, bell-crowned hat,
White as the locks on which it sat.
Never had such a sight been seen
For forty years on the village green,
Since old John Burns was a country beau,
And went to the "quiltings" long ago.

Close at his elbows all that day,
Veterans of the Peninsula,
Sunburnt and bearded, charged away;
And striplings, downy of lip and chin,
Clerks that the Home-Guard mustered in,
Glanced, as they passed, at the hat he wore,
Then at the rifle his right hand bore;
And hailed him, from out their youthful lore,
With scraps of a slangy repertoire:
"How are you, White Hat?" "Put her through!"
"Your head's level!" and "Bully for you!"
Called him "Daddy"—begged he'd disclose
The name of the tailor who made his clothes,
And what was the value he set on those;
While Burns, unmindful of jeer or scoff,
Stood there picking the rebels off,

With his long brown rifle, and bell-crowned hat,
And the swallow-tails they were laughing at.

'Twas but a moment, for that respect
Which clothes all courage their voices checked;
And something the wildest could understand
Spake in the old man's strong right hand,
And his corded throat, and the lurking frown
Of his eyebrows under his old bell-crown;
Until, as they gazed, there crept an awe
Through the ranks in whispers, and some men saw,
In the antique vestments and long white hair,
The past of the nation in battle there;
And some of the soldiers since declare
That the gleam of his old white hat afar,
Like the crested plume of the brave Navarre,
That day was their oriflamme of war.

So raged the battle. You know the rest:
How the rebels, beaten and backward pressed,
Broke at the final charge and ran.
At which John Burns—a practical man,
Shouldered his rifle, unbent his brows,
And then went back to his bees and cows.
That is the story of old John Burns;
This is the moral the reader learns:
In fighting the battle, the question's whether
You'll show a hat that's white, or a feather!

THE GETTYSBURG ADDRESS

By Abraham Lincoln

Though he was not even the main speaker at the dedication of a cemetery on the site of the bloody Gettysburg battlefield, the tantalizingly short speech Abraham Lincoln gave on November 19, 1863, is a masterpiece of both penetrating rhetoric and moral politics. These words, though few, have proven to be immortal. Carl Sandburg in 1946 hailed the address as one of the great American poems. "One may delve deeply into its unfolded meanings," he wrote, "but its poetic significance carries it far beyond the limits of a state paper. It curiously incarnates the claims, assurances, and pretenses of republican institutions, of democratic procedure, of the rule of the people. It is a timeless psalm in the name of those who fight and do in behalf of great human causes rather than talk, in a belief that men can 'highly resolve' themselves, and can mutually 'dedicate' their lives to a cause."

Fourscore and seven years ago our fathers brought forth, on this continent, a new nation, conceived in liberty, and dedicated to the proposition that all men are created equal.

Now we are engaged in a great civil war, testing whether that nation, or any nation so conceived, and so dedicated, can long endure. We are met on a great battlefield of that war. We have come to dedicate a portion of that field, as a final resting-place for those who here gave their lives, that that nation might live. It is altogether fitting and proper that we should do this.

But, in a larger sense, we can not dedicate—we can not consecrate—we can not hallow—this ground. The brave men, living and dead, who struggled here, have consecrated it far above our poor power to add or detract. The world will little note, nor long remember what we say here, but it can never forget what they did here. It is for us the living, rather, to be dedicated here to the unfinished work which they who fought here have thus far so nobly advanced. It is rather for us to be here dedicated to the great task remaining before us—that from these honored dead we take increased devotion to that cause for which they here gave the last full measure of devotion—that we here highly resolve that these dead shall not have died in vain—that this nation, under God, shall have a new birth of freedom—and that government of the people, by the people, for the people, shall not perish from the earth.

MUSIC IN CAMP

By John Reuben Thompson

The human dimensions of a war that pitted brother against brother remain among the most arresting aspects of the War between the States. In this popular lament the full impact of those emotions are grippingly brought to life.

T wo armies covered hill and plain,
    Where Rappahannock's waters
Ran deeply crimsoned with the stain
    Of battle's recent slaughters.

The summer clouds lay pitched like tents
    In meads of heavenly azure;
And each dread gun of the elements
    Slept in its hid embrasure.

The breeze so softly blew it made
    No forest leaf to quiver,
And the smoke of the random cannonade
    Rolled slowly from the river.

And now, where circling hills looked down
    With cannon grimly planted,
O'er listless camp and silent town
    The golden sunset slanted.

When on the fervid air there came
    A strain—now rich, now tender;
The music seemed itself aflame
    With day's departing splendor.

A Federal band, which, eve and morn,
    Played measures brave and nimble,
Had just struck up, with flute and horn
    And lively clash of cymbal.

Down flocked the soldiers to the banks,
    Till, margined with its pebbles,

One wooded shore was blue with "Yanks,"
    And one was gray with "Rebels."

Then all was still, and then the band
    With movement light and tricksy,
Made stream and forest, hill and strand,
    Reverberate with "Dixie."

The conscious stream with burnished glow
    Went proudly o'er its pebbles,
But thrilled throughout its deepest flow
    With yelling of the Rebels.

Again a pause, and then again
    The trumpets pealed sonorous,
And "Yankee Doodle" was the strain
    To which the shore gave chorus.

The laughing ripple shoreward flew,
    To kiss the shining pebbles;
Loud shrieked the swarming Boys in Blue
    Defiance to the Rebels.

And yet once more the bugles sang
    Above the stormy riot;
No shout upon the evening rang—
    There reigned a holy quiet.

The sad, slow stream its noiseless flood
    Poured o'er the glistening pebbles;
All silent now the Yankees stood,
    And silent stood the Rebels.

No unresponsive soul had heard
    That plaintive note's appealing,
So deeply "Home, Sweet Home" had stirred
    The hidden founts of feeling.

Or Blue or Gray, the soldier sees,
    As by the wand of fairy,
The cottage 'neath the live-oak trees,
    The cabin by the prairie.

Or cold or warm his native skies
  Bend in their beauty o'er him;
Seen through the tear-mist in his eyes,
  His loved ones stand before him.

As fades the iris after rain
  In April's tearful weather,
The vision vanished, as the strain
  And daylight died together.

But memory, waked by music's art,
  Expressed in simplest numbers,
Subdued the sternest Yankee's heart,
  Made light the Rebel's slumbers.

And fair the form of music shines,
  That bright, celestial creature,
Who still, 'mid war's embattled lines,
  Gave this one touch of Nature.

THE EMANCIPATION PROCLAMATION

By Abraham Lincoln

*Despite the fact that much of the conflict between North and South revolved
around the slavery issue, the North never adopted an abolitionist stance during
the lifetime of Abraham Lincoln. In his first inaugural speech he admitted that in
his view the freeing of slaves was not only inexpedient and impolitic but perhaps
even unconstitutional. To reinforce that position, several of the states that
remained in the northern Union were slave states—including Missouri,
Maryland, West Virginia, East Tennessee, and northern Kentucky. Thus, when the
administration finally did act on the issue of chattel slavery on January 1, 1863,
it did not actually free any slaves within the jurisdiction of its governmental
authority. This document was essentially symbolic, designed to placate certain
sectors within the Republicans' abolitionist constituency and provide certain
strategic wartime advantages. Nevertheless, the decree did lay the groundwork
for freedom for the slaves, which would come with the ratification of the
Thirteenth, Fourteenth, and Fifteenth Amendments to the Constitution.*

January 1, 1863, by the President of the United States of America: A proclamation: Whereas, on the twenty-second day of September, in the year of our Lord one thousand eight hundred and sixty-two, a proclamation was issued by the President of the United States, containing, among other things, the following to wit:

That on the first day of January, in the year of our Lord one thousand eight hundred and sixty-three, all persons held as slaves within any State or designated part of a State, the people whereof shall then be in rebellion against the United States, shall be then, thenceforward, and forever free; and the Executive Government of the United States, including the military and naval authority thereof, will recognize and maintain the freedom of such persons, and will do no act or acts to repress such persons, or any of them, in any efforts they may make for their actual freedom.

That the Executive will, on the first day of January aforesaid, by proclamation, designate the States and parts of States, if any, in which the people thereof, shall on that day be, in good faith, represented in the Congress of the United States by members chosen thereto at elections wherein a majority of the qualified voters of such State shall have participated, shall in the absence of strong countervailing testimony, be deemed conclusive evidence that such State, and the people thereof, are not then in rebellion against the United States.

Now, therefore, I, Abraham Lincoln, President of the United States, by virtue of the power in me invested as Commander-in-Chief of the Army and Navy of the United States in time of actual armed rebellion against authority and government of the United States, and as a fit and necessary war measure for suppressing said rebellion, do, on this first day of January, in the year of our Lord one thousand eight hundred and sixty three, and in accordance with my purpose so to do publicly proclaimed for the full period of one hundred days, from the day first above mentioned, order and designate as the States and parts of States wherein the people thereof respectively, are this day in rebellion against the United States the following to wit:

Arkansas, Texas, Louisiana (except the Parishes of St. Bernard, Plaquemines, Jefferson, St. Johns, St. Charles, St. James, Ascension, Assumption, Terrebone, Lafourche, St. Mary, St. Martin, and Orleans, including the City of New Orleans), Mississippi, Alabama, Florida, Georgia, South Carolina, North Carolina, and Virginia (except the forty-eight counties designated as West Virginia, and also the counties of Berkley, Accomac, Northampton, Elizabeth City, York, Princess Ann, and Norfolk, including the cities of Norfolk and Portsmouth, and which excepted parts are, for the present, left precisely as if this proclamation were not issued).

And by virtue of the power, and for the purpose aforesaid I do order and declare that all persons held as slaves within said designated States, and parts of States, are, and henceforward shall be free; and the Executive government of the United States, including the military and naval authorities thereof, will recognize and maintain the freedom of said persons.

And I hereby enjoin upon the people so declared to be free to abstain from all violence, unless in necessary self-defence; and I recommend to them that, in all cases when allowed, they labor faithfully for reasonable wages.

And I further declare and make known that such persons of suitable condition will be received into the armed service of the United States to garrison forts, positions, stations, and other places, and to man vessels of all sorts in said service.

And upon this act, sincerely believed to be an act of justice, warranted by the Constitution, upon military necessity, I invoke the considerate judgment of mankind, and the gracious favor of Almighty God.

In witness whereof, I have hereunto set my hand and caused the seal of the United States to be affixed.

Done at the City of Washington, the first day of January, in the year of our Lord one thousand eight hundred and sixty-three, and of the Independence of the United States of America the eighty-seventh.

O CAPTAIN! MY CAPTAIN!

By Walt Whitman

In death Abraham Lincoln was far more popular than he was in life. Partly it was a matter of contrasts; the men who came to power following his tragic assassination were more extreme and susceptible to the pressure of special interests. But whatever the reasons, the aftermath of his death brought adulation where before there had been only grudging acceptance. This poem, by one of the era's finest verse stylists, was instrumental in helping create the aura of Lincoln's almost ethereal saintliness.

O Captain! my Captain! our fearful trip is done,
The ship has weather'd every rack, the prize we sought is won.

The port is near, the bells I hear, the people all exulting,
While follow eyes the steady keel, the vessel grim and daring;

But O heart! heart! heart!
O the bleeding drops of red,
Where on the deck my Captain lies,
Fallen cold and dead.

O Captain! my Captain! rise up and hear the bells;
Rise up—for you the flag is flung—for you the bugle trills,
For you bouquets and ribbon'd wreaths—for you the shores
     a-crowding,
For you they call, the swaying mass, their eager faces turning;

Here, Captain! dear father!
This arm beneath your head!
It is some dream that on the deck,
You've fallen cold and dead.

My Captain does not answer, his lips are pale and still,
My father does not feel my arm, he has no pulse nor will,
The ship is anchor'd safe and sound, its voyage closed and done,
From fearful trip the victor ship comes in with object won;

Exult, O shores! and ring, O bells!
But I with mournful tread,
Walk the deck my Captain lies,
Fallen cold and dead.

RECONSTRUCTION ORATION

By Senator Benjamin Hill

The struggle between the sections did not end with the cessation of hostilities on the battlefield. Because of the decade-long reconstruction policies of the federal government, the open wounds of war failed to heal in many places for generations. Expressing outrage at the continued suppression of their region by government policy, several southern leaders warned that war could very easily erupt once again. In this prophetic speech, delivered on the floor of the Senate in 1873, the tensions and frustrations of the people were all too evident.

I tell you, the American people will not always be deceived. They will rise in defense of their constitution—and traitors will tremble. They who rallied three million strong to defeat when they considered an armed assault on the Constitution and Union will not sleep until a few hundred traitors from behind the masked battery of congressional oaths and deceptive pretensions of loyalty shall utterly batter down the Constitution and Union forever.

I warn you, boastful, vindictive Radicals, by the history of your own fathers, by every instinct of manhood, by every right of liberty, by every impulse of justice, that the day is coming when you will feel the power of an outraged and betrayed people. Go on confiscating! Arrest without warrant or probable cause; destroy habeas corpus, deny trial by jury; abrogate state governments; defile your own people and flippantly say the Constitution is dead! On, on, with your work of ruin, ye hell-born rioters in sacred things! But remember for all these things you will be called to judgment.

Ah! What an issue you have made for yourselves. Succeed and you destroy the Constitution! Fail, and you have covered the land with mourning. Succeed, and you bring ruin on yourselves and all the country! Fail, and you bring infamy upon yourselves and all your deluded followers! Succeed, and you are the perjured assassins of liberty! Fail, and you are defeated, despised traitors forever! Ye who aspire to be Radical governors and judges, I paint before you this day your destiny. You are but cowards and knaves, and the time will come when you will call upon the rocks and mountains to fall on you and the darkness to hide you from an outraged people.

A struggle is coming. It may be a long and bloody one, and you who advocate this wicked scheme will perish in it, unless the people now arouse and check its consummation.

Let every true, law-loving man rally at once to the standard of the Constitution of his country. Come. Do not abandon your rights. Defend them. Talk for them, and if need be, before God and the country, fight and die for them. Do not talk or think of secession or disunion, but come up to the good old platform of our fathers—the Constitution. Let all, North and South, come and swear before God that we will abide by it in good faith, and oppose everything that violates it.

I am willing, anxious to welcome among us good and true men from the North, who come to help build up our country and add to its prosperity. I wish they would come on and come in multitudes. They will find us friends. But when I see the low, dingy creatures—hatched from the venomous eggs of treason—coming here as mere adventurers to get offices through servile votes—to ride into power on the shoulders of the deluded—and creeping into secret leagues with a few renegades, and talking flippantly about disfranchising the wisest and best men of the land, because they know it is the only possible chance for knaves and fools like themselves to get place, I can but feel ashamed that such monsters are to be considered as belonging to the human species.

And now, my friends, of all races, of all colors, of all nations, of all sexes, of all ages, let us resolve to stand by our Constitution and surrender it to no enemy. This is our country. Let us resolve that we will never be driven from it nor be ostracized in it.

ODE TO THE CONFEDERATE DEAD

By Alan Tate

Lament for the lost cause, the lost sons, and the lost innocence of antebellum America haunted writers from both North and South well into the twentieth century. In this poignant tribute, one of the South's most gifted poets expressed the great tragedy the war wrought on the whole fabric of the culture.

Row after row with strict impunity
The headstones yield their names to the element,
The wind whirs without recollection;
In the riven troughs the splayed leaves
Pile up, of nature the casual sacrament
To the seasonal eternity of death;
Then driven by the fierce scrutiny
Of heaven to their election in the vast breath,
They sough the rumor of mortality.

Autumn is desolation in the plot
Of a thousand acres where these memories grow
From the inexhaustible bodies that are not
Dead, but feed the grass row after rich row.
Think of the autumns that have come and gone!
Ambitious November with the humors of the year,
With a particular zeal for every slab,
Staining the uncomfortable angels that rot
On the slabs, a wing chipped here, an arm there:

The brute curiosity of an angel's stare
Turns you, like them, to stone,
Transforms the heaving air
Till plunged to a heavier world below
You shift your sea-space blindly
Heaving, turning like the blind crab.

Dazed by the wind, only the wind
The leaves flying, plunge

We shall say only the leaves whispering
In the improbable mist of nightfall
That flies on multiple wing;
Night is the beginning and the end

And in between the ends of distraction
Waits mute speculation, the patient curse
That stones the eyes, or like the jaguar leaps
For his own image in a jungle pool, his victim.

What shall we say who have knowledge
Carried to the heart? Shall we take the act
To the grave? Shall we, more hopeful, set up the grave
In the house? The ravenous grave?

Leave now
The shut gate and the decomposing wall:
The gentle serpent, green in the mulberry bush,
Riots with his tongue through the hush
Sentinel of the grave who counts us all!

MY COUNTRY 'TIS OF THEE

By Samuel Smith

Actually written prior to the war, this hymnlike patriotic song became an anthem of healing in the years immediately following the conflict. In fact, due to its universal popularity it very nearly became the national anthem at the end of the nineteenth century during the Spanish-American War. It seemed to express both an appreciation of the past and an optimism for the future.

My country 'tis of thee
Sweet land of liberty:
Of thee I sing.
Land where my fathers died
Land of the Pilgrims' pride
From every mountainside
Let freedom ring.

My native country thee
Land of the noble free
Thy name I love;
I love thy rocks and rills
Thy woods and templed hills
My heart with rapture thrills
Like that above.

Let music swell the breeze
And ring from all the trees
Sweet freedom's song
Let all that breathe partake
Let mortal tongues awake
Let rocks their silence break
The sound prolong.

Our fathers' God to thee
Author of liberty
To thee we sing
Long may our land be bright
With freedom's holy light
Protect us by thy might
Great God, our King.

AMENDMENTS TO THE CONSTITUTION

Almost immediately, the new government found discrepancies or omissions in its constitutional framework. As a result, a series of amendments were proposed; between 1798 and 1870 five were ratified. The first two rectified omissions in the original charter concerning legal actions and the orderly election of the chief executive. The other three were rather more dramatic adjustments of the charter wrought as a result of the War between the States and Reconstruction.
Amendment XI was ratified in 1798, Amendment XII in 1804, Amendment XIII in 1865, Amendment XIV in 1868, and Amendment XV in 1870.

AMENDMENT XI

The Judicial power of the United States shall not be construed to extend to any suit in law or equity, commenced or prosecuted against one of the United States by Citizens of another State, or by Citizens or Subjects of any Foreign State.

AMENDMENT XII

The Electors shall meet in their respective States and vote by ballot for President and Vice-President, one of whom, at least, shall not be an inhabitant of the same State with themselves; they shall name in their ballots the person voted for as President, and in distinct ballots the person voted for as Vice-President, and they shall make distinct lists of all persons voted for as President, and of all persons voted for as Vice-President, and of the number of votes for each, which lists they shall sign and certify, and transmit sealed to the seat of the government of the United States, directed to the President of the Senate; The President of the Senate shall, in the presence of the Senate and House of Representatives, open all the certificates and the votes shall then be counted; The person having the greatest number of votes for President, shall be the President, if such number be a majority of the whole number of Electors appointed; and if no person have such majority, then from the persons having the highest numbers not exceeding three on the list of those voted for as President, the House of Representatives shall choose immediately, by ballot, the President. But in choosing the President, the votes shall be taken by states, the representation from each state having one vote; a quorum for this purpose shall consist of a member or members from two-thirds of the states, and a majority of all the states shall be necessary to a choice. And if the House of Representatives shall not choose a President whenever the right of choice shall devolve upon them, before the fourth day of March next following, then the Vice-President shall act as President, as in the case of the death or other constitutional disability of the President. The person having the greatest number of votes as Vice-President, shall be the Vice-President, if such number be a majority of the whole number of Electors appointed, and if no person have a majority, then from the two highest numbers on the list, the Senate shall choose the Vice-President; a quorum for the purpose shall consist of two-thirds of the whole number of Senators, and a majority of the whole number shall be necessary to a choice. But no person constitutionally ineligible to the office of President shall be eligible to that of Vice-President of the United States.

AMENDMENT XIII

Section 1: Neither slavery nor involuntary servitude, except as a punishment for crime whereof the party shall have been duly convicted, shall exist within the United States, or any place subject to their jurisdiction.

Section 2: Congress shall have power to enforce this article by appropriate legislation.

AMENDMENT XIV

Section 1: All persons born or naturalized in the United States, and subject to the jurisdiction thereof, are citizens of the United States and of the State wherein they reside. No State shall make or enforce any law which shall abridge the privileges or immunities of citizens of the United States; nor shall any State deprive any person of life, liberty, or property, without due process of law; nor deny to any person within its jurisdiction the equal protection of the laws.

Section 2: Representatives shall be apportioned among the several States according to their respective numbers, counting the whole number of persons in each State, excluding Indians not taxed. But when the right to vote at any election for the choice of electors for President and Vice-President of the United States, Representatives in Congress, the Executive and Judicial officers of a State, or the members of the Legislature thereof, is denied to any of the male inhabitants of such State, being twenty-one years of age, and citizens of the United States, or in any way abridged, except for participation in rebellion, or other crime, the basis of representation therein shall be reduced in the proportion which the number of such male citizens shall bear to the whole number of male citizens twenty-one years of age in such State.

Section 3: No person shall be a Senator or Representative in Congress, or elector of President and Vice-President, or hold any office, civil or military, under the United States, or under any State, who, having previously taken an oath, as a member of Congress, or as an officer of the United States, or as a member of any State legislature, or as an executive or judicial officer of any State, to support the Constitution of the United States, shall have engaged in insurrection or rebellion against the same, or given aid or comfort to the enemies thereof. But Congress may by a vote of two-thirds of each House, remove such disability.

Section 4: The validity of the public debt of the United States, authorized by law, including debts incurred for payment of pensions and bounties for services in suppressing insurrection or rebellion, shall not be questioned. But neither the United States nor any State shall assume or pay any debt or obligation incurred in aid of insurrection or rebellion against the United States, or any claim for the loss or emancipation of any slave; but all such debts, obligations, and claims shall be held illegal and void.

Section 5: The Congress shall have the power to enforce, by appropriate legislation, the provisions of this article.

AMENDMENT XV

Section 1: The right of citizens of the United States to vote shall not be denied or abridged by the United States or by any State on account of race, color, or previous condition of servitude.

Section 2: The Congress shall have power to enforce this article by appropriate legislation.

FOUNDERS' SONS

The men who served in the presidency just after the Founding Era up to the advent of modernity had the awesome task of directing the gangling young American republic toward its manifest destiny. Sadly, that task was disrupted by the greatest conflict in our nation's history: the terrible War between the States that was anything but civil. Their story reflects both the tenacity and the fragility of this great experiment in liberty.

JAMES MONROE (1758-1831)

The first extended period of peace came to our young nation with Monroe's administration–the serene years known as the Era of Good Feeling. The European nations, exhausted by the Napoleonic wars, let the new nation develop in peace, and Monroe and the U.S. made the most of it. The U.S. persuaded Britain to disarm forever along the Canadian border, purchased Florida from Spain, and asserted its growing authority by drafting the Monroe Doctrine, a warning to European nations against further conquest or colonization in the Western Hemisphere. At home the problem of slavery was temporarily solved by the Missouri Compromise, which admitted Missouri as a slave state but prohibited slavery north of the Mason-Dixon line. Before reaching the presidency, Monroe served in a variety of posts. He began as an eighteen-year-old lieutenant in the Revolution; forty years later he held the unusual Cabinet position of secretary of state and war. His long career was punctuated with controversy; as Washington's minister to France he earned Federalist disapproval and, finally, removal for his sympathy for the French cause. As Jefferson's minister to England, he concluded a treaty on naval problems that failed to uphold American rights and was, therefore, rejected by Jefferson. However, as Jefferson's minister extraordinaire in France he won a share of the credit for the purchase of Louisiana by signing the treaty that concluded the greatest of real estate transactions. Monroe's administration brought to an end almost a quarter century of rule by the close friends the Federalists called the Virginia Dynasty—Jefferson, Madison, and Monroe. Like his friends, Monroe almost exhausted his fortune in a lifetime of public service; with them he helped block the Federalists' drift toward class rule and furthered the establishment of the government according to Jeffersonian principles of democracy.

JOHN QUINCY ADAMS (1767-1848)

Monroe was the last of the southern aristocrats of the Virginia Dynasty. The man who succeeded him was the last of the northern aristocrats of the Massachusetts Dynasty—the Adams family of Braintree. Adams, though not born to the purple, was born to the red, white, and blue. He literally grew up with the country: as a boy he watched the battle of Bunker Hill from a hill near home, at fourteen he served as secretary to the minister to Russia, at sixteen he was secretary at the treaty ending the Revolution, and he later held more offices than any earlier president. The only son of a president ever to reach that office, Adams followed a career that closely resembled his father's. Both attended Harvard, studied law, and were successful ministers and peace commissioners in Europe. Both were elected president for only one term, and both became involved in party conflicts and spent their least successful years in the White House. Studious and crotchety, Adams was more successful as a diplomat and statesman than as a politician. As Monroe's secretary of state he negotiated with the Spanish for Florida and was largely responsible for the document that became known as the Monroe Doctrine. In the unusual election of 1824, four Democrat-Republicans contended for the presidency. Andrew Jackson received almost fifty thousand votes more than Adams, which was still less than the required majority. The decision thus rested with the House of Representatives, and when Henry Clay threw his support to Adams, the House elected Adams instead. Jackson felt cheated. The strong feelings that developed between Jackson and Adams ruined Adams' administration and finally drove the two men into separate parties—Adams to the National Republicans and Jackson to the Democrats. Adams was more successful in Congress, where he served for his last seventeen years. There he distinguished himself by his dedicated fight to remove the "gag rule" that prevented Congress from considering any antislavery petitions. After fourteen years of struggle he finally won. But his service did not end until he collapsed on the floor of Congress in 1848, sixty-six years after he first served his country at his father's side.

ANDREW JACKSON (1767-1845)

The first man of the people to become president, Jackson's election in 1828 stands in American history as a great divide between government by aristocrats—the rich and well-born, as Hamilton described them—and government by leaders who were drawn from and identified with the people. Under Jackson, Jefferson's democratic principles became more of a political reality, but Jackson had to reconcile those principles of political equality with the economic problems of an expanding industrial economy in a growing country. His election, like Jefferson's, marked a revolution in American democracy. A child of the western frontier, Jackson was as rough-hewn as the log walls of his birthplace. From the time he fought in the Revolution at fourteen, his life was largely one of struggle. On the frontier he studied law and gradually rose in Tennessee politics, representing the new state in Congress before he became state supreme court judge. But he gained fame not as a politician but as a military hero. In the War of 1812 he commanded the American forces that roundly defeated the British at New Orleans. Tall and with a commanding presence, Jackson had a large, devoted personal following. And his stunning victory over John Quincy Adams in 1828 helped convince him he was the champion of the people. With such a mandate he exercised his authority with a firm and sometimes reckless hand; he asserted the supremacy of the federal government when South Carolina tried to nullify tariff laws, and in his most dramatic act, he boldly vetoed the recharter of the Bank of the United States, the half-private bank that had become powerful enough to threaten the government itself. Jackson proclaimed that the government should not "make the rich richer and the potent more powerful" at the expense of the rest of society. The man who had been elected by a great popular majority—and had himself risen from the people—proved thirty years before Lincoln that American democracy could achieve government not only of and for the people, but by the people as well.

Martin Van Buren (1782-1862)

Martin Van Buren was America's first political boss. Elegant in dress, amiable and courteous in manner, "Little Van" early demonstrated such political skill that he rapidly rose to prominence in New York state politics, becoming one of the leaders of the "Albany Regency," a political machine that developed a spoils system on a large scale and gained control of state politics in the 1820s. A masterful organizer, he welded diverse regional interests into the first effective national political party—the new Democrat party that in 1828 supported Andrew Jackson for the presidency. Coming to the presidency after the fiery general, Van Buren inherited thorny financial problems; shortly after he took office, there were bread riots and failed banks—the country was caught up in the Panic of 1837. The skilled politician who had earned such names as "The Little Magician" and "The American Talleyrand" was unable to avert the financial upheaval, but he courageously attempted to improve matters. He established what later became the Treasury Department, independent of any bank. But his administration was generally held responsible for the Panic. He never regained his earlier popularity and was defeated by William Harrison in

1840. The charming little gentleman in a snuff-colored coat was no longer seen gliding through the streets of Washington in an elegantly fitted coach attended by liveried footmen. Although he remained a national figure for many years and was an unsuccessful presidential candidate for the Free Soil Party in 1848, he spent most of his time in retirement at Lindenwald, his estate at Kinderhook, the quiet little village on the Hudson where he was born.

William H. Harrison (1773-1841)

In 1840 the Whigs took the gamble of nominating the oldest man ever to run for president, sixty-eight-year-old William H. Harrison. They won the election but lost the gamble, for Harrison lived only one month after his inauguration; he had made a three-hour inaugural speech in a drenching rain and caught pneumonia. He served the shortest term of any president, but his election ended the Jacksonian reign and brought the growing Whigs to power, even though John Tyler, the vice president who succeeded Harrison, was an ex-Democrat with rather watery Whig convictions. The election of 1840 marked the beginning of elaborate national campaigns, for by then the Whigs had become established as a second party—a development that helped institutionalize the party system as the country's method of selecting candidates. Smarting from their defeat in 1836 when they were new and poorly organized, the Whigs met almost a year before the election for their first national convention. They then proceeded to build an elaborate campaign around everything but the issues: Harrison's military exploits against the Indians—especially the battle of Tippecanoe—and his service as a simple man of the West in the Ohio and Indiana Territories where he served as a civil and military leader. Campaign posters pictured Harrison as "The Hero of Tippecanoe" or "The Farmer of North Bend," hand to the plow in front of a log cabin. The catchy slogan "Tippecanoe and Tyler, too" rang out at the largest political rallies and mass meetings ever held in America. It is one of the ironies of politics that a log cabin became a potent campaign symbol for Harrison—a man who was born in a white-pillared mansion into one of the aristocratic families of tidewater Virginia. His father, Benjamin Harrison, was one of the Founding Fathers of the nation, a member of the Continental Congress, and a signer of the Declaration of Independence.

John Tyler (1790-1862)

A tall Virginia gentleman, Tyler was the first vice president to complete the unexpired term of a president, but it is almost certain that the Whigs would never have chosen him as their vice-presidential candidate had they known he was to serve all but a month of Harrison's term. By 1840 "Honest John" had clearly demonstrated that he was not a party man; during his years in Washington as a nominally Democratic congressman and senator he had followed such an independent course—fighting the Missouri Compromise, fighting high tariffs, fighting Jackson—that it finally led him, by 1833, out of the Democratic party altogether. Yet his views on states' rights and on strict construction of the Constitution would never permit him to be at home with the Whigs. The Whigs had nominated him, though, and after Harrison's death, they had to live with him—as their chief executive. It is not surprising that Tyler's years in the White House were tempestuous ones. When his stand on states' rights led him to veto a bill for a Bank of the United States, every member of Harrison's original Cabinet except Webster promptly resigned, and Webster as secretary of state was at the time deeply involved in settling the northeastern boundary dispute with Great Britain. Tyler further alienated the Whigs by repudiating the spoils system and refusing to replace some Democratic ministers abroad. Throughout his term he was unable to work in harmony with the Whig majority in Congress, who were led by Henry Clay, the actual political leader of the party. They did agree with Tyler, however, on the annexation of Texas, which was accomplished in the final days of Tyler's term. But in the election of 1844 only an irregular Democratic convention nominated Tyler, and he withdrew before election. At a time when political parties were emerging as powers on the national political scene, John Tyler left the White House a president without a party. He served in the Confederate Congress at the end of his life and was a strong supporter of southern nullification and secession.

JAMES K. POLK (1795-1849)

An Expansionist mood dominated the country in the mid-1840s, and the man who caught the spirit of the times and came from nowhere to lead the country through the period of its greatest expansion was the Tennessean Polk. In spite of this distinction, Polk has been one of the most neglected of our presidents. Emerging from comparative oblivion to become president, he has somehow managed to return there in spite of a successful administration—one called by several leading historians "the one bright spot in the dull void between Jackson and Lincoln." When the delegates to the Democratic convention met in Baltimore in 1844, Polk was not even considered for the presidency; before the convention was over he had become the first dark-horse candidate. And in the election, when the Whigs made "Who Is Polk?" their battle cry, he answered them by soundly defeating their candidate, Henry Clay, who was running in his third presidential race. As president the little-known Polk was a strong, though not radical, expansionist. During his administration the nation acquired the vast lands in the Southwest and Far West that extended the borders of the country almost to the present continental limits. He proved to be a forceful president in his direction of the Mexican War and in settling the Oregon boundary dispute with Great Britain. Yet he did not yield to those extremists who wanted all of Mexico, nor to those who cried "Fifty-four forty or fight!" and claimed the Oregon Territory clear to the Alaskan border. But the man who successfully led the country through its period of expansion strangely faded away when his work was done. Still popular at the end of his term but exhausted from overwork, Polk declined to be a candidate and returned to his home in Nashville, where he died only three months after leaving the White House—at the age of fifty-three.

Zachary Taylor (1784-1850)

Tobacco-chewing General Taylor was the first Regular Army man to become president. It was solely on the strength of his popularity as a military hero that the Whigs chose him in 1848; never had a candidate known less about government, law, or politics. "Old Rough and Ready" had practically no formal education, had spent his entire life moving from one Army post to another, and had never voted in an election in his life. Although earlier presidents had distinguished themselves in military service, none had made the Regular Army a career as Taylor did. Commissioned a first lieutenant in the infantry in 1808, he served in almost every war and skirmish for the next forty years. As a young captain in the War of 1812 he showed himself a cool and courageous leader; he won further recognition in the wars with the Black Hawks and Seminoles in later years. But it was his dramatic success in leading the American forces against the Mexican army in 1846 and 1847 that caught the imagination of the American people and made him a national hero. In battle after battle he defeated the Mexicans—at Palo Alto, Reseca de la Palma, and Monterrey—and on February 22, 1847, he won his greatest victory at Buena Vista when his troops routed a large army led by General Santa Ana. In the White House Taylor saw his job as the civilian counterpart of a military commander; untutored in politics, he tried to remain nonpartisan, leave legislative matters to Congress, and simply execute the laws himself. But running the government proved more complex, and before long he became embroiled in the issue that haunted the country: slavery. Although unskilled in politics, he was a forthright and determined leader; when southern congressmen threatened trouble over the admission of California as a free state, Taylor, who owned slaves himself, warned that he would lead the Army against them and hang any who resisted as traitors. Thus the hero of the Mexican War, who died unexpectedly in July 1850, proved that for all his lack of skill he yet was able to take a stand on the issue the country dreaded facing. No successor until Lincoln was to show such courage.

MILLARD FILLMORE (1800-1874)

When vice president Fillmore succeeded to the presidency upon the death of Zachary Taylor, he became one of the select group of presidents who made the American myth "from a log cabin to the White House" a reality. But Fillmore's rise from humble apprentice to the highest office in the land was more inspiring than his performance in that office. When the short, stocky Taylor was still in the White House, Washingtonians observed that the tall, dignified Fillmore looked more like a president than the president himself. Born in a log cabin in Cayuga County, New York, Fillmore overcame extreme handicaps: he had little formal education, worked on his father's farm, and at fifteen was apprenticed to a wool carder. While serving his apprenticeship he belatedly began his studies and gradually learned enough to teach school himself so he could afford to study law. At twenty-three he was admitted to the bar; by the time he was thirty he had established himself in Buffalo and won a seat in the New York state assembly. In politics Fillmore generally followed a moderate course, although in Congress he did espouse an unpopular cause by supporting John Quincey Adams in his fight against the "gag rule" against antislavery bills. But as president he accepted Henry Clay's compromise measures on slavery and signed his political life away when he endorsed the Fugitive Slave Act. Part of the Compromise of 1850, the Act permitted slave owners to seize Negroes in the North as fugitives without process of law. The Act aroused extreme bitterness in the North; instead of improving conditions, it drove the North and South ever farther apart. Although Fillmore could not then have realized it, his political career was practically over. The man who looked the part of a president was not even nominated by his own party to play the role again—though he continued to be a third-party threat for nearly another quarter century.

FRANKLIN PIERCE (1804-1869)

"I would rather be right than President," Henry Clay said, and he was often right but never president. But Franklin Pierce, a genial New Hampshire lawyer who said that the presidency would be "utterly repugnant" to him became president in spite of himself—without ever making a single campaign speech. Like Polk, Pierce had not even been considered a candidate before the Democratic convention, but he was reluctantly pushed into the role of compromise candidate when the convention reached a stalemate at the thirty-fifth ballot. Although he served honorably in his state legislature and in the House and Senate, Pierce gradually developed a marked distaste for politics; in 1842 he resigned from the Senate to return to private practice and later he refused several opportunities to return to office. Handsome, friendly Pierce had retired from politics for life until he was caught up in the swirl of events that suddenly put him in the White House. In 1853 slavery was still a dominating issue. Pierce took office with the belief that he should support the Compromise of 1850, and like Fillmore he alienated the North by enforcing the Fugitive Slave Act. The Kansas-Nebraska Act, which created new territories in 1854, simply provided a new arena for the great struggle. In these new territories nothing was settled as abolitionists and proslavery groups resorted to force and bloodshed: "Bleeding Kansas" became an open wound. On other fronts Pierce fared little better. Part of his expansionist policy was a plan to purchase Cuba, but he was forced to denounce three of his ministers—one of them his successor, James Buchanan—when they declared in the Ostend Manifesto that America should take Cuba if Spain refused to sell it. However, Pierce was able to purchase land from Mexico, which gave us our present southwest border and completed our expansion in the West. Pierce was probably grateful when his party neglected to nominate him for another term. At last he could have his privacy.

JAMES BUCHANAN (1791-1868)

Having the distinction of being our only bachelor president, Buchanan did little else to distinguish his administration. Like Fillmore and Pierce he futilely tried to satisfy both North and South in their intensifying conflict. It is one of the ironies of fate—and of politics—that Buchanan, who was a brilliant young lawyer in the 1820s and a promising political figure in the 1830s, was passed over when he first sought the presidential nomination in the 1840s and finally selected to run only when he had become a tired and indecisive old man, becoming the second-oldest president ever elected. History has not dealt kindly with "Old Buck," whose record might have looked far better had he never reached the White House. His career as congressman and senator, as minister to Russia and Great Britain, and especially as secretary of state under Polk earned him a respectable, though far from outstanding, place in history. But he had the misfortune of reaching the nation's highest office well past his prime and at a time of impending crisis. And it was his further misfortune that the remedy of compromise, that in the past had at least maintained a surface calm, was no longer sufficient; the problem had outgrown this kind of "solution." The test the nation had been avoiding almost since its beginning was upon it, and the old nostrums simply wouldn't work. Unsure of himself, engrossed in legalistic details, Buchanan pursued a course that history has most dramatically demonstrated to be the wrong one. And it is his unhappy fate to be forever thrust into the shadows by the towering figure of his successor, the man who proved him wrong.

ABRAHAM LINCOLN (1809-1865)

A villain to some, a hero to others, Lincoln has undoubtedly attained greatness—but only in retrospect. In all history there is no more dramatic example of the times making a man, rather than a man making the times, than the legendary rise of Abraham Lincoln from obscurity to the presidency of the shattered Union. Every conceivable obstacle was there before him: humble birth, ignorance, poverty, and life in the wilderness of the frontier. He was completely without advantages or connections. He was too human to ever be a favorite of the professional politicians; he was too enigmatic, too philosophical, too humorous to be a great popular figure. But somehow Lincoln was nominated for the presidency—as the second choice of many—and with less than a majority of the popular vote he managed to be elected in 1860. Out of those early years of poverty and trial emerged a man uniquely prepared to wage a devastating war against many of his former friends and colleagues—a man of haunting transparency, a man with a probing conscience and penetrating intellect, and a man of deep humanity. After the first ineffectual and indecisive eighteen months in office Lincoln became a strong, effective leader—firm, unrelenting, and brutal in the prosecution of both war and politics. But above all he proved to be a man of vision. He saw the United States in its largest dimension, as a noble experiment in self-determination that had to be preserved even if it meant violating the principles of self-determination. After a long history of tyranny and oppression, he believed that American democracy was man's great hope and that it must be saved even if he had to resort to nondemocratic coercion. To him the great ideal of democracy overshadowed the practical realities of democracy. Lincoln's profound conviction of the enduring value of this experiment in a unified government sustained him throughout the long years of war. On the battlefield at Gettysburg it moved him to give the world a glimpse of his vision of the country's true greatness: "a nation conceived in liberty and dedicated to the proposition that all men are created equal." And it moved him to enunciate his ultimate reason for striving to preserve the Union: that "government of the people, by the people, and for the people shall not perish from the earth." One of the truly great political and human statements of all time, the Gettysburg Address reveals both the ironic complexity and the coarse nobility that mark Lincoln as a legendary figure in American life and culture.

ANDREW JOHNSON (1808-1875)

Few men who have reached the presidency have been less prepared for that high office than Johnson. It is reported that he never spent a single day in a schoolroom. Bound as apprentice to a tailor when only a boy of ten, Johnson spent his youth working long hours in the shop. Only after he had established himself as a tailor in the mountain town of Greenville, Tennessee, and married, did he—with the help of his wife—make progress with his education. But, determined as he was, he never achieved the polish of the formally educated. Unfortunately, he also lacked the complex human qualities of his predecessor. Yet this rough-hewn politician who was plagued with political handicaps of background and personality left his mark on history, for through all his faults and failings shone the integrity and courage that command universal respect. Never in sympathy with the southern aristocracy, Johnson alone of the twenty-two southern senators refused to leave his senate seat in 1861 when his state seceded from the Union. Firm in his resolve, he served the Union as military governor of Tennessee until he was elected vice president in 1864. And after Lincoln's death, the presidency provided him further occasions for courageous action. Fighting radical Republicans who wanted to grind the war-torn South under their Northern boots, Johnson fearlessly brought the wrath of the Republican Congress on his own head and narrowly missed impeachment—the only president ever to be involved in impeachment proceedings. But he survived that ordeal, and six years after leaving office, he had the pleasure of being elected once again to the Senate, where he fought against the crushing tyranny of Reconstruction policies put into effect after his tenure in the White House.

ULYSSES S. GRANT (1822-1885)

General Grant was one of the nation's greatest military heroes but one of its most unsuccessful presidents. Decisive and masterful on the battlefield, a dynamic leader and a horseman of great prowess, he proved to be ingenuous in the political arena. Raised on a farm, he early developed a love of horses and seemed always at his best on horseback. As leader of the victorious forces of the North, Grant was considered one of the saviors of the Union. After Johnson's unhappy term, Republicans turned readily to

Grant even though he knew nothing about politics. Innocent and sincere, Grant committed errors of judgment from the beginning; he appointed two unknowns from his hometown in Illinois to Cabinet positions. Later he allowed himself to be entertained by two stock manipulators—Jay Gould and Jim Fisk—who tried to corner the gold market, a mistake which left him open to charges of incompetence and corruption. As the years passed, the evidences of corruption in his administration were such that Grant lost much of the popularity that first brought him into office. However, he managed to be re-elected to another term, one tarnished by even more corruption and scandal. In spite of the scandals, Grant scored a few victories. Passage of the Amnesty Bill in 1872 restored civil rights to many southerners, relieving some of the harsh conditions of Reconstruction. And against considerable opposition, Grant took courageous steps to fight the growing threat of inflation. But the battle-torn country was still in distress; the General who had brought the great uncivil war to a successful close was not the man to bind up the nation's wounds.

PART IV
THE AMERICAN DREAM

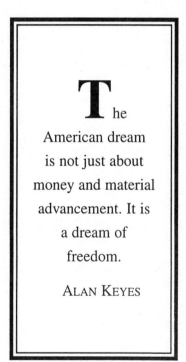

The American dream is not just about money and material advancement. It is a dream of freedom.

ALAN KEYES

SENECA FALLS DECLARATION

By Elizabeth Cady Stanton

In the summer of 1848 five ardent Quaker reformers met at the obscure village of Seneca Falls, New York, to discuss the social, civil, and religious rights of women. Elizabeth Cady Stanton, Lucretia Mott, Martha Wright, Jane Hunt, and Mary Ann McClintock were all veterans of the abolitionist and temperance movements. Influenced by the clarity of the Declaration of Independence, they together helped Stanton draft a manifesto that initiated a groundswell of support for women's rights. Later that summer, they held a convention, where the draft resolution was resoundingly affirmed. Though written and adopted prior to the War between the States, it was one of the first great political documents of the new postbellum age of modernity.

Whereas, the great precept of nature is conceded to be that "man shall pursue his own true and substantial happiness." Blackstone in his Commentaries remarks that this law of nature being coeval with mankind, and dictated by God himself, is of course superior in obligation to any other. It is binding over all the globe, in all countries and at all times; no human laws are of any validity if contrary to this, and such of them as are valid, derive all their force, and all their validity, and all their authority, immediately from this original; therefore:

Resolved, that all laws which prevent woman from occupying such a station in society as her conscience shall dictate, or which place her in a position inferior to that of man, are contrary to the great precept of nature, and therefore of no force or authority.

Resolved, that woman is man's equal—was intended to be so by the Creator, and the highest good of the race demands that she should be recognized as such.

Resolved, that the women of this country ought to be enlightened in regard to the laws under which they live, that they may no longer publish their degradation by declaring themselves satisfied with their present position, nor their ignorance by asserting that they have all the rights they want.

Resolved, that inasmuch as man, while claiming for himself intellectual superiority, does accord to woman moral superiority, it is preeminently his duty to encourage her to speak and teach, as she has an opportunity, in all religious assemblies.

Resolved, that the same amount of virtue, delicacy, and refinement of behavior that is required of woman in the social state, should also be required of man, and the same transgressions should be visited with equal severity on both man and woman.

Resolved, that the objection of indelicacy and impropriety, which is so often brought against woman when she addresses a public audience, comes with a very ill grace from those who encourage, by their attendance, her appearance on the stage, in the concert, or in feats of the circus.

Resolved, that woman has too long rested satisfied in the circumscribed limits which corrupt customs and a perverted application of the Scriptures have marked out for her, and that it is time she should move in the enlarged sphere which her great Creator has assigned her.

Resolved, that it is the duty of the women of this country to secure to themselves their sacred right to the elective franchise.

Resolved, that the equality of human rights results necessarily from the fact of the identity of the race in capabilities and responsibilities.

Resolved, that the speedy success of our cause depends upon the zealous and untiring efforts of both men and women, for the overthrow of the monopoly of the pulpit, and for the securing to women an equal participation with men in the various trades, professions, and commerce.

Resolved, therefore, that, being invested by the Creator with the same capabilities, and the same consciousness of responsibility for their exercise, it is demonstrably the right and duty of woman, equally with man, to promote every righteous cause by every righteous means; and especially in regard to the great subjects of morals and religion, it is self-evidently her right to participate with her brother in teaching them, both in private and in public, by writing and by speaking, by any instrumentalities proper to be used, and in any assemblies proper to be held; and this being a self-evident truth growing out of the divinely implanted principles of human nature, any custom or authority adverse to it, whether modern or wearing the hoary sanction of antiquity, is to be regarded as a self-evident falsehood, and at war with mankind.

PLEDGE OF ALLEGIANCE

By Francis Bellamy

This patriotic vow was written by a journalist to commemorate the four-hundredth anniversary of the discovery voyage of Christopher Columbus in 1892. Though it was first publicly recited at the Columbian Exposition in Chicago that year, it was not officially recognized until 1954. At that time the original was revised to include the words "under God." Usually recited at the opening of public ceremonies or events, it is a kind of national covenantal commitment.

I pledge allegiance
To the flag of the United States of America
And to the republic for which it stands,
One nation under God,
Indivisible, with liberty, and justice for all.

ATLANTA EXPOSITION ADDRESS

By Booker T. Washington

Born into slavery, Booker T. Washington literally pulled himself up by his own bootstraps to become one of the most articulate and influential educators in the nation. Founder of the Tuskegee Institute, author of a number of books, and a popular speaker, he always emphasized the importance of education, hard work, and self-discipline for the advancement of African-Americans. Washington's audience at the Cotton States' Exposition on September 18, 1895, included both white and black southerners, and his speech received enormous attention throughout the country; it helped galvanize public opinion in favor of black self-improvement.

Mr. President and Gentlemen of the Board of Directors and Citizens: One-third of the population of the South is of the Negro race. No enterprise seeking the material, civil, or moral welfare of this section can disregard this element of our population and reach the highest success. I but convey to you, Mr. President and directors, the sentiment of the masses of my race when I say that in no way have the value and manhood of the American Negro been more fittingly and generously recognized than by the managers of this magnificent exposition at every stage of its progress. It is a recognition that will do more to cement the friendship of the two races than any occurrence since the dawn of our freedom.

Not only this, but the opportunity here afforded will awaken among us a new era of industrial progress. Ignorant and inexperienced, it is not strange that in the first years of our new life we began at the top instead of at the bottom; that a seat in Congress or the state legislature was more sought than real estate or industrial skill; that the political convention or stump speaking had more attractions than starting a dairy farm or truck garden.

A ship lost at sea for many days suddenly sighted a friendly vessel. From the mast of the unfortunate vessel was seen a signal, "Water, water; we die of thirst!" The answer from the friendly vessel at once came back, "Cast down your bucket where you are." And a third and fourth signal for water was answered, "Cast down your bucket where you are." The captain of the distressed vessel, at last heeding the injunction, cast down his bucket, and it came up full of fresh, sparkling water from the mouth of the Amazon River. To those of my race who depend on bettering their condition in a foreign land or who underestimate the importance of cultivating friendly relations with the Southern white man, who is their next-door neighbor, I would say: "Cast down your bucket where you are"—cast it down in making friends in every manly way of the people of all races by whom we are surrounded.

Cast it down in agriculture, mechanics, in commerce, in domestic service, and in the professions. And in this connection it is well to bear in mind that whatever other sins the South may be called to bear, when it comes to business, pure and simple, it is in the South that the Negro is given a man's chance in the commercial world, and in nothing is this exposition more eloquent than in emphasizing this chance. Our greatest danger is that in the great leap from slavery to freedom we may overlook the fact that the masses of us are to live by the productions of our hands, and fail to keep in mind that we shall prosper in proportion as we learn to dignify and glorify common labor and put brains and skill into the common occupations of life; shall prosper in proportion as we learn to draw the line between the superficial and the substantial, the ornamental gew-gaws of life and the useful. No race can prosper till it learns that there is as much dignity in tilling a field as in writing a poem. It is at the bottom of life we must begin, and not at the top. Nor should we permit our grievances to overshadow our opportunities.

To those of the white race who look to the incoming of those of foreign birth and strange tongue and habits for the prosperity of the South, were I permitted I would repeat what I say to my own race, "Cast down your bucket where you are." Cast it down among the eight millions of Negroes whose habits you know, whose fidelity and love you have tested in days when to have proved treacherous meant the ruin of your firesides. Cast down your bucket among these people who have, without strikes and labor wars, tilled your fields, cleared your forests, built your railroads and cities, and brought forth treasures from the bowels of the earth, and helped make possible this magnificent representation of the progress of the South. Casting down your bucket among my people, helping and encouraging them as you are doing on these grounds, and to education of head, hand, and heart, you will find that they will buy your surplus land, make blossom the waste places in your fields, and run your factories. While doing this, you can be sure in the future, as in the past, that you and your families will be surrounded by the most patient, faithful, law-abiding, and unresentful people that the world has seen. As we have proved our loyalty to you in the past, in nursing your children, watching by the sick-bed of your mothers and fathers, and often following them with tear-dimmed eyes to their graves, so in the future, in our humble way, we shall stand by you with a devotion that no foreigner can approach, ready to lay down our lives, if need be, in defense of yours, interlacing our industrial, commercial, civil, and religious life with yours in a way that shall make the interests of both races one. In all things that are purely social we can be as separate as the fingers, yet one as the hand in all things essential to mutual progress.

There is no defense or security for any of us except in the highest intelligence and development of all. If anywhere there are efforts tending to curtail the fullest growth of the Negro, let these efforts be turned into stimulating, encouraging, and making him the most useful and intelligent citizen. Effort or means so invested will pay a thousand percent interest. These efforts will be twice blessed—"blessing him that gives and him that takes."

There is no escape through law of man or God from the inevitable:

The laws of changeless justice bind
Oppressor with oppressed;
And close as sin and suffering joined
We march to fate abreast.

Nearly sixteen millions of hands will aid you in pulling the load upward; or they will pull against you the load downward. We shall constitute one-third and more of the ignorance and crime of the South, or one-third its intelligence and progress; we shall contribute one-third to the business and industrial prosperity of the South, or we shall prove a veritable body of death, stagnating, depressing, retarding every effort to advance the body politic. Gentlemen of the exposition, as we present to you our humble effort at an exhibition of our progress, you must not expect overmuch. Starting thirty years ago with ownership here and there in a few quilts and pumpkins and chickens (gathered from miscellaneous sources), remember the path that has led from these to the inventions and production of agricultural implements, buggies, steam engines, newspapers, books, statuary, carving, paintings, the management of drugstores and banks, has not been trodden without contact with thorns and thistles. While we take pride in what we exhibit as a result of our independent efforts, we do not for a moment forget that our part in this exhibition would fall far short of your expectations but for the constant help that has come to our educational life, not only from the Southern states, but especially from Northern philanthropists, who have made their gifts a constant stream of blessing and encouragement.

The wisest among my race understand that the agitation of questions of social equality is the extreme folly, and that progress in the enjoyment of all the privileges that will come to us must be the result of severe and constant struggle rather than of artificial forcing. No race that has anything to contribute to the markets of the world is long in any degree ostracized. It is important and right that all privileges of the law be ours, but it is vastly more important that we be prepared for the exercises of these privileges. The opportunity to earn a dollar in a factory just now is worth infinitely more than the opportunity to spend a dollar in an opera house.

In conclusion, may I repeat that nothing in thirty years has given us more hope and encouragement, and drawn us so near to you of the white race, as this opportunity offered by the exposition; and here bending, as it were, over the altar that represents the results of the struggles of your race and mine, both starting practically empty-handed three decades ago, I pledge that in your effort to work out the great and intricate problem which God has laid at the doors of the South, you shall have at all times the patient, sympathetic help of my race; only let this be constantly in mind, that, while from representations in these buildings of the product of field, of forest, of mine, of factory, letters, and art, much good will come, yet far above and beyond material benefits will be that higher good, that, let us pray God, will come, in a blotting out of sectional differences and racial animosities and suspicions, in a determination to administer absolute justice, in a willing obedience among all classes to the mandates of law. This, this, coupled with our material prosperity, will bring into our beloved South a new heaven and a new earth.

CROSS OF GOLD

By William Jennings Bryan

This speech, delivered at the Democratic National Convention in Chicago on July 9, 1896, was quite probably the most effective oration in the history of American party politics. Bryan, then only thirty-six, had come to Chicago as a leader of the Nebraska delegation with the avowed intention of vaulting from this relatively obscure role into the presidential nomination. And that he did. The great issue before the convention was whether the party should take its place behind President Cleveland and the conservative Democrats in a continued defense of the gold standard or yield to the fervent demand of populists in the West for free coinage of silver—a remedy for depressed prices, unemployment, and the blight of depression. Bryan was perhaps the most articulate advocate of the silver strategy, which essentially called for the government to inflate the money supply. Though he was ultimately defeated by William McKinley in the general election, he had established himself as a political force to be contended with.

I would be presumptuous, indeed, to present myself against the distinguished gentlemen to whom you have listened if this were a mere measuring of abilities; but this is not a contest between persons. The humblest citizen in all the land, when clad in the armor of a righteous cause, is stronger than all the hosts of error. I come to speak to you in defense of a cause as holy as the cause of liberty—the cause of humanity.

When this debate is concluded, a motion will be made to lay upon the table the resolution offered in commendation of the administration, and also the resolution offered in condemnation of the administration. We object to bringing this question down to the level of persons. The individual is but an atom; he is born, he acts, he dies; but principles are eternal; and this has been a contest over a principle.

Never before in the history of this country has there been witnessed such a contest as that through which we have just passed. Never before in the history of American politics has a great issue been fought out as this issue has been, by the voters of a great party. On the fourth of March, 1895, a few Democrats, most of them members of Congress, issued an address to the Democrats of the nation, asserting that the money question was the paramount issue of the hour; declaring that a majority of the Democratic party had the right to control the action of the party on this paramount issue; and concluding with the request that the believers in the free coinage of silver in the Democratic party should organize, take charge of, and control the policy of the Democratic party. Three months later, at

Memphis, an organization was perfected, and the silver Democrats went forth openly and courageously proclaiming their belief, and declaring that, if successful, they would crystallize into a platform the declaration which they had made. They began the conflict. With a zeal approaching the zeal which inspired the crusaders who followed Peter the Hermit, our silver Democrats went forth from victory unto victory until they are now assembled, not to discuss, not to debate, but to enter up the judgment already rendered by the plain people of this country. In this contest brother has been arrayed against brother, father against son. The warmest ties of love, acquaintance and association have been disregarded; old leaders have been cast aside when they have refused to give expression to the sentiments of those whom they would lead, and new leaders have sprung up to give direction to this cause of truth. Thus has the contest been waged, and we have assembled here under as binding and solemn instructions as were ever imposed upon representatives of the people.

We do not come as individuals. As individuals we might have been glad to compliment the gentleman from New York but we know that the people for whom we speak would never be willing to put him in a position where he could thwart the will of the Democratic party. I say it was not a question of persons; it was a question of principle, and it is not with gladness, my friends, that we find ourselves brought into conflict with those who are now arrayed on the other side.

The gentleman who preceded me spoke of the State of Massachusetts; let me assure him that not one present in all this convention entertains the least hostility to the people of the State of Massachusetts, but we stand here representing people who are the equals, before the law, of the greatest citizens in the State of Massachusetts. When you, turning to the gold delegates, come before us and tell us that we are about to disturb your business interests, we reply that you have disturbed our business interests by your course.

We say to you that you have made the definition of a business man too limited in its application. The man who is employed for wages is as much a business man as his employer; the attorney in a country town is as much a business man as the corporation counsel in a great metropolis; the merchant at the cross-roads store is as much a business man as the merchant of New York; the farmer who goes forth in the morning and toils all day—who begins in the spring and toils all summer—and who by the application of brain and muscle to the natural resources of the country creates wealth, is as much a business man as the man who goes upon the board of trade and bets upon the price of grain; the miners who go down a thousand feet into the earth, or climb two thousand feet upon the cliffs, and bring forth from their hiding places the precious metals to be poured into the channels of trade are as much business men as the few financial magnates who, in a back room, corner the money of the world. We come to speak for this broader class of business men.

Ah, my friends, we say not one word against those who live upon the Atlantic coast, but the hardy pioneers who have braved all the dangers of the wilderness, who have made the desert to blossom as the rose—the pioneers away out there who rear their children near to Nature's heart, where they can mingle their voices with the voices of the birds—out there where they have erected schoolhouses for the education of their young, churches where they praise their Creator, and cemeteries where rest the ashes of their dead—these people, we say, are as deserving of the consideration of our party as any people in this country. It is for these that we speak. We do not come as aggressors. Our war is not a war of conquest; we are fighting in the defense of our homes, our families, and posterity. We have petitioned, and our petitions have been scorned; we have entreated, and our entreaties have been disregarded; we have begged, and they have mocked when our calamity came. We beg no longer; we entreat no more; we petition no more. We defy them.

The gentleman from Wisconsin has said that he fears a Robespierre. My friends, in this land of the free you need not fear that a tyrant will spring up from among the people. What we need is an Andrew Jackson to stand, as Jackson stood, against the encroachments of organized wealth.

They tell us that this platform was made to catch votes. We reply to them that changing conditions make new issues; that the principles upon which Democracy rests are as everlasting as the hills, but that they must be applied to new conditions as they arise. Conditions have arisen, and we are here to meet those conditions. They tell us that the income tax ought not to be brought in here; that it is a new idea. They criticize us for our criticism of the Supreme Court of the United States. My friends, we have not criticized; we have simply called attention to what you already know. If you want criticisms, read the dissenting opinions of the court. There you will find criticisms. They say that we passed an unconstitutional law; we deny it. The income tax law was not unconstitutional when it was passed; it was not unconstitutional when it went before the Supreme Court for the first time; it did not become unconstitutional until one of the judges changed his mind, and we cannot be expected to know when a judge will change his mind. The income tax is just. It simply intends to put the burdens of government justly upon the backs of the people. I am in favor of an income tax. When I find a man who is not willing to bear his share of the burdens of the government which protects him, I find a man who is unworthy to enjoy the blessings of a government like ours.

They say that we are opposing national bank currency; that is true. If you will read what Thomas Benton said, you will find he said that, in searching history, he could find but one parallel to Andrew Jackson; that was Cicero, who destroyed the conspiracy of Cataline and saved Rome. Benton said that Cicero only did for Rome what Jackson did for us when he destroyed the bank conspiracy and saved America. We say in our platform that we believe that the right to coin and issue money is a function of government. We believe it. We believe that it is a part of sovereignty, and can no more with safety be delegated to private individuals than we could afford to delegate to private individuals the power to make penal statutes or levy taxes. Mr. Jefferson, who was once regarded as good Democratic authority, seems to have differed in opinion from the gentleman who has addressed us on the part of the minority. Those who are opposed to this proposition tell us that the issue of paper money is a function of the bank, and that the Government ought to go out of the banking business. I stand with Jefferson rather than with them, and tell them, as he did, that the issue of money is a function of government, and that the banks ought to go out of the governing business.

They complain about the plank which declares against life tenure in office. They have tried to strain it to mean that which it does not mean. What we oppose by that plank is the life tenure which is being built up in Washington, and which excludes from participation in official benefits the humbler members of society.

Let me call your attention to two or three important things. The gentleman from New York says that he will propose an amendment to the platform providing that the proposed change in our monetary system shall not affect contracts already made. Let me remind you that there is no intention of affecting those contracts which according to present laws are made payable in gold; but if he means to say that we cannot change our monetary system without protecting those who have loaned money before the change was made, I desire to ask him where, in law or in morals, he can find justification for not protecting the debtors when the act of 1873 was passed, if he now insists that we must protect the creditors.

He says he will also propose an amendment which will provide for the suspension of free coinage if we fail to maintain the party within a year. We reply that when we advocate a policy which we believe will be successful, we are not compelled to raise a doubt as to our own sincerity by suggesting what we shall do if we fail. I ask him, if he would apply his logic to us, why he does not apply it to himself. He says he wants this country to try to secure an international agreement. Why does he not tell us what he is going to do if he fails to secure an international agreement? There is more reason for him to do that than there is for us to provide against the failure to maintain the party. Our opponents have tried for twenty years to secure an international agreement, and those are waiting for it most patiently who do not want it at all.

And now, my friends, let me come to the paramount issue. If they ask us why it is that we say more on the money question than we say upon the tariff question, I reply that, if protection has slain its thousands, the gold standard has slain its tens of thousands. If they ask us why we do not embody in our platform all the things that we believe in, we reply that when we have restored the money of the Constitution all other necessary reforms will be possible; but that until this is done there is no other reform that can be accomplished.

Why is it that within three months such a change has come over the country? Three months ago, when it was confidently asserted that those who believe in the gold standard would frame our platform and nominate our candidates, even the advocates of the gold standard did not think that we could elect a president. And they had good reason for their doubt, because there is scarcely a State here today asking for the gold standard which is not in the absolute control of the Republican party. But note the change. Mr. McKinley was nominated at St. Louis upon a platform which declared for the maintenance of the gold standard until it can be changed into bimetallism by international agreement. Mr. McKinley was the most popular man among the Republicans, and three months ago everybody in the Republican party prophesied his election. How is it today? Why, the man who was once pleased to think that he looked like Napoleon—that man shudders today when he remembers that he was nominated on the anniversary of the battle of Waterloo. Not only that, but as he listens he can hear with ever-increasing distinctness the sound of the waves as they beat upon the lonely shores of St. Helena.

Why this change? Ah, my friends, is not the reason for the change evident to any one who will look at the matter? No private character, however pure, no personal popularity, however great, can protect from the avenging wrath of an indignant people a man who will declare that he is in favor of fastening the gold standard upon this country, or who is willing to surrender the right of self-government and place the legislative control of our affairs in the hands of foreign potentates and powers.

We go forth confident that we shall win. Why? Because upon the paramount issue of this campaign there is not a spot of ground upon which the enemy will dare to challenge battle. If they tell us that the gold standard is a good thing, we shall point to their platform and tell them that their platform pledges the party to get rid of the gold standard and substitute bimetallism. If the gold standard is a good thing, why try to get rid of it? I call your attention to the fact that some of the very people who are in this convention today and who tell us that we ought to declare in favor of international bimetallism—thereby declaring that the gold standard is wrong and that the principle of bimetallism is better—these very people four months ago were open and avowed advocates of the gold standard, and were then telling us that we could not legislate two metals together, even with the aid of all the world. If the gold standard is a good thing, we ought to declare in favor of its retention and not in favor of abandoning it; and if the gold standard is a bad thing why should we wait until other nations are willing to help us to let go? Here is the line of battle, and we care not upon which issue they force the fight; we are prepared to meet them on either issue or on both. If they tell us that the gold standard is the standard of civilization, we reply to them that this, the most enlightened of all the nations of the earth, has never declared for a gold standard and that both the great parties this year are declaring against it. If the gold standard is the standard of civilization, why, my friends, should we not have it? If they come to meet us on that issue we can present the history of our nation. More than that; we can tell them that they will search the pages of history in vain to find a single instance where the common people of any land have ever declared themselves in favor of the gold standard. They can find where the holders of the fixed investments have declared for a gold standard, but not where the masses have.

Mr. Carlisle said in 1878 that this was a struggle between "the idle holders of idle capital" and "the struggling masses, who produce the wealth and pay the taxes of the country;" and, my friends, the question we are to decide is: Upon which side will the Democratic party fight; upon the side of "the idle holders of idle capital" or upon the side of "the struggling masses"? That is the question which the party must answer first, and then it must be answered by each individual hereafter. The sympathies of the Democratic party, as shown by the platform, are on the side of the struggling masses who have ever been the foundation of the Democratic party. There are two ideas of government. There are those who believe that if you will only legislate to make the well-to-do prosperous, their prosperity will leak through on those below. The Democratic idea, however, has been that if you legislate to make the masses prosperous, their prosperity will find its way up through every class which rests upon them.

You come to us and tell us that the great cities are in favor of the gold standard; we reply that the great cities rest upon our broad and fertile prairies. Burn down your cities and leave our farms, and your cities will spring up again as if by magic; but destroy our farms and the grass will grow in the streets of every city in the country.

My friends, we declare that this nation is able to legislate for its own people on every question, without waiting for the aid or consent of any other nation on earth; and upon that issue we expect to carry every State in the Union. I shall not slander the inhabitants of the fair State of Massachusetts nor the inhabitants of the State of New York by saying that, when they are confronted with the proposition, they will declare that this nation is not able to attend to its own business. It is the issue of 1776 over again. Our ancestors, when, but three millions in number, had the courage to declare their political independence of every other nation; shall we, their descendants, when we have grown to seventy millions, declare that we are less independent than our forefathers? No, my friends, that will never be the verdict of our people. Therefore, we care not upon what lines the battle is fought. If they say bimetallism is good, but that we cannot have it until other nations help us, we reply that, instead of having a gold standard because England has, we will restore bimetallism, and then let England have bimetallism because the United States has it. If they dare to come out in the open field and defend the gold standard as a good thing, we will fight them to the uttermost. Having behind us the producing masses of this nation and the world, supported by the commercial interests, the laboring interests, and the toilers everywhere, we will answer their demand for a gold standard by saying to them: You shall not press down upon the brow of labor this crown of thorns, you shall not crucify mankind upon a cross of gold.

CUBA TO COLUMBIA

By Will Carleton

Patriotic fervor ran high during the brief Spanish-American War. Uniting the nation for the first time since the calamity of the War between the States and Reconstruction, the war was heralded in songs like this one as an emblem of America's new vitality.

A voice went over the waters
    A stormy edge of the sea;
Fairest of Freedom's daughters,
    Have you no help for me?
Do you not hear the rusty chain
    Clanking about my feet?

Have you not seen my children slain,
  Whether in cell or street?
Oh, if you were sad as I,
  And I as you were strong,
You would not have to call or cry
  You would not suffer long!

"Patience?" Have I not learned it,
  Under the crushing years?
Freedom—have I not earned it,
  Toiling with blood and tears?
"Not of you?" My banners wave
  Not on Egyptian shore,
Or by Armenia's mammoth grave,
  But at your very door,
Oh, if you were needy as I,
  And I as you were strong,
You should not suffer, bleed, and die,
  Under the hoofs of wrong!

Is it that you have never
  Felt the oppressor's hand,
Fighting, with fond endeavor,
  To cling to your own sweet land?
Were you not half dismayed,
  There in the century's night,
Till to your view a sister's aid
  Came, like a flash of light?
Oh, what gift could ever be grand
  Enough to pay the debt,
If out of the starry Western land,
  Should come my Lafayette!

THE MEN OF THE MAINE

By Clinton Scollard

Spanish-American relations—already tense due to reports of brutal human rights abuses in the European powers' few remaining colonies—were transformed into open conflict when an American battle cruiser was mysteriously destroyed by a mine while peacefully anchored in the Havana harbor. The men aboard who lost their lives became the martyrs in a national crusade for honor and vindication.

Not in the dire, ensanguined front of war,
Conquered or conqueror,
'Mid the dread battle-peal, did they go down
To the still under-seas, with fair Renown
To weave for them the hero-martyr's crown.
They struck no blow
'Gainst an embattled foe;
With valiant-hearted Saxon hardihood
They stood not as the Essex sailors stood,
So sore bestead in that far Chilian bay;
Yet no less faithful they,
These men who, in a passing of the breath,
Were hurtled upon death.

No warning the salt-scented sea-wind bore,
No presage whispered from the Cuban shore
Of the appalling fate
That in the tropic night-time lay in wait
To bear them whence they shall return no more.
Some lapsed from dreams of home and love's clear star
Into a realm where dreams eternal are;
And some into a world of wave and flame
Where-through they came
To living agony that no words can name.
Tears for them all,
And the low-tuned dirge funereal!

Their place is now
With those who wear, green-set about the brow,

The deathless immortelles,
The heroes torn and scarred
Whose blood made red the barren ocean dells,
Fighting with him the gallant Ranger bore,
Daring to do what none had dared before,
To wave the New World banner, freedom-starred,
At England's very door!
Yea, with such noble ones their names shall stand
As those who heard the dying Lawrence speak
His burning words upon the Chesapeake,
And grappled in the hopeless hand-to-hand;
With those who fell on Erie and Champlain
Beneath the pouring, pitiless battle-rain:
With such as these, our lost men of the Maine!

What though they faced no storm of iron hail
That freedom and the right might still prevail?
The path of duty it was theirs to tread
To death's dark vale through ways of travail led,
And they are ours—our dead!
If it be true that each loss holds a gain,
It must be ours through saddened eyes to see
From out this tragic holocaust of pain
The whole land bound in closer amity!

BATTLE SONG

By Robert Burns Wilson

*The Spanish military, once the greatest in the world, was no match for the
vigorous American expeditionary force—especially since it was so distantly
separated from its supply lines. Thus the battle songs of the Americans were
invariably songs of invincibility and victory.*

When the vengeance wakes, when the battle breaks,
    And the ships sweep out to sea;
When the foe is neared, when the decks are cleared,
    And the colors floating free;
When the squadrons meet, when it's fleet to fleet
    And front to front with Spain,

From ship to ship, from lip to lip,
    Pass on the quick refrain,
"Remember, remember the Maine!"

When the flag shall sign, "Advance in line;
    Train ships on an even keel";
When the guns shall flash and the shot shall crash
    And bound on the ringing steel;
When the rattling blasts from the armored masts
    Are hurling their deadliest rain,
Let their voices loud, through the blinding cloud,
    Cry ever the fierce refrain,
"Remember, remember the Maine!"

God's sky and sea in that storm shall be
    Fate's chaos of smoke and flame,
But across that hell every shot shall tell
    Not a gun can miss its aim;
Not a blow shall fail on the crumbling mail,
    And the waves that engulf the slain
Shall sweep the decks of the blackened wrecks,
    With the thundering, dread refrain,
"Remember, remember the Maine!"

DEWEY IN MANILA BAY

By R. V. Risley

Though the Rough Riders charging up San Juan Hill received the most publicity, the greatest military victory came at sea far from the Western theater—off the coast of the Philippines. This popular song celebrates the valor, ingenuity, and quick victory of Commodore Dewey at Manila Bay.

He took a thousand islands and he didn't lose a man
    (Raise your heads and cheer him as he goes!)
He licked the sneaky Spaniard till the fellow cut and ran,
    For fighting's part of what a Yankee knows.

He fought 'em and he licked 'em, without any fuss or flame
    (It was only his profession for to win),
He sank their boats beneath 'em, and he spared 'em as they swam,
    And then he sent his ambulances in.

He had no word to cheer him and had no bands to play,
    He had no crowds to make his duty brave;
But he risked the deep torpedoes at the breaking of the day,
    For he knew he had our self-respect to save.

He flew the angry signal crying justice for the Maine,
    He flew it from his flagship as he fought.
He drove the tardy vengeance in the very teeth of Spain,
    And he did it just because he thought he ought.

He busted up their batteries and sank eleven ships
    (He knew what he was doing, every bit);
He set the Maxims going like a hundred cracking whips,
    And every shot that crackled was a hit.

He broke 'em and he drove 'em, and he didn't care at all,
    He only liked to do as he was bid;
He crumpled up their squadron and their batteries and all—
He knew he had to lick 'em and he did.
And when the thing was finished and they flew the frightened flag,
    He slung his guns and sent his foot ashore,
And he gathered in their wounded, and he quite forgot to brag,
    For he thought he did his duty, nothing more.

Oh, he took a thousand islands and he didn't lose a man
    (Raise your heads and cheer him as he goes!)
He licked the sneaky Spaniard till the fellow cut and ran,
    For fighting's part of what a Yankee knows !

THE NEW COLOSSUS

By Emma Lazarus

Written in 1883, this poem gained fame after it was inscribed on the Statue of Liberty in 1903. Thereafter it became a beacon light of hope to the oppressed peoples of the world. To this day it conveys the exceptionalism of the American experiment in national life—one that is rooted first and foremost in a set of ideas about freedom.

Not like the brazen giant of Greek fame,
With conquering limbs astride from land to land;
Here at our sea-washed, sunset gates shall stand
A mighty woman with a torch, whose flame
Is the imprisoned lightning, and her name
Mother of Exiles. From her beacon-hand
Glows worldwide welcome; her mild eyes command
The air-bridged harbor that twin cities frame.

"Keep, ancient lands, your storied pomp!" cries she
With silent lips. "Give me your tired, your poor,
Your huddled masses yearning to breathe free,
The wretched refuse of your teeming shore.
Send these, the homeless, tempest-tost to me,
I lift my lamp beside the golden door!"

PANAMA

By James Roche

The construction of the Panama Canal was not only a remarkable feat of engineering prowess, thrusting the American republic to the forefront of the world stage, but it was a great economic, diplomatic, and administrative achievement as well. As this popular poem illustrates, the dynamic leadership of Theodore Roosevelt had already made an impression upon the energetic nation—and this singular accomplishment of his only added to the luster of America's new sterling reputation.

Here the oceans twain have waited
    All the ages to be mated
Waited long and waited vainly,
    Though the script was written plainly:
"This, the portal of the sea,
    Open for him who holds the key;
Here the empire of the earth
    Waits in patience for its birth."
But the Spanish monarch, dimly
    Seeing little, answered grimly:
"North and South the land is Spain's,
    As God gave it, it remains.
He who seeks to break the tie,
    By mine honor, he shall die!"
So the centuries rolled on,
    And the gift of great Colon,
Like a spendthrift's heritage,
    Dwindled slowly, age by age,
Till the flag of red and gold
    Fell from hands unnerved and old.
And the granite-pillared gate
    Waited still the key of fate.
Who shall hold that magic key
    But the child of destiny,
In whose veins has mingled long
    All the best blood of the strong?
He who takes his place by grace
    Of no single tribe or race,
But by many a rich bequest
    From the bravest and the best.
Sentinel of duty, here
    Must he guard a hemisphere.
Let the old world keep its ways;
    Naught to him its blame or praise;
Naught its greed, or hate, or fear;
    For all swords be sheathed here.
Yea, the gateway shall be free
    Unto all, from sea to sea;
And no fratricidal slaughter
    Shall defile its sacred water;

But—the hand that opened the gate
Shall forever hold the key!

THE MAN WITH THE MUCK-RAKE

By Theodore Roosevelt

_One of the most popular men who ever held the highest political office in the
land, Theodore Roosevelt made his reputation as a reformer. His entire career
was a kind of crusade against systemic corruption and injustice. Unlike most
reformers, however, he was profoundly committed to conservative principles; his
reforms were designed to preserve the heritage of Christendom rather than to
merely innovate. That unique combination of progressivism and conservatism is
especially evident in this speech, which he delivered to the House of
Representatives on April 14, 1906._

Over a century ago Washington laid the cornerstone of the Capitol
in what was then little more than a tract of wooded wilderness
here beside the Potomac. We now find it necessary to provide
by great additional buildings for the business of the government. This
growth in the need for the housing of the government is but a proof and
example of the way in which the nation has grown and the sphere of action
of the national government has grown. We now administer the affairs of a
nation in which the extraordinary growth of population has been
outstripped by the growth of wealth and the growth in complex interests.
The material problems that face us today are not such as they were in
Washington's time, but the underlying facts of human nature are the same
now as they were then. Under altered external form we war with the same
tendencies toward evil that were evident in Washington's time, and are
helped by the same tendencies for good. It is about some of these that I
wish to say a word today.

In Bunyan's Pilgrim's Progress you may recall the description of the
Man with the Muck-rake, the man who could look no way but downward,
with the muck-rake in his hand; who was offered a celestial crown for his
muck-rake, but who would neither look up nor regard the crown he was
offered, but continued to rake to himself the filth of the floor.

In Pilgrim's Progress the Man with the Muck-rake is set forth as the
example of him whose vision is fixed on carnal instead of on spiritual

things. Yet he also typifies the man who in this life consistently refuses to see aught that is lofty and fixes his eyes with solemn intentness only on that which is vile and debasing. Now, it is very necessary that we should not flinch from seeing what is vile and debasing. There is filth on the floor, and it must be scraped up with the muck-rake: and there are times and places where this service is the most needed of all the services that can be performed. But the man who never does anything else, who never thinks or speaks or writes save of his feats with the muck-rake, speedily becomes, not a help to society, not an incitement to good, but one of the most potent forces for evil.

There are, in the body politic, economic, and social, many and grave evils, and there is urgent necessity for the sternest war upon them. There should be relentless exposure of and attack upon every evil man, whether politician or business man, every evil practice, whether in politics, in business, or in social life. I hail as a benefactor every writer or speaker, every man who, on the platform, or in book, magazine, or newspaper, with merciless severity makes such attack, provided always that he in his turn remembers that the attack is of use only if it is absolutely truthful. The liar is no whit better than the thief, and if his mendacity takes the form of slander, he may be worse than most thieves. It puts a premium upon knavery untruthfully to attack an honest man, or even with hysterical exaggeration to assail a bad man with untruth. An epidemic of indiscriminate assault upon character does no good but very great harm.

My plea is not for immunity to, but for the most unsparing exposure of the politician who betrays his trust, of the big-business man who makes or spends his fortune in illegitimate or corrupt ways. There should be a resolute effort to hunt every such man out of the position he has disgraced. Expose the crime, and hunt down the criminal; but remember that even in the case of crime, if it is attacked in sensational, lurid, and untruthful fashion, the attack may do more damage to the public mind than the crime itself. It is because I feel that there should be no rest in the endless war against the forces of evil that I ask that the war be conducted with sanity as well as with resolution. The men with the muck-rakes are often indispensable to the well-being of society; but only if they know when to stop raking the muck, and to look upward to the celestial crown above them, to the crown of worthy endeavor. There are beautiful things above and round about them; and if they gradually grow to feel that the whole world is nothing but muck, their power of usefulness is gone. If the whole picture is painted black, there remains no hue whereby to single out the rascals for distinction from their fellows. Such painting finally induces a kind of moral colorblindness; and people affected by it come to the conclusion that no man is really black, and no man really white, but that all are gray.

To assail the great and admitted evils of our political and industrial life with such crude and sweeping generalizations as to include decent men in the general condemnation means the searing of the public conscience. There results a general attitude either of cynical belief in and indifference to public corruption or else of a distrustful inability to discriminate between the good and the bad. Either attitude is fraught with untold damage to the country as a whole. The fool who has not sense to discriminate between what is good and what is bad is well-nigh as dangerous as the man who does discriminate and yet chooses the bad. There is nothing more distressing to every good patriot, to every good American, than the hard, scoffing spirit which treats the allegation of dishonesty in a public man as a cause for laughter.

There is any amount of good in the world, and there never was a time when loftier and more disinterested work for the betterment of mankind was being done than now. The forces that tend for evil are great and terrible but the forces of truth and love and courage and honesty and generosity and sympathy are also stronger than ever before. It is a foolish and timid, no less than a wicked, thing to blink the fact that the forces of evil are strong, but it is even worse to fail to take into account the strength of the forces that tell for good. Hysterical sensationalism is the very poorest weapon wherewith to fight for lasting righteousness. The men who, with stern sobriety and truth, assail the many evils of our time, whether in the public press, or in magazines, or in books, are the leaders and allies of all engaged in the work for social and political betterment. But if they give good reason for distrust of what they say, if they chill the ardor of those who demand truth as a primary virtue, they thereby betray the good cause, and play into the hands of the very men against whom they are nominally at war.

We can no more and no less afford to condone evil in the man of capital than evil in the man of no capital. The wealthy man who exults because there is a failure of justice in the effort to bring some trust magnate to an account for his misdeeds is as bad as, and no worse than, the so-called labor leader who clamorously strives to excite a foul class feeling on behalf of some other labor leader who is implicated in murder. One attitude is as bad as the other and no worse; in each case the accused is entitled to exact justice; and in neither case is there need of action by others which can be construed into an expression of sympathy for crime. There is nothing more antisocial in a democratic republic like ours than such vicious class-consciousness.

It is important to this people to grapple with the problems connected with the amassing of enormous fortunes, and the use of those fortunes, both corporate and individual, in business. We should discriminate in the sharpest way between fortunes well won and fortunes ill won; between those gained as an incident to performing great services to the community as a whole, and those gained in evil fashion by keeping just within the limits of mere law-honesty. Of course no amount of charity in spending such fortunes in any way compensates for misconduct in making them. As a matter of personal conviction, and without pretending to discuss the details or formulate the system, I feel that we shall ultimately have to consider the adoption of some such scheme as that of a progressive tax on all fortunes, beyond a certain amount, either given in life or devised or bequeathed upon death to any individual—a tax so framed as to put it out of the power of the owner of one of these enormous fortunes to hand on more than a certain amount to any one individual.

The eighth commandment reads "Thou shalt not steal." It does not read "Thou shalt not steal from the rich man." It does not read "Thou shalt not steal from the poor man." It reads, simply and plainly, "Thou shalt not steal." No good whatever will come from that warped and mock morality which denounces the misdeeds of men of wealth and forgets the misdeeds practiced at their expense; which denounces bribery, but blinds itself to blackmail; which foams with rage if a corporation secures favors by improper methods, and merely leers with hideous mirth if the corporation is itself wronged. The only public servant who can be trusted honestly to protect the rights of the public against the misdeeds of a corporation is that public man who will just as surely protect the corporation itself from wrongful aggression. If a public man is willing to yield to popular clamor and do wrong to the men of wealth or to rich corporations, it may be set down as certain that if the opportunity comes he will secretly and furtively do wrong to the public in the interest of a corporation.

More important than aught else is the development of the broadest sympathy of man for man. The welfare of the wage-worker, the welfare of the tiller of the soil—upon this depends the welfare of the entire country; their good is not to be sought in pulling down others; but their good must be the prime object of all our statesmanship.

Materially we must strive to secure a broader economic opportunity for all men, so that each shall have a better chance to show the stuff of which he is made. Spiritually and ethically we must strive to bring about clean living and right thinking. We appreciate that the things of the body are important; but we appreciate also that the things of the soul are immeasurably more important. The foundation stone of national life is, and ever must be, the high individual character of the average citizen.

HAVE FAITH IN MASSACHUSETTS

By Calvin Coolidge

_This speech, delivered on January 7, 1914, to the state senate of Massachusetts,
was the crowning plea of scholarly conservatism in a day of reaction and
radicalism. Its laconic style and quiet confidence thrust the taciturn Calvin
Coolidge upon the national stage and established a new platform for traditional
civic restraint. In many ways it heralded the advent of a fresh new conservative
movement. The speech, a simple Vermont performance, was like the man—
immovable but majestic granite._

This Commonwealth is one. We are all members of one body. The
welfare of the weakest and the welfare of the most powerful are
inseparably bound together. Industry cannot flourish if labor
languish. Transportation cannot prosper if manufactures decline. The
general welfare cannot be provided for in any one act, but it is well to
remember that the benefit of one is the benefit of all, and the neglect of one
is the neglect of all. The suspension of one man's dividends is the
suspension of another man's pay envelope.

Men do not make laws. They do but discover them. Laws must be
justified by something more than the will of the majority. They must rest
on the eternal foundation of righteousness. That state is most fortunate in
its form of government which has the aptest instruments for the discovery
of laws. The latest, most modern, and nearest perfect system that
statesmanship has devised is representative government. Its weakness is
the weakness of us imperfect human beings who administer it. Its strength
is that even such administration secures to the people more blessings than
any other system ever produced. No nation has discarded it and retained
liberty. Representative government must be preserved.

Courts are established, not to determine the popularity of a cause, but to
adjudicate and enforce rights. No litigant should be required to submit his
case to the hazard and expense of a political campaign. No judge should be
required to seek or receive political rewards. The courts of Massachusetts
are known and honored wherever men love justice. Let their glory suffer
no diminution at our hands. The electorate and judiciary cannot combine.
A hearing means a hearing. When the trial of causes goes outside the court-
room, Anglo-Saxon constitutional government ends.

The people cannot look to legislation generally for success. Industry,
thrift, character, are not conferred by act or resolve. Government cannot

relieve from toil. It can provide no substitute for the rewards of service. It can, of course, care for the defective and recognize distinguished merit. The normal must care for themselves. Self-government means self-support. Man is born into the universe with a personality that is his own. He has a right that is founded upon the constitution of the universe to have property that is his own. Ultimately, property rights and personal rights are the same thing. The one cannot be preserved if the other be violated. Each man is entitled to his rights and the rewards of his service be they ever so large or never so small.

History reveals no civilized people among whom there were not a highly educated class, and large aggregations of wealth, represented usually by the clergy and the nobility. Inspiration has always come from above. Diffusion of learning has come down from the university to the common school—the kindergarten is last. No one would now expect to aid the common school by abolishing higher education.

It may be that the diffusion of wealth works in an analogous way. As the little red schoolhouse is builded in the college, it may be that the fostering and protection of large aggregations of wealth are the only foundation on which to build the prosperity of the whole people. Large profits mean large pay rolls. But profits must be the result of service performed. In no land are there so many and such large aggregations of wealth as here; in no land do they perform larger service; in no land will the work of a day bring so large a reward in material and spiritual welfare.

Have faith in Massachusetts. In some unimportant detail some other States may surpass her, but in the general results, there is no place on earth where the people secure, in a larger measure, the blessings of organized government, and nowhere can those functions more properly be termed self-government.

Do the day's work. If it be to protect the rights of the weak, whoever objects, do it. If it be to help a powerful corporation better to serve the people, whatever the opposition, do that. Expect to be called a stand-patter, but don't be a stand-patter. Expect to be called a demagogue, but don't be a demagogue. Don't hesitate to be as revolutionary as science. Don't hesitate to be as reactionary as the multiplication table. Don't expect to build up the weak by pulling down the strong. Don't hurry to legislate. Give administration a chance to catch up with legislation.

We need a broader, firmer, deeper faith in the people—a faith that men desire to do right, that the Commonwealth is founded upon a righteousness which will endure, a reconstructed faith that the final approval of the people is given not to demagogues, slavishly pandering to their selfishness, merchandising with the clamor of the hour, but to statesmen, ministering to their welfare, representing their deep, silent, abiding convictions.

Statutes must appeal to more than material welfare. Wages won't satisfy, be they never so large. Nor houses; nor lands, nor coupons, though they fall thick as the leaves of autumn. Man has a spiritual nature. Touch it, and it must respond as the magnet responds to the pole. To that, not to selfishness, let the laws of the Commonwealth appeal. Recognize the immortal worth and dignity of man. Let the laws of Massachusetts proclaim to her humblest citizen, performing the most menial task, the recognition of his manhood, the recognition that all men are peers, the humblest with the most exalted, the recognition that all work is glorified. Such is the path to equality before the law. Such is the foundation of liberty under the law. Such is the sublime revelation of man's relation to man—Democracy.

THE AMERICAN LANGUAGE

By H. L. Mencken

In the course of his remarkable career in journalism, criticism, and punditry, H. L. Mencken poleaxed many a cultural sacred cow and deftly needled many a political windbag, but this essay—which prefaced his 1919 magnum opus, The American Language—*reflects primarily his concern with the speech of what he liked to refer to as this "Great Republic." It highlights the "salient differences between the English of England and the English of America." His opinions on language, like those he expressed on other subjects, have given rise to much comment and controversy, but their influence has been greater than perhaps any other American writer except perhaps Noah Webster.*

The aim of this book is best exhibited by describing its origin. I am, and have been since early manhood, an editor of newspapers, magazines and books, and a critic of the last named. These occupations have forced me into a pretty wide familiarity with current literature, both periodical and within covers, and in particular into a familiarity with the current literature of England and America. It was part of my daily work, for a good many years, to read the principal English newspapers and reviews; it has been part of my work, all the time, to read the more important English novels, essays, poetry and criticism. An American born and bred, I early noted, as everyone else in like case must note, certain salient differences between the English of England and the English of America as practically spoken and written—differences in vocabulary, in syntax, in the shades and habits of idiom, and even, coming to the common speech, in grammar. And I noted too, of course, partly during visits to England but more largely by a somewhat wide and intimate intercourse with English people in the United States, the obvious differences between English and American pronunciation and intonation.

Greatly interested in these differences—some of them so great that they led me to seek exchanges of light with Englishmen—I looked for some work that would describe and account for them with a show of completeness, and perhaps depict the process of their origin. I soon found that no such work existed, either in England or in America—that the whole literature of the subject was astonishingly meagre and unsatisfactory. There were several dictionaries of Americanisms, true enough, but only one of them made any pretension to scientific method, and even that one was woefully narrow and incomplete. The one more general treatise, the work of a man foreign to both England and America in race and education, was more than 40 years old, and full of palpable errors. For the rest, there was only a fugitive and inconsequential literature—an almost useless mass of notes and essays, chiefly by the minor sort of pedagogues, seldom illuminating, save in small details, and often incredibly ignorant and inaccurate. On the large and important subject of American pronunciation, for example, I could find nothing save a few casual essays. On American spelling, with its wide and constantly visible divergencies from English usages, there was little more. On American grammar there was nothing whatever. Worse, an important part of the poor literature that I unearthed was devoted to absurd efforts to prove that no such thing as an American variety of English existed—that the differences I constantly encountered in English and that my English friends encountered in American were chiefly imaginary, and to be explained away by denying them.

Still intrigued by the subject, and in despair of getting any illumination from such theoretical masters of it, I began a collection of materials for my own information, and gradually it took on a rather formidable bulk. My interest in it being made known by various articles in the newspapers and magazines, I began also to receive contributions from other persons of the same fancy, both English and American, and gradually my collection fell into a certain order, and I saw the workings of general laws in what, at first, had appeared to be mere chaos. The present book then began to take form—its preparation a sort of recreation from other and far different labor. It is anything but an exhaustive treatise upon the subject; it is not even an exhaustive examination of the materials. All it pretends to do is to articulate some of those materials—to get some approach to order and coherence into them, and so pave the way for a better work by some more competent man. That work calls for the equipment of a first rate philologist, which I am surely not. All I have done here is to stake out the field, sometimes borrowing suggestions from other inquirers and sometimes, as in the case of American grammar, attempting to run the lines myself.

That it should be regarded as an anti-social act to examine and exhibit the constantly growing differences between English and American, as certain American pedants argue sharply—this doctrine is quite beyond my understanding. All it indicates, stripped of sophistry, is a somewhat childish effort to gain the approval of Englishmen—a belated efflorescence of the colonial spirit, often commingled with fashionable aspiration. The plain fact is that the English themselves are not deceived, nor do they grant the approval so ardently sought for. On the contrary, they are keenly aware of the differences between the two dialects, and often discuss them, as the following pages show. Perhaps one dialect, in the long run, will defeat and absorb the other; if the two nations continue to be partners in great adventures it may very well happen. But even in that case, something may be accomplished by examining the differences which exist today. In some ways, as in intonation, English usage is plainly better than American. In others, as in spelling, American usage is plainly better than English. But in order to develop usages that the people of both nations will accept it is obviously necessary to study the differences now visible. This study thus shows a certain utility. But its chief excuse is its human interest, for it prods deeply into national idiosyncrasies and ways of mind, and that sort of prodding is always entertaining.

I am thus neither teacher, nor prophet, nor reformer, but merely inquirer. The exigencies of my vocation make me almost completely bilingual; I can write English, as in this clause, quite as readily as American, as in this here one. Moreover, I have a hand for a compromise dialect which embodies the common materials of both, and is thus free from offense on both sides of the water—as befits the editor of a magazine published in both countries. But that compromise dialect is the living speech of neither. What I have tried to do here is to make a first sketch of the living speech of These States. The work is confessedly incomplete, and in places very painfully so, but in such enterprises a man must put an arbitrary term to his labors, lest some mischance, after years of diligence, take him from them too suddenly for them to be closed, and his laborious accumulations, as Ernest Walker says in his book on English surnames, be "doomed to the waste-basket by harassed executors."

If the opportunity offers in future I shall undoubtedly return to the subject. For one thing, I am eager to attempt a more scientific examination of the grammar of the American vulgar speech, here discussed briefly in Chapter VI. For another thing, I hope to make further inquiries into the subject of American surnames of non-English origin. Various other fields invite. No historical study of American pronunciation exists; the influence of German, Irish-English, Yiddish and other such immigrant dialects upon American has never been investigated; there is no adequate treatise on American geographical names. Contributions of materials and suggestions for a possible revised edition of the present book will reach me if addressed to me in care of the publisher at 220 West Forty-second Street, New York. I shall also be very grateful for the correction of errors, some perhaps typographical but others due to faulty information or mistaken judgment.

In conclusion I borrow a plea in confession and avoidance from Ben Jonson's pioneer grammar of English, published in incomplete form after his death. "We have set down," he said, "that that in our judgment agreeth best with reason and good order. Which notwithstanding, if it seem to any to be too rough hewed, let him plane it out more smoothly, and I shall not only not envy it, but in the behalf of my country most heartily thank him for so great a benefit; hoping that I shall be thought sufficiently to have done my part if in tolling this bell I may draw others to a deeper consideration of the matter; for, touching myself, I must needs confess that after much painful churning this only would come which here we have devised."

WAR MESSAGE

By Woodrow Wilson

Despite having run on a platform of determined neutrality, President Woodrow Wilson found his administration being drawn inexorably toward war. On March 5, 1917, he delivered his second inaugural address as the nations of the world engaged in a great global war. "The tragical events of the thirty months of vital turmoil through which we have just passed have made us citizens of the world. There can be no turning back. All nations are equally interested in the peace of the world and in the political stability of free peoples, and equally responsible for their maintenance." Less than a month later, the president, citing Germany's policy of unlimited submarine warfare against its enemies as well as neutral countries, including the United States, asked Congress for a declaration of war against the Imperial German government. The United States entered the First World War on April 6, 1917.

I have called the Congress into extraordinary session because there are serious, very serious, choices of policy to be made, and made immediately, which it was neither right nor constitutionally permissible that I should assume the responsibility of making.

On the third of February last, I officially laid before you the extraordinary announcement of the Imperial German government that on and after the first day of February it was its purpose to put aside all restraints of law or of humanity and use its submarines to sink every vessel that sought to approach either the ports of Great Britain and Ireland, or the western coasts of Europe, or any of the ports controlled by the enemies of Germany within the Mediterranean.

That had seemed to be the object of the German submarine warfare earlier in the war; but since April of last year the Imperial government had somewhat restrained the commanders of its undersea craft in conformity with its promise then given to us that passenger boats should not be sunk and that due warning would be given to all other vessels which its submarines might seek to destroy, when no resistance was offered or escape attempted, and care taken that their crews were given at least a fair chance to save their lives in their open boats. The precautions taken were meager and haphazard enough, as was proved in distressing instance after instance in the progress of the cruel and unmanly business, but a certain degree of restraint was observed.

The new policy has swept every restriction aside. Vessels of every kind, whatever their flag, their character, their cargo, their destination, their errand, have been ruthlessly sent to the bottom without warning and without thought of help or mercy for those on board—the vessels of friendly neutrals along with those of belligerents. Even hospital ships and ships carrying relief to the sorely bereaved and stricken people of Belgium, though the latter were provided with safe conduct through the proscribed areas by the German government itself and were distinguished by unmistakable marks of identity, have been sunk with the same reckless lack of compassion or of principle.

I was for a little while unable to believe that such things would in fact be done by any government that had hitherto subscribed to the humane practices of civilized nations. International law had its origin in the attempt to set up some law which would be respected and observed upon the seas, where no nation had right of dominion and where lay the free highways of the world. By painful stage after stage has that law been built up, with meager enough results, indeed, after all was accomplished that could be accomplished, but always with a clear view, at least, of what the heart and conscience of mankind demanded.

This minimum of right the German government has swept aside under the plea of retaliation and necessity and because it had no weapons which it could use at sea except those which it is impossible to employ as it is employing them without throwing to the winds all scruples of humanity or of respect for the understandings that were supposed to underlie the intercourse of the world. I am not now thinking of the loss of property involved, immense and serious as that is, but only of the wanton and wholesale destruction of the lives of noncombatants, men, women, and children, engaged in pursuits which have always, even in the darkest periods of modern history, been deemed innocent and legitimate. Property can be paid for; the lives of peaceful and innocent people cannot be. The present German submarine warfare against commerce is a warfare against mankind.

It is a war against all nations. American ships have been sunk, American lives taken, in ways which it has stirred us very deeply to learn of, but the ships and people of other neutral and friendly nations have been sunk and overwhelmed in the waters in the same way. There has been no discrimination. The challenge is to all mankind. Each nation must decide for itself how it will meet it. The choice we make for ourselves must be made with a moderation of counsel and a temperateness of judgment befitting our character and our motives as a nation. We must put excited feeling away. Our motive will not be revenge or the victorious assertion of the physical might of the nation, but only the vindication of right, of human right, of which we are only a single champion.

With a profound sense of the solemn and even tragical character of the step I am taking, and of the grave responsibilities which it involves, but in unhesitating obedience to what I deem my constitutional duty, I advise that the Congress declare the recent course of the Imperial German government to be in fact nothing less than war against the government and people of the United States; that it formally accept the status of belligerent which has thus been thrust upon it; and that it take immediate steps not only to put the country in a more thorough state of defense, but also to exert all its power and employ all its resources to bring the government of the German Empire to terms and end the war.

We have no quarrel with the German people. We have no feeling toward them but one of sympathy and friendship. It was not upon their impulse that their government acted in entering this war. It was not with their previous knowledge or approval. It was a war determined upon as wars used to be determined upon in the old, unhappy days when peoples were nowhere consulted by their rulers and wars were provoked and waged in the interest of dynasties or little groups of ambitious men who were accustomed to use their fellow men as pawns and tools.

A steadfast concert for peace can never be maintained except by a partnership of democratic nations. No autocratic government could be trusted to keep faith within it or observe its covenants. It must be a league of honor, a partnership of opinion. Intrigue would eat its vitals away; the plottings of inner circles who could plan what they would and render account to no one would be a corruption seated at its very heart. Only free peoples can hold their purpose and their honor steady to a common end and prefer the interests of mankind to any narrow interest of their own.

One of the things that has served to convince us that the Prussian autocracy was not and could never be our friend is that from the very outset of the present war it has filled our unsuspecting communities and even our offices of government with spies and set criminal intrigues everywhere afoot against our national unity of counsel, our peace within and without, our industries and our commerce.

We are glad, now that we see the facts with no veil of false pretense about them, to fight thus for the ultimate peace of the world and for the liberation of its peoples, the German peoples included, for the rights of nations great and small and the privilege of men everywhere to choose their way of life and of obedience. The world must be made safe for democracy. Its peace must be planted upon the tested foundations of political liberty. We have no selfish ends to serve. We desire no conquest, no dominion. We seek no indemnities for ourselves, no material compensation for the sacrifices we shall freely make. We are but one of the champions of the rights of mankind. We shall be satisfied when those rights have been made as secure as the faith as the freedom of nations can make them.

It is a distressing and oppressive duty, gentlemen of the Congress, which I have performed in thus addressing you. There are, it may be, many months of fiery trial and sacrifice ahead of us. It is a fearful thing to lead this great peaceful people into war, into the most terrible and disastrous of all wars, civilization itself seeming to be in the balance. But the right is more precious than peace, and we shall fight for the things which we have always carried nearest our hearts—for democracy, for the right of those who submit to authority to have a voice in their own governments, for the rights and liberties of small nations, for a universal dominion of right by such a concert of free peoples as shall bring peace and safety to all nations and make the world itself at last free. To such a task we can dedicate our lives and our fortunes, everything that we are and everything that we have, with the pride of those who know that the day has come when America is privileged to spend her blood and her might for the principles that gave her birth and happiness and the peace which she has treasured. God helping her, she can do no other.

FOURTEEN POINTS

By Woodrow Wilson

The Great War—as the First World War was called by contemporaries—ended on November 11, 1918, and President Wilson brought to the Paris Peace Conference an outline for peace composed of fourteen points that he had presented in an address to Congress eleven months earlier. The speech had met with great enthusiasm on both sides of the Atlantic, and when the Treaty of Versailles was signed on June 28, 1919, Wilson's cornerstone proposal—the establishment of a League of Nations—was included. The president embarked on a cross-country speaking tour to take his case for Senate ratification of the League of Nations Covenant directly to the people. On September 26, in the midst of the tour, Wilson suffered a stroke from which he never recovered. The Senate rejected the covenant in March 1920, and the United States never joined the League of Nations.

We entered this war because violations of right had occurred which touched us to the quick and made the life of our own people impossible unless they were corrected and the world secured once for all against their recurrence. What we demand in this war, therefore, is nothing peculiar to ourselves. It is that the world be made fit and safe to live in—and particularly that it be made safe for every peace-loving nation which, like our own, wishes to live its own life, determine its own institutions, be assured of justice and fair dealing by the other peoples of the world as against force and selfish aggression. All the peoples of the world are in effect partners in this interest, and for our own part we see very clearly that unless justice be done to others it will not be done to us. The program of the world's peace, therefore, is our program; and that program, the only possible program, as we see it, is this:

1. Open covenants of peace, openly arrived at, after which there shall be no private international understandings of any kind but diplomacy shall proceed always frankly and in the public view.

2. Absolute freedom of navigation upon the seas, outside territorial waters, alike in peace and in war, except as the seas may be closed in whole or in part by international action for the enforcement of international covenants.

3. The removal, so far as possible, of all economic barriers and the establishment of an equality of trade conditions among all the nations consenting to the peace and associating themselves for its maintenance.

4. Adequate guarantees given and taken that national armaments will be reduced to the lowest point consistent with domestic safety.

5. A free, open-minded, and absolutely impartial adjustment of all colonial claims, based upon a strict observance of the principle that in determining all such questions of sovereignty the interests of the populations concerned must have equal weight with the equitable claims of the government whose title is to be determined.

6. The evacuation of all Russian territory and such a settlement of all questions affecting Russia as will secure the best and freest cooperation of the other nations of the world in obtaining for her an unhampered and unembarrassed opportunity for the independent determination of her own political development and national policy and assure her of a sincere welcome into the society of free nations under institutions of her own choosing—and, more than a welcome, assistance also of every kind that she may need and may herself desire.

7. Belgium, the whole world will agree, must be evacuated and restored, without any attempt to limit the sovereignty which she enjoys in common with all other free nations.

8. All French territory should be freed and the invaded portions restored, and the wrong done to France by Prussia in 1871 in the matter of Alsace-Lorraine, which has unsettled the peace of the world for nearly fifty years, should be righted, in order that peace may once more be made secure in the interest of all.

9. A readjustment of the frontiers of Italy should be effected along clearly recognizable lines of nationality.

10. The peoples of Austria-Hungary, whose place among the nations we wish to see safeguarded and assured, should be accorded the freest opportunity of autonomous development.

11. Rumania, Serbia, and Montenegro should be evacuated; occupied territories restored; Serbia accorded free and secure access to the sea; and the relations of the several Balkan states to one another determined by friendly counsel along historically established lines of allegiance and nationality; and international guarantees of the political and economic independence and territorial integrity of the several Balkan states should be entered into.

12. The Turkish portions of the present Ottoman Empire should be assured a secure sovereignty, but the other nationalities which are now under Turkish rule should be assured an undoubted security of life and an absolutely unmolested opportunity of autonomous development, and the Dardanelles should be permanently opened as a free passage to the ships and commerce of all nations under international guarantees.

13. An independent Polish state should be erected which should include

the territories inhabited by indisputably Polish populations, which should be assured a free and secure access to the sea, and whose political and economic independence and territorial integrity should be guaranteed by international covenant.

14. A general association of nations must be formed under specific covenants for the purpose of affording mutual guarantees of political independence and territorial integrity to great and small states alike.

For such arrangements and covenants we are willing to fight and to continue to fight until they are achieved; but only because we wish the right to prevail and desire a just and stable peace such as can be secured only by removing the chief provocations to war, which this program does not remove. We have no jealousy of German greatness, and there is nothing in this program that impairs it.

We have spoken now, surely, in terms too concrete to admit of any further doubt or question. An evident principle runs through the whole program I have outlined. It is the principle of justice to all peoples and nationalities, and their right to live on equal terms of liberty and safety with one another, whether they be strong or weak. Unless this principle be made its foundation no part of the structure of international justice can stand. The people of the United States could act upon no other principle; and to the vindication of this principle they are ready to devote their lives, their honor, and everything that they possess. The moral climax of this the culminating and final war for human liberty has come, and they are ready to put their own strength, their own highest purpose, their own integrity and devotion to the test.

VICTORY BELLS

By Grace Conkling

The Great War was the most brutal and devastating war the civilized world had ever witnessed. As a result, when peace finally came, there was much rejoicing on both sides of the battle lines. This poem, set to a popular jazz tune, highlighted the exultant relief of a world once again at peace.

I heard the bells across the trees,
I heard them ride the plunging breeze
Above the roofs from tower and spire,
And they were leaping like a fire,
And they were shining like a stream
With sun to make its music gleam.
Deep tones as though the thunder tolled,
Cool voices thin as tinkling gold,
They shook the spangled autumn down
From out the tree-tops of the town;
They left great furrows in the air
And made a clangor everywhere
As of metallic wings. They flew
Aloft in spirals to the blue
Tall tent of heaven and disappeared.
And others, swift as though they feared
The people might not heed their cry
Went shouting "victory up" the sky.
They did not say that war is done,
Only that glory has begun
Like sunrise, and the coming day
Will burn the clouds of war away.
There will be time for dreams again,
And home-coming for weary men.

LEAGUE OF NATIONS

By Mary Siegrist

The Great War was supposed to be the "war to end all wars." Part of that idealistic hope stemmed from optimism for a new council of nations where states would have the opportunity to work out their differences over an arbitrated negotiating table. Although the League of Nations failed, its aspiration and inspiration were preserved in hearts and minds and were given new life with the advent of the United Nations a quarter century later.

Lo, Joseph dreams his dream again,
And Joan leads her armies in the night,
And somewhere, the Master from His cross
Lifts his hurt hands and heals the world again!
For from the great red welter of the world,
Out from the tides of its red suffering
Comes the slow sunrise of the ancient dream
Is flung the glory of its bright imaging.
See how it breaks in beauty on the world,
Shivers and shudders on its trembling way
Shivers and waits and trembles to be born!

America, young daughter of the gods, swing out,
Strong in the beauty of virginity,
Fearless in thine unquestioned leadership,
And hold the taper to the nations' torch,
And light the hearth fires of the halls of home.
Thine must it be to break an unpathed way,
To light the torch for world's in-brothering
To bring to birth this child of all the earth,
Formed of the marriage of all nations;
Else shall we go, the head upon the breast,
A Cain without a country, a Judas at the board!

THE NEW CRUSADE

By Katherine Lee Bates

The entry of America into the First World War was accompanied by an almost eschatological optimism. It was believed that this would indeed be the "war to end all wars." It took on all the elements of a crusade. As a result, much of the popular lyricism of the day reflected a confident new idealistic nationalism—as this song so aptly illustrates.

Life is a trifle;
Honor is all;
Shoulder the rifle;
Answer the call.

A nation of traders
We'll show what we are,
Freedom's crusaders
Who war against war.

Battle is tragic;
Battle shall cease;
Ours is the magic
Mission of Peace.

Gladly we barter
Gold of our youth
For Liberty's charter
Blood—sealed in truth.

Sons of the granite,
Strong be our stroke,
Making this planet
Safe for all folk.

Life is but passion,
Sunshine on dew.
Forward to fashion
The old world anew!

A nation of traders
We'll show what we are,
Freedom's crusaders
Who war against war.

MARCHING SONG

By Dana Burnet

Like all foreign wars, the First World War was attended by an atmosphere of romance and adventure. Many of the songs of the day reflected both the riotous optimism and the zealous valor of that peculiar perspective. This song, popular among the troops in France and Belgium, takes an ironic look at such military adventurism.

When Pershing's men go marching into Picardy.
Marching, marching into Picardy

With their steel aslant in the sunlight and their great gray hawks a-wing
And their wagons rumbling after them like thunder in the Spring

> *Tramp, tramp, tramp, tramp,*
> *Till the earth is shaken*
> *Tramp, tramp, tramp, tramp,*
> *Till the dead towns waken!*

And flowers fall and shouts arise from Chaumont to the sea—
When Pershing's men go marching, marching into Picardy.

Women of France, do you see them pass to the battle in the North?
And do you stand in the doorways now as when your own went forth?

Then smile to them and call to them, and mark how brave they fare
Upon the road to Picardy that only youth may dare!

> *Tramp, tramp, tramp, tramp,*
> *Till the earth is shaken*
> *Tramp, tramp, tramp, tramp,*
> *Such is Freedom's passion*

And oh, take heart, ye weary souls that stand along the Lys,
For the New World is marching, marching into Picardy!

April's sun is in the sky and April's in the grass
And I doubt not that Pershing's men are singing as they pass

For they are very young men, and brave men, and free,
And they know why they are marching, marching into Picardy.

> *Tramp, tramp, tramp, tramp,*
> *Till the earth is shaken*
> *Tramp, tramp, tramp, tramp,*
> *Through the April weather.*

And never Spring has thrust such blades against the light of dawn.
As yonder waving stalks of steel that move so shining on!

I have seen the wooden crosses at Ypres and Verdun,
I have marked the graves of such as lie where the Marne waters run,

And I know their dust is stirring by hill and vale and lea,
And their souls shall be our captains who march to Picardy.

> *Tramp, tramp, tramp, tramp,*
> *Till the earth is shaken*
> *Tramp, tramp, tramp, tramp,*
> *Forward, and forever!*

And God is in His judgment seat, and Christ is on His tree
And Pershing's men are marching, marching into Picardy.

THE FIRST THREE

By Clinton Scollard

All was not adventure and romance in the war, of course. Indeed, the brutality and widespread devastation of the First World War outstripped anything anyone had ever seen. In this lament, the tragedy of this brutal war is memorialized.

"Somewhere in France," upon a brown hillside,
They lie, the first of our brave soldiers slain;
Above them flowers, now beaten by the rain,
Yet emblematic of the youths who died
In their fresh promise. They who, valiant-eyed,
Met death unfaltering have not fallen in vain;
Remembrance hallows those who thus attain
The final goal; their names are glorified.
Read then the roster—Gresham! Enright! Hay!
No bugle call shall rouse them when the flower
Of morning breaks above the hills and dells,
For they have grown immortal in an hour,
And we who grieve and cherish them would lay
Upon their hillside graves our immortals!

LEAGUE OF NATIONS SPEECH

By Henry Cabot Lodge

When the esteemed Senate majority leader addressed the Senate on August 12, 1919, the nation was already in the midst of a "Great Debate" over its future foreign policy. The Great War had just ended. Should the country now join the new League of Nations that President Wilson had hammered into shape at the Versailles Peace Conference, or should the nation retain its traditional commitment to neutrality—as articulated in Washington's hallowed Farewell Address? Utilizing carefully measured phrases and appealing to the mood of the audience, this speech somehow bridged the gap between the two positions and unleashed a storm of applause from the packed galleries. A group of marines just returned from France pounded their helmets enthusiastically against the gallery railing, and men and women cheered, whistled, and waved handkerchiefs and hats. It was minutes before order could be restored, and when a Democratic

senator attempted to reply to Lodge's arguments, his remarks were greeted with
boos and hisses. In the end the policy Lodge elaborated became the foundation of
American foreign relations for the rest of the century.

I object in the strongest possible way to having the United States agree, directly or indirectly, to be controlled by a league which may at any time, and perfectly lawfully and in accordance with the terms of the covenant, be drawn in to deal with internal conflicts in other countries, no matter what those conflicts may be. We should never permit the United States to be involved in any internal conflict in another country, except by the will of her people expressed through the Congress which represents them.

With regard to wars of external aggression on a member of the league, the case is perfectly clear. There can be no genuine dispute whatever about the meaning of the first clause of article 10. In the first place, it differs from every other obligation in being individual and placed upon each nation without the intervention of the league. Each nation for itself promises to respect and preserve as against external aggression the boundaries and the political independence of every member of the league.

It is, I repeat, an individual obligation. It requires no action on the part of the league, except that in the second sentence the authorities of the league are to have the power to advise as to the means to be employed in order to fulfill the purpose of the first sentence. But that is a detail of execution, and I consider that we are morally and in honor bound to accept and act upon that advice. The broad fact remains that if any member of the league suffering from external aggression should appeal directly to the United States for support the United States would be bound to give that support in its own capacity and without reference to the action of other powers, because the United States itself is bound, and I hope the day will never come when the United States will not carry out its promises. If that day should come, and the United States or any other great country should refuse, no matter how specious the reason, to fulfill both in letter and spirit every obligation in this covenant, the United States would be dishonored and the league would crumble into dust, leaving behind it a legacy of wars. If China should rise up and attack Japan in an effort to undo the great wrong of the cession of the control of Shantung to that power, we should be bound under the terms of article 10 to sustain Japan against China, and a guaranty of that sort is never involved except when the question has passed beyond the stage of negotiation and has become a question for the application of force. I do not like the prospect. It shall not come into existence by any vote of mine.

Any analysis of the provisions of this league covenant, however brings out in startling relief one great fact. Whatever may be said, it is not a league of peace; it is an alliance, dominated at the present moment by five great powers, really by three, and it has all the marks of an alliance. The development of international law is neglected. The court which is to decide disputes brought before it fills but a small place. The conditions for which this league really provides with the utmost care are political conditions, not judicial questions, to be reached by the executive council and the assembly, purely political bodies without any trace of a judicial character about them. Such being its machinery, the control being in the hands of political appointees whose votes will be controlled by interest and expedience it exhibits that most marked characteristic of an alliance that its decisions are to be carried out by force. Those articles upon which the whole structure rests are articles which provide for the use of force; that is, for war. This league to enforce peace does a great deal for enforcement and very little for peace. It makes more essential provisions looking to war than to peace for the settlement of disputes.

Taken altogether, these provisions for war present what to my mind is the gravest objection to this league in its present form. We are told that of course nothing will be done in the way of warlike acts without the assent of Congress. If that is true let us say so in the covenant. But as it stands there is no doubt whatever in my mind that American troops and American ships may be ordered to any part of the world by nations other than the United States, and that is a proposition to which I for one can never assent. It must be made perfectly clear that no American soldiers, not even a corporal's guard, that no American sailors, not even the crew of a submarine, can ever be engaged in war or ordered anywhere except by the constitutional authorities of the United States. To Congress is granted by the Constitution the right to declare war, and nothing that would take the troops out of the country at the bidding or demand of other nations should ever be permitted except through congressional action. The lives of Americans must never be sacrificed except by the will of the American people expressed through their chosen Representatives in Congress. This is a point upon which no doubt can be permitted. American soldiers and American sailors have never failed the country when the country called upon them. They went in their hundreds of thousands into the war just closed. They went to die for the great cause of freedom and of civilization. They went at their country's bidding and because their country summoned them to service. We were late in entering the war. We made no preparation, as we ought to have done, for the ordeal which was clearly coming upon us; but we went and we turned the wavering scale. It was done by the American soldier, the American sailor, and the spirit and energy of the

American people. They overrode all obstacles and all shortcomings on the part of the administration of Congress and gave to their country a great place in the great victory. It was the first time we had been called upon to rescue the civilized world. Did we fail? On the contrary, we succeeded, succeeded largely and nobly, and we did it without any command from any league of nations. When the emergency came, we met it and we were able to meet it because we had built up on this continent the greatest and most powerful nation in the world, built it up under our own politics, In our own way, and one great element of our strength was the fact that we had held aloof and had not thrust ourselves into European quarrels; that we had no selfish interest to serve. We made great sacrifices. We have done splendid work. I believe that we do not require to be told by foreign nations when we shall do work which freedom and civilization require. I think we can move to victory much better under our own command than under the command of others. Let us unite with the world to promote the peaceable settlement of all international disputes. Let us try to develop international law. Let us associate ourselves with the other nations for these purposes. But let us retain in our own hands and in our own control the lives of the youth of the land. Let no American be sent into battle except by the constituted authorities of his own country and by the will of the people of the United States.

Those of us, Mr. President, who are either wholly opposed to the league, or who are trying to preserve the independence and the safety of the United States by changing the terms of the league, and who are endeavoring to make the league, if we are to be a member of it, less certain to promote war instead of peace have been reproached with selfishness in our outlook and with a desire to keep our country in a state of isolation. So far as the question of isolation goes, it is impossible to isolate the United States. I well remember the time 20 years ago, when eminent Senators and other distinguished gentlemen who were opposing the Philippines and shrieking about imperialism sneered at the statement made by some of us, that the United States had become a world power. I think no one now would question that the Spanish war marked the entrance of the United States into world affairs to a degree which had never obtained before. It was both an inevitable and an irrevocable step, and our entrance into the war with Germany certainly showed once and for all that the United States was not unmindful of its world responsibilities. We may set aside all this empty talk about isolation. Nobody expects to isolate the United States or to make it a hermit Nation, which is a sheer absurdity. But there is a wide difference between taking a suitable part and bearing a due responsibility in world affairs and plunging the United States into every controversy and conflict on the face of the globe. By meddling in all the differences which may arise among any portion or fragment of humankind we simply fritter away our influence and injure ourselves to no good purpose. We shall be of far more value to the world and its peace by occupying, so far as possible, the situation which we have occupied for the last 20 years and by adhering to the policy of Washington and Hamilton, of Jefferson and Monroe, under which we have risen to our present greatness and prosperity. The fact that we have been separated by our geographical situation and by our consistent policy from the broils of Europe has made us more than any one thing capable of performing the great work which we performed in the war against Germany and our disinterestedness is of far more value to the world than our eternal meddling in every possible dispute could ever be.

Now, as to our selfishness, I have no desire to boast that we are better than our neighbors, but the fact remains that this Nation in making peace with Germany had not a single selfish or individual interest to serve. All we asked was that Germany should be rendered incapable of again breaking forth, with all the horrors, incident to German warfare, upon an unoffending world, and that demand was shared by every free nation and indeed by humanity itself. For ourselves we asked absolutely nothing. We have not asked any government or governments to guarantee our boundaries or our political independence. We have no fear in regard to either. We have sought no territory, no privileges, no advantages, for ourselves. That is the fact. It is apparent on the face of the treaty. I do not mean to reflect upon a single one of the powers with which we have been associated in the war against Germany, but there is not one of them which has not sought individual advantages for their own national benefit. I do not criticize their desires at all. The services and sacrifices of England and France and Belgium and Italy are beyond estimate and beyond praise. I am glad they should have what they desire for their own welfare and safety. But they all receive under the peace territorial and commercial benefits. We are asked to give, and we in no way seek to take. Surely it is not too much to insist that when we are offered nothing but the opportunity to give and to aid others we should have the right to say what sacrifices we shall make and what the magnitude of our gifts shall be. In the prosecution of the war we gave unstintedly American lives and American treasure. When the war closed we had 3,000,000 men under arms. We were turning the country into a vast workshop for war. We advanced ten billions to our allies. We refused no assistance that we could possibly render. All the great energy and power of the Republic were put at the service of the good cause. We have not been ungenerous. We have been devoted to the cause of freedom, humanity, and civilization everywhere. Now we are asked, in the making of peace, to sacrifice our Sovereignty in important respects, to involve ourselves almost without limit in the affairs of other nations and to yield up policies and rights which we have maintained throughout our history. We are asked to incur liabilities to an unlimited extent and furnish assets at the same time which no man can measure. I think it is not only our right but our duty to determine how far we shall go. Not only must we look carefully to see where we are being led into endless disputes and entanglements, but we must not forget that we have in this country millions of people of foreign birth and parentage.

Our one great object is to make all these people Americans so that we may call on them to place America first and serve America as they have done in the war just closed. We cannot Americanize them if we are continually thrusting them back into the quarrels and difficulties of the countries from which they came to us. We shall fill this land with political disputes about the troubles and quarrels of other countries. We shall have a large portion of our people voting not on American questions and not on what concerns the United States but dividing on issues which concern foreign countries alone. That is an unwholesome and perilous condition to force upon this country. We must avoid it. We ought to reduce to the lowest possible point the foreign questions in which we involve ourselves. Never forget that this league is primarily—I might say overwhelmingly—a political organization, and I object strongly to having the politics of the United States turn upon disputes where deep feeling is aroused but in which we have no direct interest. It will all tend to delay the Americanization of our great population, and it is more important not only to the United States but to the peace of the world to make all these people good Americans than it is to determine that some piece of territory should belong to one European country rather than to another. For this reason I wish to limit strictly our interference in the affairs of Europe and of Africa. We have interests of our own in Asia and in the Pacific which we must guard upon our own account, but the less we undertake to play the part of umpire and thrust ourselves into European conflicts the better for the United States and for the world.

It has been reiterated here on this floor, and reiterated to the point of weariness, that in every treaty there is some sacrifice of sovereignty. That is not a universal truth by any means, but it is true of some treaties and it is a platitude which does not require reiteration. The question and the only question before us here is how much of our sovereignty we are justified in sacrificing. In what I have already said about other nations putting us into war I have covered one point of sovereignty which ought never to be yielded—the power to send American soldiers and sailors everywhere, which ought never to be taken from the American people or impaired in the slightest degree. Let us beware how we palter with our independence. We have not reached the great position from which we were able to come down into the field of battle and help to save the world from tyranny by being guided by others. Our vast power has all been built up and gathered together by ourselves alone. We forced our way upward from the days of the Revolution, through a world often hostile and always indifferent. We owe no debt to anyone except to France in that Revolution, and those policies and those rights on which our power has been founded should never be lessened or weakened. It will be no service to the world to do so and it will be of intolerable injury to the United States. We will do our share. We are ready and anxious to help in all ways to preserve the world's peace. But we can do it best by not crippling ourselves.

I am as anxious as any human being can be to have the United States render every possible service to the civilization and the peace of mankind, but I am certain we can do it best by not putting ourselves in leading strings or subjecting our policies and our sovereignty to other nations. The independence of the United States is not only more precious to ourselves but to the world than any single possession. Look at the United States to-day. We have made mistakes in the past. We have had shortcomings. We shall make mistakes in the future and fall short of our own best hopes. But none the less is there any country today on the face of the earth which can compare with this in ordered liberty, in peace, and in the largest freedom? I feel that I can say this without being accused of undue boastfulness, for it is the simple fact, and in making this treaty and taking on these obligations all that we do is in a spirit of unselfishness and in a desire for the good of mankind. But it is well to remember that we are dealing with nations every one of which has a direct individual interest to serve, and there is grave danger in an unshared idealism. Contrast the United States with any country on the face of the earth to-day and ask yourself whether the situation of the United States is not the best to be found. I will go as far as anyone in world service, but the first step to world service is the maintenance of the United States. You may call me selfish if you will, conservative or reactionary, or use any other harsh adjective you see fit to apply, but an American I was born, an American I have remained all my life. I can never be anything else but an American, and I must think of the United States first, and when I think of the United States first in an arrangement like this I am thinking of what is best for the world, for if the United States fails the best hopes of mankind fail with it. I have never had but one allegiance—I cannot divide it now. I have loved but one flag and I cannot share that devotion and give affection to the mongrel banner invented for a league. Internationalism, illustrated by the Bolshevik and by the men to whom all countries are alike provided they can make money out of them, is to me repulsive. National I must remain, and in that way I, like all other Americans, can render the amplest service to the world. The

United States is the world's best hope, but if you fetter her in the interests and quarrels of other nations, if you tangle her in the intrigues of Europe, you will destroy her power for good and endanger her very existence. Leave her to march freely through the centuries to come as in the years that have gone. Strong, generous, and confident, she has nobly served mankind. Beware how you trifle with your marvelous inheritance, this great land of ordered liberty, for if we stumble and fall, freedom and civilization everywhere will go down in ruin.

We are told that we shall "break the heart of the world" if we do not take this league just as it stands. I fear that the hearts of the vast majority of mankind would beat on strongly and steadily and without any quickening if the league were to perish altogether. If it should be effectively and beneficiently changed, the people who would lie awake in sorrow for a single night could be easily gathered in one not very large room, but those who would draw a long breath of relief would reach to millions.

We hear much of visions and I trust we shall continue to have visions and dream dreams of a fairer future for the race. But visions are one thing and visionaries are another, and the mechanical appliances of the rhetorician designed to give a picture of a present which does not exist and of a future which no man can predict are as unreal and shortlived as the steam or canvas clouds, the angels suspended on wires and the artificial lights of the stage. They pass with the monument of effect and are shabby and tawdry in the daylight. Let us at least be real. Washington's entire honesty of mind and his fearless look into the face of all facts are qualities which can never go out of fashion and which we should all do well to imitate.

Ideals have been thrust upon us as an argument for the league until the healthy mind which rejects cant revolts from them. Are ideals confined to this deformed experiment upon a noble purpose, tainted, as it is, with bargains and tied to a peace treaty which might have been disposed of long ago to the great benefit of the world if it had not been compelled to carry this rider on its back? "Post equitem sedet atra cura," Horace tells us, but no blacker care ever sat behind any rider than we shall find in this covenant of doubtful and disputed interpretation as it now perches upon the treaty of peace.

No doubt many excellent and patriotic people see a coming fulfillment of noble ideals in the words "league for peace." We all respect and share these aspirations and desires, but some of us see no hope, but rather defeat, for them in this murky covenant. For we, too, have our ideals, even if we differ from those who have tried to establish a monopoly of idealism. Our first ideal is our country, and we see her in the future, as in the past, giving service to all her people and to the world. Our ideal of the future is that she should continue to render that service of her own free will. She has great problems of her own to solve, very grim and perilous problems, and a right solution, if we can attain to it, would largely benefit mankind. We would have our country strong to resist a peril from the West, as she has flung back the German menace from the East. We would not have our politics distracted and embittered by the dissensions of other lands. We would not have our country's vigor exhausted or her moral force abated, by everlasting meddling and muddling in every quarrel, great and small, which afflicts the world. Our ideal is to make her ever stronger and better and finer, because in that way alone, as we believe, can she be of the greatest service to the world's peace and to the welfare of mankind.

PEARL HARBOR ADDRESS

By Franklin Delano Roosevelt

On Sunday morning, December 7, 1941, the Japanese military conducted a surprise attack on the American naval base at Pearl Harbor, Hawaii, resulting in the loss of more than two thousand American lives and the destruction of the bulk of the Pacific fleet. The next day the president addressed Congress and the nation in a broadcast heard worldwide. He branded December 7 "a date which will live in infamy." The speech was a call for a declaration of war against Japan—as well as its Axis allies in Europe. Later that afternoon, Congress passed the resolution.

Yesterday, December 7, 1941—a date which will live in infamy— the United States of America was suddenly and deliberately attacked by naval and air forces of the Empire of Japan.

The United States was at peace with that nation and, at the solicitation of Japan, was still in conversation with its government and its emperor looking toward the maintenance of peace in the Pacific. Indeed, one hour after Japanese air squadrons had commenced bombing in Oahu, the Japanese ambassador to the United States and his colleague delivered to the secretary of state a formal reply to a recent American message. While this reply stated that it seemed useless to continue the existing diplomatic negotiations, it contained no threat or hint of war or armed attack.

It will be recorded that the distance of Hawaii from Japan makes it obvious that the attack was deliberately planned many days or even weeks ago. During the intervening time the Japanese government had deliberately sought to deceive the United States by false statements and expressions of hope for continued peace.

The attack yesterday on the Hawaiian Islands has caused severe damage to American naval and military forces. Very many American lives have been lost. In addition American ships have been reported torpedoed on the high seas between San Francisco and Honolulu.

Yesterday the Japanese government also launched an attack against Malaya.

Last night Japanese forces attacked Hong Kong.

Last night Japanese forces attacked Guam.

Last night Japanese forces attacked the Philippine Islands.

Last night the Japanese attacked Wake Island.

This morning the Japanese attacked Midway Island.

Japan has, therefore, undertaken a surprise offensive extending throughout the Pacific area. The facts of yesterday speak for themselves. The people of the United States have already formed their opinions and well understand the implications to the very life and safety of our nation.

As commander in chief of the army and navy I have directed that all measures be taken for our defense.

Always will we remember the character of the onslaught against us. No matter how long it may take us to overcome this premeditated invasion, the American people in their righteous might will win through to absolute victory.

I believe I interpret the will of the Congress and of the people when I assert that we will not only defend ourselves to the uttermost but will make very certain that this form of treachery shall never endanger us again.

Hostilities exist. There is no blinking at the fact that our people, our territory, and our interests are in grave danger.

With confidence in our armed forces—with the unbounded determination of our people—we will gain the inevitable triumph—so help us God.

I ask that the Congress declare that since the unprovoked and dastardly attack by Japan on Sunday, December 7, a state of war has existed between the United States and the Japanese Empire.

THE MARSHALL PLAN

By George C. Marshall

On June 5, 1947, Secretary of State George C. Marshall delivered the commencement address at Harvard University. In this address he formulated what would later be called the Marshall Plan. In concert with the Truman Doctrine—a commitment to support democracy abroad—the plan was to undertake economic reconstruction of all of Europe, East and West alike, following the devastation of the Second World War. Eventually the plan became official policy as the European Recovery Program. It had an immediate galvanizing effect in Europe. The economic and political recovery of the modern world can well be said to have begun the day after this speech.

I need not tell you gentlemen that the world situation is very serious. That must be apparent to all intelligent people. I think one difficulty is that the problem is one of such enormous complexity that the very mass of facts presented to the public by press and radio make it exceedingly difficult for the man in the street to reach a clear appraisement of the situation. Furthermore, the people of this country are distant from the troubled areas of the earth and it is hard for them to comprehend the plight and consequent reactions of the long-suffering peoples, and the effect of those reactions on their governments in connection with our efforts to promote peace in the world.

In considering the requirements for the rehabilitation of Europe, the physical loss of life, the visible destruction of cities, factories, mines, and railroads was correctly estimated but it has become obvious during recent months that this visible destruction was probably less serious than the dislocation of the entire fabric of European economy. For the past ten years conditions have been highly abnormal. The feverish preparation for war and the more feverish maintenance of the war effort engulfed all aspects of national economies. Machinery has fallen into disrepair or is entirely obsolete. Under the arbitrary and destructive Nazi rule, virtually every possible enterprise was geared into the German war machine. Long-standing commercial ties, private institutions, banks, insurance companies, and shipping companies disappeared, through loss of capital, absorption through nationalization, or by simple destruction. In many countries, confidence in the local currency has been severely shaken. The breakdown of the business structure of Europe during the war was complete. Recovery has been seriously retarded by the fact that two years after the close of hostilities a peace settlement with Germany and Austria has not been agreed upon. But even given a more prompt solution of these difficult problems, the rehabilitation of the economic structure of Europe quite evidently will require a much longer time and greater effort than had been foreseen.

There is a phase of this matter which is both interesting and serious. The farmer has always produced the foodstuffs to exchange with the city dweller for the other necessities of life. This division of labor is the basis of modern civilization. At the present time it is threatened with breakdown. The town and city industries are not producing adequate goods to exchange with the food-producing farmer. Raw materials and fuel are in short supply. Machinery is lacking or worn out. The farmer or the peasant cannot find the goods for sale which he desires to purchase. So the sale of his farm produce for money which he cannot use seems to him an unprofitable transaction. He, therefore, has withdrawn many fields from crop cultivation and is using them for grazing. He feeds more grain to stock and finds for himself and his family an ample supply of food, however short he may be on clothing and the other ordinary gadgets of civilization. Meanwhile people in the cities are short of food and fuel. So the governments are forced to use their foreign money and credits to procure these necessities abroad. This process exhausts funds which are urgently needed for reconstruction. Thus a very serious situation is rapidly developing which bodes no good for the world. The modern system of the division of labor upon which the exchange of products is based is in danger of breaking down.

The truth of the matter is that Europe's requirements for the next three or four years of foreign food and other essential products—principally from America—are so much greater than her present ability to pay that she must have substantial additional help or face economic, social, and political deterioration of a very grave character.

The remedy lies in breaking the vicious circle and restoring the confidence of the European people in the economic future of their own countries and of Europe as a whole. The manufacturer and the farmer throughout wide areas must be able and willing to exchange their products for currencies the continuing value of which is not open to question.

Aside from the demoralizing effect on the world at large and the possibilities of disturbances arising as a result of the desperation of the people concerned, the consequences to the economy of the United States should be apparent to all. It is logical that the United States should do whatever it is able to do to assist in the return of normal economic health in the world, without which there can be no political stability and no assured peace. Our policy is directed not against any country or doctrine but against hunger, poverty, desperation, and chaos. Its purpose should be the revival of a working economy in the world so as to permit the emergence of political and social conditions in which free institutions can exist. Such assistance, I am convinced, must not be on a piecemeal basis as various crises develop. Any assistance that this Government may render in the future should provide a cure rather than a mere palliative. Any government that is willing to assist in the task of recovery will find full cooperation, I am sure, on the part of the United States Government. Any government which maneuvers to block the recovery of other countries cannot expect help from us. Furthermore, governments, political parties, or groups which seek to perpetuate human misery in order to profit therefrom politically or otherwise will encounter the opposition of the United States.

It is already evident that, before the United States Government can proceed much further in its efforts to alleviate the situation and help start the European world on its way to recovery, there must be some agreement among the countries of Europe as to the requirements of the situation and the part those countries themselves will take in order to give proper effect to whatever action might be undertaken by this Government. It would be neither fitting nor efficacious for this Government to undertake to draw up unilaterally a program designed to place Europe on its feet economically. This is the business of the Europeans. The initiative, I think, must come from Europe. The role of this country should consist of friendly aid in the drafting of a European program and of later support of such a program so far as it may be practical for us to do so. The program should be a joint one, agreed to by a number of, if not all, European nations.

An essential part of any successful action on the part of the United States is an understanding on the part of the people of America of the character of the problem and the remedies to be applied. Political passion and prejudice should have no part. With foresight, and a willingness on the part of our people to face up to the vast responsibility which history has clearly placed upon our country, the difficulties I have outlined can and will be overcome.

NOBEL PRIZE ACCEPTANCE

By William Faulkner

By the end of 1950, when William Faulkner was awarded the Nobel Prize for Literature, he had published twenty books, which were widely known in Europe and Asia as well as in the United States. Southerners noted that he was the first writer from that region to win the prize and praised his brilliant and articulate colloquialism. All his life Faulkner had avoided speeches and insisted that he not be taken as a man of letters. "I'm just a farmer who likes to tell stories," he once said. Because of his known aversion to making formal pronouncements, there was much interest in what he would say in the speech that custom obliged him to deliver when he traveled to Stockholm to receive the prize on December 10, 1950. He evidently wanted to set the record straight concerning the place of the regionalist poet in the discourse of a wider culture—and that he did.

I feel that this award was not made to me as a man but to my work— a life's work in the agony and sweat of the human spirit, not for glory and least of all for profit, but to make out of the material of the human spirit something which was not there before; so this award is only mine in trust. It will not be hard to find a dedication for the money part of it to commemorate with the purpose and the significance of its origin but I would like to do the same with the acclaim too by using this fine moment as a pinnacle from which I might be listened to by the young man or young woman, already dedicated to the same anguish and sweat, who will some day stand here where I am standing.

Our tragedy today is a general and universal physical fear so long sustained by now that we can even bear it. There are no longer problems of the spirit. There is only the question: When will I be blown up? Because of this, the young man or woman writing today has forgotten the problems of the human heart in conflict with itself which alone can make good writing because only that is worth writing about; worth the agony and the sweat.

He must learn them again, he must teach himself that the basest of all things is to be afraid, and teaching himself that, forget it forever leaving no room in his workshop for anything but the old verities and truths of the heart, the old universal truths lacking which any story is ephemeral and doomed—love and honor and pity and pride and compassion and sacrifice. Until he does so, he labors under a curse. He writes not of love but of lust, of defeats in which nobody loses anything of value, of victories without hope and, worst of all, without pity or compassion. His griefs grieve on no universal bones, leaving no scars. He writes not of the heart but of the gland.

Until he relearns these things, he will write as though he stood among and watched the end of man. I do not believe in the end of man.

It is easy enough to say that man is immortal simply because he will endure: then when the last ding-dong of doom has clanged and faded from the last worthless rock hanging tideless in the last red and dying evening, that even then there will still be one more sound: that of his puny inexhaustible voice still talking.

I believe more than this. I believe man will not merely endure, he will prevail. He is immortal, not because he, alone among creatures, has an inexhaustible voice but because he has a soul, a spirit, capable of compassion and sacrifice and endurance.

The poet's—the writer's—duty is to write about these things. It is his privilege to help man endure by lifting his heart, by reminding him of courage and honor and hope and pride and compassion and pity and sacrifice which have been the glory of his past.

The poet's voice need not merely be the record of man, it can be one of the props to help him endure and prevail.

BROWN V. BOARD OF EDUCATION OF TOPEKA

By Earl Warren

"All men are created equal" the framers of the Declaration had proclaimed as self-evident truth in 1776. Lincoln at Gettysburg had reaffirmed this as the distinctive proposition of American national dedication. In 1868 the Fourteenth Amendment had written the proposition plainly into the Constitution of the United States: "nor shall any State deny to any person within its jurisdiction the equal protection of the laws." Nevertheless, racial segregation and discrimination persisted throughout the nation until this Supreme Court decision in 1954. Thurgood Marshall, then chief counsel of the NAACP, argued before the court that the standard of "separate but equal" schools was little more than a cover for rank prejudice and injustice. Chief Justice Earl Warren's opinion was upheld unanimously by the other justices. This landmark case paved the way for virtually all civil rights gains afterward.

These cases come to us from the States of Kansas, South Carolina, Virginia, and Delaware. They are premised on different facts and different local conditions, but a common legal question justifies their consideration together in this consolidated opinion.

In each of the cases, minors of the Negro race, through their legal representatives, seek the aid of the courts in obtaining admission to the public schools of their community on a nonsegregated basis. In each instance, they had been denied admission to schools attended by white children under laws requiring or permitting segregation according to race. This segregation was alleged to deprive the plaintiffs of the equal protection of the laws under the Fourteenth Amendment. In each of the cases other than the Delaware case, a three judge federal district court denied relief to the plaintiffs on the so-called "separate but equal" doctrine announced by this Court in Plessy v. Ferguson, 163 U.S. 537. Under that doctrine, equality of treatment is accorded when the races are provided substantially equal facilities, even though these facilities be separate. In the Delaware case, the Supreme Court of Delaware adhered to that doctrine, but ordered that the plaintiffs be admitted to the white schools because of their superiority to the Negro schools.

The plaintiffs contend that segregated public schools are not "equal" and cannot be made "equal," and that hence they are deprived of the equal protection of the laws. Because of the obvious importance of the question presented, the Court took jurisdiction. Argument was heard in the 1952 Term, and reargument was heard this Term on certain questions propounded by the Court.

Reargument was largely devoted to the circumstances surrounding the adoption of the Fourteenth Amendment in 1868. It covered exhaustively consideration of the Amendment in Congress, ratification by the states, then existing practices in racial segregation, and the views of proponents and opponents of the Amendment. This discussion and our own investigation convince us that, although these sources cast some light, it is not enough to resolve the problem with which we are faced. At best, they are inconclusive. The most avid proponents of the post-War Amendments undoubtedly intended them to remove all legal distinctions among "all persons born or naturalized in the United States." Their opponents, just as certainly, were antagonistic to both the letter and the spirit of the Amendments and wished them to have the most limited effect. What others in Congress and the state legislatures had in mind cannot be determined with any degree of certainty.

An additional reason for the inconclusive nature of the Amendment's history, with respect to segregated schools, is the status of public education at that time. In the South, the movement toward free common schools, supported by general taxation, had not yet taken hold. Education of white children was largely in the hands of private groups. Education of Negroes was almost non-existent, and practically all of the race were illiterate. In fact, any education of Negroes was forbidden by law in some states. Today, in contrast, many Negroes have achieved outstanding success in the arts and sciences as well as in the business and professional world. It is true that public school education at the time of the Amendment had advanced further in the North, but the effect of the Amendment on Northern States was generally ignored in the congressional debates. Even in the North, the conditions of public education did not approximate those existing today. The curriculum was usually rudimentary; ungraded schools were common in rural areas; the school term was but three months a year in many states; and compulsory school attendance was virtually unknown. As a consequence, it is not surprising that there should be so little in the history of the Fourteenth Amendment relating to its intended effect on public education.

In the first cases in this Court construing the Fourteenth Amendment, decided shortly after its adoption, the Court interpreted it as proscribing all state-imposed discriminations against the Negro race. The doctrine of "separate but equal" did not make its appearance in this Court until 1896 in the case of Plessy v. Ferguson, supra, involving not education but transportation. American courts have since labored with the doctrine for over half a century. In this Court, there have been six cases involving the "separate but equal" doctrine in the field of public education. In Cumming v. Board of Education of Richmond County, 175 U.S. 528, and Gong Lum v. Rice, 275 U.S. 78, the validity of the doctrine itself was not challenged. In more recent cases, all on the graduate school level, inequality was found in that specific benefits enjoyed by white students were denied to Negro students of the same educational qualifications. Missouri ex ref. Gaines v. Canada, 305 U.S. 337; Sipuel v. Board of Regents of University of Oklahoma, 332 U.S. 631; Sweatt v. Painter, 339 U.S. 629; McLaurin v. Oklahoma State Regents, 339 U.S. 637. In none of these cases was it necessary to re-examine the doctrine to grant relief to the Negro plaintiff. And in Sweatt v. Painter, supra, the Court expressly reserved decision on the question whether Plessy v. Ferguson should be held inapplicable to public education.

In the instant cases, that question is directly presented. Here, unlike Sweatt v. Painter, there are findings below that the Negro and white schools involved have been equalized, or are being equalized, with respect to buildings, curricula, qualifications and salaries of teachers, and other "tangible" factors. Our decision, therefore, cannot turn on merely a comparison of these tangible factors in the Negro and white schools involved in each of the cases. We must look instead to the effect of segregation itself on public education.

In approaching this problem, we cannot turn the clock back to 1868 when the Amendment was adopted, or even to 1896 when Plessy v. Ferguson was written. We must consider public education in the light of its full development and its present place in American life throughout the nation. Only in this way can it be determined if segregation in public schools deprives these plaintiffs of the equal protection of the laws.

Today, education is perhaps the most important function of state and local governments. Compulsory school attendance laws and the great expenditures for education both demonstrate our recognition of the importance of education to our democratic society. It is required in the performance of our most basic public responsibilities, even service in the armed forces. It is the very foundation of good citizenship. Today it is a principal instrument in awakening the child to cultural values, in preparing him for later professional training, and in helping him to adjust normally to his environment. In these days, it is doubtful that any child may reasonably be expected to succeed in life if he is denied the opportunity of an education. Such an opportunity, where the state has undertaken to provide it, is a right which must be made available to all on equal terms.

We come then to the question presented: does segregation of children in public schools solely on the basis of race, even though the physical facilities and other "tangible" factors may be equal, deprive the children of the minority group of equal educational opportunities? We believe that it does.

In Sweatt v. Painter, supra, in finding that a segregated law school for Negroes could not provide them equal educational opportunities, this Court relied in large part on "those qualities which are incapable of objective measurement but which make for greatness in a law school." In McLaurin v. Oklahoma State Regents, supra, the Court, in requiring that a Negro admitted to a white graduate school be treated like all other students again resorted to intangible considerations: "...his ability to study, to engage in discussions and exchange views with other students, and, in general, to learn his profession." Such considerations apply with added force to children in grade and high schools. To separate them from others of similar age and qualifications solely because of their race generates a feeling of inferiority as to their status in the community that may affect their hearts and minds in a way unlikely ever to be undone. The effect of this separation on their educational opportunities was well stated by a finding in the Kansas case by a court which nevertheless felt compelled to rule against the Negro plaintiffs:

Segregation of white and colored children in public schools has a detrimental effect upon the colored children. The impact is greater when it has the sanction of the law; for the policy of separating the races is usually interpreted as denoting the inferiority of the negro group. A sense of inferiority affects the motivation of a child to learn. Segregation with the sanction of law, therefore, has a tendency to retard the educational and mental development of Negro children and to deprive them of some of the benefits they would receive in a racially integrated school system.

Whatever may have been the extent of psychological knowledge at the time of Plessy v. Ferguson, this finding is amply supported by modern authority. Any language in Plessy v. Ferguson contrary to this finding is rejected.

We conclude that in the field of public education the doctrine of "separate but equal" has no place. Separate educational facilities are inherently unequal. Therefore, we hold that the plaintiffs and others similarly situated for whom the actions have been brought are, by reason of the segregation complained of, deprived of the equal protection of the laws guaranteed by the Fourteenth Amendment. This disposition makes unnecessary any discussion whether such segregation also violates the Due Process Clause of the Fourteenth Amendment.

Because these are class actions, because of the wide applicability of this decision, and because of the great variety of local conditions, the formulation of decrees in these cases presents problems of considerable complexity. On reargument, the consideration of appropriate relief was necessarily subordinated to the primary question—the constitutionality of segregation in public education. We have now announced that such segregation is a denial of the equal protection of the laws. In order that we may have the full assistance of the parties in formulating decrees, the cases will be restored to the docket, and the parties are requested to present further argument on Questions 4 and 5 previously propounded by the Court for the reargument this Term. The Attorney General of the United States is again invited to participate. The Attorneys General of the states requiring or permitting segregation in public education will also be permitted to appear as amici curiae upon request to do so by September 5, 1954, and submission of briefs by October 1, 1954.

INAUGURAL ADDRESS

By John F. Kennedy

This inaugural address outlined the idealistic priorities of an energetic new administration that entered office in the midst of booming national prosperity and optimism. Its premise: helping poorer citizens. Kennedy called for an "alliance for progress" with the Latin American nations, and a new "quest for peace, before the dark powers of destruction unleashed by science engulf all humanity in planned or accidental self-destruction." Though written by a crack team of ghost-writers, the closing words of the address—"Ask not what your country can do for you, ask what you can do for your country"—became synonymous with the memory of the martyred president.

Wwe observe today not a victory of party but a celebration of freedom—symbolizing an end as well as a beginning, signifying renewal as well as change. For I have sworn before you and Almighty God the same solemn oath our forebears prescribed nearly a century and three-quarters ago.

The world is very different now. For man holds in his mortal hands the power to abolish all forms of human poverty and all forms of human life. And yet the same revolutionary beliefs for which our forebears fought are still at issue around the globe: the belief that the rights of man come not from the generosity of the state but from the hand of God.

We dare not forget today that we are the heirs of that first revolution. Let the word go forth from this time and place, to friend and foe alike, that the torch has been passed to a new generation of Americans—born in this century, tempered by war, disciplined by a hard and bitter peace, proud of our ancient heritage—and unwilling to witness or permit the slow undoing of those human rights to which this nation has always been committed, and to which we are committed today at home and around the world.

Let every nation know, whether it wishes us well or ill, that we shall pay any price, bear any burden, meet any hardship, support any friend, oppose any foe to assure the survival and the success of liberty.

This much we pledge—and more.

To those old allies whose cultural and spiritual origins we share, we pledge the loyalty of faithful friends. United, there is little we cannot do in a host of cooperative ventures. Divided, there is little we can do—for we dare not meet a powerful challenge at odds and split asunder.

To those new states whom we welcome to the ranks of the free, we pledge our word that one form of colonial control shall not have passed away merely to be replaced by a far more iron tyranny. We shall not always expect to find them supporting our view. But we shall always hope to find them strongly supporting their own freedom—and to remember that, in the past, those who foolishly sought power by riding the back of the tiger ended up inside.

To those people in the huts and villages of half the globe struggling to break the bonds of mass misery, we pledge our best efforts to help them help themselves, for whatever period is required—not because the Communists may be doing it, not because we seek their votes, but because it is right. If a free society cannot help the many who are poor, it cannot save the few who are rich.

To our sister republics south of the border, we offer a special pledge: to convert our good words into good deeds—in a new alliance for progress— to assist free men and free governments in casting off the chains of poverty. But this peaceful revolution of hope cannot become the prey of hostile powers. Let all our neighbors know that we shall join with them to oppose aggression or subversion anywhere in the Americas. And let every other power know that this hemisphere intends to remain the master of its own house.

To that world assembly of sovereign states, the United Nations, our last best hope in an age where the instruments of war have far outpaced the instruments of peace, we renew our pledge of support—to prevent it from becoming merely a forum for invective, to strengthen its shield of the new and the weak, and to enlarge the area in which its writ may run.

Finally, to those nations who would make themselves our adversary, we offer not a pledge but a request: that both sides begin anew the quest for peace, before the dark powers of destruction unleashed by science engulf all humanity in planned or accidental self-destruction.

We dare not tempt them with weakness. For only when our arms are sufficient beyond doubt can we be certain beyond doubt that they will never be employed.

But neither can two great and powerful groups of nations take comfort from our present course—both sides overburdened by the cost of modern weapons, both rightly alarmed by the steady spread of the deadly atom, yet both racing to alter that uncertain balance of terror that stays the hand of mankind's final war.

So let us begin anew, remembering on both sides that civility is not a sign of weakness, and sincerity is always subject to proof. Let us never negotiate out of fear. But let us never fear to negotiate.

Let both sides explore what problems unite us instead of belaboring those problems which divide us.

Let both sides, for the first time, formulate serious and precise proposals for the inspection and control of arms—and bring the absolute power to destroy other nations under the absolute control of all nations.

Let both sides seek to invoke the wonders of science instead of its terrors. Together let us explore the stars, conquer the deserts, eradicate disease, tap the ocean depths, and encourage the arts and commerce.

Let both sides unite to heed in all corners of the earth the command of Isaiah—to "undo the heavy burdens and let the oppressed go free."

And if a beachhead of cooperation may push back the jungle of suspicion, let both sides join in creating a new endeavor, not a new balance of power, but a new world of law, where the strong are just and the weak secure and the peace preserved.

All this will not be finished in the first one hundred days. Nor will it be finished in the first one thousand days, nor in the life of this administration, nor even perhaps in our lifetime on this planet. But let us begin.

In your hands, my fellow citizens, more than mine, will rest the final success or failure of our course. Since this country was founded, each generation of Americans has been summoned to give testimony to its national loyalty. The graves of young Americans who answered the call to service surround the globe.

Now the trumpet summons us again—not as a call to bear arms, though arms we need; not as a call to battle, though embattled we are—but a call to bear the burden of a long twilight struggle, year in and year out, "rejoicing in hope, patient in tribulation," a struggle against the common enemies of man: tyranny, poverty, disease, and war itself.

Can we forge against these enemies a grand and global alliance, north and south, east and west, that can assure a more fruitful life for all mankind? Will you join in that historic effort?

In the long history of the world, only a few generations have been granted the role of defending freedom in its hour of maximum danger. I do not shrink from this responsibility—I welcome it. I do not believe that any of us would exchange places with any other people or any other generation. The energy, the faith, the devotion which we bring to this endeavor will light our country and all who serve it—and the glow from that fire can truly light the world.

And so, my fellow Americans: Ask not what your country can do for you—ask what you can do for your country.

My fellow citizens of the world: Ask not what America will do for you, but what together we can do for the freedom of man.

Finally, whether you are citizens of America or citizens of the world, ask of us here the same high standards of strength and sacrifice which we ask of you. With a good conscience our only sure reward, with history the final judge of our deeds, let us go forth to lead the land we love, asking His blessing and His help, but knowing that here on earth God's work must truly be our own.

LETTER FROM THE BIRMINGHAM JAIL

By Martin Luther King Jr.

In 1963, during the most intense days of the struggle for civil rights, Martin Luther King Jr. wrote this remarkable open letter to his fellow clergymen around the nation, who had criticized and condemned his relentless assault on prejudice, discrimination, segregation, and injustice as "unwise and untimely." The effect was galvanizing. A tidal wave of support soon insured that civil rights would be legally extended to every citizen—rich or poor, black or white, hale or infirm, young or aged, man or woman.

My dear Fellow Clergymen: While confined here in the Birmingham City Jail, I came across your recent statement calling our present activities "unwise and untimely." Since I feel that you are men of genuine goodwill and your criticisms are sincerely set forth, I would like to answer your statement in what I hope will be patient and reasonable terms.

I think I should give the reason for my being in Birmingham, since you have been influenced by the argument of "outsiders coming in." Several months ago our local affiliate here in Birmingham invited us to be on call to engage in a nonviolent direct action program if such were deemed necessary. So I am here, along with several members of my staff, because we were invited here. I am here because I have basic organizational ties here.

Beyond this, I am in Birmingham because injustice is here. Just as the eighth-century prophets left their little villages and carried their "thus saith the Lord" far beyond the boundaries of their home towns; and just as the Apostle Paul left his little village of Tarsus and carried the gospel of Jesus Christ to practically every hamlet and city of the Graeco-Roman world, I too am compelled to carry the gospel of freedom beyond my particular home town. Like Paul, I must constantly respond to the Macedonian call for aid.

Moreover, I am cognizant of the interrelatedness of all communities and states. I cannot sit idly by in Atlanta and not be concerned about what happens in Birmingham. Injustice anywhere is a threat to justice everywhere. We are caught in an inescapable network of mutuality, tied in a single garment of destiny. Whatever affects one directly affects all indirectly. Never again can we afford to live with the narrow, provincial "outside agitator" idea. Anyone who lives inside the United States can never be considered an outsider anywhere in this country.

You deplore the demonstrations that are presently taking place in Birmingham. But I am sorry that your statement did not express a similar concern for the conditions that brought the demonstrations into being. I am sure that each of you would want to go beyond the superficial social analyst who looks merely at effects, and does not grapple with underlying causes. I would not hesitate to say that it is unfortunate that so called demonstrations are taking place in Birmingham at this time, but I would say in more emphatic terms that it is even more unfortunate that the white power structure of this city left the Negro community with no other alternative.

Birmingham is probably the most thoroughly segregated city in the United States. Its ugly record of police brutality is known in every section of this country. Its unjust treatment of Negroes in the courts is a notorious reality. There have been more unsolved bombings of Negro homes and churches in Birmingham than in any city in this nation. These are the hard, brutal, and unbelievable facts. On the basis of these conditions Negro leaders sought to negotiate with the city fathers. But the political leaders consistently refused to engage in good-faith negotiation.

You may well ask, "Why direct action? Why sit-ins, marches, etceteras? Isn't negotiation a better path?" You are exactly right in your call for negotiation. Indeed, this is the purpose of direct action. Nonviolent direct action seeks to create such a crisis and establish such creative tension that a community that has constantly refused to negotiate is forced to confront the issue. It seeks so to dramatize the issue that it can no longer be ignored. I just referred to the creation of tension as a part of the work of the nonviolent resister. This may sound rather shocking. But I must confess that I am not afraid of the word tension. I have earnestly worked and preached against violent tension, but there is a type of constructive nonviolent tension that is necessary for growth. Just as Socrates felt that it was necessary to create a tension in the mind so that individuals could rise from the bondage of myths and half-truths to the unfettered realm of creative analysis and objective appraisal, we must see the need of having nonviolent gadflies to create the kind of tension in society that will help men to rise from the dark depths of prejudice and racism to the majestic heights of understanding and brotherhood. So the purpose of the direct action is to create a situation so crisis-packed that it will inevitably open the door to negotiation. We, therefore, concur with you in your call for negotiation. Too long has our beloved Southland been bogged down in the tragic attempt to live in monologue rather than dialogue.

My friends, I must say to you that we have not made a single gain in civil rights without determined legal and nonviolent pressure. History is the long and tragic story of the fact that privileged groups seldom give up their privileges voluntarily. Individuals may see the moral light and voluntarily give up their unjust posture; but as Reinhold Neibuhr has reminded us, groups are more immoral than individuals.

We know through painful experience that freedom is never voluntarily given by the oppressor; it must be demanded by the oppressed. Frankly, I have never yet engaged in a direct-action movement that was "well timed," according to the timetable of those who have not suffered unduly from the disease of segregation. For years now I have heard the word "Wait!" It rings in the ear of every Negro with a piercing familiarity. This "wait" has almost always meant "never." It has been a tranquilizing thalidomide, relieving the emotional stress for a moment, only to give birth to an ill-formed infant of frustration. We must come to see with the distinguished jurist of yesterday that "justice too long delayed is justice denied." We have waited for more than three hundred and forty years for our constitutional and God-given rights. The nations of Asia and Africa are moving with jet-like speed toward the goal of political independence, and we still creep at horse and buggy pace toward the gaining of a cup of coffee at a lunch counter. I guess it is easy for those who have never felt the stinging darts of segregation to say, "Wait." But when you have seen vicious mobs lynch your mothers and fathers at will and drown your sisters and brothers at whim, when you have seen hate-filled policemen curse, kick, brutalize, and even kill your black brothers and sisters with impunity; when you see the vast majority of your twenty million Negro brothers smothering in an airtight cage of poverty in the midst of an affluent society; when you suddenly find your tongue twisted and your speech stammering as you seek to explain to your six-year-old daughter why she can't go to the public amusement park that has just been advertised on television, and see tears welling up in her little eyes when she is told that Funtown is closed to colored children, and see the depressing clouds of inferiority begin to form in her little mental sky, and see her begin to distort her little personality by unconsciously developing a bitterness toward white people; when you have to concoct an answer for a five-year-old son asking in agonizing pathos: "Daddy, why do white people treat colored people so mean?"; when you take a cross country drive and find it necessary to sleep night after night in the uncomfortable corners of your automobile because no motel will accept you, when you are humiliated day in and day out by nagging signs reading "white" and "colored"; when your first name becomes "nigger" and your middle name becomes "boy" (however old you are) and your last name becomes "John," and when your wife and mother are never given the respected title "Mrs."; when you are harried by day and haunted at night by the fact that you are a Negro, living constantly at tip-toe stance never quite knowing what to expect next, and plagued with inner fears and outer resentments; when you are forever fighting a degenerating sense of "nobodiness"; then you will understand why we find it difficult to wait. There comes a time when the cup of endurance runs over, and men are no longer willing to be plunged into an abyss of injustice where they experience the blackness of corroding despair. I hope, sirs, you can understand our legitimate and unavoidable impatience.

You express a great deal of anxiety over our willingness to break laws. This is certainly a legitimate concern. Since we so diligently urge people to obey the Supreme Court's decision of 1954 outlawing segregation in the public schools, it is rather strange and paradoxical to find us consciously breaking laws. One may well ask, "How can you advocate breaking some laws and obeying others?" The answer is found in the fact that there are two types of laws: There are just and there are unjust laws. I would agree with Saint Augustine that "an unjust law is no law at all."

Now what is the difference between the two? How does one determine when a law is just or unjust? A just law is a man-made code that squares with the moral law or the law of God. An unjust law is a code that is out of harmony with the moral law. To put it in the terms of Saint Thomas Aquinas, an unjust law is a human law that is not rooted in eternal and natural law. Any law that uplifts human personality is just. Any law that degrades human personality is unjust. All segregation statutes are unjust because segregation distorts the soul and damages the personality. It gives the segregator a false sense of superiority, and the segregated a false sense of inferiority. To use the words of Martin Buber, the great Jewish philosopher, segregation substitutes an "I-it" relationship for the "I-thou" relationship, and ends up relegating persons to the status of things. So segregation is not only politically, economically, and sociologically unsound, but it is morally wrong and sinful. Paul Tillich has said that sin is separation. Isn't segregation an existential expression of man's tragic separation, an expression of his awful estrangement, his terrible sinfulness? So I can urge men to disobey segregation ordinances because they are morally wrong.

There are some instances when a law is just on its face and unjust in its application. For instance, I was arrested Friday on a charge of parading without a permit. Now there is nothing wrong with an ordinance which requires a permit for a parade, but when the ordinance is used to preserve segregation and to deny citizens the First Amendment privilege of peaceful assembly and peaceful protest, then it becomes unjust.

I hope you can see the distinction I am trying to point out. In no sense do I advocate evading or defying the law as the rabid segregationist would do. This would lead to anarchy. One who breaks an unjust law must do it openly, lovingly (not hatefully as the white mothers did in New Orleans when they were seen on television screaming "nigger, nigger, nigger"), and with a willingness to accept the penalty. I submit that an individual who breaks a law that conscience tells him is unjust, and willingly accepts the penalty by staying in jail to arouse the conscience of the community over its injustice, is in reality expressing the very highest respect for law.

Of course, there is nothing new about this kind of civil disobedience. It was seen sublimely in the refusal of Shadrach, Meshach, and Abednego to obey the laws of Nebuchadnezzar because a higher moral law was involved. It was practiced superbly by the early Christians who were willing to face hungry lions and the excruciating pain of chopping blocks, before submitting to certain unjust laws of the Roman empire. To a degree academic freedom is a reality today because Socrates practiced civil disobedience.

We can never forget that everything Hitler did in Germany was "legal" and everything the Hungarian freedom fighters did in Hungary was "illegal." It was "illegal" to aid and comfort a Jew in Hitler's Germany. But I am sure that if I had lived in Germany during that time, I would have aided and comforted my Jewish brothers even though it was illegal. If I lived in a Communist country today, where certain principles dear to the Christian faith are suppressed, I believe I would openly advocate disobeying these anti-religious laws. I must make two honest confessions to you, my Christian and Jewish brothers. First, I must confess that over the last few years I have been gravely disappointed with the white moderate. I have almost reached the regrettable conclusion that the Negro's great stumbling block in the stride toward freedom is not the White Citizen's Councilor or the Ku Klux Klanner, but the white moderate who is more devoted to "order" than to justice; who prefers a negative peace which is the absence of tension to a positive peace which is the presence of justice; who constantly says "I agree with you in the goal you seek, but I can't agree with your methods of direct action"; who paternalistically feels that he can set the timetable for another man's freedom; who lives by the myth of time and who constantly advises the Negro to wait until a "more convenient season." Shallow understanding from people of goodwill is more frustrating than absolute misunder-standing from people of ill will. Lukewarm acceptance is much more be-wildering than outright rejection.

I had hoped that the white moderate would understand that law and order exist for the purpose of establishing justice, and that when they fail to do this they become dangerously structured dams that block the flow of social progress. I had hoped that the white moderate would understand that the present tension in the South is merely a necessary phase of the transition from an obnoxious negative peace, where the Negro passively accepted his unjust plight, to a substance-filled positive peace, where all men will respect the dignity and worth of human personality. Actually, we who engage in nonviolent direct action are not the creators of tension. We merely bring to the surface the hidden tension that is already alive. We bring it out in the open where it can be seen and dealt with. Like a boil that can never be cured as long as it is covered up but must be opened with all its pus-flowing ugliness to the natural medicines of air and light, injustice must likewise be exposed, with all of the tension its exposing creates, to the light of human conscience and the air of national opinion before it can be cured.

In your statement you asserted that our actions, even though peaceful, must be condemned because they precipitate violence. But can this assertion be logically made? Isn't this like condemning the robbed man because his possession of money precipitated the evil act of robbery? Isn't this like condemning Socrates because his unswerving commitment to truth and his philosophical delvings precipitated the misguided popular mind to make him drink the hemlock? Isn't this like condemning Jesus because His unique God-Consciousness and never-ceasing devotion to His will precipitated the evil act of crucifixion? We must come to see, as federal courts have consistently affirmed, that it is immoral to urge an individual to withdraw his efforts to gain his basic constitutional rights because the quest precipitates violence. Society must protect the robbed and punish the robber.

I had also hoped that the white moderate would reject the myth of time. I received a letter this morning from a white brother in Texas which said: "All Christians know that the colored people will receive equal rights eventually, but it is possible that you are in too great of a religious hurry. It has taken Christianity almost two thousand years to accomplish what it has. The teachings of Christ take time to come to earth." All that is said here grows out of a tragic misconception of time. It is the strangely irrational notion that there is something in the very flow of time that will inevitably cure all ills. Actually time is neutral. It can be used either destructively or constructively. I am coming to feel that the people of ill-will have used time much more effectively than the people of good will. We will have to repent in this generation not merely for the vitriolic words and actions of the bad people, but for the appalling silence of good people. We must come to see that human progress never rolls in on wheels of inevitability. It comes through the tireless efforts and persistent work of men willing to be coworkers with God, and without this hard work time itself becomes an ally of the forces of social stagnation. We must use time creatively, and forever realize that the time is always ripe to do right. Now is the time to make real the promise of democracy, and transform our pending national elegy into a creative psalm of brotherhood. Now is the time to lift our national policy from the quicksand of racial injustice to the solid rock of human dignity.

I stand in the middle of two opposing forces in the Negro community. One is a force of complacency made up of Negroes who, as a result of long years of oppression, have been so completely drained of self-respect and a sense of "somebodiness" that they have adjusted to segregation, and of a few Negroes in the middle class who, because of a degree of academic and economic security, and because at points they profit by segregation, have unconsciously become insensitive to the problems of the masses. The other force is one of bitterness and hatred, and comes perilously close to advocating violence. It is expressed in the various black-nationalist groups that are springing up over the nation, the largest and best known being

Elijah Muhammad's Muslim movement. This movement is nourished by the contemporary frustration over the continued existence of racial discrimination. It is made up of people who have lost faith in America, who have absolutely repudiated Christianity, and who have concluded that the white man is an incurable "devil." I have tried to stand between these two forces, saying that we need not follow the "do-nothingism" of the complacent or the hatred and despair of the black nationalists. There is the more excellent way of love and nonviolent protest. I'm grateful to God that, through the Negro church, the dimension of nonviolence entered our struggle. If this philosophy had not emerged, I am convinced that by now many streets of the South would be flowing with floods of blood. And I am further convinced that if our white brothers dismiss as "rabble-rousers" and "outside agitators" those of us who are working through the channels of nonviolent direct action and refuse to support our nonviolent efforts, millions of Negroes, out of frustration and despair, will seek solace and security in black nationalist ideologies, a development that will lead inevitably to a frightening racial nightmare.

Oppressed people cannot remain oppressed forever. The urge for freedom will eventually come. This is what happened to the American Negro. Something within has reminded him of his birthright of freedom; something without has reminded him that he can gain it. Consciously, and unconsciously, he has been swept in by what the Germans call the Zeitgeist, and with his black brothers of Africa, and his brown and yellow brothers of Asia, South America, and the Caribbean, he is moving with a sense of cosmic urgency toward the promised land of racial justice. Recognizing this vital urge that has engulfed the Negro community, one should readily understand public demonstrations. The Negro has many pent-up resentments and latent frustrations. He has to get them out. So let him march sometime; let him have his prayer pilgrimages to the city hall; understand why he must have sit-ins and freedom rides. If his repressed emotions do not come out in these nonviolent ways, they will come out in ominous expressions of violence. This is not a threat; it is a fact of history. So I have not said to my people "get rid of your discontent." But I have tried to say that this normal and healthy discontent can be channelized through the creative outlet of nonviolent direct action. Now this approach is being dismissed as extremist. I must admit that I was initially disappointed in being so categorized.

But as I continued to think about the matter I gradually gained a bit of satisfaction from being considered an extremist. Was not Jesus an extremist in love? "Love your enemies, bless them that curse you, pray for them that despitefully use you." Was not Amos an extremist for justice? "Let justice roll down like water and righteousness like a mighty stream." Was not Paul an extremist for the gospel of Jesus Christ? "I bear in my body the marks of the Lord Jesus." Was not Martin Luther an extremist? "Here I stand; I can do none other so help me God." Was not John Bunyan an extremist? "I will stay in jail to the end of my days before I make a butchery of my conscience." Was not Abraham Lincoln an extremist? "This nation cannot survive half slave and half free." Was not Thomas Jefferson an extremist? "We hold these truths to be self-evident, that all men are created equal." So the question is not whether we will be extremist but what kind of extremist will we be. Will we be extremists for hate—or will we be extremists for love? Will we be extremists for the preservation of injustice—or will we be extremists for the cause of justice? In that dramatic scene on Calvary's hill, three men were crucified. We must not forget that all three were crucified for the same crime—the crime of extremism. Two were extremists for immorality, and thusly fell below their environment. The other, Jesus Christ, was an extremist for love, truth, and goodness, and thereby rose above his environment. So, after all, maybe the South, the nation, and the world are in dire need of creative extremists.

I hope the church as a whole will meet the challenge of this decisive hour. But even if the church does not come to the aid of justice, I have no despair about the future. I have no fear about the outcome of our struggle in Birmingham, even if our motives are frequently misunderstood. We will reach the goal of freedom in Birmingham and all over the nation, because the goal of America is freedom. Abused and scorned though we may be, our destiny is tied up with the destiny of America. Before the pilgrims landed at Plymouth we were here. Before the pen of Jefferson etched across the pages of history the majestic words of the Declaration of Independence, we were here. For more than two centuries our fore-parents labored in this country without wages; they made cotton king, and they built the homes of their masters in the midst of brutal injustice and shameful humiliation—and yet out of a bottomless vitality they continued to thrive and develop. If the inexpressible cruelties of slavery could not stop us, the opposition we now face will surely fail. We will win our freedom because the sacred heritage of our nation and the eternal will of God are embodied in our echoing demands.

ROE V. WADE

By Harry A. Blackmun

In perhaps its most divisive and controversial decision since Dred Scott, the Supreme Court overturned the homicide laws in abortion cases in all fifty states. Delivered on January 22, 1973, the decision sent shock waves throughout the nation—the effects of which are still felt. In a remarkably argued majority opinion, Associate Justice Blackmun introduced several creative constitutional innovations, including a heretofore unrecognized "right to privacy." Like the Dred Scott decision before it, this case actually only exacerbated the debate the court set out to resolve.

We forthwith acknowledge our awareness of the sensitive and emotional nature of the abortion controversy, of the vigorous opposing views, even among physicians, and of the deep and seemingly absolute convictions that the subject inspires. One's philosophy, one's experiences, one's exposure to the raw edges of human existence, one's religious training, one's attitudes toward life and family and their values, and the moral standards one establishes and seeks to observe, are all likely to influence and to color one's thinking and conclusions about abortion.

In addition, population growth, pollution, poverty, and racial overtones tend to complicate and not to simplify the problem.

Our task, of course, is to resolve the issue by constitutional measurement, free of emotion and of predilection. We seek earnestly to do this, and, because we do, we have inquired into, and in this opinion place some emphasis upon, medical and medical-legal history and what that history reveals about man's attitudes toward the abortion procedure over the centuries. We bear in mind, too, Mr. Justice Holmes' admonition in his now-vindicated dissent in Lochner v. New York: "The Constitution is made for people of fundamentally differing views, and the accident of our finding certain opinions natural and familiar or novel and even shocking ought not to conclude our judgment upon the question whether statutes embodying them conflict with the Constitution of the United States."

Jane Roe, a single woman who was residing in Dallas County, Texas, instituted this federal action in March 1970 against the District Attorney of the county. She sought a declaratory judgment that the Texas criminal abortion statutes were unconstitutional on their face, and an injunction restraining the defendant from enforcing the statutes.

Roe alleged that she was unmarried and pregnant; that she wished to terminate her pregnancy by an abortion "performed by a competent, licensed physician, under safe, clinical conditions"; that she was unable to get a "legal" abortion in Texas because her life did not appear to be threatened by the continuation of her pregnancy; and that she could not afford to travel to another jurisdiction in order to secure a legal abortion under safe conditions. She claimed that the Texas statutes were unconstitutionally vague and that they abridged her right of personal privacy, protected by the First, Fourth, Fifth, Ninth, and Fourteenth Amendments. By an amendment to her complaint Roe purported to sue "on behalf of herself and all other women" similarly situated.

The principal thrust of appellant's attack on the Texas statutes is that they improperly invade a right, said to be possessed by the pregnant woman, to choose to terminate her pregnancy. Appellant would discover this right in the concept of personal "liberty" embodied in the Fourteenth Amendment's Due Process Clause, or in personal, marital, familial, and sexual privacy said to be protected by the Bill of Rights or its penumbras.

It perhaps is not generally appreciated that the restrictive criminal abortion laws in effect in a majority of states today are of relatively recent vintage. Those laws, generally proscribing abortion or its attempt at any time during pregnancy except when necessary to preserve the pregnant woman's life, are not of ancient or even of common-law origin. Instead, they derive from statutory changes effected, for the most part, in the latter half of the 19th century.

It is thus apparent that in common law, at the time of the adoption of our Constitution, and throughout the major portion of the 19th century, abortion was viewed with less disfavor than under most American statutes currently in effect. Phrasing it another way, a woman enjoyed a substantially broader right to terminate a pregnancy than she does in most States today. At least with respect to the early stage of pregnancy, and very possibly without such a limitation, the opportunity to make this choice was present in this country well into the 19th century. Even later, the law continued for some time to treat less punitively an abortion procured in early pregnancy.

The Constitution does not explicitly mention any right of privacy. In a line of decisions, however, going back perhaps as far as Union Pacific v. Botsford (1891), the Court has recognized that a right of personal privacy, or a guarantee of certain areas or zones of privacy, does exist under the Constitution. In varying contexts, the Court or individual Justices have, indeed, found at least the roots of that right in the First Amendment; in the Fourth and Fifth Amendments; in the penumbras of the Bill of Rights, in the Ninth Amendment; or in the concept of liberty guaranteed by the first section of the Fourteenth Amendment. These decisions make it clear that only personal rights that can be deemed "fundamental" or "implicit in the concept of ordered liberty," are included in this guarantee of personal privacy. They also make it clear that the right has some extension to activities relating to marriage; procreation; contraception; family relationships; and child rearing and education.

This right of privacy, whether it be founded in the Fourteenth Amendment's concept of personal liberty and restrictions upon state action, as we feel it is, or, as the District Court determined, in the Ninth Amendment's reservation of rights to the people, is broad enough to encompass a woman's decision whether or not to terminate her pregnancy. The detriment that the State would impose upon the pregnant woman by denying this choice altogether is apparent. Specific and direct harm medically diagnosable even in early pregnancy may be involved. Maternity, or additional offspring, may force upon the woman a distressful life and future. Psychological harm may be imminent. Mental and physical health may be taxed by child care. There is also the distress, for all concerned, associated with the unwanted child, and there is the problem of bringing a child into a family already unable, psychologically and otherwise, to care for it. In other cases, as in this one, the additional difficulties and continuing stigma of unwed motherhood may be involved. All these are factors the woman and her responsible physician necessarily will consider in consultation.

On the basis of elements such as these, appellant and some amici argue that the woman's right is absolute and that she is entitled to terminate her pregnancy at whatever time, in whatever way, and for whatever reason she alone chooses. With this we do not agree. Appellant's arguments that Texas either has no valid interest at all in regulating the abortion decision, or no interest strong enough to support any limitation upon the woman's sole determination, is unpersuasive. The Court's decisions recognizing a right of privacy also acknowledge that some state regulation in areas protected by that right is appropriate. As noted above, a State may properly assert important interests in safeguarding health, in maintaining medical standards, and in protecting potential life. At some point in pregnancy, these respective interests become sufficiently compelling to sustain regulation of the factors that govern the abortion decision. The privacy right involved, therefore, cannot be said to be absolute. In fact, it is not clear to us that the claim asserted by some amici that one has an unlimited right to do with one's body as one pleases bears a close relationship to the right of privacy previously articulated in the Court's decisions. The Court has refused to recognize an unlimited right of this kind in the past.

We, therefore, conclude that the right of personal privacy includes the abortion decision, but that this right is not unqualified and must be considered against important state interests in regulation.

We note that those federal and state courts that have recently considered abortion law challenges have reached the same conclusion.

Although the results are divided, most of these courts have agreed that the right of privacy, however based, is broad enough to cover the abortion decisions; that the right, nonetheless, is not absolute and is subject to some limitations; and that at some point the state interests as to protection of health, medical standards, and prenatal life, become dominant. We agree with this approach.

The appellee and certain amici argue that the fetus is a "person" within the language and meaning of the Fourteenth Amendment. In support of this, they outline at length and in detail the well-known facts of fetal development. If this suggestion of personhood is established, the appellant's case, of course, collapses, for the fetus' right to life is then guaranteed specifically by the amendment. The appellant conceded as much on reargument. On the other hand, the appellee conceded on reargument that no case could be cited that holds that a fetus is a person within the meaning of the Fourteenth Amendment.

The Constitution does not define "person" in so many words. The use of the word is such that it has application only postnatally. None indicates, with any assurance, that it has any possible pre-natal application.

All this, together with our observation, supra, that throughout the major portion of the 19th century prevailing legal abortion practices were far freer than they are today, persuades us that the word "person," as used in the Fourteenth Amendment, does not include the unborn.

Texas urges that, apart from the Fourteenth Amendment, life begins at conception and is present throughout pregnancy and that therefore the State has a compelling interest in protecting that life from and after conception. We need not resolve the difficult question of when life begins. When those trained in the respective disciplines of medicine, philosophy, and theology are unable to arrive at any consensus, the judiciary, at this point in the development of man's knowledge, is not in a position to speculate as to the answer.

In areas other than criminal abortion, the law has been reluctant to endorse any theory that life, as we recognize it, begins before live birth or to accord legal rights to the unborn except in narrowly defined situations and except when the rights are continent upon live birth. In short, the unborn have never been recognized in the law as persons in the whole sense.

In view of all this, we do not agree that, by adopting one theory of life, Texas may override the rights of the pregnant woman that are at stake. We repeat, however, that the State does have an important and legitimate interest in preserving and protecting the health of the pregnant woman.

With respect to the State's important and legitimate interest in the health of the mother, the "compelling" point, in the light of present medical knowledge, is at approximately the end of the first trimester. This is so because of the now-established medical fact, that until the end of the first trimester mortality in abortion may be less than mortality in normal childbirth. It follows that, from and after this point, a State may regulate the abortion procedure to the extent that the regulation reasonably relates to the preservation and protection of maternal health. Examples of permissible state regulation in this area are requirements as to the qualifications of the person who is to perform the abortion; as to the licensure of that person; as to the facility in which the procedure is to be performed, that is, whether it must be a hospital or may be a clinic or some other place of less-than-hospital status; as to the licensing of the facility; and the like.

With respect to the State's important and legitimate interest in potential life, the "compelling" point is at viability. This is so because the fetus then presumably has the capability of meaningful life outside the mother's womb. State regulation protective of fetal life after viability thus has both logical and biological justifications. If the State is interested in protecting fetal life after viability, it may go so far as to proscribe abortion during that period, except when it is necessary to preserve the life or health of the mother.

Measured against these standards, Article 1196 of the Texas Penal Code, in restricting legal abortions to those "procured or attempted by medical advice for the purpose of saving the life of the mother," sweeps too broadly. The statute makes no distinction between abortions performed early in pregnancy and those performed later, and it limits to a single reason, "saving" the mother's life, the legal justification for the procedure. The statute, therefore, cannot survive the constitutional attack made upon it here.

INAUGURAL ADDRESS

By Ronald Reagan

Ushered into the presidency by a roiling discontent with the course of modern liberalism, Ronald Reagan initiated a remarkable new era of conservatism in American political life. His inauguration was a celebration of the original intentions of the Founders: small, limited, and accountable civil prerogatives. Although his administration's domestic successes were actually rather limited— particularly in reining in the size and cost of government—the moral resolve manifested here ultimately resulted in the greatest foreign policy victory in this century: the collapse of Communism's "Evil Empire." In all respects, there can be little doubt that this manifesto of optimism ultimately set the stage for the political debate through the end of the century.

These United States are confronted with an economic affliction of great proportions. We suffer from the longest and one of the worst sustained inflations in our national history. It distorts our economic decisions, penalizes thrift and crushes the struggling young and the fixed-income elderly alike. It threatens to shatter the lives of millions of our people.

Idle industries have cast workers into unemployment, human misery and personal indignity. Those who do work are denied a fair return for their labor by a tax system which penalizes successful achievement and keeps us from maintaining full productivity.

But great as our tax burden is, it has not kept pace with public spending. For decades we have piled deficit upon deficit, mortgaging our future and our children's future for the temporary convenience of the present.

To continue this long trend is to guarantee tremendous social, cultural, political and economic upheavals. You and I, as individuals, can, by borrowing, live beyond our means, but for only a limited period of time. Why then should we think that collectively, as a nation, we are not bound by that same limitation? We must act today in order to preserve tomorrow. And let there be no misunderstanding—we're going to begin to act beginning today.

The economic ills we suffer have come upon us over several decades. They will not go away in days, weeks or months, but they will go away. They will go away because we as Americans have the capacity now, as we have had in the past, to do whatever needs to be done to preserve this last and greatest bastion of freedom.

In this present crisis, government is not the solution to our problem, government is the problem.

From time to time we've been tempted to believe that society has become too complex to be managed by self-rule, that government by an elite group is superior to government for, by and of the people. But if no one among us is capable of government himself, then who among us has the capacity to govern someone else?

All of us together—in and out of government—must beat the burden. The solutions we seek must be equitable with no one group singled out to pay a higher price. We hear much of special interest groups. Our concern must be for a special interest group that has been too long neglected. It knows no sectional boundaries, or ethnic and racial divisions and it crosses political party lines. It is made up of men and women who raise our food, patrol our streets, man our mines and factories, teach our children, keep our homes and heal us when we're sick.

Professionals, industrialists, shopkeepers, clerks, cabbies and truck drivers. They are, in short, "We the people." This breed called Americans.

This administration's objective will be a healthy, vigorous, growing economy that provides equal opportunities for all Americans with no barriers born of bigotry or discrimination. Putting America back to work means putting all Americans back to work. Ending inflation means freeing all Americans from the terror of runaway living costs. All must share in the productive work of this "new beginning " and all must share in the bounty of a revived economy.

With the idealism and fair play which are the core of our system and our strength, we can have a strong, prosperous America at peace with itself and the world.

So as we begin, let us take inventory.

We are a nation that has a government—not the other way around. And this makes us special among the nations of the earth.

Our government has no power except that granted it by the people. It is time to check and reverse the growth of government which shows signs of having grown beyond the consent of the governed. It is my intention to curb the size and influence of the federal establishment and to demand recognition of the distinction between the powers granted to the federal government and those reserved to the states or to the people.

All of us—all of us need to be reminded that the federal government did not create the states; the states created the federal government. Now, so there will be no misunderstanding, it's not my intention to do away with government. It is rather to make it work—work with us, not over us; to stand by our side, not ride on our back. Government can and must provide opportunity, not smother it; foster productivity, not stifle it.

If we look to the answer as to why for so many years we achieved so much, prospered as no other people on earth, it was because here in this land we unleashed the energy and individual genius of man to a greater extent than has ever been done before.

Freedom and the dignity of the individual have been more available and assured here than in any other place on earth. The price for this freedom at times has been high, but we have never been unwilling to pay that price.

It is no coincidence that our present troubles parallel and are proportionate to the intervention and intrusion in our lives that result from unnecessary and excessive growth of government.

It is time for us to realize that we are too great a nation to limit ourselves to small dreams. We're not, as some would have us believe, doomed to an inevitable decline; I do not believe in a fate that will fall on us no matter what we do. I do believe in a fate that will fall on us if we do nothing.

So, with all the creative energy at our command let us begin an era of national renewal. Let us renew our determination, our courage and our strength. And let us renew our faith and our hope. We have every right to dream heroic dreams.

Your dreams, your hopes, your goals are going to be the dreams, the hopes and the goals of this administration, so help me God.

We shall reflect the compassion that is so much a part of your makeup. How can we love our country and not love our countrymen? And loving them reach out a hand when they fall, heal them when they're sick and provide opportunity to make them self-sufficient so they will be equal in fact and not just in theory?

Can we solve the problems confronting us? The answer is an unequivocal and emphatic yes. To paraphrase Winston Churchill, I did not take the oath I've just taken with the intention of presiding over the dissolution of the world's strongest economy.

In the days ahead I will propose removing the roadblocks that have slowed our economy and reduced productivity. Steps will be taken aimed at restoring the balance between the various levels of government. Progress may be slow—measured in inches and feet, not miles—but we will progress. It is time to reawaken this industrial giant, to get government back within its means and to lighten our punitive tax burden.

And these will be our first priorities, and on these principles there will be no compromise.

I believe we the Americans of today are ready to act worthy of ourselves, ready to do what must be done to insure happiness and liberty for ourselves, our children and our children's children.

And as we renew ourselves here in our own land we will be seen as having greater strength throughout the world. We will again be the exemplar of freedom and a beacon of hope for those who do not now have freedom.

To those neighbors and allies who share our freedom, we will strengthen our historic ties and assure them of our support and firm commitment. We will match loyalty with loyalty. We will strive for mutually beneficial relations. We will not use our friendship to impose on their sovereignty, for our own sovereignty is not for sale.

As for the enemies of freedom, those who are potential adversaries, they will be reminded that peace is the highest aspiration of the American people. We will negotiate for it, sacrifice for it, we will not surrender for it—now or ever.

Our forbearance should never be misunderstood. Our reluctance for conflict should not be misjudged as a failure of will. When action is required to preserve our national security we will act. We will maintain sufficient strength to prevail if need be, knowing that if we do so we have the best chance of never having to use that strength.

Above all we must realize that no arsenal or no weapon in the arsenals of the world is so formidable as the will and moral courage of free men and women.

It is a weapon our adversaries in today's world do not have. It is a weapon that we as Americans do have. Let that be understood by those who practice terrorism and prey upon their neighbors.

God bless you all. And God bless the United States of America.

AMENDMENTS TO THE CONSTITUTION

The twentieth century has seen more adjustment of the nation's constitutional structure than at any other time in our history. Several amendments have radically altered the nature and function of the government. Two of the farthest reaching amendments, Amendments XVI and XVII, were ratified in a single year: 1913. Another, Amendment XVIII, was ratified in 1919 only to be repealed by another—Amendment XXI—that was ratified in 1933. Amendment XIX, giving the franchise to women, was ratified in 1920, and Amendment XX, regulating the terms of federal officials, was ratified in 1933. Amendment XXII was ratified in 1951, and Amendment XXIII was ratified ten years later in 1961. Amendment XXIV, guaranteeing all citizens civil and voting rights, was ratified in 1964. Amendment XXV, providing for orderly succession in the White House, was ratified in 1967, and Amendment XXVI, which lowered the legal voting age, was ratified in 1971. Amendment XXVII has had perhaps the most interesting route to ratification. It was first proposed in 1789. Nevertheless, it was not ratified until more than two hundred years later in 1992.

AMENDMENT XVI

The Congress shall have power to lay and collect taxes on incomes, from whatever source derived, without apportionment among the several States, and without regard to any census or enumeration.

AMENDMENT XVII

The Senate of the United States shall be composed of two Senators from each State, elected by the people thereof, for six years; and each Senator shall have one vote. The electors in each State shall have the qualifications requisite for electors of the most numerous branch of the State legislatures.

When vacancies happen in the representation of any State in the Senate, the executive authority of such State shall issue writs of election to fill such vacancies: Provided, That the legislature of any State may empower the executive thereof to make temporary appointments until the people fill the vacancies by election as the legislature may direct.

This amendment shall not be so construed as to affect the election or term of any Senator chosen before it becomes valid as part of the Constitution.

AMENDMENT XVIII

Section 1. After one year from the ratification of this article the manufacture, sale, or transportation of intoxicating liquors within, the importation thereof into, or the exportation thereof from the United States and all territory subject to the jurisdiction thereof for beverage purposes is hereby prohibited.

Section 2. The Congress and the several States shall have concurrent power to enforce this article by appropriate legislation.

Section 3. This article shall be inoperative unless it shall have been ratified as an amendment to the Constitution by the legislatures of the several States, as provided in the Constitution, within seven years from the date of the submission hereof to the States by the Congress.

AMENDMENT XIX

The right of citizens of the United States to vote shall not be denied or abridged by the United States or by any State on account of sex.

Congress shall have power to enforce this article by appropriate legislation.

AMENDMENT XX

Section 1. The terms of the President and Vice-President shall end at noon on the 20th day of January, and the terms of Senators and

Representatives at noon on the 3rd day of January, of the years in which such terms would have ended if this article had not been ratified; and the terms of their successors shall then begin.

Section 2. The Congress shall assemble at least once in every year, and such meeting shall begin at noon on the 3rd day of January, unless they shall by law appoint a different day.

Section 3. If, at the time fixed for the beginning of the term of the President, the President elect shall have died, the Vice-President elect shall become President. If a President shall not have been chosen before the time fixed for the beginning of his term, or if the President elect shall have failed to qualify, then the Vice-President elect shall act as President until a President shall have qualified; and the Congress may by law provide for the case wherein neither a President elect nor a Vice-President elect shall have qualified, declaring who shall then act as President, or the manner in which one who is to act shall be selected, and such person shall act accordingly until a President or Vice-President shall have qualified.

Section 4. The Congress may by law provide for the case of the death of any of the persons from whom the House of Representatives may choose a President whenever the right of choice shall have devolved upon them, and for the case of the death of any of the persons from whom the Senate may choose a Vice-President whenever the right of choice shall have devolved upon them.

Section 5. Sections 1 and 2 shall take effect on the 15th day of October following the ratification of this article.

Section 6. This article shall be inoperative unless it shall have been ratified as an amendment to the Constitution by the legislatures of three-fourths of the several States within seven years from the date of its submission.

Amendment XXI

Section 1. The eighteenth article of amendment to the Constitution of the United States is hereby repealed.

Section 2. The transportation or importation into any State, Territory, or possession of the United States for delivery or use therein of intoxicating liquors, in violation of the laws thereof, is hereby prohibited.

Section 3. This article shall be inoperative unless it shall have been ratified as an amendment to the Constitution by conventions in the several States, as provided in the Constitution, within seven years from the date of the submission hereof to the States by the Congress.

Amendment XXII

No person shall be elected to the office of the President more than twice, and no person who has held the office of President, or acted as President, for more than two years of a term to which some other person was elected President shall be elected to the office of the President more than once.

But this Article shall not apply to any person holding the office of President when this Article was proposed by the Congress, and shall not prevent any person who may be holding the office of President, or acting as President, during the term within which this Article becomes operative from holding the office of President or acting as President during the remainder of such term.

Amendment XXIII

Section 1. The District constituting the seat of Government of the United States shall appoint in such manner as the Congress may direct:

A number of electors of President and Vice-President equal to the whole number of Senators and Representatives in Congress to which the District would be entitled if it were a State, but in no event more than the least populous State; they shall be in addition to those appointed by the States, but they shall be considered, for the purposes of the election of President and Vice President, to be electors appointed by a State; and they shall meet in the District and perform such duties as provided by the twelfth article of amendment.

Section 2. The Congress shall have power to enforce this article by appropriate legislation.

Amendment XXIV

Section 1. The right of citizens of the United States to vote in any primary or other election for President or Vice-President, for electors for President or Vice-President, or for Senator or Representative in Congress, shall not be denied or abridged by the United States or any State by reason of failure to pay any poll tax or other tax.

Section 2. The Congress shall have the power to enforce this article by appropriate legislation.

Amendment XXV

Section 1. In case of the removal of the President from office or his death or resignation, the Vice-President shall become President.

Section 2. Whenever there is a vacancy in the office of the Vice-President, the President shall nominate a Vice-President who shall take the office upon confirmation by a majority vote of both houses of Congress.

Section 3. Whenever the President transmits to the President pro tempore of the Senate and the Speaker of the House of Representatives his written declaration that he is unable to discharge the powers and duties of his office, and until he transmits to them a written declaration to the contrary, such powers and duties shall be discharged by the Vice-President as Acting President.

Section 4. Whenever the Vice-President and a majority of either the principal officers of the executive departments, or of such other body as Congress may by law provide, transmit to the President pro tempore of the Senate and the Speaker of the House of Representatives their written declaration that the President is unable to discharge the powers and duties of his office, the Vice-President shall immediately assume the powers and duties of the office as Acting President.

Thereafter, when the President transmits to the President pro tempore of the Senate and the Speaker of the House of Representatives his written declaration that no inability exists, he shall resume the powers and duties of his office unless the Vice-President and a majority of either the principal officers of the executive departments, or of such other body as Congress may by law provide, transmit within four days to the President pro tempore of the Senate and the Speaker of the House of Representatives their written declaration that the President is unable to discharge the powers and duties of his office. Thereupon Congress shall decide the issue, assembling within 48 hours for that purpose if not in session. If the Congress, within 21 days after receipt of the latter written declaration, or, if Congress is not in session, within 21 days after Congress is required to assemble, determines by two-thirds vote of both houses that the President is unable to discharge the powers and duties of his office, the Vice-President shall continue to discharge the same as Acting President; otherwise, the President shall resume the powers and duties of his office.

AMENDMENT XXVI

Section 1. The right of citizens of the United States, who are 18 years of age or older, to vote shall not be denied or abridged by the United States or any state on account of age.

Section 2. The Congress shall have the power to enforce this article by appropriate legislation.

AMENDMENT XXVII

No law varying the compensation for the services of the Senators and Representatives, shall take effect until an election of Representatives shall have intervened.

FATHERS OF THE FUTURE

From the end of Reconstruction to the present, the men who have held the highest civic office in the land have been a very eclectic group; some of them, like Theodore Roosevelt, Calvin Coolidge, Franklin Roosevelt, and Ronald Reagan, undoubtedly attained greatness while others, like Woodrow Wilson, Warren Harding, Herbert Hoover, and Richard Nixon, attained little more than ignominy. Nevertheless, their stories have become an integral part of our national heritage.

RUTHERFORD B. HAYES (1822-1893)

After the scandals of the Grant administration, the Republican Party was concerned about choosing an especially upright candidate. They found him in Hayes—a devout, conscientious Midwesterner whose Puritan ancestors had come from New England. In his third term as governor of Ohio in 1876, Hayes was known for an honest administration, constructive reforms, and a strong stand on sound money, one of the leading issues of the day. In addition, he had an outstanding military record, having performed gallantly and emerging a major general. He was apparently above reproach, yet it is one of the quirks of history that such a man should reach the White House through the very questionable settlement of a disputed election; the settlement was in the hands of a special electoral commission that happened to have a majority of Republicans (although most historians believe that Hayes himself was not personally involved). But the Republicans had chosen well—better than some of them knew. For President Hayes proved to be too honest and forthright for many of them, who could hardly wait to get him out of office. Despite political undercurrents, Hayes made good use of his one term to stabilize the government on several fronts. He officially ended Reconstruction, withdrew federal troops from the occupied southern states, established reforms in civil service, took courageous steps to settle the railroad strike of 1877, and stood firm in enforcing a sound money policy—all in the face of vigorous opposition. The man chosen to remove the taint of scandal from the government proved to be surprisingly resolute and effective; his dedication to principle and his courageous and forthright actions won him the kind of praise earned by very few one-term presidents.

JAMES A. GARFIELD (1831-1881)

He was the last of the presidents to go from a log cabin to the White House. Left fatherless when only an infant, Garfield was forced to work from his earliest years on the family farm in Ohio. Besides helping his widowed mother, he also succeeded in earning enough—as a canal boat driver, carpenter, and teacher—to put himself through college. His love of learning led him into a teaching career, serving as a professor of Latin and Greek and later as a college president. The initiative that catapulted Garfield into the scholarly ranks ultimately carried him into public life as well. He became known as a powerful antislavery speaker and grew active in local politics. A brilliant career in the Union Army (he was a brigadier general by the time he was thirty) was interrupted when he resigned after being elected to Congress. There he served for eighteen years, emerging in 1880 as the leader of his party. Nevertheless, when the Republicans met in Chicago in 1880, Garfield was not considered a presidential contender. The struggle was between Grant, who was willing to try a third term, and Senator James Blaine from Maine. But as had happened before, the convention was so divided that neither could win; it was not until the thirty-sixth ballot that the dark-horse candidate Garfield was nominated. The surprise gift of the highest office in the land was not one that Garfield could enjoy for very long. In the White House he showed signs of being a strong executive, independent of party as was Hayes. But he was in office less than four months when he was fatally shot by an assassin on September 19, 1831, as he was about to catch a train in the Washington depot. Like that earlier log-cabin president, Garfield left the White House a martyr, having spent less time in office than any president except Harrison.

CHESTER A. ARTHUR (1830-1886)

Although the nomination and election of the dark-horse Garfield surprised many Americans, the nomination of Chester Arthur as vice president was even more of a shock. Many a citizen feared the worst when Garfield died with three and a half years of his term remaining. And for good reason. Arthur, who loved fine clothes and elegant living, had been associated with the corrupt New York political machine for almost twenty years. In 1878 he had even been removed from his post as collector of the port of New York by President Hayes, who became alarmed at his misuse of patronage. But in spite of his questionable record, Arthur was nominated as vice president largely to appease the powerful party establishment. When Arthur became president, there was every expectation that the free-wheeling spoils system that had reigned in New York would be firmly established in Washington. But Chester Arthur fooled everyone—friends and enemies alike. Somehow the responsibilities of that high office seemed to transform this corrupt petty politician into a man sincerely dedicated to the good of the country. Courageously he established his independence by vetoing a graft-laden rivers-and-harbors bill, by breaking with his former machine cronies, and by vigorously prosecuting members of his own party accused of defrauding the government. And, most important, instead of a spoils system, he supported a federal civil service based on competitive examinations and a nonpolitical merit system. With his courageous acts Arthur won over many who had first feared his coming to power, but he lost the support of the political bosses. Although he was not an inspiring leader of men, he earned the nation's gratitude as the champion of the civil service system.

GROVER CLEVELAND (1837-1908)

The only man to ever serve two nonconsecutive terms as president, Cleveland performed the greatest comeback in American politics: He succeeded his successor. With a limited formal education, Cleveland managed to study law and establish himself as a scrupulously honest office-holder in Buffalo and western New York state. By 1882 his reputation as a dedicated and effective administrator won him the governorship of New York, a post in which he gained further renown by fighting the New York City Democratic machine in cooperation with a young assemblyman, Theodore Roosevelt. "We love him for the enemies he has made," said the delegate nominating Cleveland for the presidency at the 1884 Democratic convention, for Grover the Crusader had not hesitated to stamp out corruption in his own party. To many of both parties he was the incarnation of clean, honest government. After the corruption, oppression, injustice, and outright tyranny of the Reconstruction era, it was time for a change, and "Grover the Good" was elected in 1884, the first Democratic president in twenty-four years. In office Cleveland was a doer, and he continued to make enemies; he made civil service reform a reality by courageously placing a number of political jobs under the protection of civil service, and he stood firmly against a high protective tariff—moves that contributed to his defeat in 1888. While out of office Cleveland assumed the role of party spokesman and became an active critic of the Harrison administration. In 1892 he soundly defeated the man who had replaced him in the White House. But he returned to power in grim times with a depression cutting deeply into the nation's economy. Strong measures were called for, and in forcing repeal of silver legislation and halting the Pullman labor strike, Cleveland demonstrated a firm hand. Throughout a difficult term he remained an honest, independent leader—a man who left office with the hard-won respect of members of both parties.

BENJAMIN HARRISON (1833-1901)

Grandson of a president and great-grandson of a signer of the Declaration of Independence, Benjamin Harrison carried a distinguished

American name into the White House. Most historians generally agree, however, that he added very little distinction to it during his stay there. Harrison's early years were filled with promise and success—admitted to the Indiana bar at age twenty, he became one of the state's ablest lawyers, and he interrupted his law career only to become a brigadier general for the Union Army in the War between the States at the age of thirty-two. But the success that marked his early years became rather spotty when he entered politics after the war. Shortly after returning to Indiana, he was defeated in a run for governor. After one term in the U.S. Senate, he failed to be re-elected in 1887, and his victory over Cleveland in the presidential election of 1888 was matched by a defeat at Cleveland's hands when the two ran against each other in 1892. Although he performed bravely on the battlefield, Harrison was not a bold president. Strongly supported and influenced by the mammoth trusts and other business interests, he signed into law one of the highest protective tariffs the country has ever known. When a bill to curb the trusts—the Sherman Anti-Trust Act—managed to pass, his administration did virtually nothing to enforce it. In spite of such concessions to big business, the economy grew worse. Harrison permitted the country's gold reserves to be severely depleted by a questionable pension plan for war veterans, and by the close of his administration the signs of depression had multiplied. As is almost always the case, what was good for the huge corporate trusts had not proved to be good for the nation. The cautious man who was afraid of the new electric lights in the White House had failed to convince the country he could lead on to better times; once again the country turned to Cleveland.

WILLIAM McKINLEY (1843-1901)

Although a kind, gentle man beloved by the American people, McKinley did not earn a place in history as a champion of the people. Instead his administration was closely identified with monopolies, trusts, corporations, and special interests. At a time when the expanding West and the agrarian South were developing populist movements of growing political significance, the dignified Midwestern lawyer represented the bankers, mercantilists, and industrialists who formed the most powerful bloc in the Republican party establishment. Both economically and politically, McKinley was a conservative; on the three burning issues of the day—the tariff, currency, and Cuba—he took a conservative position. The McKinley Tariff Bill, passed in 1890, was one of the highest protective tariffs in U.S. history. As president, McKinley supported the gold standard and for a time resisted those who wanted to stampede the U.S. into war with Spain in order to rescue an oppressed Cuba (although McKinley had been elected on a platform supporting Cuban independence). American investments in sugar plantations and trade with Cuba were at stake, and the newspapers kept stories of Spanish atrocities in Cuba before the eyes of the public. The pressure for American intervention, especially after the sinking of the battle cruiser Maine in Havana harbor, finally moved McKinley to go to war. The remarkable victories of servicemen like Teddy Roosevelt on the field and Dewey on the seas brought Puerto Rico, Guam, and the Philippines into American hands. Ironically, the conservative McKinley launched the nation as a global power. With McKinley's re-election in 1900, big business seemed secure for four more years; but a series of accidents dramatically altered this serene picture. In the 1900 campaign the progressive governor of New York, Theodore Roosevelt, was put on the ticket as vice president by rival New York Republican leaders who hoped that post would be his political graveyard. But only six months after the inauguration, McKinley was fatally shot by an anarchist at the Pan-American Exposition in Buffalo on September 14, 1901. The era of free-wheeling big business died with McKinley, the third martyred president.

THEODORE ROOSEVELT (1858-1919)

Before his fiftieth birthday he had served as a New York state legislator, as the under-secretary of the Navy, as the police commissioner for the city of New York, as a U.S. civil service commissioner, as the governor of the state of New York, as vice president under William McKinley, as a colonel in the U.S. Army, and for two terms as the president of the United States. In addition he had run a cattle ranch in the Dakota Territories, served as a reporter and editor for several journals, newspapers, and magazines, and conducted scientific expeditions on four continents. He read at least five books every week of his life and wrote nearly fifty on an astonishing array of subjects—from history and biography to natural science and social criticism. He enjoyed hunting, boxing, and wrestling and was an amateur taxidermist, botanist, ornithologist, and astronomer. He was a devoted family man who lovingly raised six children, and he enjoyed a life-long romance with his wife. During his long and varied career Roosevelt was hailed by supporters and rivals alike as the greatest man of the age—perhaps one of the greatest of all ages. A reformer and fighter, he was the most colorful and the most controversial president since Lincoln and the most versatile since Jefferson. Born to wealth, Roosevelt was imbued with a strong sense of public service; in every position he held, he fought for improvement and reform. His was largely a moral crusade; he saw his chief enemy as non-Christian corruption and weakness, and he vigorously fought it wherever he found it—in business or in government. In the White House the many-sided personality of Roosevelt captured the American imagination. The youngest man to become president, this dynamic reformer who combined a Harvard refinement with the toughness of a Dakota cowboy was a totally new kind of president. Fighting the "malefactors of great wealth," Roosevelt struck out against the mammoth trusts that appeared beyond government regulation. The railroads, the food and drug industries, and enterprises using the natural wealth of the public lands were all subjected to some form of regulation for the protection of the public interest. Many conservation practices began with Roosevelt. A reformer at home, he was an avowed expansionist abroad. He supported the Spanish War and led his "Rough Riders" to fame; when president, he acquired the Canal Zone from Panama and sent U.S. battleships on a world cruise to show off America's growing strength. Perhaps most notable were Roosevelt's efforts to end the Russo-Japanese War, an achievement that won him the Nobel Peace Prize. This peacemaker, soldier, explorer, hunter, scientist, writer, and progressive statesman left many a mark upon history. To government he brought the fresh winds of reform and the courage, vigor, and tenacity to make his reforms an enduring part of the American scene.

WILLIAM H. TAFT (1857-1930)

Most Americans were saddened (though the Republican establishment was relieved) when Roosevelt announced he would not seek a third term. His successor was the country's largest president, a jovial, warm-hearted mountain of a man with a brilliant legal mind—an excellent administrator but a poor politician. He served with distinction as the first governor of the Philippines and as Roosevelt's secretary of war, positions in which his amiable nature served to advantage. But it was Taft's great misfortune to succeed such a dazzling political figure as Roosevelt in the presidency. Probably no successor could have pleased Roosevelt, but the fall from grace of the devoted friend Roosevelt had practically placed in the White House is one of the most tragic affairs in the history of the presidency. Near the end of Taft's administration, when it was clear that he had not completely supported Roosevelt's Square Deal and had made concessions to the monopolists, Roosevelt fiercely attacked him in speeches and articles. In the 1912 election Roosevelt won every primary and was poised to sweep back into office when the Republican establishment stripped the credentials of hundreds of delegates and denied the great man the opportunity. They renominated the compliant Taft instead. Roosevelt helped organize the Progressive Party and nearly won the day anyway. With less than a month to go in the campaign, however, a nearly successful assassination effectively took Roosevelt out of the race, and the Democratic opponent, Woodrow Wilson, was able to barely eke out a win. Taft and the bosses of the Republican party establishment were humiliated.

In spite of the fiasco in his party, Taft continued to serve his country. After teaching law at Yale, he was appointed in 1921 by President Harding to the post he had long sought, one that probably meant more to him than the presidency: chief justice of the Supreme Court. He was only man ever to hold both offices.

WOODROW WILSON (1856-1924)

Although Wilson held only one political office before he became president, his years as a professor of history provided him with a detailed knowledge of political processes; as president of Princeton University and governor of New Jersey, he proved himself an able, dedicated administrator, unafraid to institute reforms. Thus while Wilson's philosophy, knowledge, and ability uniquely equipped him for the nation's highest office, it was ironic that his policies were for the most part dictated by a secretive band of political cronies and conspirators led by a man named Colonel House. The administration's energies were first directed toward domestic issues—including the establishment of the Internal Revenue Service and the Federal Reserve Act—thus greatly centralizing the economy and the control of money through the establishment of a semiprivate national bank and the collection of income taxes. But the country that had emerged as a world power under McKinley and Roosevelt could not long ignore the conflict in Europe—so war ultimately overshadowed domestic concerns. America's sympathy with the Allies made Wilson's ostensible neutrality difficult to maintain. "To make the world safe for democracy," Wilson finally led the nation into war in 1917. In directing the military effort, he cooperated with a Congress that gave him vast emergency powers. While mobilizing the industrial, as well as the military, forces of the nation, he labored over plans for peace; his great hope was for a multinational government called the League of Nations. But his dedication to the noble ideal of the League's Covenant led to a bitter conflict with Congress when the Covenant, already signed by the European powers, was before them for approval. When Congress rejected it, he suffered his greatest defeat. During the last several months of his administration he was deathly ill, and his cronies ran what they could of the government as their personal fiefdom.

WARREN G. HARDING (1865-1923)

Promising a nation weary of war and big-government social experiments "a return to normalcy," the good-natured, undistinguished senator from Ohio was swept into office in 1920. The dark-horse Republican candidate, Harding received over seven million votes more than the Democrat James Cox who ran on Wilson's dismal record. The genial Harding had run on Theodore Roosevelt's platform, pledging "not heroics, but healing; not nostrums, but normalcy." The editor of a small-town newspaper, Harding was an easy-going politician who seemed to be everybody's friend. In the eyes of his clever manager Harry Daugherty, Harding had one great asset: He looked like a president. Handsome, with dignified bearing and easy charm, Harding was an impressive figure, and it was as a figurehead, as ceremonial chief of state, that he best filled the office of president. He was the first "packaged" president, though certainly not the last. Neither a leader nor a man of ideas, he seemed to represent the mood and temper of the McKinley administration rather than the two decades of progressive government that had followed; high protective tariffs were established, and both the regulation and taxation of business were reduced. Once again the government seemed to be at the service of the privileged few. Ironically, with the return to "normalcy" came rumors of corruption in high places—at the cabinet level. Daugherty, who had become attorney general, was later discovered to have freely sold his influence, and secretary of the interior Albert Fall was eventually convicted for accepting a hundred thousand dollars from private oil interests. But the public, as well as the president himself, knew nothing of these scandals in the summer of 1923 when Harding took a trip to Alaska. Harding learned the details on his return trip, and then he died in San Francisco only a few days later under very suspicious conditions that were never resolved. The country mourned the passing of the warm-hearted man who had symbolized tranquil, prewar America, perhaps sensing that such "normalcy" was as irrevocably lost as was their president.

CALVIN COOLIDGE (1872-1933)

The sixth vice president to reach the White House through the death of a president, Coolidge differed markedly from the man he succeeded. Harding was easygoing and chatty, Coolidge shy and reserved; Harding was an inexperienced executive, Coolidge a proven administrator. Harding was a man ruled by few defined principles; Coolidge was a taciturn Yankee with a passion for economy and efficiency. Both believed in less rather than more government, and both favored business. "The business of America is business," said Coolidge in a statement as lengthy as almost any he made. Somehow the pious, businesslike Coolidge was never associated with the scandals of Harding's administration, and he managed to establish his own tenure as thoroughly honest and efficient. In every position he held—from mayor of Northampton, Massachusetts, to vice president—he demonstrated what he meant by efficient government by working long hours himself. "We need more of the office desk and less of the show window in politics." The times were good, business prospered, the size and cost of government was cut drastically, and the industrious New Englander in the White House gained public favor. In 1924 the country showed its approval by electing him for another term. In the years that followed he continued to effect economies in government. In August 1927, with characteristic brevity, he announced, "I do not choose to run for president in 1928." Though by now enormously popular, no one could change his mind. The man who had worked to maintain stability was determined to leave the White House while the country was enjoying stable and prosperous times.

HERBERT HOOVER (1874-1964)

He was one of those men, like both of the Adamses, Jefferson, and Madison, whose greatest contribution to the nation was not made in the White House. For Hoover, an extraordinarily successful mining engineer and administrator, the presidency was a time of trial; he was elected on a prosperity platform during the 1928 boom, but the stock market crash and the grinding depression that followed proved to be harsh contradictions to his innate optimism. Orphaned at nine, Hoover learned the Quaker virtues and rewards of hard work at an early age. He put himself through the first class at Stanford and became a phenomenal success as a mining engineer before he was thirty. Known and respected in international mining circles, he gained worldwide fame when he directed emergency relief activities in Europe during the First World War. By the end of that terrible conflict he held a unique place in the eyes of the world as a dedicated administrator in the service of the cause of humanity. Success continued to be Hoover's lot when he served as secretary of commerce in the Harding and Coolidge cabinets, where he reorganized and expanded the Commerce Department. Running against the popular governor of New York, Alfred E. Smith, in 1928, Hoover was again successful, gaining more popular votes than any previous candidate. But when Hoover took office, vast forces were at work: the stock market collapsed, the booming industrial complex of the United States broke down, and no individual—not even Hoover with all the powers of the presidency—could cope with the disaster. He instituted measures to stimulate business with government aid, but the depression continued throughout his years in office. He was overwhelmingly defeated when he ran for re-election in 1932.

FRANKLIN D. ROOSEVELT (1882-1945)

Two figures have dominated the American political scene in the twentieth century. The first was Theodore Roosevelt. The second, remarkably, was his young cousin Franklin. Both men possessed great personal charisma, keen political instincts, penetrating social consciences, seemingly boundless energy, and brilliantly diverse intellects. Both of them left a lasting impress upon the world in which we live, but that is where the similarity between the two ends. In every other way, they could not have been more different. Franklin was the patriarch of the Hyde Park side of the family. A Harvard-educated lawyer, he began his political career as a Democratic party reformer in the New York state senate. His vigorous campaign on behalf of Wilson—against his famous cousin—during the 1912 presidential election earned him an appointment as assistant secretary of the Navy. In 1920 he was the vice-presidential running mate on the losing Democratic ticket. Eight years later, after a crippling bout with polio, he was elected to the first of two terms as New York's governor. Finally, in 1932, he ran for the presidency against the Depression-plagued Herbert Hoover and won overwhelmingly. During his record four terms, he directed the ambitious transformation of American government, created the modern system of social welfare, guided the nation through World War II, and laid the foundations for the United Nations. Theodore Roosevelt was a conservative social reformer who firmly and faithfully wanted to reestablish the "Old World Order." Franklin on the other hand, was a liberal social revolutionary who boldly and unashamedly wanted to usher in the "New World Order." Theodore's motto was "Speak softly and carry a big stick." Franklin's motto was "Good neighbors live in solidarity." Both men understood the very critical notion that ideas have consequences. As a result, the twentieth century in America has largely been the tale of two households—of the Roosevelts of Sagamore Hill and of the Roosevelts of Hyde Park. In his tenure in office, Franklin introduced far-reaching social and economic changes in the form and function of government to stimulate the economy and relieve the distress of millions of unemployed. In thus extending the influence of the federal government farther than ever before into the social and economic life of the country, he transformed the republic from limited representationalism to bureaucratic interventionism. The only president to serve more than two terms, Roosevelt was re-elected in 1936, 1940, and 1944. Domestic problems dominated his first term, but by the middle of the second, he began to recognize the aggressiveness of the Axis powers as a serious threat to world peace. Roosevelt offered American aid to the Allied powers and, after the attack on Pearl Harbor, directed the greatest total war effort—military and civilian—in all history. Supposedly to make America "the arsenal of democracy," the government took on war powers to regulate every aspect of industrial production and civilian consumption. Thus America was ruled with much of the same centralized control as the rest of the nations of the earth during the difficult days of the Second World War. Though already ailing, Roosevelt met with Churchill and Stalin at Teheran in 1943 to plan strategy and in 1945 at Yalta to plan for peace. Roosevelt was in Warm Springs, Georgia, preparing a speech for the San Francisco United Nations Conference when he died suddenly.

HARRY S TRUMAN (1884-1972)

In succeeding to the office that Roosevelt held through twelve years of depression, world tension, and war, Harry Truman faced the greatest challenge ever to confront an American vice president. Thrust without warning into the role of world leader, he was immediately burdened with two almost overwhelming tasks: leading the nation to final victory in the war and planning a sound world peace. Truman emerged from the shadow of his predecessor, dealt courageously with these problems, and in 1948 established himself as president in his own right when he upset all predictions and defeated Governor Thomas E. Dewey of New York. As a young man Truman had farmed, served in World War I as an artillery captain, and been partner in a haberdashery; in 1929 he entered politics. After studying law and serving as county judge, he was elected to the Senate in 1934. During the Second World War, the Truman Committee became known for its careful investigation of defense spending; Harry Truman won national prominence and in 1944 the vice-presidential nomination. Truman's administration was filled with momentous events; in the first year he met with Churchill and Stalin at Potsdam, he made the historic decision to use the atomic bomb, Germany and Japan surrendered, and America ratified the United Nations' Charter. In the following years came the Marshall Plan and aid for Europe, aid and technical assistance for under-developed countries, the establishment of NATO, and in 1950 the Korean War—the most dramatic step the nation had taken to try to contain Communism. Sending troops to Korea to fight a "limited" war and deciding to use the atomic bomb represented totally new kinds of decisions for a president; in making them, the man who said "The buck stops here" forced the country face to face with the two greatest problems of the day— nuclear power and the threat of Communism.

DWIGHT D. EISENHOWER (1890-1969)

He was the popular hero of the Second World War and thus was drafted by the Republican party to run for president in 1952. In that year the genial "Ike," whose apparent sincerity and goodwill captured the country, took his place alongside other American military heroes who have been elevated to the presidency; like Zachary Taylor and Ulysses Grant, Eisenhower was a professional soldier who had never held a political office. In the Army Eisenhower distinguished himself in planning and staff work, and during the 1930s he served as special assistant to General Douglas MacArthur and assisted him when he became military adviser to the Philippines. During the Second World War, Eisenhower commanded the North African invasion and later became famous as the man who devised the D-Day invasion and then welded the armies of the allied nations into a mighty force that eventually won the war against the Nazis. Elected on a platform of peace, Eisenhower used the powers of the presidency to reduce world tension. In his first year in office he brought the Korean War to an end, and after both American and Russian scientist developed H-bombs, he proposed an "open-skies" plan for disarmament, as well as plans for an international atom pool for peaceful use. Despite such efforts, the problem of containing Communism continued to be a major concern throughout his administration; North Vietnam fell to the Communists in 1954, and in 1956 Russian troops crushed an uprising for freedom in Hungary. The enormous popularity that carried Eisenhower into the White House remained undiminished in 1956 when he again defeated Adlai Stevenson of Illinois. During his second term racial segregation became a consuming domestic issue–one that reached a climax in September 1957 when he sent troops to Little Rock, Arkansas, to ensure safety to black school children. With the Communist threat continuing to dominate the world scene, Eisenhower made a dramatic world tour for peace. In 1961, when he retired to his Gettysburg farm, the nation had reached a state of unparalleled prosperity.

JOHN F. KENNEDY (1917-1963)

The youngest man ever elected president—and the youngest to die in office—Kennedy defeated vice president Richard Nixon in the first presidential election to feature candidates in formal television debates before millions of voters across the nation. A naval hero during the Second World War, he was the first Catholic to be elected president. Kennedy was born into a family with a political history; both his grandfathers were active in politics, and his father served as the nation's ambassador to Great Britain. But Kennedy first won acclaim as an author when his Harvard honors thesis, published as *Why England Slept,* became a best-seller. In the war he was decorated for saving his PT-boat crew when a Japanese destroyer cut his boat in two. In 1946 he entered politics and was elected to Congress from Massachusetts. Six years later he became a senator. Publication of Kennedy's book *Profiles in Courage,* which won the Pulitzer prize despite the fact that it was ghost-written, coincided with his emergence on the national political scene. In 1956 he narrowly missed the Democratic nomination for vice president; and by 1960 he was a leading contender for the presidency. He defeated Nixon in one of the closest elections in the nation's history—less than one vote per precinct separated them. On taking office, Kennedy delivered a stirring inaugural address written by the same ghosts who had garnered his literary fame. He appealed to all peoples for restraint and cooperation in building a safe and free world in the age of nuclear weapons. In his first year he introduced a number of new social welfare programs, weathered the Bay of Pigs disaster, and met Communist challenges throughout the world. His space program bore fruit in 1962 when astronaut John Glenn orbited the earth. By challenging the Communist build-up in Cuba, Kennedy effected the first significant Russian retreat of the Cold War. In 1963 he reached an agreement with Russia to limit nuclear tests and offered controversial civil-rights and tax bills to Congress. On November 22, before Congress acted and while President Kennedy was in Dallas, Texas, on a speaking tour with his wife, he was assassinated by a sniper—a tragedy that shocked the world.

LYNDON B. JOHNSON (1908-1973)

He was the eighth vice president to take the place of a president who died in office and the fourth to be elected to a new term afterwards. One of the most experienced national political figures ever elected vice president, he was sworn into office in Dallas shortly after President Kennedy was assassinated. Like his predecessor, Johnson was born into a family with a political heritage; his father and grandfather were both in politics. Indeed, when he was born, his grandfather predicted he would be a U.S. senator. By the time he was forty, Johnson had achieved what his grandfather had predicted, although the manipulative means by which he did remained a scandal throughout his career. In the Senate his abilities to lead and persuade were felt; as Senate majority leader during President Eisenhower's administrations, Johnson established himself as a skilled and commanding political leader. He provided the Republican president bipartisan support for such critical legislation as the civil-rights bill that was passed in 1957, the first civil-rights legislation in over eighty years. In 1960 Johnson surprised many political friends when he ran as vice president on the Kennedy ticket. After becoming president, he moved firmly to stabilize the government and support Kennedy programs at home and abroad. In November 1964 Johnson won a landslide election that pitted his own New Deal liberalism against Senator Barry Goldwater's conservatism. In 1965 he sent Congress his programs to build "The Great Society." One of the most productive in congressional history, that session turned into law bills on Medicare, school and college aid, voting rights, and antipoverty measures. During 1965 Johnson also increased the nation's commitment in Southeast Asia and in December he directed the first air raid against North Vietnam. The bombing and the continued increases of troops in Vietnam led to large, occasionally violent, demonstrations. The country was also torn by riots in predominantly Negro sections of major cities. On March 31, 1968, President Johnson stunned the nation by announcing he would not run for re-election. In October he announced a bombing halt that led to more serious peace talks in Paris. The closing days of his administration saw a flawless Apollo flight to the moon and indications from the Paris talks of improved prospects for peace in Vietnam.

RICHARD M. NIXON (1918-1995)

The first president to resign from office, Nixon removed himself from the presidency on August 9, 1974, after it became clear he could not survive the impeachment proceedings then in progress. One month later he was granted an unqualified pardon by his successor. It was an ignominious end to a rather spectacular political career. He first won national attention in 1948 when, as a member of the House Un-American Activities Committee, he forced the confrontation that led to the perjury conviction of Alger Hiss. As vice president in 1959, he conducted the famous "kitchen debate" with the Russian dictator Khrushchev in Moscow. He was defeated for the presidency by Kennedy in 1960, but after a seven-year absence, he returned to national office in 1968 when he defeated vice president Hubert Humphrey, finally attaining the office of chief executive. During his first term, an American became the first man to walk on the moon, opposition to U.S. participation in Vietnam took the form of mass demonstrations all across the nation, and the Soviet Union entered into strategic arms limitations talks. Most significant were Nixon's efforts to resolve international problems and promote world peace; he was a brilliant foreign policy expert. In February 1972 he became the first president ever to visit Communist China. His talks with Premier Chou En-lai and Chairman Mao Tse-tung led to a historic agreement pledging peaceful co-existence. In May 1972 Nixon and Chairman Brezhnev of the Soviet Union signed a treaty that reduced antiballistic missile deployment and limited the number of offensive strategic weapons—the first significant action to limit the nuclear arms race. On June 17, 1972, four men were arrested for breaking into the Democratic National Headquarters in the Watergate, but Nixon and his aides denied involvement, and the incident did not become a significant issue in the 1972 election, which Nixon easily won. In 1973 he began withdrawing all troops from Vietnam. During the next eighteen months, the Senate Watergate hearings, the revelation of secretly recorded White House tapes, the trials of over twenty Nixon aides, and finally the Supreme Court's 8-0 decision forcing Nixon to surrender crucial tapes to the special prosecutor, convinced him that he faced impeachment if he did not resign.

GERALD R. FORD (1913-)

America's first un-elected president, Ford assumed that office on August 9, 1974, when President Nixon resigned. Eight months before, Ford had become the first appointed vice president. He assumed both positions under the provisions of the Constitution's Amendment XXV. An exceptional football player at the University of Michigan, Ford coached football at Yale while studying law there. In the Second World War he served as a naval officer in the Pacific. In 1948 he won a seat in Congress and soon gained a reputation for his ability to deal with the complexities of defense budgets. He built a record over the next two decades that was moderate to conservative. During those years, he declined to run for both the governorship and the Senate, preferring to remain in the House. In 1960 he won the position of GOP conference chairman. Two years later he was elected minority leader. Ford began his presidency with immense popular support. His sudden pardon of Nixon, though, brought sharp criticism. On taking office, he stated he would not be a candidate in 1976, but in July 1975 he reversed himself and announced he would run. That year he signed the Helsinki accords with the Soviets and thirty other nations and met with Chinese leaders in Peking, seeking to maintain stable, if limited, relations. By early 1976 it was clear that Ford had succeeded in bringing the country out of a recession, and his "peace and prosperity" campaign brought him early primary victories. But although he presided over a glorious Bicentennial Fourth of July and the economic recovery continued, he narrowly defeated Ronald Reagan for the party's nomination. Although the nation's economic recovery slowed during the campaign and Democratic candidate Carter dominated the first presidential television debates since 1960, Ford came from behind to make a very close race of the election. Ford was the first incumbent since Herbert Hoover to lose a presidential election.

JAMES E. CARTER (1924-)

In only the second presidential election involving nationally televised debates, Carter came from comparative obscurity to capture the Democratic nomination and the presidency, the first man from the Deep South elected president since before the War between the States. As a young naval officer, he served in the nuclear submarine program under Admiral Hyman Rickover. After his father died Carter resigned from the Navy and returned to Georgia to operate the family farm. His father had served in the Georgia senate, and Carter's first public service was on the local school board. In 1967, as a little-known candidate, he defeated an experienced state senator, winning a disputed election in which his opponent used illegal tactics. In 1966 Carter ran for the Democratic nomination for governor, but lost to Lester Maddox. In 1970 he finally won the governor's office. Carter's presidency was marked by a continuing commitment to human rights, a quest for Arab-Israeli peace, and at the end, an interminable hostage crisis. In 1977 Carter proposed a comprehensive Energy Program—calling the problem "the moral equivalent of war"— created a new Energy Department, and signed the controversial treaties that relinquished control of the Panama Canal. In 1978 he helped bring together Egypt's Anwar Sadat and Israel's Menachen Begin to agree on the historic Camp David Accords, establishing a "framework for peace" in the Middle East. In 1979 he established diplomatic relations with Communist China and ended relations with Taiwan. That year world oil prices more than doubled, and inflation soared to double digits. The Iranian seizure of Americans at the embassy in Tehran in November 1979 created a crisis that dominated the nation's concerns until they were released almost a year and a half later. To protest the Soviet's invasion of Afghanistan, Carter instituted a grain and trade embargo and enforced a boycott of the 1980 Olympics in Moscow. Though he proclaimed himself a "born again" Christian, his administration's policies on abortion on demand, radical feminism, and homosexual advocacy cost him the support of many conservative Christians who voted for him in 1976. Carter barely survived the challenge of Senator Edward Kennedy for his party's nomination, and in the election he was roundly defeated by Republican Ronald Reagan.

RONALD W. REAGAN (1911-)

Twice winning landslide elections—by the greatest electoral margin since Franklin Roosevelt defeated Alfred Landon in 1936—Reagan ushered in a new era of conservatism and traditionalism after the long tenure of liberals in the highest office in the land. A comparative latecomer to politics, Reagan achieved national recognition as a leading man in more than four dozen Hollywood movies and as a network television host. He served six terms as president of the Screen Actors Guild and two terms as president of the Motion Picture Industry Council. He emerged suddenly on the national political scene in 1964 when he delivered a rousing speech on television supporting presidential candidate Barry Goldwater. Two years later he was elected governor of California. Reagan's victory over incumbent Jimmy Carter in 1980 represented a profound political shift toward conservatism across the country. In Washington on March 30, 1981, President Reagan was shot and wounded in an assassination attempt. After successful surgery, he was able to continue to function as president. That year he won congressional approval of a tax cut and appointed the first woman—Sandra O'Connor—to the Supreme Court. After a recession in 1982, the U.S. economy began a remarkably strong recovery that endured to the end of his second term. After his landslide victory in 1984, won in large part because he had mobilized the emerging religious right, he continued to set a conservative pace, including a tax-reform bill and a strong defense system. His strong opposition to terrorism and Communism—including the bombing of Libya, the liberation of Grenada, and tough economic pressures on the Soviet bloc—won general approval at home, but criticism abroad. His meetings with the new leader of the Soviet Union, Mikhail Gorbachev, in 1985 and 1988 led to historic agreements on the banning of intermediate range nuclear missiles. The American economy continued to expand—but the federal government's budget deficit soared to unprecedented heights. Reagan left office the most popular president since Theodore Roosevelt.

GEORGE BUSH (1924-)

The first incumbent vice president since Martin Van Buren to be elected president, Bush defeated Democratic candidate Michael Dukakis, governor of Massachusetts, by a landslide, enjoying the benefit of President Reagan's popularity and by reinforcing his party's ties to the religious right. Though his election provided continuity to the conservative "Reagan Revolution," the Democratic party remained securely in control of Congress. Bush came to the presidency with extensive experience in government and politics, having served in Congress and in the military, diplomatic, and intelligence arms of the executive branch, and as chairman of the Republican national committee before becoming vice president. His father, Prescott Bush, was U.S. senator from Connecticut from 1952 to 1962. In 1942, at age eighteen, Bush volunteered for service as a naval pilot, becoming the youngest in the Navy. He flew fifty-eight combat missions in the Pacific during the Second World War. He was shot down but was later rescued by an American submarine. After the war he took his degree at Yale in three years—and captained the baseball team. He first entered politics in 1962. Working in Houston in the oil business, he was elected chairman of the Harris County Republican party. Two years later, he ran an unsuccessful campaign for the Senate. In 1968, while serving his first term in Congress, he faced a crisis when he voted for an open-housing bill, which many of his white constituents opposed. His speech in Houston defending his vote, won him support, and he was re-elected. However, in running for the Senate in 1970, he lost to Democrat Lloyd Bentsen. Over the next decade, Bush represented the United States at the United Nations and in China and served as director of the Central Intelligence Agency. He campaigned for the presidency in 1980 but settled for vice president under Ronald Reagan. And though he had won office as the heir to the Reagan Revolution, he quickly abandoned the basic principles of the grassroots conservative ground-swell that put him in office. He supported major tax increases and allowed the budget deficit to continue soaring. He gained immense popularity between 1989 and 1991 when the old Soviet bloc began to fall apart and Communism lost power. That popularity was enhanced even more when the Gulf War against Iraq's incursions in Kuwait proved overwhelmingly successful. But his weak domestic policy and his unwillingness to maintain the core support of conservatives and the religious right cost him the 1992 election.

WILLIAM JEFFERSON CLINTON (1946-)

Attaining the highest office in the land despite losing more than fifty-seven percent of the electoratal vote, Clinton's tenure in the White House got off to a rockier start than any other president since the time of the War between the States. Taking a proactive liberal stance—on his first day in office he institutionalized an unpopular pro-abortion policy and a still more unpopular policy regarding homosexual practice—he quickly plunged into the heated "culture war" debates that already raged throughout the nation. His rise to power was meteoric—evidence of his extraordinary political instincts. Rising from poverty and a broken home, he became an excellent student and a Rhodes Scholar. In 1977, just five years out of school, he was elected attorney general of Arkansas. Two years later he was elected governor of the state. His aggressive, ideological style proved to be a bit much for that conservative state, and he was defeated in 1981 during his re-election bid. During the next two years he reinvented himself and with his new image was able to convince the electorate he had changed. He won back the governorship and held it for four more terms. Then, overcoming a spate of lurid rumors, he won the Democratic nomination in 1992. The general election later that year was marked by much apathy, malaise, and a massive defection from the two major parties; more than twenty-one million votes went to third party candidates. Clinton's lack of an electoral mandate was highlighted by the defeat of his health care reform plan and his setback in the 1994 elections when his party lost their majority tenure in both the House and the Senate for the first time in a half century. Nevertheless, exploiting the Republicans' lack of decisive leadership, his extraordinary political gifts were enough to enable him to overcome a myriad of plaguing scandals and retain the support of his core constituencies to win a second term.

THE MESSAGE OF FREEDOM

By Alan Keyes

Whether on the stump, in print, over the airwaves, or in animated one-on-one conversation, this remarkably eloquent African-American spokesman for traditional mores is likely to remind his listeners that America's special blessings are the result of generations-long adherence to a set of special principles—the very principles that first launched America's great experiment in liberty. They are also likely to hear him proclaim that if we are to overcome our current cultural woes, we will have to return to that adherence—and posthaste. This Lindoln Day speech electified the nation when it was repeatedly broadcast on radio and telvision and reprinted in journals, newspapers, and magazines across the land.

America has once again arrived at a momentous crossroads. We are going to have to decide—as we have had to decide so many times in the past—whether we shall only speak of justice and speak of principle, or whether we shall stand and fight for them. We are going to have to decide whether we shall quote the words of the Declaration of Independence with real conviction, or whether we shall take that document and throw it on the ash heap of history as we adopt the message of those who insist that we stand silent in the face of injustice.

When it comes to deciding whether we shall stand by the great principle that declares that all human beings are "created equal" and "endowed by their Creator" with the "right to life," it seems to me, there is no choice for silence.

Again, there is no choice for silence.

Thus, for instance, those so-called Conservatives who are recommending that we avoid the pro-life issue in our public discourse and civic responsibilities are actually recommending—as some people decided in the Whig Party, in the years before the Civil War, that they would be silent on the great issue of principle that faced this nation—we should be silent.

And you remember what happened to the Whigs—once the most powerful political force in America. They vanished altogether.

Modern cultural and political Conservatism grew up as a movement aimed first and foremost at dealing with that kind of moral irresponsibility—standing on the principle that Lincoln articulated: you cannot have the right to do what is wrong.

In the public arena, there are innumerable spokesmen clamoring for public attention today. Whether from the Right or the Left, the focus and crux of their message is basically the same. They talk about money. They talk about budgets, deficits, gross national products, and trade imbalances. "It's the economy, stupid," is their mantra.

But you and I both know, if we are willing to look ourselves in the eye, what the truth is. America's problems are not merely economic.

Why is it that we spend so much money dealing with welfare and illegitimacy? Why is it that we spend so much money dealing with crime and violence in our streets? Why is it even that we spend so much money dealing with the problems of irresponsible behaviors that contribute to the decline of the health of this nation? I think you know in your heart what the real answer is.

We don't have money problems. We have moral problems. And it is time we stood up and faced that truth.

But, I don't know how we're going to face that truth if, as has been so often suggested, we can look our daughters in the eye and tell them that it is somehow consistent with freedom for them to trample on the human rights of their unborn offspring.

We are going to have to find the courage one of these days to tell people that freedom is not an easy discipline. Freedom is not a choice for those who are lazy in their heart and in their respect for their own moral capacities.

Freedom requires that at the end of the day, we accept the constraint that is required, the respect for the laws of nature and nature's God that say unequivocally that our daughters do not have the right to do what is wrong, that our sons do not have the right to do what is wrong. We do not have the right to steal bread from the mouths of the innocent, they do not have the right to steal life from the womb of the unborn.

Some people may say that if we stand up and we speak out and we fight for this basic principle, we'll be dividing the nation and the burgeoning Conservative movement. But I don't think so. The Republican Party, for instance, was born on a clear commitment to principle. It was founded by those who had the courage to stand before the American people and in the face of the threat of a greater division than we'll ever face, insist that we had to respect the principles that make us great, the principles that make us strong, the principles that make us free.

Here we are more than a hundred years later and I'll tell you, we're going to have to do it again.

Look at what is happening in the streets of our cities. Look at what is happening to our families today. Do you think that the decline of marriage and the moral dissolution of the family is a money problem? Or do you think it is a problem that comes from putting the self first, from deciding that there are no obligations that have to be respected, and that at the end of the day freedom is just another kind of empty licentiousness?

We know better and our Founders knew better and it is time that we get back to the truth. The men and women who first launched the great experiment in liberty we enjoy to this day did not tell us that freedom would be an easy road. They offered us a hard-won vision of the future of America. It was not a vision of licentious freedom and stupid self indulgence. Instead, it was a vision of freedom based upon the fear of God and the respect for law.

So why is it that out of the mouths of all our contemporary statesmen we hear all kinds of great emotional words, slogans, and sound bites—but not the simple truths that our Founders from Washington and Jefferson to Lincoln and all of their successors spoke right up until we got to our own cowardly times? Whatever became of the undiluted message of true freedom?

I talk about abortion not just because of the issue in and of itself, but because I think it epitomizes the deeper issue, which is the corruption of our idea of freedom—a corruption that is really killing us. I think abortion is a very dramatic example of that corruption and its consequences, because obviously that has direct consequences for the heart that we need to sustain the family. If we harden our hearts against our offspring, and if we aggrandize our self-fulfillment to the extent that we are even willing to kill our offspring, that is the extreme case of the self-centered and egotistical and self-worshipping concept of freedom I think is being promoted in various ways in the society.

We are not going to remain a free people if we insist on being a corrupt and licentious people. We are not going to remain a free people if we arrogate to ourselves the right to destroy the rights of others. And that is exactly what we are doing when we embrace the so-called "pro-choice" agenda—which is actually just the pro-abortion agenda.

I think it is empty to praise the courage of the men and women who have died in the service of this country's freedom and its principles and yet decide that we simply cannot muster the courage to stand up for them ourselves. Many or few—or even alone if we must—it is essential that we deny the legitimacy of that kind of compromise. It was moral courage that built America. That is the true foundation of freedom.

The vaunted American Dream was not, as some would have us believe, a dream of material progress and prosperity, and great cities suffused in mountains of money. Not at all. Economics is important, but in the long life of a nation, it is ultimately subordinate to the moral facts.

To be sure, I am glad that we have achieved that prosperity, even though it came at much expense to some of my forebears. But even those who toiled in the depths of slavery had an understanding of the real dream of American freedom.

It was and is the dream of moral dignity that comes from respecting our true moral capacity. It was and is the dream of self-government that comes from respecting the fact that in the end, freedom is not just a choice, it is not just an opportunity. It can be a burden and a sacrifice and an obligation. And, above all, it is the obligation to respect the truth of our moral identity.

That moral identity can unite us across every line of race and color and creed, so long as we have the courage to stand for it.

And I think you know by now, looking at the overall dismal state of our culture, that if we abandon that line of principle, there is little hope left for America.

At every point in our history when we have had the choice between right and wrong, in the end we have chosen what is right. For that we can certainly be grateful. But, I believe we shall do it again. I believe we shall do it again because deep down we know that the real heroes in America are those who, in their families and in their daily lives, respect the truth that we must meet the obligations and sacrifices of freedom before we claim its privileges and benefits. Deep down we know that come what may—even if it means that we must sacrifice in our personal lives—we have to stand where our Founders stood: on the belief that no none has the right to do what is wrong, that if we build self-government on a true adherence to the principles of justice, then we shall hold up a beacon of right and hope for all of humankind to understand the true destiny of mankind.